I R I S H
F A M I L Y
HISTORIES

For my grandchildren

Not to be aware of the past is to be forever a child

Man is the sum of his ancestors

Emerson

IRISH
FAMILY
HISTORIES

Ida Grehan

Foreword by
Desmond FitzGerald
29th Knight of Glin

Heraldry in Ireland by
Donal Begley
Chief Herald at the Irish Genealogical Office

TOWN HOUSE, DUBLIN

Published in the United States by Roberts Rinehart Publishers,
5455 Spine Road, Boulder, Colorado 80301

ISBN 1—57098—041—1

Published in Ireland by Town House and Country House Publishers,
Trinity House, Charleston Road, Ranelagh, Dublin 6, Ireland

ISBN 1—86059—003—9

Library of Congress card number 93—85474

A CIP record for this book is available from the British Library

Typesetting:
Red Barn Publishing, Skeagh, Skibbereen, Co. Cork, Ireland

Set in Bembo 11/12½

Printed in the United States of America

Contents

Acknowledgments

For their help in the compilation of this book I should like to thank:
The staff of the National Library, the National Gallery and the National Museum, the Office of Public Works and the Philatelic Section of the Department of Posts and Telegraphs. Bord Fáilte (the Irish Tourist board); the Royal Irish Academy; the Royal Dublin Society; Trinity College, Dublin; the Irish Architectural Archive; P.J. Carroll Ltd.; Desmond FitzGerald, 29th Knight of Glin; Donal Begley, Chief Herald; Nellie O Brien de Lacy of Buenos Aires; the late Sir Dermot MacDermot, Prince of Coolavin; The O Morchoe of Wexford; Sir John Nugent; O Conor Don; the late Rupert J. Coughlan for his help with the O Donnells; Donal O Donovan; the late Edward Moore O Ferrall; The (late) O Grady of Kilballyowen; Count Walter O Kelly; Peter Tynan O Mahony; the Lord O Neill of Shane's Castle; the Irish Genealogical Association of Belfast; the late Baron Brian de Breffny and James O Rourke for their help with the O Rourkes; Harman Murtough of the Irish Military Society and *The Irish Sword*; the Irish Georgian Society; the Northern Ireland Tourist Board, Belfast; Tomas Graves, for advice on the Guinness Museum Archive; Irish Distillers International Limited; Belleek Pottery Ltd.; Michael Grehan Dover, my son and honorary literary adviser.

A book of this nature is a potential minefield of inaccuracies. I acknowledge mine but would mention that the *Dictionary of National Biography*, no less than our wealth of Irish records, often disagree.

Acknowledgments for illustrations

Argentinian Embassy: 13; Bord Fáilte: 9, 20, 35, 66, 153, 184; Irish Genealogical Office: for the Coats of Arms; *The Irish Sword*: 97; Mercier Press: 87; George Morrison: 26; National Gallery: 28, 33, 44, 56 top, 79, 85, 123 top, 128, 146, 186, 189, 197, 205 top, 213, 215 bottom, 226 top, 240 bottom, 251; National Library: xxii, 4, 5, 8, 10, 11, 12, 16, 17, 18, 19, 21, 30, 31, 36, 37, 41, 48, 49, 55 top, 58, 61, 63, 64, 67, 68, 75, 82, 84, 92, 95, 98, 99, 101, 102, 107, 108, 113, 120, 124 bottom, 130, 132, 133, 134, 137, 139, 149, 150, 151, 155, 163, 164, 166, 170, 171, 173, 175, 184, 193, 204, 209, 210, 218, 220, 226, 234, 236, 240, 243, 245; National Museum: 59, 83, 227; the Northern Ireland Tourist Board: 121; Cynthia O Connor Gallery: 248; Office of Public Works: x, 29, 39, 53, 105, 148, 187, 192; Radio Telefís Éireann: 156; Sotheby's, London: 2; Trinity College, Dublin: vii; United Press Photos: 195; United States Embassy, Dublin: 90.

ṁē cellaig
clann grīle
Fergus m dublṁē
ṁē gilla clm
ṁē ceilball
ṁē cethernaig
ṁē azaile
ṁē duibdoinn
Hemplan
ṁē ceilball
ṁē cethernaig
ṁē congaile
ṁē duib duinn
Mael cellaig
ṁē corcrain
ṁē echdach
ṁē congaile
Gelban m mail
ṁē echdach
ṁē congaile
Clann phiadaig
Cu allaid m phiazail
J mathgamain

pniszal clann core
Formzal use ech
cherzjm
ṁē domnaill
ṁē longmm
ṁē corcin
ṁē mail canuch
ṁē ozain
ṁē flacdbenzanē
ṁē duib chuain
ṁē mirza
ṁē becan nch
ṁē oinin
ṁē arn
ṁē gilonain
ṁē lochain
ṁē punizz
ṁē sairt
ṁē corolan
chunt beizzan
Pino mē cnaio
ṁē ozain
ṁē beizzan

Fillā duib
ṁē flor am
ṁē connch
ṁē mijnec
ṁē byr am
ṁē paichs
ṁē ozan
clann plann
zenolla
Ceilball m
zezm
ṁē mail mc
ṁē laujar
ṁē mailcn
ṁē ceilbal
ṁē plam
ṁē flacbe
ṁē duibcu
clann plaid
zaile
Conzran
rōmmun
ṁē oiann

Foreword

Talking recently to a Texan about his visit to Ireland, he told me how he had become interested in his Irish roots. He remembered that, when he was a child, a gaitered Anglican Canon who wore a wide-brimmed hat came to call at his parents' house. The Canon spread out a vast genealogical chart on the floor and, evidently with some satisfaction, pointed out two names on the Texan's family tree and told the boy that one was a sheep thief and the other had killed a bishop!

My Texan friend who, needless to say, remembered only these two dramatic revelations, accused his parents of wasting time delving into the past. It was only years later, when he had become a distinguished engineer, that he returned to County Fermanagh to search for the relics of his Scotch-Irish background and he regretted not paying more attention to the old clergyman.

There are many other people of southern Irish descent who look back on Irish history with its tales of violence, famine and the devious politics of "our most distressful country" with understandable sadness and distaste. Emigrants often remember only the dark side. Their memories can stretch over an extraordinarily great length of time. A Virginian friend told me that, when he was acting as best man to a friend marrying a Catholic in the early 1950s, the priest became extremely annoyed during the wedding rehearsal. Some of the Protestant members of the congregation were not following the service and had taken to chatting in the pews. My friend, attempting to calm him down, said, "Father, I am a sort of Irishman myself: my name is FitzGerald".

Desmond FitzGerald, 29th Knight of Glin

"Ha", said the priest, not in the least mollified. "I remember when there were so many FitzGeralds hanging from the trees in Ireland that it was thought theirs was the name of the berry!" This folk memory undoubtedly goes back to Elizabethan times, when so many of the Geraldines of Desmond in the province of Munster were hanged by the English invaders.

The study of family history and the search for origins has been burgeoning in the United States and, more recently, in Australia and England—countries in which millions of people of Irish descent live. A former Chief Herald, Edward MacLysaght, who died in 1986, aroused great interest with the publication of his four books on Irish family history. Ida Grehan has consolidated much of MacLysaght's material and has expanded it. We find here the stories of soldiers, actresses, adulterers, politicians, statesmen and writers galore. She has also found many interesting illustrations which give the book a great deal of life. She has concentrated on 80 Irish families of Gaelic or Anglo-Norman descent and has woven a tapestry of facts around each name.

I cannot help thinking that our author would have had some sympathy with The MacDermot, Prince of Coolavin, who Arthur Young described in his Irish tour of 1776 as having only £100 a year and never permitting his children to sit down in his presence. Young had probably read Boswell's *Tour of the Hebrides* describing a journey he had taken with Dr Johnson in 1773, as he repeats the story of a visit by some of the Prince's neighbours, including Mr O Hara of Sligo and three men of settler descent, Mr Sandford, Lord Kingsborough and Mr Ponsonby.

Script taken from the early Irish genealogies compiled in the tenth century. This copy was written by Lucas O Dallain, a scribe of one of the learned Irish families, and is reproduced from a manuscript in Trinity College, Dublin.

The Prince of Coolavin addressed them, "O Hara, you are welcome. Sandford, I am glad to see that you are your mother's son [his mother was an O Brien]. As to the rest of ye, come in as ye can". This shows vividly what he thought of a scion of the new Irish peerage (Ponsonby was the son of Lord Bessborough, a member of one of the important ruling ascendancy families in Ireland which had arrived in Cromwellian times).

Gaelic pride in pedigree is remarkable. Professor John Barry, in 1967, in one of the annual series known as the O Donnell lectures, took as his subject "The study of family history in Ireland". He pointed out that Ireland's Gaelic aristocracy was almost entirely dispossessed during the seventeenth century, and though many fled abroad forming the famous "Wild Geese", others moved down the social scale becoming tenants and even servants of the new colonial ruling class. Barry suggested that the dignity, hospitality and easy good manners of the Irish people, so often commented on by foreign travellers, was one of the consequences of this leavening of the mass of the people. Family ties had cemented society in aristocratic Gaelic Ireland, and genealogy survived as a major concern in the Irish countryside.

Professor Barry cited a professional genealogist, Bridget FitzGerald, in the barony of Barrymore, County Cork. "Her genealogical knowledge of the leading families of the neighbourhood was immense. An Earl of Barrymore who once visited her house at Loughnaphreaghaun, between Castlelyons and Rathcormac, was informed that she considered his descent to be less honourable than that of some other of the Barrys. Stung by this, the Earl is reputed to have replied, "Have the honour, but I'll have the land", and deprived her of her farm. The aspersion which she cast on the descent of the Earls of Barrymore was apparently the bigamy of James Barry of Ibaune in the fifteenth century! Daniel Corkery, the influential Cork novelist, relates the story of an old man accused of playing the fool who retorted, "I am no fool, I know my genealogy".

All these stories are underlined by the unknown, probably English writer describing a tour in 1674, who states that "The people in general are great admirers of their pedigree and have got their genealogy so exactly by heart that though it be two hours work for them to repeat the names from which they are descended lineally, yet will they not omit one word in half a dozen and several repetitions, from which I gather they say them instead of their paternosters in their evening and morning prayers".

The Irish abroad seem to have carried on this tradition. For instance, Thackeray's "Barry Lyndon" told a Prussian officer that he was a descendant of Brian Boru. "I have never met an Irishman who was not a descendant of kings", the Prussian officer observed sarcastically. Thackeray had a keen but jaundiced eye for the pretensions of the Irish, as he had come to know them first hand through his ghastly Irish mother-in-law who had County Cork landed family connections. She was the original for all the overbearing boastful snobs who gave their daughters ideas of grandeur by telling them stories of titled relations and (often mythical) Irish estates. It was perhaps no surprise to learn that an Englishman, John Loveday, in his Irish tour of 1732, recounted that even among the peasantry "So great is ye pride of these common people that if a woman be ye same name as some noble family she'll retain it in marriage unless her husband has as distinguished a name".

A clearly exasperated editor, Arthur Charles Fox Davies, in his preface to *Burke's Landed Gentry of Ireland 1812*, lamented that "My most vehement correspondent seems to fancy that Burke is edited by Hans Andersen". He goes on to say, "one knows that every Irishman is the descendant of countless kings, princes and other minor celebrities... also that every family is the oldest in County Galway, or County Sligo or somewhere else". This particular form of Irish pride has probably a great deal to do with the confiscation of practically all of the lands of the native Irish in the seventeenth century and those of Norman descent, known as "The Old English". This also meant that many of this ancient aristocracy were too proud to seek useful work and go into trade.

The problem of these two worlds, as it were, was brilliantly summed up by John Fitzgibbon, the Lord Chancellor, in his famous Union speech in 1800. His family background (he was the descendant of a decayed "old English family") gave him added sensitivity. "The whole property of this country", he said, "has been conferred by successive monarchs of England upon an English colony composed of three sets of English adventurers who poured into this country at the termination of three successive rebellions. Confiscation is their title, and from their first settlement they have been hemmed in on every side by the old inhabitants of Ireland brooding over their discontent in sullen indignation".

Ida Grehan's introduction to the study of these Irish families should tempt many people of Irish descent from all over the world to make the picturesque, though often grim, voyage back through Ireland's long history. The new Genealogical Office and Heraldic Museum, which are housed in the old Kildare Street Club building, are now open to the public, providing a very important research centre. There a visitor in search of his or her roots can consult a staff member, look at reference books, and be put in touch with other repositories of information. Parish records exist all over the country and local heritage societies are springing up, region by region. Soon you will be able to go to the area from which you think your family originated and get the local archivists on the trail. You can also pursue the quest down many a leafy lane and in many a nettle-filled graveyard! Even if nothing relevant turns up, the seeker will have had the unique experience of discovering the out-of-the-way places in our beautiful land.

by Desmond FitzGerald, 29th Knight of Glin

Ruins of the early medieval monastic settlement on Skellig Michael, off the Kerry coast. It was in remote locations such as this that Christianity survived during the Dark Ages.

How to Read this Book

Not everyone will want to read this book from cover to cover. It is for dipping into and finding what interests you. The eighty families are arranged in alphabetical order in the Irish way, which means that where an O or Mac prefix is prevalent in Ireland, it is given in this book. For instance, if your name is Reilly, you will not find it under R, but under O for O Reilly, and similarly with Sullivan, which is more commonly O Sullivan in Ireland. Other families may never have lost their Irish prefix, or may have retrieved it since the passing of the bad old days when Irish surnames were outlawed, when MacGowan was changed to Smith, and Ó Morchoe to Murphy. Prefixes denote descent: Mac means son of, while O indicates that the name derives from a grandfather or earlier ancestor. Because many names came into being before the standardization of spelling, and because of the influx of many nationalities and the Anglicization of Irish names, there are many different ways of spelling the same name. MacEnenany is spelled in at least 25 different ways, but most of them came about when the family went to the United States.

Because of a turbulent history, Irish archives and records are comparatively scarce. Each family is traced as far back as records will allow. Firstly, there is the originating sept, or clan, which is followed, whenever possible, through to the present day. Inevitably a family branches out, forms new allegiances or backs a new leader in the ceaseless and universal power struggle. This sometimes involves a name change, or the addition of the name of a wife or relative.

Each profile begins with the meaning of the name, followed by a general history of the family and its outstanding characters. Very often a particular family will have a special talent, such as the Butlers for administration, the O Dalys for poetry and the FitzGeralds for leadership.

From the fourth century, the Irish travelled abroad, and their exploits through the centuries cover a fairly comprehensive account of world history; there was hardly a battleground on which they did not play a prominent role. A scan through the *Key Dates in Irish History* at the end of this book might help clarify a number of important issues that led to the making or breaking of many a family.

Anyone who is interested in finding their Irish origins has to be prepared for hard work. You must find out as much as you can about your parents, grandparents or great-grandparents before you can embark on more detailed genealogical research. Here is some information that you should try to discover.

- Precise place of residence in Ireland—province, county, village, town, townland or parish.

- Religion—vital if you are to make use of church records.

- Approximate dates of birth, marriage and, where applicable, emigration.

Your local library should have a selection of books with helpful information on how to trace your ancestors and where to write for help. The late Margaret D. Fally's book, *Irish and Scotch-Irish Ancestral Research*, covers all the repositories, records and preliminary research in the United States. Your local librarian or the Board for the Certification of Genealogists (also in the US) should be able to give you the name and address of research associations near you.

Dr Edward MacLysaght, who died in 1986 just short of his one hundredth birthday, has written a number of valuable books on Irish families, their names, arms and origins. Your librarian should be able to get these for you and they will give you a good grounding. The bibliography which I have included also lists some source books.

If you cannot find the name you are looking for in this book, you should consult the index, where all the name variations are included. You might not know, for example, that some branches of the Nugent family became Gilsenan, or that MacDermot, through a different emphasis in pronunciation or spelling, could also be Kermode.

WATERCOURSE DISTILLERY.

MIDLETON DISTILLERY.

NORTH MALL DISTILLERY.

Nineteenth-century engravings of three Murphy's distilleries in Cork. All three are still in operation.

Introduction

This is my third book of Irish family histories, and, although I began only a dozen years ago, looking back I can see that the germ, though dormant, was there far longer. Driving through Irish towns and cities, I always looked out for the signs over the small shops, tossing the names around in my imagination, wondering where they originated from. One summer, when I was maybe ten, I frequently visited the market garden in County Meath run by a Mr Comiskey. Always alerted by the exotic, I liked to think that Mr Comiskey had come from far away Russia—or perhaps it would have been Poland, because of that final "ski", rather than the Russian "off", as in Romanoff. I now know that Comiskey is an ancient Gaelic name which is spelled Mac Cumascaigh, meaning son (*mac*) of the confuser (*cumascach*). Perhaps because my own name, Grehan, is an obscure one whose origins my Connacht-born father was forever trying to discover, names were something I viewed as deliberately as others might a stamp collection.

One day a colleague at the *Irish Times* asked if I would consider taking on a book she had neither the time nor the inclination to tackle. When she explained that it was about the history of Irish family names, I agreed without hesitation. She has since become a best-selling novelist, while I still track generations of Irish families in libraries and archives around the world, in the many countries to which they dispersed in a continual wave of emigration.

The book that I was commissioned to write was intended to follow one on Scottish families, and the editor suggested I send him a few samples of the histories of the one hundred leading families. I think I sent him the O Neills, O Kellys, O Sullivans and Butlers. He telephoned from Edinburgh, "Cut the number down to fifty and expand. We had no idea Irish families were so interesting."

With the manic devotion of a compulsive gambler, I have become addicted to the pursuit of family history. Whether in Tokyo or Toronto, Madrid or New York, I leaf through the telephone directories looking for Irish names. Not a very expensive addiction, mine is, however, a fairly solitary occupation. Accuracy—as far as humanly possible—is essential. Scholars and historians lie in wait to pounce on the mildest error—particularly Irish ones. No matter how thorough the research, history is a minefield.

Submitting my work to the present-day representatives of a family, they point out mistakes, mainly in dates, titles and relationships: sister not aunt, mistress not wife. Few bother nowadays about skeletons being discovered in cupboards!

I am told genealogy is a science. I like to think that the writing of family history is a creative, though constricted art. Emerson got it right when he said, "Man is the sum of his ancestors", and, in Ireland, we are well-acquainted with our first, second and third cousins, even those once, twice or further removed. From earliest times, in biblical fashion, every clan—or sept, as the Irish scholars prefer it—had its own bard who, apart from his poetry, could also recite the family pedigree, which was passed down orally from generation to generation. Later, with the spread of writing, this was recorded on parchment. Intense interest in every aspect of our history may well explain why surnames were formalized early in Ireland. A literary race, we have surnames that are colourful, which describe an occupation or, sometimes cruelly, highlight a physical defect. For instance, *cruitín* is a hunchback in Irish, whence MacCurtin, son of the hunchback. Until comparatively recently, our history, perhaps because it has been harsh, inclined to mythology and romance. In recent years however, it has been severely demythologized.

Digging for family roots unearths facts. Following families from one generation, or one period in history, to another, you see them mesh together, the predominant ones interwoven in a tapestry of power struggle, intermarriage, land aggrandizement, politics, raids and counter-raids. It is also a sorry story of Burke against FitzGerald, O Rourke against MacMurrough, MacDermot against Costello and O Neill against O Neill.

Geographically Ireland is closest to Britain and now also speaks the same language. In every period of its history the Irish have migrated there. Freed from the restrictions imposed by the colonists in Ireland, they have often risen to eminence in their adopted country and integrated like the Normans. Emigration grew to such high proportions, especially in the early days of the newly independent but poor state, that Britain came to be called "Ireland's backdoor".

Canada, which received Irish emigrants hospitably, particularly during the Famine, has two million people of Irish descent in the state of Ontario alone. Since 1791, when the first convicts landed, the Irish have been emigrating to Australia and New Zealand, where it is estimated that about 40% of the immigrants are Irish. They have played distinguished roles in the social, commercial, political and artistic lives of these countries.

In the early eighteenth and nineteenth centuries, Irish soldiers and statesmen were prominent in several South American countries, particularly Argentina, where they were early settlers in rural areas. In the USA, forty million people claim Irish ancestry, third in the ethnic list following the English and Germans. A factor which helped the Irish preserve their identity there was that their women also emigrated with them.

Irish family names first came into use in the twelfth century, not long after the death of King Brian Boru, who is believed by some to have invented them. Certainly, his name is well-perpetuated in the O Brien family. In 1522, the Irish Office of Arms was formed in Dublin Castle by the Anglo-Norman administrators. Through the vicissitudes of history it has filled a useful role, especially when Irishmen were gaining prominence in the armies and courts of Europe. Unless they could prove noble descent, they could not attain high rank. To obtain this proof, they wrote home to the Office of Arms and, upon receiving their pedigree showing descent from the Irish aristocracy, these ranks were open to them.

The modern state of Ireland has no titles of nobility—only titles of courtesy. A Chief of his Name, to qualify for the designation, must satisfy the Chief Herald—the civil servant who is today head of the Genealogical Office—with an authentic account of his ancestry. It could well be that he is not, as he thought, one of the royal O Conors of Connacht or the noble O Briens of Thomond, but merely a descendant of one of their followers who had adopted his chieftain's name.

The last official authentication of the chieftains was in 1943, since when some have lapsed, or become dormant. The following are those which still exist: The O Callaghan; O Conor Don; MacDermot, Prince of Coolavin; The O Donoghue of the Glens; The O Donovan; The O Grady of Kilballyowen; The O Kelly of Gallagh; The O Morchoe (Murphy); The O Neill of Clannaboy; The O Brien of Thomond; The O Donnell of Tirconnell.

The once dreaded Dublin Castle, former seat of the English governors of Ireland, is now a showplace and a venue for meetings of the European Economic Community which Ireland joined in 1973. Some years ago, the Genealogical Office in Dublin Castle moved to Kildare Street, close to the National Library of Ireland.

I have included a short sketch of Irish history, in an effort to clarify the origin of surnames. The real history of Ireland, however, is to be found in the family histories that follow.

In the nineteenth century in particular, a number of the prominent families closed ranks and kept their lands in the family. It was commonplace for a landowner to marry his first cousin, and it was not at all strange to find uncles marrying their nieces.

There have been many surges of emigration, and many immigrants have enriched our race. Since the seventeenth century at least, we have had Jews and Huguenots, Italians, Palatines, Quakers, Scots and Scandinavians, and lately the industrious Chinese.

Ireland is divided geographically into four provinces, each with its distinctive geographical features and surnames. There is an old Celtic saying which is not without a grain of truth: "Ulster for battle; Leinster for learning; Munster for farming; Connacht for magic".

Too small an island to contain its wealth of talent, the Irish have long learned to adapt—to become governors in British colonies, brigadiers or admirals in their services, or to control more than 35% of corporate America. British broadcasting and television is sometimes said to be the best in the world, and many of its most popular performers have graduated from broadcasting in Ireland.

There are over 4,000 Irish surnames, many with a variety of different spellings and forms. The criteria for the eighty I have selected for this book were that they had to be to the fore for at least five hundred years and to be names that are still numerous. The Usshers, for instance, had a long and distinguished line of academics and archbishops, but they are very scarce today. There are many families with ancient Gaelic names who are numerous. They are undoubtedly fine people who have never murdered kings, written masterpieces, climbed the Himalayas, been Prime Minister of Australia or discovered new worlds, and so they have not been included in the records. They have no history and may well be all the happier for that!

In this 1581 woodcut by Derrick, a MacSweeney chieftain feasts while his bard recites to the accompaniment of a harper.

A Short History of Ireland

Beginning at the beginning—if that were possible—Irish history is a kaleidoscope of folklore and of the assimilation of different races. In earliest times there were the mysterious Tuatha de Danaan, god-like warriors of pre-history, their servants, the squat, dark Firbolgs, and their sea-going henchmen, the Formorians. By the sixth century BC they had disappeared, probably annihilated by King Milesius and his forces from Spain. In about 350 BC, the Celts who had marched across Europe came to a halt in Ireland, the farthest outpost of Europe. Around the first century AD, the Gaels began to emerge, having absorbed the myths—and genes—of all those who had preceded them.

Ireland was pagan until the fifth century AD, when Saint Patrick introduced Christianity. He had been preceded by Palladius, who is believed to have been sent to Ireland, which was then known as Scotia, by Pope Celestine I. Little trace of Palladius remains, however. There are conflicting theories concerning St Patrick, he may have been Roman, or Welsh, or French, or there may even have been two Patricks! In any case, his impact on Ireland has been profound and enduring and he is shared by Catholics and Protestants alike.

Christianity ushered in Ireland's Golden Age. Schools were opened, laws were formulated, poets abounded, but so, alas, did bloodshed, although the monasteries provided a moderating influence. Beautiful metalwork, stone sculptures and books and manuscripts were produced in the monastic centres. Saints and scholars went abroad to Europe to spread the gospel, and lay people, men and women, went to tend the sick in Europe, which was then descending into the Dark Ages.

In the ninth century, the Vikings and Norsemen from Scandinavia came in their longboats, plundering the monasteries and any settlements close to the sea or rivers, carrying off their treasures and often their women. Some remained to found the ports of Dublin and Waterford—originally Vadrefjord. Many married Irish women.

In 1014, at the battle of Clontarf in Dublin, most, but by no means all, of the Norsemen were driven out by the forces of the High King, Brian Boru, progenitor of the powerful O Briens. After that victory over the foreigners, there should have been peace, but there was not. The kings of Ulster, Munster, Leinster, Connacht, and their followers, were all warring for the High Kingship.

The arrival of St Patrick and the Anglo-Norman invasion were early turning-points in Irish history. The Anglo-Norman invasion, which began in 1169, was not planned—it just happened. A bitter rivalry existed between two warrior kings, Dermot MacMurrough (see Kavanagh) of Leinster and Tiernan O Rourke of Breifne (now Cavan and west Leitrim). MacMurrough had earned O Rourke's implacable enmity by running off with his wife, Devorgilla. Although she returned to her husband after a short interval, O Rourke supported Rory O Connor, King of Connacht, in a feud against MacMurrough and his ally, Murtough MacLachlainn, the powerful King of Ulster. The sudden death of MacLachlainn left MacMurrough isolated and helpless. His palace at Ferns in County Wexford was destroyed and he fled, secretly, to Europe to seek assistance from Henry, Duke of Normandy, Count of Anjou and Maine, who had been crowned King of England at the age of 21 in 1154. Henry actively encouraged MacMurrough to recruit some of the freewheeling Normans and Flemings who had come to England after the battle of Hastings in 1066, a battle which had settled Duke William of Normandy's claim to the English throne.

Richard Fitzgilbert de Clare, Earl of Pembroke, an ambitious Norman known as "Strongbow", agreed to send an armed force to Ireland in exchange for marriage with Aoife, MacMurrough's daughter, and the right of succession to the Leinster kingdom. In May 1169, the first wave of Norman adventurers landed on a County Wexford beach, later followed by Strongbow. The Irish, aided by their allies the settled Norsemen, fought valiantly but were overcome by the invaders' superior weapons and discipline and also by a clever ruse: a herd of cattle let loose by the Normans caused hopeless confusion among the Irish troops. The Normans went on to conquer the port of Waterford, and Aoife, amidst the carnage, was duly married to Strongbow, in a bizarre ceremony recreated in a huge painting in the National Gallery of Ireland by Daniel Maclise (1805–70).

With his death a year later, in 1171, MacMurrough's ambitions came to nothing. The Normans were prospering, so Henry II, worried lest they grow too powerful, went to Ireland in 1175 and set up a centralized administration. He also built the first Dublin Castle, and introduced coinage and the jury system.

Within eight years of their arrival, the Normans had taken over most of the country, except parts of Connacht and Ulster. They built castles and fortresses, and invited Dominican, Benedictine, Franciscan and other friars to run the monasteries, which had grown lax in the wake of the devastation caused by the Scandinavian raiders. The Normans were splendid builders and administrators who brought many improvements to Ireland, but, unfortunately, they did not completely conquer the country. They integrated so well with the native Irish that the English, fearing a threat to their monarchy, instituted Poynings' Law, which was designed to prevent the Normans from speaking Irish, marrying Irish spouses and adopting Irish dress or customs.

The Irish continued with their personal vendettas and sometimes also sided profitably with the Anglo-Irish (as the influx of English and Normans began to be called). The Normans had lost their roots in Northern France and had none in either England or Wales, but in Ireland they acquired much valuable land and married local chieftains' daughters. Their names live on: Burke, Butler, FitzGerald, Cusack, Dillon, de Lacy, Martin, Nugent, Power, Roche.

To save expense and solve the difficulty of governing from a distance, the English monarchy established the FitzGeralds as governors of Ireland. Garret Mór FitzGerald, the great Earl of Kildare, an outstanding leader, was known as "the all-but-king of Ireland". His son, Garret Óg, who succeeded him in 1513, lacked his father's forcefulness and also had the arrogant young Henry VIII to contend with.

In 1541, Henry VIII boldly declared himself King of Ireland. A majority of the Irish chieftains and old Norman barons gave him token allegiance, for which they were awarded peerages. Henry had broken with Rome and also declared himself head of the Church in England and Ireland. This the Irish would not accept, remaining faithful to the international Christian Church.

There were numerous uprisings. Eventually, a strong army led by the Earl of Tyrone, Hugh O Neill, and Red Hugh O Donnell, marched south from Ulster to join a Spanish force which had sailed into Kinsale in County Cork. They were overwhelmed by the superior English forces at the battle of Kinsale, another crucial turning-point in Irish history. O Neill and O Donnell, together with more than ninety of the once most powerful men of Ulster and their families, sailed from Lough Swilly in County Donegal to permanent exile in Europe, in what became known as the "Flight of the Earls".

As always, Ireland continued to represent a threat to the political stability of England and, in 1649, Oliver Cromwell (1599–1658) descended on Ireland. His army began by capturing Drogheda, in County Louth, and the port of Wexford, before engulfing the country, wrecking monasteries and castles. He granted his soldiers confiscated land in lieu of pay, thus laying the basis of the Protestant land-owning ascendancy.

The Flight of the Earls had left a power vacuum in Ulster, which James I of England (1566–1625) filled by the plantation of Protestant immigrants, mostly from Scotland, who were given land subsidies in the six counties of Ulster. Because of its close proximity and frequent interchanges with Scotland, this north-eastern part of Ireland has always differed from the rest of the country. The importation three hundred years ago of privileged immigrants, with a distinct nationality and a rigid religious observance, could be said to have lain the foundation for the appalling situation which prevails today in Northern Ireland.

From 1695, penal laws had been introduced with the aim of destroying Catholicism as a political force, with its accompanying threat to Britain from Catholic Spain and France. Catholics were debarred from parliament, from holding government office, from the legal profession, and from commissions in the army or navy. Despite the fact that they were not even allowed to own a horse worth more than £5, some did manage to acquire wealth through trade and industry. Those who crossed over to the Established Church could attain high office in the legal profession. Most of the Old Norman and Old English families held on to their land and titles by embracing the new faith. The Irish were further compelled to Anglicize their names, to drop the prefix O or Mac, the Ni or the Ban. MacGowan, which means blacksmith, became Smith. O hIcidhe, a famous medical family, became Hickey. O Maoilriain was pared down to Ryan, and so on, as will be discovered in the family histories in this book.

King James II (1633–1700) succeeded his brother, Charles II. James II, a Catholic, after a violent and mismanaged reign fled to Ireland, where the Irish flocked to his banner and fought by his side at the battle of the Boyne in 1690. This was a power struggle between two monarchs and two faiths, rather than a battle between the Irish and the English colonizers. The Anglo-Dutch William of Orange (husband, and cousin, of James II's daughter Mary) had been invited to take over James II's throne. In July 1690, William and his 35,000-strong English and Dutch army defeated James and his army of 23,000 Irish and French troops. James fled after the battle. The Irish struggled on for a while, but defeats at Aughrim and Limerick ended their resistance. Between 1690 and 1730, it is estimated that 120,000 Irish sailed for Europe. Many of these took passage as cargo on the boats of Irish wine smugglers plying between French and Irish ports. They were registered as "Wild Geese", a name that became synonymous with the Irish emigrants whose talents were to flower abroad as they could not do at home.

In France, Spain, Italy, Portugal and Austria, they were kindly treated by Church and State. Some ventured further afield, to Scandinavia, Poland, Russia and to the Americas. Supported by their martial spirit—soldiering was the profession of the majority—they soon occupied high posts in the armies of Europe and put their administrative talents to use in the royal courts and colonies.

In 1781, the American colonies' defiance of the British parliament inspired the oppressed Irish to do likewise. Led by patriotic Ulster Protestants, they agitated for legislative independence, which they achieved in 1782. For a brief but glorious period, Ireland was an independent kingdom, though sharing the monarchy with England. A number of religious restrictions were removed. Catholics were given the vote, but were still excluded from standing for parliament and from any high legal office.

Because of the communication with Irish immigrants living in France, the philosophy of the French Revolution filtered back to the militant Irish at home. Inspired by Wolfe Tone and Lord Edward FitzGerald, an uprising, centred mainly in Dublin and Wexford, took place in 1798, but it was quickly suppressed.

In 1801, despite much opposition, and by creating many new peerages, an Act of Union with Britain was passed. Ireland lost its independent parliament to become once more a minor part of the United Kingdom. For the first and perhaps only time in history, Ireland was united. The union set the political and cultural life of the country back a hundred years and Dublin ceased to be one of Europe's leading capitals.

It was not until 1829 that Daniel O Connell won full Catholic emancipation. The Young Ireland movement, contrary to O Connell, believed that force was the only way to win the repeal of unjust land laws. In 1848, their abortive insurrection came to nothing and led to its leader, William Smith O Brien, being transported to Australia, along with Charles Gavan Duffy and many other distinguished men. Not only did these idealists enrich Australia, but their writings had a greater effect in Ireland than their attempted physical rebellion.

In 1845, the potato crop, on which the poor people were far too dependent, succumbed to a virulent blight. In five years a population of eight million people was reduced to three and a half million, by death and emigration to the Americas and Canada.

At home, despite the loss of so many leaders, the fight for Home Rule and land reform, led by Charles Stewart Parnell (1845–91), grew ever more active. In Canada and the United States it was taken up by the Irish who formed the militant Fenian Brotherhood. The career of Parnell, "the uncrowned king of Ireland", was shattered by the scandal of his liaison with Catherine O Shea. The party that he had developed into a great political force was split. He lost the leadership, which died with him, though his contribution to the reform of the land code did not.

For many, the Easter Rising in 1916 came as a surprise. Patrick Pearse and many young republican idealists were ruthlessly executed, leaving a legacy of hatred. Home Rule was finally granted, but six counties of Ulster held firm and, because of their established traditions, refused to join a united Ireland. A compromise treaty, which allowed for the partition of Ireland and separate status for Northern Ireland, was agreed upon, but the republicans who wanted a thirty-two county state refused to accept this, resulting in a tragic Civil War between those for and against this division. This long and bitter struggle continues today in the violence perpetrated by the IRA and its splinter groups.

Side by side with the rise of nationalist political movements, the period between the death of Parnell and the final withdrawal of the British in 1921 saw the banding together of a cohort of poets, painters, writers, musicians, playwrights, actors and patrons to form a new cultural renaissance. W. B. Yeats, the poet, towered over the literary movement, and, together with Lady Gregory, founded the Abbey Theatre, the national theatre of Ireland, whose plays reflected this new political fervour. Sport and music were encouraged by the Gaelic League and the Feis Ceoil, a prestigious annual music competition.

Celt, Norman, Anglo-Irish, English, Scottish, Welsh: in more than sixty years of nationhood, Irish affairs are still dominated by men and women whose very names reflect its turbulent history and the interweaving strands of conquest, plantation and assimilation.

An eighteenth-century engraving by A. O Kelly depicting an attack on a process server during the Irish Land League agitation in the 1870s.

Heraldry in Ireland

Heraldry, it is now generally agreed, was the form, unique to medieval Europe, of military symbolism which is, of course, as old as man himself. A graphic device on the banner and shield of the knight banneret at once proclaimed his identity to his followers and his opposition to his enemies. As Bartolus, the fourteenth-century Italian jurist and heraldist so neatly put it, the purpose of heraldry was *ad cognoscendum homines*—to tell one individual from another.

As to its origins, heraldry is linked with the crusading movements of the Middle Ages which were organized to counter the threat to Western civilization posed by the rise of Islam. A characteristic feature of the military equipment of the day was the use, from about 1150, of full-length protective body armour, with the head completely encased in a helmet. This development necessitated the placing of distinguishing colour and marks on shields and greatcoats for purposes of individual identification. And so, out of the peculiar conditions of medieval warfare and the critical requirements of instantly being able to tell one combatant from the next in the confusion of battle, came the birth of heraldry. Indeed, the function of heraldry remained largely military until the fifteenth century, when the introduction of gunpowder rendered the armorial service shield obsolete.

Turning to the history and development of heraldry in Ireland, it is important, at the outset, to advert to the existence of three distinct Irish heraldic traditions. These traditions, which for convenience sake we may term Norman, Anglo-Irish and Gaelic, correspond in large measure to the three main ethnic groups which over the centuries have coalesced to form the Irish people. Each group in turn brought with it to the island its own distinctive culture, which duly found expression in a variety of art forms, including heraldry.

Speak of the Normans, for example, and immediately horses, armour and castles spring to mind. It was they who dragged an unwilling Celtic Ireland into the mainstream of European life. When those adventurer knights from south Wales, with names like de Clare, Fitzstephen and FitzGerald, effected a military landing on the south coast of Wexford in May 1169, they were able to draw on the experience of the equivalent of two world wars (in the form of the first two crusades). They disdainfully brushed aside the efforts of the Irish chiefs to resist them, and, by 1250, there were few areas of the country that had not felt the impact of their presence.

It was the Normans who first introduced heraldry to Ireland. Theirs was a classical heraldry—severe and practical—designed to promote the success of their military ventures. Their service shields and banners were characterized by what we now call heraldic ordinaries, suitably tinctured. Typical examples of Norman heraldry are provided by the shields of de Clare, de Burgo, FitzGerald, Butler, Power and Barry. These shields have, for the most part, retained their pristine simplicity right through to the present day.

Anglo-Irish heraldry was a by-product of the endeavours of the Tudor kings to bring English influence to bear on their Irish possessions. The opening, in 1541, of the Irish parliament, modelled on the Westminster institution, marked an important phase in the constitutional history of the island. In July of the same year, the formal proclamation of Henry VIII as

King of Ireland was marked by striking pomp and ceremony in Dublin. In the reign of Philip and Mary, a conscious policy of settling English people on the land of Ireland began to take shape with the plantation of part of the midlands, thereafter known as King's and Queen's counties, the present-day counties Offaly and Laois.

In the circumstances of the time, some means had to be found to secure social acceptance for the Tudor settlers. Accordingly, heraldic patents were issued to the *novi homines* (new men) by the newly constituted Office of Arms for Ireland (1552). Exemplifications of arms found in the early registers of that Office reveal elaborate heraldic achievements, with individual shields often containing as many as a dozen charges. Many of the achievements reflect a preoccupation on the part of the grantees with family relationships, expressed through the medium of impaling, quartering and cadency, not overlooking the heraldic pedigree. It is with some justification that Anglo-Irish heraldry is occasionally referred to as "court" heraldry, in contrast to Norman heraldry, which is essentially military in character.

Gaelic heraldry exhibits certain characteristics that distinguish it from the other two Irish heraldic traditions. These characteristics include a noticeable lack of heraldic ordinaries, rather frequent use of the tincture vert and the recurrence of certain motifs, such as the twin rampant lions and the dexter red hand. Certainly unique to Gaelic heraldry are a number of mottoes and war cries in the Gaelic language which are inseparably attached to the arms of certain Irish families. Examples of this are *Crom Abú*, which is the FitzGerald motto and *Conland Abú* of the O Mores.

One might have expected that the heraldry of a people whose genius produced such masterpieces of Christian art as the Book of Kells and the Cross of Cong would itself be thoroughly Christian in form and content. Such, in fact, is not the case. While Gaelic heraldry undoubtedly makes use of traditional Christian symbols, like the cross and fleur de lys, its motifs, by and large, are based on pagan Celtic religion and mythology. In the context of Irish history, all three Irish heraldic traditions are complementary and afford us graphic insight into the ideals and aspirations of the people of Ireland in bygone centuries.

by Donal Begley, Chief Herald, Irish Genealogical Office, Dublin

An eighteenth-century engraving of the courtyard at Dublin Castle showing the old Genealogical Office with a flag flying from its tower. This office was closed in the 1980s and moved to its present location in Kildare Street, Dublin.

The Clans of Ireland Office

Other than those bestowed by the British before independence, Ireland, like most democracies, confers no titles. A testament to Irish nobility are the chieftains whose bloodline is authenticated by the Chief Herald at the Genealogical Office in Dublin.

Some chieftaincies have died out, a number are in abeyance and a few are held by representatives in Europe. Following intense research, several ancient chieftaincies have been revived and officially acknowledged.

Today, with the resurgence of interest in family origins and a sense of wanting to belong, clan rallies are held annually all over Ireland during the summer. A few, like the O Connors or the O Neills, can boast a direct bloodline going back a thousand years or more. There is an election of a clan chieftain (not necessarily claiming the clan name) to head the rally and contribute to its promotion at home and abroad. Breaking the ancient mould, the elected chieftain can be a woman.

To satisfy the demand for clan rallying and to help organize the gathering, the Clans of Ireland Office has been established under the auspices of Bord Fáilte (the Irish Tourist Board) and the Department of the Taoiseach (the Prime Minister). Those interested should contact Clans of Ireland Ltd., 2 Kildare Street, Dublin 2. Telephone (01) 6618811.

Officially recognized ancient Irish Chiefs of the Name

MacCarthy Mór
MacDermot, Prince of Coolavin
MacDermot Roe *(dormant since 1917)*
MacDonald of the Glens
MacGillycuddy of the Reeks
MacMurrough Kavanagh *(dormant since 1958)*
Maguire of Fermanagh
O Brien of Thomond
O Callaghan
O Conor Don
O Dochartaigh of Inis Eoghain
O Donnell of Tirconnell
O Donoghue of The Glens
O Donovan
O Grady of Kilballyowen
O Kelly of Gallagh and Tycooly
O Long of Garranelongy
O Morchoe (Murphy)
O Neill of Clannaboy
O Rourke of Breifne
O Toole of Fer Tire *(dormant since 1956)*
An Sionnach (The Fox)

Hereditary Irish knights

The Knight of Glin (FitzGerald)
The Knight of Kerry (FitzGerald)
The White Knight of Clangibbon (Fitzgibbon) (in abeyance)

Ahern

ó heachtiarna

Few Irish surnames begin with the first letter of the alphabet, and Ahern was no exception as its original Irish form was Ó hEachtighearna, which means lord of the horse. Transported into English it became O Hagerin, which was finally simplified to Ahern or Hearne. In Britain there are numerous Hearnes, some of whom may have had earlier roots in Ireland, but, since many do not, tracking this name's origins can be difficult.

The Aherns are thought to be an offshoot of the Dalcassians, an important sept whose chieftain in the tenth century was Mathghamhain, King of Thomond, an area which roughly covers the county of Clare and part of County Limerick. An elder brother of the great High King Brian Boru (*see* O Brien), Mathghamhain drove the Norsemen from Limerick. He died in battle in AD 976 and his descendants are the Aherns or Hearnes who are still rooted in Clare and Limerick.

In the Irish telephone directory the name is numerous, ranging from Ahearn, Ahern, Aherne to Hearn, Hearne and Hearns. In the nineteenth century there was a Hearn's Bank in Callan, County Kilkenny, and there is a famous old hostelry, Hearn's Hotel, in Clonmel, County Tipperary.

The Belfast Public Records Office has an account of the Hearn family dating from 1620 to 1856, while Dublin's Genealogical Office holds manuscripts following the Herron, or Heron, family from 1728 to 1940. In the eighteenth century there were many clerical and academic Ahernes in the colleges and courts of France where they had fled from religious persecution in their homeland.

John Aheron, probably born in Limerick, is regarded as the founder of Irish architecture. In 1754 he published in Dublin *A General Treatise on Architecture*, generously illustrated with his own drawings. Even in those élitist days the names of the book's subscribers included not only Sir Marcus Beresford of Waterford and the Earl of Tyrone (*see* Power), but also Mr Edward Byrne, bricklayer, John Haughton, carver, and Hughie Hanna, carpenter.

Unlike the fashion of the day which was to slavishly follow Italian Palladian architecture, which was more suited to warmer climes, John Aheron showed an appreciation of the necessity for heat insulation in his Irish houses. Among the various structures he designed for the nobility was the gazebo which can still be seen in the gardens of Dromoland Hotel in County Clare, a former castle of the kingly O Briens.

Little is known of **Samuel Hearne** other than that he was an Irishman who worked for the Hudson's Bay Company in Canada between 1769 and 1795. He explored North America extensively and, in 1809, published several volumes about his travels.

John Ahearne (1769–1806) was one of the band of revolutionary United Irishmen and a close friend of the patriot hero, Wolfe Tone. After Wolfe Tone's death in prison following the revolution of 1798, John Ahearne fled Ireland and followed a new military career as an officer in Napoleon's Irish Legion.

William Edward Hearn (1826–88) earned an international reputation in law. He was born in Belturbet, County Cavan, the son of a vicar of Killage. A remarkably versatile scholar, he transferred from Queen's College, Galway, where he was Professor of Greek, to the new University of Melbourne where he filled the unusual role of professor in four different

Aheron

Hearne

Heron

faculties. He wrote on law and economics, and, when appointed Chancellor of Melbourne University, he also represented the Legislative Council in Parliament where he introduced many new laws. He never lost touch with his homeland and wrote with concern of the economics of Ireland and the suffering caused by the several famines there in the nineteenth century.

James A. Hearne (1840–1901) was born in New York, the son of immigrants who had come from Ireland as Aherns. He learned his trade as an amateur actor before becoming a playwright. He had enormous success with his play *Hearts of Oak*, which was followed by a still more rural drama, *Share Acres*, which toured the United States for six seasons.

Patricio Lafcadio Hearn (1850–1904) was born in Greece, the son of Charles Bush Hearn, a surgeon from County Westmeath, and a Greek mother. His parents parted and he spent a lonely boyhood with relatives in Ireland. He emigrated to the USA in 1869. Journalism took him to Japan in 1890, a country which so captivated him he remained there for the rest of his life. He married a Japanese lady and became a citizen of Japan. An exotic figure among Irish literary exiles, he is celebrated not only in the USA, but most particularly in Japan, where he was Head of the English Department in Tokyo's Imperial University. He wrote prolifically, explaining Japan to the Western World. He was recently acknowledged in Ireland by the placing of a plaque on the house in Rathmines, Dublin, in which his boyhood was spent. A charming film has been made of his life in Japan.

May Ellen Ahern (1860–1938) was born of Irish parents in Indiana, where as Assistant State Librarian she was regarded as "a librarian militant".

All through her long career her theme was "libraries should be kept out of politics". Working at the time when Andrew Carnegie's philanthropy was funding the spread of libraries in many countries, she encouraged the use of the Dewey decimal system which was then in its infancy. During the First World War, she went to France for the War Library Service of the American Library Association.

Stradbally Hall, County Laois, home of the Cosby family, was designed by John Aheron.

Barry
ᴅᴇ ʙᴀʀʀᴀ

Nesta, a Welsh princess known as "the Helen of Wales" because of her numerous extramarital liaisons, was married to **Gerald de Barri**. The Barry name came from their estate in Glamorgan. Their sons went to Ireland to spearhead the Anglo-Norman invasion of 1170.

Gerald (1147–1223) was educated for the priesthood in Paris and followed his brothers to Ireland as court chaplain and chronicler. Known as Giraldus Cambrensis (of Wales), he wrote *Topography of Ireland* and *Conquest of Ireland*, both instructive chronicles of the time, yet, for a cleric, showing a remarkable lack of compassion for the invaded.

Philip de Barri settled in Ireland and established a dynasty of Barrys on the vast acreage granted to him in 1179 in County Cork. Perhaps to satisfy his conscience for this land acquired from the dispossessed Irish, Philip founded the Augustinian Abbey of Ballybeg.

At one time there were so many Barrys that they had to be distinguished by their physical appearance. There were Barry Mór (meaning big), Barry Óg (young), Barry Roe (red), Barry Maol (bald) and Barry Láidir (strong). By the end of the fifteenth century, the Barrys had worked their way into the English peerage and were titled Earls of Barrymore and Viscounts Buttevant. Buttevant, in County Cork, a town in the area where they settled, derived its name from the family motto *Boutez en avant* (strike forward), the Barry rallying cry in battle.

In 1507, **Barry Roe** and his entourage were recorded as going on a pilgrimage to Spain. On the return journey their ship was wrecked and all were lost.

Unlike the English, the Normans in Ireland quickly integrated, marrying aristocratic Irish heiresses and consequently acquiring wealth and land. In due course, to use the hackneyed expression, "they became more Irish than the Irish themselves". This inevitably led to divided loyalties.

David Fitzjames de Barry (1550–1617) joined with his Norman-Irish neighbours in the rebellion led by the 14th Earl of Desmond (*see* FitzGerald) during the Geraldine wars, an appalling period of slaying and plundering which ravaged Munster for four years from 1579. In a letter written from Cork in February 1581, Sir Walter Raleigh wrote, "David Barry has burnt all his castles and gone into rebellion". Raleigh had his eye on Barry's Court and the adjoining Fota Island. However, David Barry got himself a pardon and returned to the English side and was given much of the land belonging to the MacCarthys.

David's son, **David Fitzdavid Barry** (1605–42), inherited his father's wealth and was married at 16 to the daughter of Richard Boyle, Earl of Cork and the richest Englishman in Ireland. For his support of the royalist cause, Charles I advanced this Viscount Buttevant to 1st Earl of Barrymore. His splendid house in County Cork was Castlelyons—Lyons is a corruption of O Lehan, the family who were the former occupants of the land. With Lord Inchiquin, an O Brien, he sat on the commission for the civil government of Munster. At one of the Barry fortresses, Liscarrol, he was killed in a minor battle at the age of only 37.

The Barry pedigree is recorded unflinchingly in *Burke's Irish Family Records*. By all accounts, in their early days they were given to a great deal of violence. In the fifteenth century, a Barry who was an archdeacon killed his brother, and was burnt to death by an O Callaghan. In one of many

de Barri

Barrymore

land and title disputes—there were many illegitimate Barrys—a **David Barry** killed both his uncle and his nephew. **Lady Sheelagh Barrymore** gouged out the eyes of her brother-in-law.

James, 5th Earl of Barrymore, who died in 1773, left huge gambling debts and a young, motherless family. They moved to London where they became associated with the Regency rakes, arrogant young aristocrats who flourished during the time of the extravagant Prince Regent (1762–1830). **Richard Barry**, whom the Prince nicknamed "Hellgate", terrified London pedestrians, driving teams of horses through the streets and squares. He built a vast theatre adjoining his house and spent lavishly. When the money, which came from his Irish estates, dried up, he joined the army and died, aged 24, from gunshot wounds. "Newgate" (after the London debtors' prison) was the nickname of **Augustus**, a compulsive gambler who escaped that prison by also dying young.

Another brother, **Henry**, who had a club foot, was known as "Cripplegate". He fought duels in the nude. He gave large dinner parties and dressed as a footman so that the bailiffs would not recognize him. He escaped his debtors to die in poverty in France.

Their sister, the **Lady Caroline**, because of her rough language was called "Billingsgate" (the London fish market).

This wild family brought to an inglorious end all the Barrymore titles and many of their fine houses. There are still interesting remains around Castlelyons. The nearby Barrymore mausoleum has been restored by the Irish Georgian Society.

Other members of the Barry family went abroad, driven by oppression and insurrection, to distinguish themselves in the armies of Europe.

One such was **Gerald Barry** of Buttevant, who was born early in the seventeenth century and went to Spain for his military training. He remained there to become a colonel in the Spanish army and a military historian, highly regarded by the King of Spain who sent him to Ireland to recruit for his army. Gerald returned and was caught up in the rising of 1641. For a short while he commanded a section of the rebels, but found his Spanish training, and probably also his age, unsuitable for irregular warfare, the only type of combat available to the Irish.

Sir Edward Barry (1696–1776) graduated as physician and surgeon from Trinity College, Dublin. He was elected to the Irish House of Commons for the borough of Charleville, County Cork. His son, **Nathaniel**, also followed his father's profession. **John Milner Barry** (1768–1822) introduced vaccination to his native Cork city in 1800.

Sir David Barry (1780–1835), born in Roscommon, was a surgeon with the 58th Foot in the English army at the battle of Salamanca.

There comes a turning point in history when the action changes from the clash of constant battle to the public services and the arts. Medicine and a rich vein of acting and playwriting was a Barry characteristic.

Lodowick Barry is thought to be the first in a line of Barry dramatists. Early in the seventeenth century he wrote and produced his play, *Ram Alley*, in London.

Spranger Barry (1719–77) inherited his father's silversmithing business in Dublin, but he soon ran it into bankruptcy. He turned to the stage where he had enormous success and became "the darling of the audience" because of his beautiful voice and fine figure. The critics described his Romeo as being better than that of Garrick, which led to a corrosive rivalry between the two. In Dublin he staged lavish shows and gave huge parties, but in time he had to return to London to retrieve his fortunes, playing the Haymarket, Covent Garden and Drury Lane. He was held in

Spranger Barry

such high esteem that when he died he was awarded the distinction of burial in Westminster Abbey.

The ancestral roots of a remarkable Philadelphia acting family, dubbed "The Royal Family of America's stage and screen", were in Ireland. Their mother was Georgina Drew, daughter of John Drew (1827–1902), an actor from Dublin. She married the actor, **Maurice Barrymore** (1847–1905). Their eldest son, **John Barrymore** (1882–1942), made his stage début in 1903 and was a leading man in the Fifth Avenue Theatre run by Augustus Daly. His leading lady was the Irish star, Ada Rehan, whose real name was Grehan, from Limerick. The star of the fantasy film, *ET*, was six-year-old **Drew Barrymore**, granddaughter of John Barrymore.

The Philadelphia Story, one of New York's longest running plays in the 1900s, was written by **Philip Barry**, whose parents came from Ireland.

James Barry (1741–1806) of Cork went to sea for a while before discovering his talent for painting. In his early days he was generously encouraged by a Cork physician. His allegorical painting, *St Patrick Baptising the King of Cashel,* brought him the patronage of the Irish philosopher and statesman, Edmund Burke, who sent him to study in Italy. In England he gained a reputation as a painter of history and of portraits, and in 1782 he became Professor of Painting at the Royal Academy. An indiscreet and cantankerous man, he was expelled from the Academy. He died a recluse, leaving a rich legacy of paintings. A Barry exhibition was held in the Tate Gallery in London, in 1983.

John Barry (1745–1803), born in Wexford, went to sea at 14 and took part in a number of sea battles during the American War of Independence. For his dedication to the up-dating and improving of the navy, Commodore Barry is known as "Father of the American navy". There are fine statues of him sculpted by fellow Irishmen, one in Philadelphia and another in Washington DC. In 1956, the Irish government issued a stamp depicting the statue by William Williams which was presented to Ireland by the people of the United States and stands in Wexford Harbour.

John Barry (1790–1859), another Wexford Barry, was consecrated Catholic Bishop of Baltimore.

William Taylor Sullivan Barry (1812–68), born in Virginia of Irish parents, was a prominent Confederate statesman and soldier.

Patrick Barry (1816–90) emigrated from Belfast to Long Island where he was a pioneer of American fruit culture, in which he was followed by his son, **William C. Barry**.

Thomas Henry Barry, born in New York, graduated in 1877 from West Point to join the Irish Seventh Cavalry. By 1898 he was a colonel in the Spanish-American war. He followed this with service in the Philippines and the Boxer rising in China. He was a major-general when he returned as superintendent to the United States Military Academy.

A number of Barrys followed careers in law. **Sir Redmond Barry** (1813–80) sailed to New South Wales where he became a judge and first chancellor of the new University of Melbourne. The public library, Technological Institution, and the National Gallery of Victoria owe their origins to the energetic Redmond Barry.

Another Redmond, the **Right Honourable Redmond Barry**, was Lord Chancellor of Ireland from 1911 to 1913. His son, **Sir Patrick Barry** (d. 1972), was judge of the Queen's Bench Division in London's High Court, presiding at many notorious criminal trials, including that of Colin Jordan and the Vassal spy case.

During the 1916 uprising in Ireland, two Barry heroes contributed to the country's independence. **Kevin Barry** (1902–20), a Dublin medical

James Barry (1741–1806)

John Barry (1745–1803)

Commander Tom Barry

student, joined the Irish Republican Army and was captured during an armed raid. His ruthless execution at the age of 18 led many other students to join the movement. *Guerrilla Days in Ireland* is **Commander Tom Barry**'s account of how he led his West Cork Brigade at Crossbarry in the War of Independence, when, with 104 men, he dispersed 5,000 British troops.

Peter Barry, son of a former Lord Mayor of Cork, was a Deputy Leader of the Fine Gael party and Minister of Foreign Affairs in a coalition government. His family firm, Barry's Tea of Cork, are the country's oldest tea merchants.

The Barrys are still plentiful in their ancient homeland of Munster; it is also a numerous English name. Three main branches of the ancient Barrys remain in Ireland and can be traced in the 1976 edition of *Burke's Irish Family Records*.

Fota Island at Carrightwohill, outside Cork city, has become one of the city's proudest amenities. A former Barrymore shooting lodge, it was sold in 1975 by the Smith Barry family to University College Cork. The building, with its fine furniture and paintings (its restoration inspired and mainly funded by a philanthropic Cork business man, Richard Wood) is open to the public. The grounds are now a wildlife park used by the Royal Zoological Society of Ireland to care for animals in danger of extinction. The arboretum, planted a century ago by the Barrys, is one of the show-pieces. Fota has now been sold by University College Cork to developers and its fate hangs in the balance.

Blake
ó blácach

Blowick

Caddell

In the twelfth century, **Richard Caddell** came to Ireland from Wales with the Normans. He was known as Niger or le Blaca (the black). In time the name was transformed to Blake, a very common name today both in Ireland and England.

The Blakes were awarded large tracts of land in Connacht where they remained for six centuries, mainly around County Galway. Branching out into new families, they covered Connacht with their castles and mansions, many of which are still standing.

In medieval times, Galway was an important port with strong European links, mostly in Spain. The leading merchant families were nicknamed by the Cromwellians "The Fourteen Tribes of Galway". Blake marriage records show them intermarrying almost exclusively with their fellow merchants, notably the Lynch, Kirwan, French and Browne families. For instance, James Blake married Margery, daughter of Dominick Browne, "the richest merchant in Ireland".

The church of St Nicholas in Galway, where there is a tradition that Columbus paused to pray on his way to America, is a highly praised example of Norman-Irish architecture. It was particularly dear to the Blakes. An heiress, **Cilly Blake**, made over her inheritance in 1438 to keep up the perpetual grants made to it by her family.

Several Blakes went abroad to take part in the Crusades. In 1591, because of the anti-Catholicism of the Elizabethan age, **James Blake** went to Spain to entreat the king, Philip II, to aid the Irish by invading Galway. Philip, old and ailing, sent no troops. In 1598 he died, and when the Spaniards did arrive in 1601 they were too few and too late and shared the Irish defeat at the battle of Kinsale, which was followed by the flight of the Irish nobility to Europe. James Blake remained behind to join the victorious English and was suspected of being a spy in their pay.

For generations a Blake was Mayor or Sheriff or Burgess of Galway. During a period of religious persecution, **Robert Blake**, though Catholic, was Mayor of Galway when, it is recorded, "for the first time freemen of the town were made capable to vote". He was also the first Mayor in thirty years not to be questioned for recusancy—refusal to attend Protestant services.

Ardfry at Oranmore, County Galway, was the home of **Sir Richard Blake**, Member of Parliament for County Galway in 1639. A descendant of his, also an MP, was created Baron Wallscourt. The **3rd Baron Wallscourt** (1779–1877) was a physically powerful man whose addiction to boxing probably caused him brain damage. He had a violent temper and was given to walking around naked, carrying only a handbell provided by his distraught wife so that he at least would not frighten the servants. Ardfry was given a face-lift for the making of the film *Mackintosh Man*.

About the Blakes of Menlough many a story has been told. Valentine is a recurrent first name and, in 1622, **Valentine Blake** was created a baronet of Ireland. When Sir Valentine was killed in a duel he was succeeded by his brother, **Sir Walter Blake**. He is described in *Burke's Irish Peerage* as "the first Catholic gentleman that joined the standard of the Prince of Orange". He even raised a regiment for King William "which he maintained and clothed at his own expense".

In the eighteenth century a **Sir Valentine Blake** of Menlough, although a good landlord, like so many of his kind squandered his income

Sir Valentine Blake

on gaming and drink. He could only leave his castle on Sundays—the one day that the bailiffs could not touch him. He was so popular that influential friends arranged for his election as a Member of Parliament, which made him immune from debt collectors.

In 1875, at the burial of the 13th baronet **Sir Thomas Blake**, his heir, **Sir Valentine**, insisted on having a Protestant service despite the fact that Sir Thomas was Catholic. There was a fearful riot at the funeral. The Menlough people were very angry, their violence barely controlled by the priests, and the legal consequences were so severe that several Menlough families fled to Australia. Ironically, 37 years later when Sir Valentine died, the stonemasons set his headstone at the foot of the grave! Menlough Castle, once the setting for extravagant social occasions, was burned accidentally in the summer of 1910 and is now a romantic ruin by the River Corrib, just outside Galway city.

Harry Blake of Annaghdown, Corrandulla, County Galway (d. 1988), used to say "The Blakes have for long followed the old maxim: with debts galore, but fun far more, oh that's the man for Galway!"

The Galway mace and sword which had been in the keeping of the Blakes since they were Mayors of Galway were sold by an impoverished Blake to the American newspaper millionaire and collector, William Randolph Hearst. In the 1960s they were restored by the Hearst Foundation of the United States of America and are now on display in the Bank of Ireland in Galway's Eyre Square.

During his brief life, **Xaverius Blake** (1752–84) of Dunmacrina, County Mayo, and also of Oranmore, County Galway, got through an inheritance of £1,000,000, and a rent roll of £5,500—a fortune in those days. He married the eldest daughter of John Knox, known as "Diamond Knox", who bestowed on her the notorious "Knox Diamonds". The extravagant life style of the Blakes and the early death of Xaverius kept the lawyers busy for almost a century establishing the ownership of the gems. The descendants of this marriage would seem to be plentiful, judging by the number of entries for Blake Knox in the Irish telephone directories.

William Rufus Blake (1805–63), a descendant of the Galway Blakes, was born at Halifax, Nova Scotia, and began a promising career in light comedy but, because of his enormous girth, he was diverted to weightier parts. He acted in the leading cities of the United States and in London where he was described as "one of the most mirth-provoking actors because of his rotundity".

William Hume Blake (1809–70), who was born at Kiltegan, County Wicklow, assumed his mother's name. Having graduated in law from Trinity College, Dublin in 1823, he chartered a ship with a group of relatives and sailed from Dublin to Canada where he founded a dynasty of Toronto lawyers. His eldest son, **Edward Blake** (1833-1912), was one of the "foremost authorities on the Canadian Constitution", according to legal history. He was also an aspiring Canadian statesman who, finding Canadian politics to be not to his liking, withdrew from public life in 1890. He did however return to Ireland where, as an Irish nationalist, he sat in the British House of Commons as a Member of Parliament for South Longford. While this was a worthwhile occupation it did not live up to his hope of Home Rule for Ireland.

Samuel Hume Blake (1835–1914), another member of that family, was a Toronto judge and his son, **William Hume Blake** (1861–1924), was also a lawyer in Toronto as well as a writer.

Sir Henry Arthur Blake (1840–1918), who was born at Limerick, followed a career familiar to many of the landed Irish gentry. He was successively governor of a string of British colonies: The Bahamas, Newfoundland, Jamaica, Hong Kong and Ceylon (now Sri Lanka). Using the pen-name "Terence McGrath", he wrote books on his travels including *Pictures from Ireland*. The Chinese gates he brought back from his travels which grace his one-time home, Myrtle Grove, Youghal, County Cork, are a fitting memorial to this cosmopolitan Blake.

One of Britain's Poet Laureates, Cecil Day-Lewis (1904–72) was born in Ballintubber, County Laois, and was brought up by his aunt, a Blake of Galway. Appropriately, he chose "Nicholas Blake" as the pen-name for his numerous successful detective stories.

In County Kildare the Blakes have given their name to the town of Blakestown. The enforced Anglicization of old Gaelic names can often cause confusion. There were Blakes in the West of Ireland of earlier, Gaelic rather than Norman, origin. In Irish their name was Ó Blachmhaich which, Anglicized, became Blowick or, more usually, Blake.

The Blakes are well documented. In *The Blake Family Records 1600–1700*, compiled by **Martin J. Blake** in 1825, there is a portrait of Sir Valentine Blake of Menlough who was Mayor of Galway from 1634 to 1644.

Menlo Castle, County Galway

Boyle

ó BAOILL

Donegal is still the county of the O Boyles. Until the breakup of the old Gaelic order in the mid-seventeenth century when they also dropped the O prefix, they shared the leadership of the north-west with those other formidable chieftains of Donegal, the O Donnells and the O Dohertys (*see* Doherty).

The Boyles, the name means a pledge, are a very ancient family from the barony of Boylagh who, according to *Burke's Landed Gentry of Ireland,* settled some 200 years ago in County Derry where they had great possessions. Their castle was at Desart, County Armagh.

Since 1660, the Boyles have been connected with Limavady, also in County Derry. In 1961 **Hugh Boyle** sold Desart Castle and he now lives in London. But not all the numerous Boyles in Ireland are of Gaelic-Irish origin: many of the Boyles of Ulster came as settlers from Scotland.

In the *Dictionary of National Biography* there are accounts of fifteen Boyles. Of these, fourteen descend from the same Boyle ancestor, **Richard Boyle** (1556–1643), who came as an adventurer from a west country English family. He had but "27 shillings and threepence, a diamond ring, a bracelet and his wearing apparel" when he arrived in Ireland. He also had a keen mind and, using every opportunity, he began to manipulate the land and so made his fortune. Though he annexed ecclesiastical land from all denominations, he thought of himself as godly, with a mission to convert the natives and improve the "New English".

He populated Munster with his fifteen children (by two wives), educated them conscientiously and set them up munificently. He married them into the nobility and bribed courtiers to get them titles; he bestowed huge dowries on his daughters. As was the custom, his children were put out first for wet nursing and then fostering. Undoubtedly this branch of the Boyles is one of the most remarkable families to be harboured by Ireland.

When Sir Walter Raleigh was executed, Richard Boyle, by now 1st Earl of Cork, bought his Myrtle Grove estate at Youghal for a paltry £1000. He bought cheaply the properties of the FitzGeralds, O Mahonys, O Donovans, O Driscolls, O Learys and other native septs, and planted them with English and Scottish settlers. His principal seat was the splendid Lismore Castle in County Waterford, on the site of which, in the eighth century (during Ireland's golden age), a monastery and university had stood.

Far ahead of his time, Richard Boyle introduced ironworks, built bridges, harbours, towns and thirteen strong castles. It was said of him, "If there had been one like him in every province, it would have been impossible for the Irish to raise a rebellion". He had his brothers appointed to the bishopric of Waterford and Lismore, and another relative was made Archbishop of Tuam. His astute financial deals did not please Sir Thomas Strafford (1593–1641), Lord Lieutenant of Ireland, who made him surrender the college of Youghal, taken from FitzGerald, Earl of Desmond, and fined him £15,000 for various evasions of the law.

Showing signs of decay, the Boyle tomb in St Mary's Collegiate Church in Youghal, County Cork, depicts the Earl surrounded by miniatures of his eight daughters and seven sons and full size figures of his two wives—wives regularly succumbed during childbirth in those unscientific days. A coloured replica of the Boyle tomb also holds a prominent position in St Patrick's Cathedral in Dublin.

The Boyle tomb

Richard Boyle (1621–79), third of the seven sons of the 1st Earl of Cork, was created Baron Broghill at the age of seven. He matured to be a versatile statesman and an army general. At first a supporter of the Cromwellians, he reverted to the monarchy on the accession of Charles II who, having proclaimed himself King of Ireland in 1660, gave power and honours to former Cromwellian leaders, including Richard Boyle whom he created 1st Earl of Orrery—an orrery being a place where the stars are studied.

The only one of Boyle's talented children not to chase titles was **Robert Boyle** (1627–91), the inventor of Boyle's Law—the discovery of the elasticity of air. Despite what he described as "a lifelong torturing malady, bad eyes and a treacherous memory", he was a brilliant natural philosopher and "a linguist by necessity". This was Galileo's time, and with so much strife in Ireland, he studied in Florence. Afterwards, in England, and at his own expense, he printed bibles in the Irish, Indian and Welsh languages. He helped in founding Britain's Royal Society. Above all he was a religious man and a modest one who declined the honours of titles offered him.

Robert Boyle

Henry, **Earl of Shannon** (1682–1764), of Castlemartyr, County Cork, descended also from the 1st Earl of Cork. His mother, Lady Mary O Brien, was the daughter of Murrough O Brien, 1st Earl of Inchiquin and president of Munster. In 1729 Henry Boyle distinguished himself in the Dublin Parliament. "The king of the Irish Commons" is how Sir Robert Walpole has described him. He held many high offices, Commissioner for Revenue in Ireland, Speaker of the House of Commons, Chancellor of the Exchequer. In 1753 he was the darling of the people, stopping a proposal to appropriate a surplus in the Irish exchequer for English use. For this he suffered dismissal from all offices held under the Crown.

A great-grandson of the 1st Earl of Cork, another **Richard**, 3rd Earl of Burlington (1695–1753), promoted the fashion for Palladian architecture and reconstructed Burlington House in London, of which the poet Gray wrote, "Beauty within; without, proportion reigns". Lord Hervey, Earl Bishop of Derry, described it as "Possessed of one great hall of state, without a room to sleep or eat". Intent on his architectural embellishing, Richard ran out of money and sold his Irish estates to pay his English debts.

In more recent times, **Richard Vicars Boyle** (b. 1822), a Dubliner, was an engineer who travelled through India constructing railroads. During the mutiny of 1857 he defended his house with only 50 men against 3,000 rebels. In Japan, where he spent five years, he was engineer-in-chief to the railways.

Henry Boyle

John J. Boyle (1851–1917) was born in New York, a descendant of several generations of stonecutters from Northern Ireland. He went to Paris to study at the École des Beaux Arts and found his *métier* in huge sculptural groupings. His work has been described by critics as "elemental rather than elegant, deep emotion untainted by sentimentality". He sculpted the famous *Indian Family* in Chicago's Lincoln Park and, in 1914, the statue of Commodore John Barry for Washington DC.

William Boyle (1853–1922) was one of the earliest dramatists to write for Dublin's Abbey Theatre. Born in Dromiskin, County Louth, a civil servant turned playwright, his best-known production is probably *The Eloquent Dempsey* which was first performed at the Abbey Theatre in 1905.

Browne

ᏧᎴ ᏴᏢᎤᏅ

Brown

de Brun

Maximilian Ulysses Browne

Brown—with or without an e—is a very common name in both England and Ireland. A **Le Brun** who came from Normandy in about the twelfth century was the forefather of the Brownes of Galway, who integrated so well in that thriving Atlantic seaport that they became one of the leading families known as "The Fourteen Tribes of Galway": Athy, Blake, Bodkin, Browne, Darcy, Deane, Ffont, Ffrench, Joyce, Kirwan, Lynch, Martin, Morris and Skerrett. The Brownes intermarried with these families and also with the two powerful Connacht septs of O Flaherty and O Malley.

A Browne kinsman who had fought in the Civil War in England against Edward II escaped to Ireland to take part in the Anglo-Norman invasion of 1170. **Sir Philip Browne** of Mulrankan, County Wexford, was appointed Governor of Wexford. From this line are said to descend the Brownes who were variously ennobled as Lord Kilmaine, Marquis of Sligo, and Lord Oranmore and Browne.

The Brownes who were Earls of Kenmare descended from an Elizabethan settler. Like their Galway namesakes, they became rooted in Ireland by marriage to Irish wives.

In the seventeenth century innumerable settlers of the name came from Scotland and England to stir up the racial mixture. Depending on the side they actively supported—native or colonizer—they had their lands forfeited, or were granted lands taken from the ancient Gaelic owners. Many shared the latter's fate during the Cromwellian transplantations to Connacht.

A recitation of the vicissitudes of Irish families must inevitably include a list of those driven out by one or another of the two dynamic social factors, politics and religion. The Brownes were no exception.

Ignatius Brown (d. 1679), born in Waterford, had to be sent to Spain to be educated. There he joined the Jesuit Order and was confessor to the queen. Later he moved to France to become rector of the Irish seminary at Poitiers.

George Browne (1698–1792) was one of a number of Brownes who, to their misfortune, favoured the ill-fated Stuart King, James II. Following his defeat at the Boyne, the Brownes of Camus, County Limerick, seeing no opportunity for their young son to follow the gentlemanly occupation of arms, sent him abroad. He joined the Russian imperial army and began a life of high adventure. He was imprisoned three times after various battles. He was sold as a slave to the Turks, but was eventually released. Having shown exceptional skill and bravery, he was appointed Field Marshal to Czar Peter of Russia. As Count George Browne, he became Governor of Livonia. He had become a great favourite with the powerful Empress Catherine and she would not consider letting him go, so he remained in Russia, dying there at the age of 94.

A kinsman from the Camus family, **Maximilian Ulysses Browne** (1705–57), whose Jacobite father was exiled following the battle of the Boyne in 1690, entered the imperial service of Austria and became a Field Marshal. He was created Count of the Empire by Charles VI of Austria and was killed at the battle of Prague.

Bishop Peter Brown (d. 1735) held the diverse ecclesiastical posts of Provost of Trinity College, Dublin, and Protestant Bishop of Cork. He was famous for his strong sermons scarifying his congregation for the custom of drinking too merrily at wakes.

Perhaps the most famous of the Irish Brownes is **William Brown** (1777–1857) of Foxford, County Mayo. He emigrated with his family to Argentina and worked his way up from cabin boy in the American Mercantile Marine to the command of a merchant vessel, from which he was induced to enter the Argentine navy. Under his command it defeated two Spanish squadrons and the Brazilian fleet. In 1814 he blockaded Montevideo. In time he was appointed admiral and stayed with the Argentine navy until 1845. He died in his home near Buenos Aires.

Admiral William Brown

In August 1992, the Argentine training ship, the *Libertad*, sailed into Dublin bay. During its stay the officers entertained a party from Foxford on board. The people of Foxford reciprocated by inviting the entire crew to Foxford where they were greeted by a band and all the local dignitaries.

The Brownes frequently combined learning with travel. **Patrick Browne** (1720–90) of Woodstock, County Mayo, was a naturalist who took his medical degree at the University of Leiden in the Netherlands and became a friend of the great Swedish botanist, Linnaeus. He travelled widely and published a history of Jamaica and various catalogues of the birds, fishes, and other wildlife of his native land.

Andrew Brown (b. 1744) came from an Ulster family and studied at Trinity College, Dublin, before serving in America as an officer in the English army. He settled in Massachusetts and fought on the American side at Lexington and Bunker Hill. When peace came, he tried to set up an academy for the young ladies of Philadelphia, but he was more successful in publishing, especially his *Philadelphia Gazette*, which was the first to regularly report debates in Congress.

Another Browne family which made a contribution to the United States was descended from the **Reverend Arthur Browne**, born in 1699 in Drogheda, County Louth. He was Vicar General of the diocese of Kildare and was returned to the Irish House of Commons. His son, **Arthur Browne**, went to America where he was rector of Trinity Church, Rhode Island. His son, a third **Arthur Browne**, was sent to Dublin to study for the Bar at Trinity College. On returning to America he was one of the original fellows of Rhode Island College which, from 1804, has been known as Brown University, inspired by these gentlemen from County Louth.

The Browns are very strong in Ulster. **Alexander Brown** (1764–1834), who has been described as "one of America's first millionaires", was born in Ballymena, County Antrim. In 1800, when he left for America, he had a small linen store in Belfast. Beginning by importing linen from Ireland, the Alexander Brown house soon grew into one of the biggest business and banking companies in America. With the help of his four sons, the business branched out to Philadelphia, New York, and Liverpool in England. They built and sailed their own importing and exporting ships and were involved in every type of civic progress and social activity, including helping to found the Maryland Institute of Art. One of Alexander's sons, **George Brown** (1787–1859), was a founder of the Baltimore and Ohio Railroad. Alexander Brown & Sons is the oldest banking house in the United States today.

Brownes also spread to the southern hemisphere, where **William Henry Browne** (1800–77) of Mallow, County Cork, who had studied theology at Trinity College, Dublin, sailed in 1825 on the *Coronet* from Cork Harbour. It was eight months before he reached Hobart Town, where he was to take up his colonial chaplaincy at St John's, Launceston. Although it was far from acceptable at the time, he was ecumenically minded and encouraged a spirit of friendliness between the differing churches.

He was also very much against the British policy of transporting prisoners to Australia. One of his sons, who was ordained in 1872, was sent to the Assyrian Christians in Turkey and became so attached to his life at the court of the Assyrian Patriarch that he became an oriental scholar and remained in Turkey until he died in 1910.

The only notable Brown lady was **Frances Brown** (1816–79), the blind poet of Donegal. She educated herself by listening at school. She published volumes of poetry and novels and was granted a civil list pension, and died in London.

John Ross Browne (b. 1822), a journalist and world traveller, went wandering at an early age. He met with little success until he shipped before the mast on a whaler bound for the Indian Ocean, which gave him material for his *Etchings on a Whaling Cruise*. He finally came to rest in Oakland, California, where he reared a large family. He wrote for *Harper's* magazine, and, in 1869, was so well-respected that he was sent for two years as US Minister to China.

An earlier home of the Kerry Brownes, Ross Castle, on the lakes of Killarney, was later home to **Valentine Browne**, Viscount Castlerosse (1891–1943), the 6th and last Earl of Kenmare. He was with the Irish Guards in the First World War. A *bon viveur* and London's foremost newspaper gossip columnist in the 1920s and 1930s, he laid out a golf course on his estate at Killarney where he invited many celebrities to play. His former home is now American owned.

In the twentieth century, the Irish literary world was startled by **Christy Brown** (1932–81). Born in the slums of Dublin, one of six children, he was almost completely paralysed from birth. His persevering mother taught him to read and, using his left foot, to write and paint. His paintings were exhibited and he achieved maturity and international acclaim with his autobiography, *My Left Foot* and his novel, *Down All the Days*. A very successful film has been made of his life.

Garech Browne (b. 1939) is a descendant of the Connacht Oranmore and Browne family. He has contributed substantially to the appreciation of Irish folk music by encouraging exchanges with other Celts, of Scotland and elsewhere, and by making recordings and films of music and poetry with Claddagh Records of Dublin.

Westport House in County Mayo is one of the showplaces of Ireland. A massive Georgian mansion, it stands on the site of an ancient castle of the O Malleys (the dungeons can be visited). It commands a magnificent view over Clew Bay and the Atlantic Ocean to Achill and Clare Island and Ireland's holy mountain, Croagh Patrick. The original house was built by **Colonel John Browne** (whose ancestors came to Ireland during the Elizabethan wars) and his wife, ancestors of the present Marquess of Sligo. His wife was a great-great-granddaughter of Grace O Malley, the sea-faring pirate queen of Connacht in Elizabeth's time. The house has a fine collection of old silver and a library with many priceless books and manuscripts. There are portraits by Sir Joshua Reynolds of the Browne who was **1st Earl of Altamont**, and of the **Rt. Hon. Denis Browne**, brother of the 1st Marquess and a member of Henry Grattan's Parliament. Beechy did the portrait of the **2nd Marquess**, who spent four months in an English jail for bribing British seamen, in time of war, to bring his ship loaded with antiques from Greece—including the gates of Mycenae—back to the harbour at Westport. This same enterprising Marquess was a friend of George IV and the poet Byron.

All his life Lord Altamont, **Jeremy Browne**, son of the present Marquess, has been fighting to retain this magnificent inheritance which is threatened by taxation and recession. He opens the house to the public and has established many attractions—an art gallery, boutiques, a zoo and camping sites. Thousands of people visit Westport House every year.

Whether from Normandy, England or Scotland, whether Protestant or Catholic, the Brownes have had many prominent churchmen in their families. They can boast one of Ireland's comparatively few cardinals, **Michael David Browne** (b. 1887), from Tipperary. A learned Dominican, he held many important appointments in the Vatican.

Also from Tipperary came **Monsignor Patrick de Brun** (1889–1960). He was an outstanding scholar, linguist and a Gaelic poet, and was a president of University College, Galway.

Michael Browne (1896–1980) was the Bishop of Galway who masterminded the imposing new cathedral in that "City of the Tribes".

Former seats built by the ubiquitous Brownes are located all over Ireland, although some have been demolished, burned down or put to other use. In the eighteenth century, **Thomas Wogan Browne**, an amateur architect, designed a number of them. Clongowes Wood College, one of Ireland's premier boys' schools, was a former Castle Browne, in County Kildare. Ashford Castle, County Galway, an Oranmore and Brown home, is now a palatial hotel. It was here that President Reagan stayed during his 1983 visit and that several EC conferences have been hosted. Through marriage or inheritance, Brownes have taken on additional surnames, such as Knox-Browne, Lecky-Brown-Lecky and Browne Clayton.

Monsignor Patrick de Brun

Burke

ᴅᴇ ʙúʀᴄᴀ

Bourke

de Burgh

de Burgo

Bernard Burke (1814–92) and his father **John Burke** (1787–1848) were genealogists and publishers of a succession of weighty volumes containing the pedigree of the British and Irish aristocracy, including *Burke's Peerage* which became known as "the stud book of humanity". Bernard Burke was Ulster King of Arms at the Genealogical Office in Dublin Castle, precursor of the present day Chief Herald. The Genealogical Office is now located in Kildare Street, Dublin.

The family of de Burgh, de Burgo, or Bourke (as at different times written), Earls and Marquesses of Clanricarde, ranks amongst the most distinguished in the Kingdom, and deduces an uninterrupted line of powerful nobles from the Conquest.

John, Earl of Comyn, and Baron of Tonsburgh, in Normandy (whose descent has been deduced from Charlemagne), being general of the King's forces, and governor of his chief towns, assumed thence the surname of de Burgh.

The family of de Burgh, or Burke, has, since the reigns of Henry III and Edward I, been esteemed one of the most opulent and powerful of the Anglo-Norman settlers in Ireland, under Strongbow. It held, by conquest and regal grant, whole territories in the counties Galway, Mayo, Roscommon, Tipperary, and Limerick; and so extended were its possessions, that its very cadets became persons of wealth, and were founders of distinguished houses themselves.

This extract from *Burke's Peerage 1876* sets the scene for a Norman family which was to become highly influential in Ireland.

The history of the energetic Burke family is complex and widespread. It has been nicely encapsulated by **Eamonn Bourke** of Castlebar, County Mayo, who published *Burke People and Places*, a comprehensive paperback which covers the Burkes through the generations.

William de Burgh (known as the Conqueror of Ireland) was the progenitor of the Burkes in Ireland and brother of **Hubert de Burgh**, "the most powerful man in England next to King John". William came to Ireland in about 1185 and was made Governor of Limerick. He consolidated his social position by marrying a daughter of Donal Mór O Brien, King of Thomond (now the area around Shannon airport). He set out to conquer Connacht and after much massacre and pillaging he overcame the reigning O Conors. According to the annals "he died of a singular disease too horrible to write down". He was buried *c.* 1205 in Athassel Abbey which he had founded.

William's son, **Richard** (*c.* 1193–1243), Viceroy of Ireland and Lord of Connacht and Trim in County Meath, despite his continual assaults on the O Conor kings of Connacht, married an O Conor daughter. It is said that he founded the city of Galway. Certainly he built himself a fine house there between Lough Corrib and the Atlantic Ocean.

His eldest son, **Walter** (d. 1272), acquired the Earldom of Ulster through marriage with a daughter of Hugh de Lacy. He fortified his Ulster territory with many castles which still enliven the coast in counties Donegal, Down and Antrim. It was he who built the amazing Dunluce Castle near Portrush in County Antrim which was used in succeeding centuries by the MacQuillans and the MacDonnells.

From Walter, 1st Earl of Ulster, descend the Burkes of Limerick and Tipperary.

Richard de Burgh (c. 1193–1243)

16

The Burkes became thoroughly Irish and adopted Brehon Law. Under these old Irish laws, women were not allowed to inherit. And so, lacking a male heir, the title of Ulster went from the de Burgos to the royal family of England when **Elizabeth de Burgo**, **Countess of Ulster** (d. 1363), an only child, married **Lionel**, **Duke of Clarence**, the third son of the Yorkist king of England, Edward II. Lionel became Earl of Ulster, a title still used by the royal family.

The Burkes saw to it that no Duke of Clarence, Earl of Ulster or not, would get hold of their Connacht territory. In fact they had grabbed it from the native O Flahertys, having driven them from Galway city. They leased some land back to the O Flahertys, but, as no rent seemed to be forthcoming, a Burke was sent to collect it at the O Flaherty headquarters at the magnificent Aughanure Castle in Oughterard. They were enjoying a banquet and he was invited to join them. During the feasting he mentioned the rent. Immediately, an O Flaherty pressed a concealed flagstone which hurled Burke into the river. They cut off his head and sent it back to the Burke stronghold, describing it as "O Flaherty's rent".

Richard Burke, known as Richard an Iarainn (of the iron), possibly because of the iron mines on his Burrishoole lands, was the second husband of Grania O Malley the pirate queen, one of the outstanding Irish women of the Elizabethan age. Their son, **"Theobald of the ships"**, was born at sea just before his mother fended off marauding Turkish pirates. Theobald was taken hostage by the English and brought up to the English point of view. Like his mother, he knew how to play both sides, and when he failed to be elected to the leadership of the Burkes of Mayo, he returned to England. He fought on the English side in 1601 at the decisive battle of Kinsale. He was created 1st Viscount Mayo in 1627 by Charles I—a title which lasted only until 1767. The de Burgos had long since sprouted new family branches. Like the Irish, they appointed chieftains over their separate territories. The most prominent County Galway Burke family was that of the chiefs of Clanricarde. In 1543, **Ulick de Burgo** had submitted to Henry VIII who created him Earl of Clanricarde.

In the seventeenth century, to prevent their lands from being confiscated by the followers of William of Orange, they changed from Catholicism to Protestantism, as did many of the neighbouring families. The Clanricardes built a fine castle at Portumna which was inherited by Viscount Lascelles, the husband of Princess Mary, only daughter of George V. It came to him from a great uncle, the last **Marquess of Clanricarde** (d. 1916), an eccentric who lived in miserly squalor in rooms in London.

In Mayo, the most significant de Burgh families are the Viscounts Mayo and the Lords Mayo (and Barons Naas). In successive generations they have been politicians, bishops, priests and statesmen at home and abroad.

One of the greatest statesmen of his day, **Edmund Burke** (1729–97), was born in Dublin. A political writer and a powerful orator, while a Member of Parliament in Britain at the time of the French Revolution he exhorted diplomacy rather than bloodshed. Nor was he afraid to say that British stupidity had lost America and would lose Ireland. Although far from wealthy, when he was Privy Counsellor he reduced his own salary by three-quarters! His book, *Reflections on the Revolution in France*, was considered enormously important all over Europe. In one of his orations he said "the age of chivalry is gone. That of sophisters, economists and calculators has succeeded".

Walter Hussey Burgh, statesman and orator, was born in Kildare in 1742. He studied law at Trinity College, Dublin. It was said of him, "No modern speaker approaches him in power of stirring the passions".

Edmund Burke

Contemporary with Walter, there was **William Burgh** of Kilkenny. He went into politics in England where he bravely advocated the abolition of the slave trade and vigorously opposed the Union which he saw would tie the Irish government even more tightly to England. He lived in York, England, for many years and left his library to York Minster.

William Burke (1792–1829) of Cork was hanged as a notorious criminal. With his fellow-countryman, Hare, he lured strangers into his Edinburgh lodging house, made them drunk, suffocated them and sold their bodies for dissection. His awful work gave a new word to the English language—"to burke"—meaning to suffocate.

Robert O Hara Burke (1820–61) of St Cleran's, Craughwell, County Galway, was of the Clanricarde Burkes. He served in the Austrian army as a captain, and later joined the Australian police as an inspector. He and his companion, W. J. Wills, were the first white men to cross Australia from south to north. Their expedition was far from well planned and, on the return journey in 1861, they both died from starvation after they had covered 3,700 miles by foot and on camel back. A film of their tragic adventure, *Burke and Wills,* was made in Australia in 1986.

St Cleran's

Richard Southwell Bourke (1822–1872), 6th Earl of Mayo and also Lord Naas, was Chief Secretary for Ireland during the Fenian risings. In 1869, aged only 46, Disraeli appointed him Viceroy of India. He was regarded as being "One of the ablest administrators that ever ruled India". While on a visit to a penal settlement in the Andaman Islands he was assassinated.

Canon Ulick Bourke (1829–87) was from County Mayo. He was one of the first and most influential of the Irish language revivalists.

Thomas Henry Burke (1829–82) of Galway, while under-secretary at Dublin Castle, was walking in Phoenix Park with the newly-arrived Chief Secretary for Ireland, Lord Frederick Cavendish, on Sunday, 6 May 1882, when they were knifed to death by terrorists styling themselves "Invincibles".

Great numbers of Burkes, many of them lawyers, went to America. **Aedanus Burke** (1742–1802) of Galway went to Virginia where his law studies led to his appointment as judge. He was the first Senator to represent South Carolina at Congress. A man at cross-purposes with himself, he believed in slavery and in democracy. During the French Revolution he wrote widely disseminated pamphlets advocating the abolition of all titles of nobility. He has been nicely described in the *Dictionary of American Biography* as "an irascible man leavened with Irish wit".

Thomas Burke (*c.* 1747–83), an aristocratic Galway man, prospered in law and politics in North Carolina where he called his estate Tyaquin after the family seat in Galway. He organized the US army in its fight for independence so thoroughly that the British kidnapped him, but he escaped. Burke County, North Carolina, is named after him.

John Daly Burke (*c.* 1775–1808) added Daly to his name in gratitude to a Miss Daly who aided him, as a political refugee, to escape to America in 1796. In Boston he struggled unsuccessfully with newspaper publishing. Success came when he found a dramatic formula which suited the nationalism of his time by writing a play with a battle scene depicting Bunker Hill. The play had long runs in Boston and New York. He was killed in a duel by a Frenchman with whom he had quarrelled.

John Gregory Bourke (1826–96) of Philadelphia was over-intensively educated by his parents who had emigrated from Galway. He ran away to join the 15th Pennsylvania Cavalry and made a career in the army. He also studied the customs of the Indian tribes and was recognized as a reliable and scientific ethnologist.

Stevenson Burke (1826–1904), son of Ulster Scotch-Irish immigrants, was a lawyer who prospered in the nineteenth-century boom. He owned mines and railroads and conducted many important legal cases in Cleveland. He was the founder of the Cleveland School of Art.

Thomas Nicholas Burke (1830–83), a Dominican, preached throughout the United States of America in the mid-nineteenth century and, although his goals were chiefly Irish political ones, he was able to donate £100,000 to charities in America.

Thomas Burke (1849–1925), born in New York of Irish parents, was a self-made lawyer. He practised in Washington DC for fifty years where, it was said, "his career was synonymous with Washington's history". He expanded trade to China and Japan and organized the railroads to the Pacific, and so became a leading citizen of Seattle, Washington State.

Many Bourkes went to Australia, including **Sir Richard Bourke** (1777–1855), a relative of the great Edmund Burke with whom he stayed in London as a student. Following a military career, he retired to Thornfield, his family estate near Limerick. The Colonial Office tempted him away with a political–military post in Cape Colony, where he demonstrated an enlightened attitude towards the Kafirs. In 1828 he was appointed Governor of New South Wales. It was a period of great economic growth and exhausting controversies. Although offered a number of other high colonial appointments, he resigned in 1838.

John Burke (1842–1919) and **John Edward Burke** (1871–1947) were from a Kinsale family who sailed on the emigrant ship *Erin go Bragh* to Queensland. With their many Burke children they were very much to the fore as shipmasters and shipowners in Australia.

In medieval times, to distinguish one Burke from another, a Mac might be placed before the first name. Thus, MacWilliam, MacDavies, MacGibbon, MacHugo, MacRedmond and MacSeoinin (Anglicized to Jennings) were originally of the Burke family. De Burgo, the Latin patronymic, lingers on in ancient families whose lineage can be traced to William de Burgh and to Charlemagne.

Perhaps the strength of the powerful, well-recorded Burke presence in Ireland can best be demonstrated by the physical mark they have left on the island, where they built 16 abbeys and 62 castles in County Mayo and 121 castles in County Galway, and left at least 38 variations of the de Burgo–Burke–Bourke name!

The versatile Burkes display a diversity of aptitudes: from William de Burgh, "the conqueror of Ireland", progenitor of the Burkes in Ireland, to **Martha Jane Burke** (1852–1903) of the Wild West known as "Calamity Jane"; from the internationally acclaimed photographer, **Margaret Bourke White**, born in New York in 1906, and back home to "the gentle rock star", **Chris de Burgh**, grandson of **General Sir Eric de Burgh** of Bargy Castle, County Wexford.

In 1990, Ireland elected its first woman President, Mrs Mary Robinson. A graduate of Trinity College, Dublin, she is a distinguished lawyer. She was born in County Mayo where her father, a Bourke, is a medical doctor.

Sir Richard Bourke

Butler

ᴅᴇ ʙᴜɪᴛʟᴇɪʀ

Eoin O Mahony (q.v.), a Cork lawyer and inimitable raconteur who popularized Irish family history in his lively broadcasts from Radio Éireann, said of the Butler family: "Numerically and historically the Burkes, FitzGeralds and Butlers are the three Norman families outstanding in the moulding of the history of Ireland following the invasion of 1169. They have been remarkably consistent in producing able churchmen, soldiers and administrators. Their history brings them to the forefront of Irish history for 800 years".

They are also a very well-documented and close-knit family. The Butler Society girdles the world, and this accounts for the success of their international rally held in their castle at Kilkenny every few years.

Butler is a common name in both England and Ireland. In fact, there has usually been a Butler in both camps. The Butlers came to Ireland when **Theobald Fitzwalter** (d. 1205), whose brother was Archbishop of Canterbury, landed in Waterford in 1185 with Prince John (later to be King). Theobald was awarded generous grants of land in counties Limerick, Tipperary and Wicklow and Henry II gave him the hereditary title of Le Boitiler—the king's chief butler, a title of function.

Theobald was a popular family name. A later **Theobald** (d. 1285) was the Butler who was awarded the Royal grant of the "prisage of wines", which meant he was entitled to "about one tenth of the cargo of any wine ship that broke bulk in Ireland". In 1810, this rewarding office was declared redundant and **Walter Butler**, Marquess of Ormond, fell heir to £216,000 in compensation.

Consolidating their position, the Butlers ringed the country with castles, married noble Irish ladies, fervently built churches and abbeys and went on the Crusades. Because of their closeness to the English court, the Butlers collected at least 25 patents of nobility, so that branches of the house of Ormond—the main Butler designation—included such titles as Dunboyne, Cahir, Mountgarrett, Galmoy, Ossory. There have been a number of Butler bishops, including **Edmund**, Prior of Athassel Abbey in Tipperary for fourteen years until 1537, when Thomas Cromwell deposed him. The Butlers fell victim to the Cromwellians, who feared their power in Ireland. They were strong military men, who took part in all the main battles from Agincourt in France to the Boyne and Aughrim.

Thomas Butler, 7th Earl of Ormond (d. 1515), was grandfather to Anne Boleyn, second wife of Henry VIII, who, although she lost her head, provided him with the daughter who was to become Queen Elizabeth I. This fearsome queen features in voluminous Butler records. Her cousin, the 10th Earl of Ormond, **Thomas Butler** (d. 1614), who had been reared at the English court, built a magnificent Tudor manor at Carrick-on-Suir, County Tipperary, expecting her to visit him, which she failed to do. Lord Dunboyne, the present Butler family historian, writes in his *Butler Family History:* "The Butlers bred like rabbits immune from myxomatosis". Black Tom, as the 10th Earl of Ormond was nicknamed, was a prime example. Three times married, he had, apart from his legal offspring, twelve known illegitimate children. One of his natural sons who received considerable estates from his father, **Piers Fitzthomas Butler**, according to a strong local tradition, was the fruit of Thomas' affection for the Virgin Queen!

The Butlers and the FitzGeralds, the mighty Earls of Kildare, despite intermarrying, were constantly feuding. Between them they alternated the

The tomb of Piers and Margaret Butler in Kilkenny.

administration of Ireland. Eight Butlers held the office of Viceroy of Ireland. Because of his fidelity to the royal house of Stuart during the Cromwellian usurpations, Charles II raised **James Butler** (1610–88), the 12th Earl, to the Dukedom of Ormond, together with a variety of other titles. James played an important role in the affairs of both England and Ireland. He was Lord Lieutenant of Ireland and Chancellor of the universities of both Dublin and Oxford. He helped incorporate the College of Physicians and founded the Royal Record Office and the Genealogical Office in Dublin Castle. Another of the great Duke's benefactions was Dublin's Phoenix Park. Its 1,752 acres make it larger than all of London's parks put together and it is still greatly enjoyed by today's citizens. James, the 1st Duke of Ormond, described as a very straight man, a prime example of the remarkable talents of the Butlers in the field of administration, was awarded the distinction of burial in Westminster Abbey.

Pierce Butler, 3rd Viscount Galmoy (1652–1740), was a soldier. He took part in the siege of Derry, the battles of the Boyne and Aughrim and, with Patrick Sarsfield, he campaigned in Europe. Pierce signed the Treaty of Limerick on behalf of the Irish following the Jacobite defeat at the Boyne. A kinsman, **Sir Toby Butler** of Ballyline, County Clare, solicitor to the unfortunate King James II, drew up the Treaty.

James Butler

John Butler (1716–1800), who was Catholic Bishop of Cork in 1763, unexpectedly found himself 12th Lord Dunboyne, a very prestigious Butler title. At the age of 70 he felt he should provide an heir. He petitioned Pope Pius VI for leave to marry, but was summarily refused. He renounced the Church and married his cousin, but there was no heir. On his deathbed, aged 84, he returned to the Church and, despite family opposition to his will, managed to leave, if not his castle of Dunboyne, at least a Dunboyne endowment, to Maynooth College, County Kildare.

Eleanor Butler (1745–1829), sister of the 17th Earl, caused enormous scandal when she eloped with her neighbour, Sarah Ponsonby. They lived together for the rest of their lives in Wales where they created a world-famous and picturesque home and were known as "The Ladies of Llangollen".

The Honourable Simon Butler, born in Dublin in 1757, was the first president of the Society of United Irishmen, and a distinguished lawyer. When he had to flee to Scotland because of his political activities, he directed the Society from there. In the same unhappy period, **John Butler** (1808–54), 2nd Marquess of Ormond and 20th Earl, was greatly loved in Kilkenny, where he helped his tenants by reducing their rents, in some cases writing them off completely.

Major-General Sir William Butler (1838–1910) of Bansha, County Tipperary, who helped found the National University of Ireland, had his differences with the British government, accusing them of forcing the Boers into war. His wife was the **Lady Butler** who painted *Roll Call*, and many battle scenes of the Victorian era. One of their sons was **Dom Richard Butler**, a Benedictine monk who taught at the abbeys of Gorey, County Wexford, and Worth and Downside in England. He was a chaplain in both the First and Second World Wars.

Following the colonization of Ireland, thousands of exiled Irishmen went to Europe to earn their living as professional soldiers, and consequently they often found themselves fighting against their own countrymen who had joined the opposing army—the Irish on the English side attacking the Irish on the French or Spanish side! This happened to the Butlers too, especially to **James** (1655–1713), the 2nd Duke of Ormond, who was first colonel of Justin MacCarthy's Mountcashel Regiment in France in 1690.

Some Butlers went further east. A member of the Kilkenny family was the first to capture a Russian two-decker ship, and there is a belief that it could have been a **David Butler** who was instrumental in founding the Russian navy.

Many Butlers went to America to take part in the War of Independence. The Marquis de Lafayette once said that when he wanted anything done well he got a Butler to do it. Five high-ranking Butler brothers fought in the American War of Independence. They served again, with their sons, in the 1812 to 1814 dispute and in the American Civil War. As happened to so many families, they had gone their different ways and some were on the Confederate side and others on the Federal.

Pierce Butler (1744–1822) was the third son of **Sir Richard Butler** of Carlow. He was a Senator and a major in the 29th Regiment. Marriage settled him firmly in South Carolina, where he was active on his estate and in politics. A wealthy, dictatorial aristocrat he was also a champion of democracy.

The American Butlers were obviously admirers of Benjamin Franklin, for several of them adopted his name. **Benjamin Franklin Butler** (1818–93) was of Ulster stock—Scotch-Irish. His father, **John Butler**, had been a captain of dragoons for Jackson at New Orleans. An adventurer, he held a privateer's commission from Simón Bolívar. His son, another **Benjamin Franklin Butler**, was a congressman and Governor of Massachusetts. He also had an astounding army career. In 1861, having built up a fortune, he was appointed to be Brigadier-General of Militia. With the money and the men at the ready, he was as much in the news as Lincoln after Fort Sumpter.

In Australia there have been many Irish Butlers. A remarkable man, **Edward Butler** (1823–79), was born in Kilkenny and, though destined for the Church, was found unsuitable. He turned to nationalistic journalism, which involved him in the fiery Young Ireland movement. During the Famine years he edited the *Galway Vindicator* with great determination. In 1852, finding it increasingly difficult to exercise freedom of speech, he made the long voyage to Sydney. From journalism he turned to law and reached the Legislative Council. As Attorney-General he presided over many controversies.

In 1922, during the Civil War in Ireland, the 5th Marquess, the Earl of Ossory, and his wife were in residence in Kilkenny Castle when it was taken over by the Republicans. At the same time they were being besieged from the outside by the Free State army. The siege lasted two days, little damage was done and both sides gave themselves credit for rescuing the Butlers!

Today the 7th Marquess, **Charles Butler**, the 31st Chief Butler, who lives in Illinois in the United States, lacks a male heir and there is much speculation as to who his successor will be. Lord Dunboyne suggests that "someone with the name Butler in some modest dwelling in Ireland or overseas may, unknowingly, be the rightful eventual heir". It has to be remembered, however, that it was customary for servants to adopt their masters' names, so that there could be hundreds of Butlers without a touch of the ducal Ormond blood. There are estimated to be about 9,000 Irish Butlers, not taking into account the many who have long since emigrated.

One of the achievements of the Butler Society has been to set up the Butler Archive in the South Tower of Kilkenny Castle. Archives are an invaluable resource in providing records of the chequered history of Ireland. When President John F. Kennedy visited Ireland in 1963, the enthusiastic Irish government presented him with a fourteenth-century treaty made between the 1st Earl of Ormond and an O Kennedy chieftain.

General William Orlando Butler (1791–1880) was one of many Irish-Americans who pursued a distinguished career in the military. He served in the Mexican War, and fought for the North in the Civil War.

This treasure had been donated to the National Library by the Butler's chieftain, but many felt that it was incorrect to denude the nation of such an irreplaceable treasure, even for the President of the United States of America.

The Butlers were sound builders and many of their castles around Ireland are still standing. Kilkenny Castle and its rose gardens is in constant use for exhibitions and conventions, and important occasions such as the annual Kilkenny Arts Festival and the International Butler Rally.

Across from the impressive Kilkenny Castle are the magnificent Ormond stables. They were converted to the Kilkenny Design Workshops, a semi-state organization, since disbanded, which fulfilled its purpose by greatly raising the standards of Irish design in everything from engineering to crafts.

Other important Butler castles include Cahir Castle in County Tipperary, the largest and best-preserved late fifteenth-century castle in Ireland open to the public. Knappogue, a rugged castle near the coast in Quin, County Clare, is used for medieval banquets. Part of it was occupied by an American couple who restored it. The Butler Arms hotel in Waterville was a castle and is now a popular County Kerry hotel, once a favourite of Charlie Chaplin and his large family. Black Tom's Tudor mansion at Carrick-on-Suir, County Tipperary, which Elizabeth I never came to visit, is on view regularly.

From the widespread Butler tree descend such diverse characters as Father Theobald Mathew (1790–1856), the apostle of Irish sobriety who was a Butler kinsman. The great poet, **William Butler Yeats** (1865–1939), was proud of his connection. It was **Mary Butler** who suggested to the Irish President, Arthur Griffith (1871–1922), the name for his new Home Rule party, Sinn Féin, meaning "we ourselves", to signify Irish self-reliance.

Hubert Butler (1900–90) of Bennetsbridge, County Kilkenny, a custodian of the Butler Society, taught English in Leningrad before Stalin and worked in Vienna in 1938 helping Jews to escape the pogroms. In Yugoslavia he witnessed the "conversion" of the Serbian Orthodox Christians by Croatian Catholics, a forerunner of latter-day "ethnic cleansing". Against this varied political background he became one of the most respected essayists of this century.

Jack Butler Yeats (1871–1957) the artist brother of William Butler Yeats.

Carroll
ó cearúil

Mac Carroll

O Carroll

Carroll is a very ancient name which, translated from the Irish, *cearbhaill*, means slaughter or, preferably, warlike champion. Maolsuthian, a clerical member of the family, was Brian Boru's official confessor and accompanied him everywhere. Previously this family had been kings of Munster. They were with the High King, Brian Boru, at the victorious battle of Clontarf in 1014. **Maonuigh**, who was slain in 1022, was the first of the family to assume the surname Carroll.

At one time there were six Carroll septs. The O Carrolls of Ely lorded over thousands of acres of rich land in counties Tipperary and Offaly. (About seventeen miles north of Cloughjordan in County Tipperary, the hill of Knockshigowna is named after the fair queen, Una, who was the legendary guardian spirit of the O Carrolls.) Equally, the O Carrolls of Oriel had their vast acres in counties Louth and Monaghan. These two prominent families, as well as the lesser ones, were scattered with the arrival of the Norman Butlers towards the end of the twelfth century. Excepting Ulster, the O Carrolls, who possibly number 16,000, are to be found today in all the provinces, and especially in Munster.

It would be impossible to mention here all the outstanding O Carrolls. They have been well taken care of in Father John Gleeson's comprehensive *History of the Ely O Carroll Territory*, published in 1915 and reprinted in 1982. It contains an O Carroll genealogy, much information about local clans and a wealth of mythology and legends.

The O Carrolls, Princes of Oriel until the twelfth century, founded several monasteries including Mellifont, County Louth, a Cistercian foundation. Its impressive remains can be seen near the River Boyne. Six Carrolls were abbots of Louth; the last, at the dissolution of the monasteries, was **John O Carroll**.

Donough (d. 1377), son of **William the Fair**, Chief of Ely, had a son Teigue, who married Sara, a daughter of the O Briens, rulers of Thomond, a vast territory around the Shannon estuary. This **Teigue O Carroll** was a powerful chieftain who, at first, was on friendly terms with King Richard II. On his way home from a pilgrimage to Rome, Teigue visited him, but their friendship was sundered by politics. On his return to Ireland, Teigue died defending his territory in Fermanagh against Richard's advancing army. In this decisive battle of 1407, when 800 of his army were killed, the Anglo-Irish chroniclers reported a very strange manifestation: the sun is said to have remained stationary in the sky while Richard's victorious army marched six miles from the site of its triumph!

Thady or **Thadeus O Carroll** (d. 1421), married Joan, daughter of the 2nd Earl of Ormond (d. 1382). This Earl was a great-grandson of Edward I. Thady's second marriage was to More, daughter of Brian O Brien, King of Thomond.

Thady and More's daughter, **Margaret** (d. 1451), was one of the outstanding women of medieval times. Known as Margaret an Eirigh (Margaret the hospitable), she married Calvagh O Connor, a chief of Offaly. Even the *Annals of the Four Masters*, which give little credence to women, wrote of her as "the best woman of her time in Ireland". She was "the only woman who has made the most of preparing highways and erecting bridges, churches and mass books and all manner of things profitable to serve God and her soul", they recorded. The Chroniclers also wrote that it was her custom twice a year to give a sumptuous entertainment for 2,700 learned men, the bards and the poor, graciously assisted by Calvagh. She went on pilgrimage to Compostella in Spain. This inspiring lady had a daughter, **Finola**, who followed in her footsteps.

One of the Ely O Carroll sept married a daughter of James FitzGerald, 10th Earl of Desmond (d. 1529); from this aristocratic alliance the O Carrolls claim a connection with the Royal Plantagenets of England.

An O Carroll of Ely fought at the battle of Knocktoe, near Galway, in 1504. He was professional axeman to the Great Earl of Kildare, Gerald FitzGerald who sought revenge on his own son-in-law, Ulick de Burgh of Clanrickard.

John, son of **Donough**, a fifteenth-century Ely O Carroll chieftain who was transplanted to Galway, went to Spain where, as a lieutenant-general, he was accepted into the Spanish aristocracy. Another **Donough O Carroll** married an O Kennedy and is distinguished by having produced thirty sons. Proudly presenting them in one troop he handed them over to the Marquis of Ormond for service with Charles I.

There was continuous and savage slaughter among the O Carrolls as they squabbled for power and territory. Leap Castle, near Coolderry in Offaly, was one of their principal fortresses. **Kian O Carroll**, son of a **Teigue**, was killed when he laid siege to it while it was occupied by a rival branch of the family. Leap Castle endured until the outbreak of the lamentable burnings of 1922. It remains a sinister ruin, abhorred by the locals, who say that it is the most hideously haunted house in Ireland.

The O Carrolls who fled Ireland's troubles and went abroad with the "Wild Geese" are well-recorded in the service of England, France, Spain and Germany—wherever they could put their martial skill to rewarding use. Many went to America as early as the 1600s, where they found an enduring home. The O Carrolls of Germany are today represented by the **Baron Zidenko Hoennin O Carroll** of Regensburg in Bavaria.

By the eighteenth century, O Carroll had shed its O and **Anthony Carroll** (1722–94), who was Irish-born, studied for the Church in France and was sent to the missions in England. When the Pope suppressed the Jesuit order in 1773, he went with his cousin **John Carroll**, also a Jesuit, to Maryland. Anthony, who returned to England, fell victim to a London mugger and died there in 1794.

His cousin, **John Carroll** (1735–1815), had gone to America because he saw greater hope of religious freedom there. Through the decades he conducted many delicate diplomatic manoeuvres in establishing the independence of the Catholic Church in America. In 1788 he was consecrated Bishop of Baltimore—the first American Bishop. As in Ireland, the Catholic Church was generally legally proscribed, except in Maryland. Ironically, John had to go to England for his consecration. In the educational and cultural life of Baltimore—a city named after a small County Cork seaport—he was a leader, and helped found its university. He renounced all claims to his wealthy family estate and left it in favour of his brothers and sisters.

Charles O Carroll, who emigrated to Maryland in 1688 where he had been given a commission as Attorney-General, was the grandfather of **Charles Carroll** (1737–1832), one of the most distinguished Irish-Americans. He had studied law in France and London, and, when his father gave him the fine estate, Carrollton Manor in Maryland, he settled down to the life of a gentleman. As a Catholic he was prevented from taking part in politics. However, when a moral issue came up for debate, he could not refrain from expressing his strong views publicly. He was a member of the US Senate from 1789 to 1792, and was the last survivor of

Charles Carroll

those who had signed the Declaration of American Independence in 1775. His life and career span an important chapter in American history.

These American Carrolls traced their lineage back to Donough, son of William the Fair, chief of Ely, who died in 1377. **Daniel Carroll** (1730–96) was yet another of Donough's American descendants. He differed from the aristocratic Carrolls by going into business, which was then considered demeaning. He inherited land and wealth and played his part in political life, being a commissioner of the District of Columbia.

In the twentieth century, Ireland's outstanding Carroll was **Paul Vincent Carroll** (1900–68), who was born in Louth. Dublin's Abbey Theatre, which was founded earlier in this century, was the cradle of Irish dramatists, and Paul Vincent Carroll is recognized as one of its finest playwrights. Like many another Irish genius who found Ireland too confining, he gave up a teaching career in Dublin to emigrate to Scotland. He settled in Glasgow, teaching and writing. In 1932, his play, *Things that are Caesars*, staged at the Abbey, set him on a long and successful career. *Shadow and Substance* and *The White Steed* won him the New York Drama Critics Circle awards in 1938 and 1939. He was one of the founders of the Glasgow Citizens' Theatre. After the War he moved on to writing plays for films and television. Although long out of Ireland, like James Joyce, he had a deep understanding of the human drama generated by the Irish clergy and their flock, and wrote about it with insight and compassion.

The owners of P.J. Carroll and Company Limited, the cigarette and tobacco manufacturers who have their factory in Dundalk, County Louth, claim descent from the O Carrolls of Ely.

Dr Edward MacLysaght, the eminent historian, wrote that there is another distinct sept of MacCarroll and that the Irish MacCearbhaill is now more usually Anglicized as MacCarvill. In Ulster there is a town called Ballymaccarroll. These MacCarrolls, ever since the fourteenth century, were prominent musicians. **James MacCarroll** (1813–92) was a successful playwright and poet in the USA.

Alice in Wonderland, incidentally, has nothing to do with the Carrolls. Lewis Carroll was born Dodgson.

Leap Castle, County Laois

Cleary

ó cléirigh

Clarke

Clary

Clery

O Clery

Dunguaire Castle, almost surrounded by the sea, looks across the bay to the ancient city of Galway. Once a fortress of the seventh-century King of Connacht, Guaire the Hospitable, it has withstood the ferocity of war and weather and is today the setting for regular medieval banquets of a high literary and musical order. This is nicely in keeping with its heritage. The O Cléirighs, who descend from **King Guaire**, feature in the records not as combatants but as poets, historians and bards. There are many versions of this Gaelic name, which is among the earliest to be recorded. Anglicized it means a clerk, or a cleric. This can be misleading, especially in the British-administered parts of Ulster, where many of the settlers were named Clark. Despite the Anglicization of O Clery to Clarke and the confusions as to which Clarke is of Gaelic origin and which is not (distinctions impossible to make unless they are substantiated by almost unobtainable documentation), it would be unfair to leave out the Clarkes who have been prominent contributors to the history of Ireland.

For generations the O Clerys were overlords of Kilmacduagh, an area south of Galway, close to Gort. Perhaps because they were less than usually warlike, they were driven north to counties Donegal and Derry and south to counties Tipperary and Waterford. There are about 5,000 Clearys, O Clerys and O Clearys in Ireland and well over 14,000 Clarkes.

Michael O Cléirigh (1575–1643), or Michael O Clery, was responsible for that fount of Irish history known as *The Annals of the Four Masters*, an account dating from earliest days to 1616. O Clery, the son of a chieftain, was a historian who went to Louvain to study for the Franciscan Order. While there he was advised to return home and make a study of the lives of the Irish saints. With the assistance of his brother **Conary**, his cousin **Cucoigchriche** (Peregrine) and Fearfeasa O Mulconry, he began to record genealogies and historical events. These scribes were known as the "Four Masters". They not only recorded the lives of the Irish saints, they also wrote an invaluable history of Ireland, just when it could have been lost forever because of the annihilation of the old Gaelic order that was taking place at that time.

The *Annals* were dedicated to their patron, the then Prince of Coolavin, Fergal O Gara. On the banks of the River Eske, outside Donegal town, stand the ruins of what was once a splendid Franciscan friary. Here Michael O Clery worked with the utmost dedication, living frugally in a cottage beside the friary, which was burned down in his time.

Lughaidh, son of **Maccon**, Chief of the O Clerys of Donegal and ninth in descent from Cormac Mac Diarmada, came from a literary family. He was one of the participants in the famous Contention of Bards in 1600, when all the poets of Ireland gathered and tested each other for the quality and quantity of their literary output.

Lughaidh, dictated his life of Red Hugh O Donnell to his son, Cucoigchriche (d. 1664). The original manuscript is in The Royal Irish Academy. Cucoigchriche was also a chieftain. In 1632, being "a mere Irishman", he was dispossessed of his lands which were forfeited to the Crown, and he returned to the original O Clery territory in Mayo. Some of the books which he left to his sons **Dermot** and **John** are also in the Royal Irish Academy. After his time, the great days of the bards and musicians were over and little more is heard of them.

Julie Bonaparte Clery

Julie and **Desiree Clery**, or Clary, have a most romantic history. Their father was a silk merchant in Marseille who came from a County Limerick family which had left Ireland in the seventeenth century. Desiree was discovered by the young Napoleon, who fell passionately in love with her and wanted to marry her. Desiree was spared what her family considered an unsuitable match by the arrival of the indomitable Josephine de Beauharnais, whom Napoleon married in 1796. Two years later, Desiree married one of Napoleon's military commanders, General Bernadotte. He made her Queen of Sweden when he became Charles XIV, King of Sweden and Norway. The Swedish writer, Anne Marie Selinko, has written Desiree's biography, and, in 1970, a film was made of her life, featuring Jean Simmons and Marlon Brando.

Meanwhile, her sister Julie had eloped with Napoleon's younger brother, Joseph. During the heady days of Napoleonic power, Joseph and Julie had two short experiences of monarchy, when he was King of Naples for two years and, from 1808 to 1813, King of Spain.

It is not generally known that during his captivity Napoleon assuaged his need for mental activity by writing a novel. It was an autobiographical love story entitled *Clisson et Eugenie*, the Eugenie is obviously his early love, Bernardine Eugenie Desiree Clary, while Clisson, the young officer of the story, is Napoleon.

There was another Clary lady married to a famous man. This was **Ann Clary**, who, in 1767, married Commodore John Barry, founder of the US navy. But little is known of her origins.

Whether under the guise of Clary, Clery or Clarke, the descendants of this ancient family are found in a variety of vocations and locations. **Revd John Clarke** (1662–1723) from Kilkenny was a Jesuit missionary who looked after the spiritual welfare of the men from Ireland and Scotland who fought in the wars in Belgium and Holland. **Revd Adam Clarke** (1762–1832) was born in Derry and had a meagre hedge school education until he went to England, where he was taken up by John Wesley. He blossomed as a linguist and a popular speaker, and he wrote factual books, including a six-volume bibliographical dictionary.

Joseph Clarke (1758–1834), yet another Derry man, was the leading obstetrician in Dublin. As Master of the Rotunda Lying-in-Hospital for seven years, he reduced infantile mortality dramatically. The Rotunda, the first such hospital in the British Dominions, became a model. A handsome building designed by Cassells, it is still one of Dublin's busiest maternity hospitals.

Sir Marshall Clarke, born in 1841 in Tipperary, was for a period a colonel in the Royal Artillery. He went to South Africa where, as a magistrate and police commissioner, he was considered to be "one of the few men who won the confidence of the natives".

Sir Caspar Purdon Clarke (1846–1911) was trained as an architect in his native Dublin. In London he worked for both the South Kensington and the India museums before going to the USA, where, from 1905 to 1911, he was a director of the Metropolitan Museum of Art in New York.

Count Keyes O Clery (1849–1913), a writer and soldier from County Limerick, went to fight with the papal Zouaves and was at the bombardment of Rome in 1870. He wrote a history of Italy and the Italian revolution. In 1903, the Pope made him a hereditary Count of Rome.

Thomas Clarke (1857–1916) was one of the revolutionaries who were so outrageously executed in 1916. He had a varied youth. He was born in England and his parents took him first to South Africa, then to County Tyrone. As a youth he went to America, where he was involved in the

1858 1916

TOM CLARKE

éıRe 3p

Thomas Clarke

28

Irish Republican Brotherhood, who sent him to England. There he was arrested for subversive activities and spent fifteen bitter years in prison. Back in Ireland, he was one of those who planned the 1916 Easter Rising. He was one of the first to sign the Proclamation of the Republic, and was executed shortly afterwards.

Harry Clarke (1889–1931), although the son of an Englishman, must be recognized for his enormous contribution to the art of stained glass in Ireland. His windows in the Honan Chapel of University College, Cork, and his illustrations for Edgar Allan Poe's *Tales of Mystery and Imagination* reveal a deep feeling for Celtic art and mythology, and an ethereal sense of colour.

Austin Clarke (1896–1974) was a Dubliner whose weekly programme on Radio Éireann for many years brought poetry to the people. He was a distinguished writer of fiction and drama, and was a president of the Irish branch of PEN and a founding member of the Irish Academy of Letters.

To extend still further the genealogical possibilities of O Clery, Dr MacLysaght discovered that "there is another Gaelic surname which has become Clery in English in some places, though more usually MacCleary or MacAlary". This is MacGiolla Arraith, a branch of the O Haras, who went to County Antrim and became established there.

Dunguaire Castle, County Galway

Collins
ó coıleáın

Collins, a very numerous name, not only in Ireland, but also in England, can sometimes be difficult to pinpoint ethnologically. In Ireland the Gaelic name is Ó Coileáin—a whelp, or, more sweetly, a young dog. Until the thirteenth century, the Ó Coileáins were lords of the barony of Connello in County Limerick. From there they were driven south to Corca Laoidhe (south-west Cork) by the powerful Anglo-Norman Geraldines (*see* FitzGerald). Unfortunately, the Ó Coileáins seem to have left no visible landmarks: no castles or towns are stamped with their name.

Noteworthy figures are scarce until the sixteenth century, when **Father Dominic Collins** (1533–1602) of Cork went to Spain, where, following service in the Spanish army, he entered the Society of Jesus as a lay brother. At the late age of 69, he returned to Ireland in time to take part in the siege of Dunboy Castle. He was captured by the Crown forces who tried to bribe him into giving information. When he refused he was hanged at Youghal, near to where he was born.

Seán Ó Coileáin (1754–1817) of Corca Laoidhe was a poet in the old Gaelic tradition, when poets commanded respect and were given the hospitality of the king's castle. Unhappily for Seán, the kings had all been deposed and the people who would have been his patrons were as poor as himself. He drank, but rather than making him happy, his drinking drove away his first wife and so enraged his second that she set fire to the house. Seán was a reluctant schoolteacher, but his poetry must have been appreciated, for he was known as the "Silver Tongue of Munster". There is some mystery surrounding a strangely melancholy poem of his which has been compared to Gray's *Elegy*. Whether Ó Coileáin or an earlier poet wrote it continues to puzzle the folklorists.

David Collins (1756–1810) left his native Offaly to join the Marines, at the age of 16. Five years later he was in Boston taking part in the American War of Independence at Bunker Hill. Next he sailed to Botany Bay and became one of the founders of Sydney and Hobart and Governor of Tasmania.

William Collins was born in County Wicklow, about 1740. Although he earned a living in London by writing, he is best remembered for being the father and grandfather of two famous men, both London born: **William Collins** (1788–1847) was a landscape painter and Royal Academician, and his son, **William Wilkie Collins** (1824–89), was a writer famous for his novel, *The Woman in White*, and what is said to be the first detective story in English, *The Moonstone*.

Edward Knight Collins' (1802–78) forbears preceded him to America where, in 1635, they settled in and around Cape Cod. Edward began his career clerking in the West Indies and Mexico. Then he worked on the shipping lines from Vera Cruz to New Orleans, which he greatly improved. He went into competition with the mighty Cunards when he set up his own Dramatic fleet to sail between New York and London. He had the imagination to foresee that sail would be ousted by steam, something the US government was slow to grasp. When it eventually did, he was given what he wanted—the contract to carry the US mails, which had been the making of the Cunard Line. He built four magnificent ships and called them the Collins Line, which, in 1850, began service from New York to London. Other Collins ships followed, and beat the Cunard sailing record

Father Dominic Collins

by one day, and soon became very popular with high society. Then tragedy struck. The *Arctic* sank in thick fog with many lives lost, including Collins' wife and daughter. Other disasters followed; state subsidies melted away. Cornelius Vanderbilt got into the shipping business and the once dynamic Collins company faded away without ever having paid a dividend. Undefeated, Edward turned his attention to Ohio, where he owned coal and iron works. He is commemorated by a statue in Boston.

Patrick Andrew Collins (1844–1905) was born on a farm at Ballinafauna near Fermoy in County Cork. When he was four, Patrick and his widowed mother sailed to Boston to escape the Famine. He had a miserable childhood, harassed by the violent bigotry of the Boston "know nothings", whose attitude the young Patrick equated with that of the English towards the Irish at home. He tried his hand at many things: farm labourer, coal miner, trade unionist. He joined the Fenians, but was disenchanted with their militancy, convinced that violence would do nothing for Ireland. Instead he developed his intellect and combined it with his ability as an actor. He was elected to the Lower House of the Senate, where he fought verbally for the abolition of the limiting "Catholic Oath" and for Catholic chaplains to be appointed to jails and hospitals. Like so many of his fellow Irish immigrants, he saw the immense value of a legal training. At the age of 37, he graduated in law from Harvard and began a meteoric career, rising to Judge Advocate General and election to Congress. He served three terms in Washington DC, where the superficial life gave him little satisfaction. He subsequently agreed to accept a consul generalship in London on condition that the ex-Fenians would not be interfered with by the British government. His monument in Boston, where he was Democratic Mayor from 1902 to 1905, is a tribute not only to the penniless Irish boy who had formerly been so badly treated, but also to the city of Boston, which had matured with him.

Jerome Collins, who died in 1850, followed a rare calling for an Irishman: he was an Arctic explorer.

Michael Collins (1890–1922), the son of a farmer from Clonakilty in West Cork, was affectionately known as The Big Fellow. A man of great physical strength and courage, his untimely death deprived Ireland of a most promising leader. Ten years in accountancy and stockbroking in the heart of the Empire in London was a sound education for a future Minister of Finance in the new Irish Free State, which came into being after the 1916 rising. This led to the eventual British withdrawal from the 26 counties. Though Michael Collins had taken part in the rising he did not approve of it as a military operation. He was one of the signatories of the Anglo-Irish Treaty, which he saw only as a stepping-stone and, prophetically, said that he was signing his death warrant. (Eamon de Valera and his Republicans opposed the Treaty, which led later to the Civil War.) Superlatives were used to describe Michael Collins: "blazingly intelligent"—"a capacity to get things done"—"a man of extraordinary vision and culture". He was responsible for the Dáil's first, most successful, Home Loan. In the 1918 general election he topped the polls for his party, Sinn Féin. He devised an intelligence system that baffled the British. In 1922, with the outbreak of the Civil War, he was appointed Commander-in-Chief, with a price of £10,000 on his head. When the President, Arthur Griffith, died in August, Michael Collins took over as head of state and the army. Ten days later he was shot in an ambush in his beloved West Cork at Beal-na-Blath, the Mouth of the Flowers.

Michael Collins

Thomas Collins

For 42 years, *Dublin Opinion* reflected the comedies and tragedies and political posturings of the new Irish nation. **Thomas Collins** (1894–1972) was joint editor, contributing poems, stories and articles until its monthly publication ceased in 1968.

Patrick Collins, born in 1909, is a major artist who represented Ireland in 1958 in the Guggenheim Award Exhibition. In 1982, his high standing in the international art world was acknowledged by a retrospective exhibition held by the Arts Council in Dublin.

One of the best-known training establishments in Kildare is run by **Con Collins**, who was born there in 1924. He has trained winning horses for many of the big names in international racing.

In recent years, the Collins name has become prominent in the Irish business and political scene. It would be hard to find a family which could surpass the record held by **John Collins** of Drogheda, County Louth, a firm of building and agricultural engineers, one of only two Irish firms that can boast of passing from father to son for seven generations.

Connolly

ó conᵹhaιle

In Irish the name is Ó Conghaile, which means the valorous. The English version has settled down to Connolly. Spelling was not too exact in earlier days, so that Connolly has sometimes been confused with a number of other surnames, like Kinnealy and Conneely. Ballyconneely, the popular Connacht seaside village, could have a connection with the Connollys, for that was one of the areas populated by this Gaelic family, which separated into three septs, one going north to Monaghan and one south into the province of Munster, while the Connacht sept was of the Uí Máine, the clan which also included the O Maddens.

The Monaghan Connellys were high on the social scale. They belonged to "The Four Tribes of Tara" and were thus related to the Munster O Neills, who had been driven north by the Anglo-Normans.

O Connola was another ancient spelling and, in 1591, **Tirlogha O Connola** is mentioned in the records, not only as a chieftain, but also as vice-marshall of one of the militant McMahon clan of Connacht. The most notorious Connolly was **Owen O Connolly**, the traitor who contributed to the failure of the rising of 1641 by leaking the plans to the Crown forces. In Bordeaux, the Connollys who had fled Ireland to escape strife in the seventeenth century ran into difficulties during the French Revolution because they were considered to be aristocrats.

The leading Connolly in the "Wild Geese" era was probably **Charles**, who spelled his name **Connely**. He is recorded as having been in Spain's Ultonia Regiment in around 1767. He saw much service in Mexico before returning to Spain where, strangely, although he is in the records as having been a serving captain, he held the rank of lieutenant-colonel.

In the seventeenth century there were not many wealthy Irishmen, but **William Conolly** (1662–1729) is always described as the richest man in Ireland at the time. He was born in Ballyshannon, County Donegal, where his parents, who owned an inn, had converted to the Protestant religion, which meant that he could study law. He soon rose high in public life, practising as attorney in Ulster. A very shrewd financier, he acquired wealth by dealing in the lands and properties forfeited by old Irish families following the battle of the Boyne in 1690. He married Katherine Conyngham, daughter of a Williamite general, who brought him a goodly fortune. He held many powerful appointments, especially Commissioner for Revenue. He was Speaker in the Irish House of Commons and deputized for the Lord Justice of Ireland in his absence.

Speaker Conolly's name lives on, not so much for his great wealth or high position, but for the Palladian mansion, Castletown in County Kildare, which he and his wife engaged Allesandro Galilei to design in 1722. It was far from being finished when he died. He was accorded a state funeral and as a special tribute to his profession the mourners wore white linen scarves, a fashion which caught on as a custom.

Castletown was not completed until nearly thirty years after his death. In 1758, Speaker Conolly's great nephew, the patriotic **Tom Conolly**, married Lady Louisa Lennox, sister of the Duchess of Leinster of the FitzGerald family. Lady Louisa and her sister played an important role in embellishing the house. In 1967, as it was drifting into decay, Desmond Guinness was instrumental in buying it for the Irish Georgian Society. Groups of volunteer workers, many from the USA, have helped restore it,

Connely

Conolly

O Connola

O Connolly

William Conolly

33

and the house and grounds have become an elegant centre for balls, concerts, dinners, lectures and all kinds of gatherings. It is now a charitable trust and is open to the public.

In the dining room, visitors are shown huge cracks on the hearthstone and the mirror. The story is that Tom Conolly, while out hunting, met a dark stranger and invited him back to supper. During the evening, the stranger removed his boots, revealing exceedingly hairy feet. Realizing he was supping with the devil, Conolly called a priest, who threw his breviary at him, missing and cracking the mirror. The devil disappeared through the hearthstone, leaving behind the remarkable crack!

There were two Connolly bishops in North America. **John Connolly** (1750–1825), born in Slane, County Meath, studied in the Dominican college in Rome. His talents were in the invaluable field of clerical diplomacy. Pope Pius VII appointed him Bishop of New York, making him the second prelate to hold this unique office. There he had to combine both pastoral and missionary work. There was then much racial hostility, not least between the French and the Irish. He engaged the Sisters of Charity to open a much needed orphanage. **Thomas Louis Connolly** (1815–76) left his County Cork home to study for the priesthood in Rome. He arrived in Nova Scotia in 1842, and from 1859 until his death, he was Archbishop of Halifax. He deplored the futility of the Fenian movement compared to confederation.

Henry Connolly (1800–66) was appointed the first Governor of New Mexico by Lincoln, in 1861. His parents had come from Ireland and he was born in Kentucky.

Many Connollys went to England, where **John Connolly** (1794–1866) was born of Irish parents. He studied medicine at Edinburgh and was one of the founders of the British Medical Association. He pioneered for the humane treatment of insanity.

In the nineteenth century, the **Pierce Connolly** family of Philadelphia became notorious because of their religious ambivalence. When they converted to Roman Catholicism, **Cornelia Connolly** (1809–79) became a nun and founded the Society of the Holy Child Jesus, while her husband became a priest. He later left the priesthood, gaining considerable notoriety. In their married days they had a son, **Pierce Francis Connolly**, born in 1841 in Louisiana, who was a much admired sculptor.

In the world of sport, "Little Mo" had a meteoric career in lawn tennis. Born in San Diego, California, **Maureen Connolly** (1934–69) won every match from 1951 to 1953 with the USA Wightman Cup team. She was the star tennis player in matches in France and Australia. At Wimbledon, she won the championships for three years. A riding accident put a tragic end to her brilliant career.

Another expatriate, this time a literary one, was **Cyril Vernon Connolly** (1903–74), a man of letters, founder of *Horizon*, the leading literary magazine of the 1940s, and author of *The Rock Pool*, *Enemies of Promise* and many other novels and essays. His family home, Clontarf Castle, which belonged to his maternal grandparents, the Vernons, is now a Dublin hotel.

James Connolly (1870–1916) pioneered socialism in Ireland. Born to poor Irish parents in Edinburgh, he may have served for a time in the army in Britain, possibly even in India, though his poor physique makes this doubtful. In Ireland, where he became a very active socialist and trade union leader, he has been described as a green Marxist. He toured Britain as a journalist and lecturer and, for a while, settled in the USA, where he founded a number of magazines and socialist and trade union organizations.

James Connolly

His return to Ireland coincided with the clash between the employers and the unions which led to the lock-out in 1913. This turned James Connolly towards politics; he formed the Citizens Army and was commander of the Republican forces in Dublin at the time of the 1916 Easter Rising. He was one of the seven signatories of the Proclamation of the Irish Republic, and was afterwards executed. His writings on labour relations reached textbook status for socialist revolutionaries.

Sybil Connolly (b. 1921) has been a trail-blazer. She opened the first couture workshop in Ireland and showed her collection in the USA in 1953. At various times she has been ranked as Woman of the Year in Great Britain, one of the Ten Best Dressed Women in the World, and one of the Best Ten Designers in the World. She helped lift Irish handmade crochet and handwoven tweed from a cottage industry to couture status. By pleating it extremely finely, she developed a new image for fine linen and, for a period, even made a fashion garment out of the Connemara women's red petticoat! Latterly she has had a major influence on the designs of Tiffany's, the New York store on Fifth Avenue.

In all four provinces, the Connolly name is a very numerous one today.

Sybil Connolly

Castletown House, County Kildare

Cullen
ó cuilinn

Cuillinane

Culhoun

MacCollin

Mac Cuilinn

MacQuillan

Cardinal Paul Cullen

The Cullens are very numerous; there could be 10,000 of them in Ireland alone, mostly still in their age-old territories of Dublin, Meath, Wicklow and Wexford. They stood little chance against the powerful O Tooles and O Byrnes, whose jealously-guarded territory was too close to the peaceful Cullens. They were dispersed to Kildare, where they gave their name to Kilcullen, a town on the borders of Kildare and Wicklow. In a manuscript written in 1598, Cullenstown in County Wexford is listed as being the homeland of the Cullen gentry.

Cullen in Irish is Ó Cuilinn, which probably derives from the word for holly, *cuileann*. There are a number of similar names, less common today, which could have been simplified to Cullen, such as Culhoun, Culloon, MacCuilinn, MacCollin, Cuillinane and even MacQuillan.

A remarkable characteristic of the Cullens is the number of religious they have given to the Church, both at home and overseas. The Cullens admit that the steady flow of priestly blood came when they married into the Maher family. **Patrick O Cullen**, a Bishop of Clogher between 1517 and 1542, was a revered composer of hymns, and there are many accounts of **Luke Cullen**, "The Monk of Clondalkin", in County Dublin, who wrote copiously of his contemporaries who fought in the disastrous rising of 1798. Their former family seats are scattered around the Midlands: Tara Hall, Prospect, Craan, and Liscarton Castle near Kells in County Meath, where the younger brother of the famed Cardinal Cullen once lived. It is now a sad ruin, a shelter for cows by the River Blackwater.

Paul Cullen (1803–78) was the son of **Hugh** and **Judith Cullen**, who were farmers of Ballytore on the flat grassland of County Kildare, where many members of the Society of Friends, or Quakers, had settled. Paul Cullen received his early education at the local Quaker school, where a distinguished predecessor was the great Edmund Burke. In 1820, he went to Rome to study for the priesthood. A brilliant scholar, he became rector of the Irish College in Rome and later was rector of the important Propaganda College. In 1849, when Mazzini headed the Republican government in Rome, Paul Cullen was ordered to disperse his pupils because some of them were Americans. Using admirable diplomacy, he appealed to the American Consul, who saved the college by having it declared a literary institution under American protection.

While in Rome, he was a liaison official between the Irish bishops and Pope Gregory XVI. In 1850, he was sent back to Ireland, to the highest bishopric, Armagh. Although Catholic emancipation had been granted in 1828, the Catholic Church in Ireland was very poor. Bishop Cullen launched a dynamic campaign to build schools, churches, convents, colleges and hospitals. By 1869, while he was Archbishop of Dublin, he had become an ardent agitator for much-needed land reform, although he forbade priests to take part in political movements. He was opposed to the Fenians and reviled them at home and in the USA. Yet, in 1859, he had helped to organize the Irish Brigade that went to the Papal States to defend Pope Pius IX, whose sovereignty was under attack.

In 1860, he was made a Cardinal—the first Irishman ever to reach this princely rank. He regularly visited the Vatican and was a member of the council concerned with defining papal infallibility. He was one of the founders of the Catholic University of Ireland, which is now University College, Dublin.

As there are links between the Irish language and the Scots' Gaelic, so there are many Cullens in Scotland who may share roots with the O Cullens. The Cullens of Corry in County Leitrim and Thornhill in nearby County Cavan, claim to descend from the O Cuilleans who, for a time, perhaps, emigrated to Scotland. During the troubled reign of Charles I they returned and acquired much land in Leitrim. They had become Anglicans and so were able to act as Members of Parliament and Justices of the Peace.

Several Cullen pedigrees and manuscripts are in the Genealogical Office in Dublin, including letters written in 1775 by a **Viscount Cullen**, suggesting the dispatch of Irish troops serving in France to serve in America with Catholic Canadian officers.

In the early nineteenth century there were many Irish in South America, particularly in Argentina. In 1830, **Domingo Cullen** of Santa Fe went to Buenos Aires to represent his region at national level. **José Maria Cullen**, also of the Santa Fe family, was one of the official deputies who arranged peace terms for the newly independent government of Buenos Aires. For this he was greatly praised and was elected provincial governor.

As recently as 1992, a **J.M. Cullen**, descendant of José Maria Cullen of Buenos Aires, and also of his predecessor, **William Cullen** of Lisbigny, County Offaly, sent to Dublin Castle for a confirmation of his arms.

Father John Cullen (1814–91) of Dublin went to Buenos Aires with the Sisters of Mercy in 1856. In those days there were no railways, and Father Cullen did the circuit of his vast parish on horseback.

Thomas Murray, in his book, *The Story of the Irish in Argentina*, published in New York in 1919, relates how the Irish went to Argentina as priests, nuns, soldiers and sailors. They built churches, schools and colleges and many took to sheepfarming in a big way. Some also had come south from the USA. He lists the names of the many Irish who had become Argentinians—the spellings of some of these names had so changed as to be barely recognizable as of Irish origin.

Cullen's Castle

The Cullens also went to the Canary Islands, but they have not featured prominently in the USA. However, in Australia they have more recently come to the fore. **Sir William Portus Cullen** (1855–1935) was the seventh son of an Irish farmer who scorned his son's longing for education. Against many odds, William schooled himself, and achieved that most useful adjunct, a legal degree. He spent his life in Sydney, where he was Chief Justice of New South Wales and an active politician. In the Balmoral suburb of Sydney, he built himself a grand home with a very fine garden. The tree, *Eucalyptus Cullenii,* is named after him.

There was also **Edward Cullen** (1861–1950)—son of a Scottish Cullen and an Irish mother, Fanny Moore—who as engineer in the Department of Harbours and Rivers, discovered, in 1887, Port Musgrave and Cullen Point, a promontory named after him.

John Cullen (1883–1970) of Wicklow was followed to Tasmania by two brothers, **Arthur** and **Joseph**; all three were priests. Father John managed to keep a foot in both countries and wrote much about the Irish, both at home and in Australia. He was a lifelong friend of Eamon de Valera.

Louis Cullen, who was born in 1932 in New Ross, County Wexford, is one of Ireland's foremost historians. A lecturer in Modern History at Trinity College, Dublin, he has written a number of important books on Irish social and economic history.

Curtin

mac cuirtín

MacCruitin

MacCruttin

MacCuertin

MacCurtain

One of the fascinations of researching family history is the discovery of a vein of maybe genius, maybe eccentricity, which descends through families from generation to generation. Take the Curtins, or more properly, MacCurtins. They have a definite talent for learning. The MacCurtins are descended from ancient Irish stock, rooted in County Clare on the Atlantic seaboard. They were connected with the powerful O Briens, descendants of the High King Brian Boru (926–1014) who had his palace at Kincora, not far from Lough Derg, one of Shannon's vast lakes. This legendary territory, once known as Thomond, is rich in classical folk tales, many of them passed on orally by the MacCurtins who, with the MacBradys, were hereditary ollaves (scholars) to the O Briens, whose name is never absent from the pages of Irish history.

Cruitin means a hunchback in Irish, and in earliest times there must have been one in the Curtin family to give them the name, which has been variously spelt MacCruitin or MacCuertin and was once Anglicized to MacCruttin. Today the Mac has mostly been dropped, and it is plain Curtin in counties Cork and Limerick where they are especially numerous.

Between the fourteenth and fifteenth centuries, the Four Masters have recorded four MacCurtins who were remarkable for their poetry, music and Gaelic scholarship. **Hugh Buidhe** (yellow or blond) **MacCruitin** (1680–1755) was not only chief of his sept, but was also a poet and a lexicographer of stature. He had been born near the famous Corcomroe Abbey in Clare and like his cousin **Aindrias MacCruitin**, he was for a time chronicler to the O Briens. He served with Sarsfield at the siege of Limerick and afterwards accompanied him to France, where he served with the Irish Brigade.

Lord Clare's Irish Brigade had been founded by an ancestor of Charles O Brien, the 6th Viscount Clare. Recognizing not only the valour of Hugh MacCruitin, but also his scholarship, Lord Clare appointed him as tutor to his children. This expatriate O Brien aristocrat, who was to become Marshal of France, moved in court circles and was probably responsible for Hugh MacCruitin's also being asked to tutor the royal children.

In 1714 he returned and wrote a satirical book which so displeased the rulers of Dublin Castle that he was imprisoned. There he wrote a book about the Irish language. Later, back in Paris, assisted by an Irish priest, Conor Begley, he produced his great opus, an English-Irish Dictionary. On learning that his cousin Aindrias had died, he returned to Ireland to fulfill the MacCruitin post as hereditary scholar and poet to the O Briens. His poems have been published in various national collections.

France was also the refuge of other members of the MacCurtin family. **Jeremiah Curtin** was there during the Revolution, when he was the Irish signatory to the National Convention.

A contemporary, **Major-General Benjamin Curtin**, was a leader of the Catholic, counter-revolutionary, Royalist Vendeans in 1793.

In the nineteenth century, the Curtins went to America, where **Jeremiah Curtin** (1840–1906) continued the scholarly tradition in a modern context. His parents had emigrated from Ireland to Detroit where he was born and became a translator in the service of the United States government. From 1864 to 1870 he was seconded to St Petersburg. On his return from Russia he was appointed to the staff of the Smithsonian Institute in Washington, specializing in ethnology. He made frequent visits to Ireland, and, although his knowledge of that language was limited, he amassed a valuable and enduring collection of Irish folk tales.

Andrew Gregg Curtin (*c.* 1815–94) could be said also to follow the family scholasticism. Born at Bellefonte, Pennsylvania, he combined the two essentials for making progress in the United States of his time—law and politics. He was also a philanthropist in that he promoted schools and the welfare of young soldiers, and he supported the union. In 1869 he was sent as US envoy to Russia and in his later years he was a Democratic congressman.

In 1941, **John Curtin** (1885–1945) was Prime Minister of Australia. His parents had emigrated from their farm in County Cork and John was born in Victoria. He grew up a socialist who believed in Australian sovereignty; his portrait hangs in Canberra's Parliament House.

It is a long jump through the centuries from the Gaelic bards and scholars to **Tomás MacCurtain** (1895–1920), a nationalist hero who was born at Ballyknockane, County Cork. He went fresh from school into politics, becoming secretary of the Gaelic League at the age of 18. He became an active member of the young Sinn Féin party and wrote for the radical Fianna Fáil newspaper published by Terence MacSwiney, the freedom fighter and poet who was member for West Cork of the first Dáil Éireann.

Although Tomás MacCurtain obeyed the order of Eoin MacNeill, his Chief of Staff, to disperse the Volunteers, the 1916 Easter Rising went ahead in Dublin, and inflamed the country. Tomás MacCurtain was imprisoned. After his release in 1920, he was elected to Cork North West and became a Sinn Féin councillor. Shortly afterwards he was elected Lord Mayor of Cork. He was also Commandant of the Cork Brigade of the IRA. Despite warnings of reprisal by the police, he considered it was his duty to remain at home with his wife and five children while attending to his public duties. In the early hours of 20 March, the Royal Irish Constabulary broke into his home and shot him dead. Terence MacSwiney immediately took his place as Lord Mayor of Cork. At his inquest, the British government acknowledged that he was wilfully murdered under circumstances of most callous brutality by the Royal Irish Constabulary. As Dorothy MacArdle wrote in her classic, *The Irish Republic*, it was "a vicious circle of violence... the effects of the British attempt to settle the Irish question at this time".

Tomás MacCurtain

Corcomroe Abbey, County Clare

Cusack

cíosóg

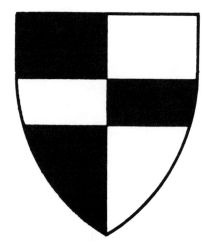

de Cussac

MacIsog

MacIssac

The Cusacks are a fine example of a Norman family which has been totally absorbed into Ireland. Originally from the Province of Guienne in south-west France, they arrived with King John during the Anglo-Norman invasion, and were given tracts of rich lands in Meath, Kildare and other areas inside The Pale. Though not quite on a par with the powerful Butlers or FitzGeralds, the Cusacks were prominent in the administration of both the country and the Church. They lost their eminence only in the early eighteenth century, when the majority of them refused to convert to the religious beliefs of their colonial overlords.

At first they were called de Cussac, from the French town of their origin. In Irish this became Cíomhsóg, but in Clare it was transformed into MacIosog or MacIsog, while those who settled in Scotland were known as MacIssac. The Cusacks, who are no longer very numerous, are found mostly now in Munster. They do not appear to have gone abroad in any significant numbers, other than to Europe, where their name appears on the roll call of many armies.

The two Cusack brothers who had come with King John in 1211 were **Geoffrey** and **André**. They married well-born Irish women and so founded a long line of landed gentry, statesmen and clergymen. Towards the end of the twelfth century, **Nicholas Cusack** was Bishop of Kildare for twenty years. **Thomas Cusack** was Mayor of Dublin in 1409.

In an early charter of St Mary's Abbey, Dublin, they are recorded as lords of Killeen, Gerardstown, Foleystown and Clonard—one of their major seats. In the twelfth century another branch wrested the territory of Tirawley in County Mayo from the Uí Fiachrach, one of the most powerful septs in that territory.

Sir John Cusack, 2nd Lord of Gerardstown and many other territories was the ancestor of a distinguished line of Cusacks in Ireland. With his brothers, he defeated Edward Bruce at the battle of Dundalk in 1318.

A century later, the split in Christianity was having its effect in Ireland, and another **Thomas Cusack** (1490–1571), benefiting from the dissolution of the monasteries, was granted Lismullen, outside Navan in County Meath, part of the estate of the Augustinian nuns. This Thomas was a lawyer, and, although he was appreciative of Irish traditions and culture, he worked zealously to abolish the Irish Brehon Code in favour of English law and for this he was knighted in 1541. He was also Master of the Rolls. His career spanned three English reigns: Edward VI appointed him Lord Chancellor; Queen Mary ordered him to restore Dublin's St Patrick's Cathedral, Queen Elizabeth acceded to his plea for a pardon for Shane O Neill, the rebellious chief of Ulster. Sir Thomas Cusack is recorded as having been married twice and divorced once.

James Cusack (b. 1656) of Clonard was one of the very many Irish officers who fought with the ill-fated James II at the battle of the Boyne.

Nicholas Cusack lost his head when he joined one of the risings against Elizabeth I. Later, when Cromwell's army came to savage the country, **Patrick Cusack** led the opposing confederate Catholics.

Following the disastrous battle of the Boyne, like so many of their Irish compatriots, the Cusacks emigrated to join the armies of Europe. For some of them it must have been a return to their origins, perhaps especially for so distinguished a soldier as the **General Chevalier Richard Edmond de Cusack** (1687–1770).

There was the notorious "Grand Pyrite", **Captain George Cusack** (d. 1674). He was a son of the Cusacks of Granstown, County Meath, and, according to a contemporary account, he was "Bred as a scholar and disposed by his parents for a Fryer, but the wildness of his youth not agreeing with the religious life he first robbed his kinsmen of £60 and a watch and fled to Dublin". He soldiered in Flanders, where the severity of the discipline convinced him to try the navy. And thus began a wildly adventurous career, first as a gunner's mate, then as captain in a variety of privateers. He took part in innumerable Mediterranean mutinies, using a different name for each ship he commanded. Nor was he averse to "putting the crew overboard, denying them the longboats". His diary, which includes an episode in London's Marshalsea prison, makes gripping reading.

James William Cusack (1788–1861) was born at Laragh, near Maynooth. One of Ireland's most distinguished nineteenth-century men of medicine, he was Professor of Religion at his alma mater, Trinity College Dublin, as well as being Queen Victoria's surgeon in Ireland, surely an undemanding appointment! He had a large practice, and at one time had as many as 78 apprentices, as was then the custom. One of these was Charles Lever, the doctor who later wrote an abundance of comic Irish novels and died as British Consul in Trieste. James Cusack's portrait hangs in the Royal College of Surgeons in Ireland, of which he was twice president.

James William Cusack

His niece **Margaret Anne Cusack** (1832–99) was the daughter of **Dr Samuel Cusack**, an impecunious younger son. She also had the misfortune to be born a woman and ahead of her time. She showed enormous compassion and insight and, very unpopular in those Victorian days, the strength of character to follow through her ideas. A great handicap was her difficulty in finding a branch of Christianity to suit her emancipated views. For a while she was an Anglican nun in London. Then she joined the ascetic Catholic order of the Poor Clares and founded a branch in Kenmare, County Kerry, where she was very active in feeding the poor during the famine of 1879. She eventually left the Poor Clares, inspired with the idea of opening a new order, to be called the Sisters of Peace, at Knock in County Mayo, where an apparition of the Virgin Mary had been seen—the same shrine which Pope John Paul II made a point of visiting in 1979. The local clergy failed to support her, so instead, with the approval of Pope Leo XIII she sailed for the USA, to found there the Sisters of Peace and to look after the welfare of the much neglected immigrant Irish servant girls. She received little support from the clergy in America, so she left for England, where she tried several versions of the Anglican or Episcopalian faith. She wrote her autobiography, *The Nun of Kenmare*, in 1889. She also wrote a succession of biographies and pamphlets to support her Kenmare convent. Today, in Ireland, "The Nun of Kenmare" is revered as Ireland's first suffragette and campaigner for Home Rule.

Michael Cusack (1860–1907) came from the Burren, a strange lunar landscape of rocks and rare flowers in County Clare. He was an experienced schoolteacher and he taught for several years in America before returning to Ireland where he was on the staff of several of Ireland's more famous boys' schools. He saw a gap in the education system and filled it with resounding success when he opened his Civil Service Academy, a Dublin cramming school for young men who aspired to white collar jobs.

Working with young people who had athletic as well as patriotic ambitions inspired him to form an athletic association. In November 1884, with other nationalists, he founded the Gaelic Athletic Association (GAA) at Hayes' Commercial Hotel in Thurles, County Tipperary. He received encouragement from Thomas Croke, the Archbishop of Cashel and Emly, who helped develop it into the force it remains in rural Ireland today. Parnell and Michael Davitt were also patrons, and when the GAA playing fields were opened in North Dublin they were named Croke Park and one of the stands is called the Cusack stand.

Cyril Cusack (1910–92) was actor, poet and playwright. His appearance in any theatre, especially Dublin's Abbey Theatre, drew discerning crowds. He acted internationally in films and on television. **Sorcha**, **Sineád** and **Niamh Cusack** have followed in their distinguished father's footsteps.

Daly

ó dálaigh

From the eleventh to the seventeenth centuries there were no less than thirty outstanding O Daly poets. "There is certainly no family to which the bardic literature of Ireland is more deeply indebted than that of O Daly", wrote the historian John O Donovan (1805–61). Their family history goes back to earliest recorded times. They claim descent from one of Ireland's epic heroes, Niall of the Nine Hostages, the High King who ruled from his palace at Tara from AD 380 to 405. He was ancestor of the O Neills of Tyrone and the O Donnells of Tirconnell, whose lengthy pedigrees are in Dublin's Genealogical Office. From the Dalys came several kings of Meath, who in time branched out to Thomond and to Connacht. The surname derives from the Irish word *dáil*, a place where councils are held. (Thus Dáil Éireann, the Irish Parliament, got its name.)

The first of this gifted family of leaders in Irish bardic literature was **Cuconnacht na Scoile** (Cuconnacht of the school), who died at Clonard in 1139. His was a school for bards—poets and minstrels. From Westmeath they fanned out, becoming official poets to the leading families of the land.

In Cavan they were resident bards with the powerful O Reillys. Numerous O Dalys scattered north to follow their poetic vocation with the foremost Ulster family, the O Neills. In West Cork they served Munster's ruling family, the MacCarthys. In Connacht the kingly O Connors could boast an O Daly bard and there they were also hereditary poets to the O Loghlins, Lords of Corcomroe.

Also in Connacht, **Donogh Mór O Daly** (d. 1244) of Kinvarra wrote such fine poetry that he has been fulsomely described as "the Irish Ovid". He is buried in the Cistercian Abbey in Boyle, County Roscommon, now an ivy clad ruin near the main road by the River Boyle.

Poets can be excessively temperamental beings. In 1213, **Muiredagh O Daly** from Lough Derravaragh (the Lake of the Oaks) in County Westmeath, where the legendary children of Lir were turned into swans, went to pay a visit to the O Donnells of Drumcliff, near Sligo. One of their stewards provoked him so severely that the poet retaliated by killing him! For this appalling behaviour, Muiredagh was pursued all over Ireland by the enraged O Donnells. He fled to Scotland where, in time, he repented and wrote a poem so disarming that he was forgiven by the O Donnells and was able to return home.

Aengus O Daly of Cork was a renegade. He allowed himself to be employed by the English to write *The Tribes of Ireland*, a bitter satire on his own people. Foolishly, he returned to Ireland where, in 1617, he was stabbed to death by a Meagher of Roscrea, who had been vilified in the book.

Daniel O Daly (1595–1662) of Kerry was an outstanding European scholar. To escape religious persecution he went to Europe to study for the priesthood. He founded a Dominican college in Louvain, and, in Lisbon, a college and a convent for Irish religious exiles. His considerable diplomatic skill was recognized by diverse monarchs. The then Prince of Wales, later Charles I of England, even tried to use him, though unsuccessfully, when he was seeking the hand of Philip IV of Spain's daughter. In Portugal, in 1640, he was prominent in the revolution which freed it from Spain. An international traveller, he was summoned to Paris in 1650 by Charles II and

Daley

Dally

Dawley

O Daly

his mother, Queen Henrietta Maria, where they urged him to use his influence to effect a coalition of Irish Royalists against the Parliamentarians. As a result, Dominic de Rosario (O Daly's religious name) wrote to Ormond, Lord Lieutenant of Ireland, assuring him of his readiness to serve the royal cause both in Ireland and Spain. But he insisted he must have the assurance of Charles II that Ireland would be established as a free nation. Portugal was lucky, but not Ireland, although he had done his utmost. Earlier, he had been an envoy from Portugal to Louis XIV in Paris, advising on military matters concerning the Irish who were seeking allies for a revolt. This versatile and learned Irish Dominican, who died at Lisbon in 1662, left many ecclesiastical writings.

With the submergence of Irish culture and aristocracy in the seventeenth century, there was little outlet for the O Daly poetic vein. They found other methods for creative self-expression. The stage, for instance. **Richard Daly** (1750–1813) was an actor manager. A second son of Connacht landed gentry who had survived by conforming to the Anglican faith, he was sent to Trinity College, Dublin, where his addiction to duelling and gambling frittered away his inheritance. A young blood of "striking stature and elegance", he turned very successfully to the stage. In the 1780s, when Dublin was the second city of the Empire, Richard Daly found his *métier* in management and brought over Kemble and Mrs Siddons to his famous Smock Alley Theatre. He owned several theatres and may have inspired Daly's Club in College Street (now an office), much favoured by the gambling bloods. Richard's career was a stormy one, especially with the critics, against one of whom he won an important libel case.

By the eighteenth century, the Dalys who descended from the poet Donogh More O Daly, "the Irish Ovid", had become politicians, men of the law, and Barons of Dunsandle and Clan Conal in County Galway. In the thirty years up to 1720, there were at least six mayors of Galway who were Dalys, including **Denis Bowes Daly**, who was six times mayor of Galway.

Denis Daly (1747–91), a Member of Parliament for Galway, won government office and £1,200 a year for opposing a measure for independence. He was also against Flood's Bill for Parliamentary Reform. Despite these rigid views, his friendship with Henry Grattan, leader of the Irish Opposition, remained unbroken. Although often inclined to indolence, when he spoke he could be dynamic. Grattan described his death, at the age of 44, as an irretrievable loss to Ireland: "Had Daly lived there would probably have been no insurrection. He would have spoken to the people with authority and would have restrained them".

His eldest son, **James Daly** (1782–1847), who was created Baron Dunsandle and Clan Conal in 1845, was Member of Parliament for County Galway.

Denis St George Daly (1810–93), James's eldest son, was a captain in the 7th Hussars. He had two natural sons whose heirs moved about between the various Daly properties in Ireland, eventually settling in England, where they pursued successful military careers.

The 4th and last Baron of Dunsandle and Clan Conal, **James Daly** (1848–1911), was Private Secretary to a succession of British Prime Ministers.

Major Denis Bowes Daly (b. 1900), once of Dunsandle (demolished in 1954), was father of **Lieutenant-Colonel Denis James Daly** of the Blues and Royals. His son, **Lieutenant Anthony Daly**, died, aged 23, in July 1982 in the IRA massacre of the Household Cavalry in Hyde Park, London.

Denis Daly (1747–91)

There are over 30,000 Dalys in Ireland today, mostly in Munster, followed closely by Leinster, with a sprinkling in Ulster. Some have reverted to their ancient O prefix.

Prominent among them was the Irish language devotee **Cearbhaill Ó Dalaigh**. Born in modest circumstances in Bray, County Wicklow, he became a judge in the Court of Justice of the European Communities and, for a short time, was President of Ireland. He resigned in dramatic circumstances and died shortly afterwards in 1978.

Like many Irish men and women who sought wider horizons, the Dalys went far afield. There is a Daly's Cove in Jamaica, named after one of their Irish homes, and a Dunsandle in the former Tanganyka.

The Dalys found plenty of scope in Australia. **Sir Dominick Daly** (1798–1868) of County Galway, after a successful career in Canada where, in 1841, he was elected to the Legislative Assembly following the Union of the Canadas, subsequently became Governor of South Australia. A century later, **Sir Thomas Daly** was Australia's Chief of General Staff.

In the mid-nineteenth century, America was rapidly developing her vast potential. The Dalys were there to help with this process.

Charles Patrick Daly (1816–99) was born in New York to poor, immigrant parents. He spent three years before the mast and saw fighting when the French took Algiers in 1830. On returning to New York, he worked by day as an apprentice carpenter, while at night he studied law. Assisted by various benefactors, he entered a law office from where his brilliance saw him through to the Bar in less than the usual time. He practised in New York, joined the Democratic party and, at the age of only 28, was made a judge. He was Chief Justice for almost 42 years. His early experience of travel remained with him, and for years he was president of the American Geographical Society.

John Augustus Daly (1838–99) was born in Plymouth, North Carolina, the son of **Captain Denis Daly**, a shipowner whose family had come from Ireland. John Augustus was the founder of one of New York's best-known theatres, Daly's Fifth Avenue Theatre, where Ada Rehan (1860–1916), the Limerick-born actress, was leading lady for many years. It was this Daly who introduced melodrama to the theatre, anticipating the cinema. He held his audience entranced, waiting for the rescue of seemingly helpless victims bound to railroad tracks in the path of the onrushing train. He was also an eminent Shakespearean producer.

It seems fitting that an Irish-American should first promote the plays of George Bernard Shaw in America. This was **Arnold Daly** (1875–1927), Brooklyn-born of Irish parents. In 1903 he staged a single matinée performance of *Candida* at the Prince's Theatre, New York, with Dorothy Donnelly as leading lady and himself as Marchbanks. It was such a success that he rented the Berkeley Lyceum, where *Candida* ran for 150 performances. This began the Shaw vogue in America. He produced many Shaw plays, including *Mrs Warren's Profession*, which caused him to be arrested for violating the law! He was acquitted and continued to stage Shaw revivals, although his main interest was in the theatre of ideas. He never used newspaper advertising or gave free seats to critics. Eventually he ran into financial troubles, a victim, it was said, of his own irascibility.

Marcus Daly (1841–1900) emigrated to America with his impoverished parents. At 15 he was working as a pick-and-shovel man, but his innate ability was recognized by mining experts who sent him to Butte, Montana. Here he progressed so rapidly that he entered a partnership to buy the Alice Silver Mine and the Anaconda Silver Mine. When the silver gave out, he caught the great copper boom and amassed a fortune.

A man of wide interests, he developed fruit-growing in Montana and owned and trained some of the finest racehorses. Success did not go to his head. He never lost touch with his former pick-and-shovel friends to whom he gave considerable help.

Chicago has been regarded as one of the best-run cities in the United States and some of the credit must be given to **Mayor Richard Daley**, who dominated its civic institutions for several decades. Richard Daley (1902–76) was the son of Lillian Dunne of Limerick and **Michael Daley**, a sheet metal worker from Waterford, who followed so many of their fellow countrymen to America.

In ecclesiastical terms the island of Ireland is treated as one—the boundaries go far back in history. **Cathal Daly** was born in Loughuile, County Armagh, in 1917. He was created Cardinal and Primate of all Ireland in 1991. A graduate of Queen's University Belfast, he had a distinguished academic career at home and abroad. As the leading Catholic prelate he is outspoken against the violence in what is probably the most continuously troubled see in Christendom. Despite the sectarian divide he is strongly opposed to the integration of schools.

Dillon
⌀íolún

Dillon is a prime example of a Norman name which has become thoroughly accepted as Irish. Their lineage in Ireland began in 1185, when **Sir Henry de Leon** came from Brittany as secretary to Prince (later King) John of England and France. Dispossessing the MacCarrons, MacGeoghegans and the O Melaghlins, Prince John awarded him large tracts of land in the midlands. Sir Henry married the daughter of John de Courcy, another Norman, and Earl of Ulster. Their marriage was most fruitful, and so numerous were their descendants that vast territories of Longford, Westmeath and Kilkenny became known as Dillon's Country.

The prolific Dillons became Barons of Drumrany, Earls of Roscommon, Lords of Clonbrock, County Galway, Viscounts Dillon of Costello-Galen in County Sligo, and Counts Dillon in France.

In 1343, **Sir Henry Dillon**, described as the "Premier Dillon, Lord Baron Drumrany", founded the Franciscan Abbey in Athlone. He was the ancestor of a remarkable line of distinguished bishops, priors, abbots, nuns, priests and soldiers.

One of his descendants, **Sir Theobold Dillon**, commanded an independent troop in the reign of Queen Elizabeth I. His reward was to be created Viscount Dillon of Costello-Galen and Lord President of Connacht. The 1st Viscount Dillon died at a great age. He had such a large progeny that, at his last family reunion, he was able to assemble in his house over 100 of his descendants.

Thomas, 4th Viscount Dillon of Costello-Galen (1614–84), forfeited his Catholic religion because it made him ineligible to take his parliamentary seat in London. He returned to Ireland as Lieutenant-General and as joint President of Connacht.

He changed his allegiance later and was received back into the Catholic Church with great ceremony by the Papal Nuncio, Rinuccini. What promised to be a successful Irish revolution was brewing and Thomas joined the army of James Butler, Duke of Ormond. They were defeated outside Dublin by Cromwell's Roundheads. Thomas's estates were confiscated and he fled to France. He returned after the restoration of Charles II and regained most of his extensive lands.

Although the sea crossing was slow and often perilous in the seventeenth century, the numerous Dillons moved freely between Ireland and England. **James Dillon**, one of the family who were Earls of Roscommon, married Elizabeth Wentworth, the sister of Thomas, Earl of Strafford, who had been sent by Charles I to subdue Ireland. (In this he was far from successful and, later, lost his head for alleged treason.)

James Dillon, 3rd Earl of Roscommon, was succeeded by his son **Wentworth** (1633–84) as 4th Earl of Roscommon. He was sent to France to be educated because of religious unrest both in England and Ireland. He married a granddaughter of Richard Boyle, the self-made millionaire and 1st Earl of Cork. When Charles II was restored to the throne, Wentworth Dillon regained his lands, but he stayed in London, a literary dilettante of such eminence he was considered worthy of burial in Westminster Abbey.

Sir James Dillon, who had been a Member of Parliament for County Wicklow from 1639 to 1642, had to flee to France from the rampaging Cromwellians. In fact, less than six generations after they had left France for Ireland, many of the Dillons were back there again, but this time they were distinctly Irish. It was this Sir James Dillon who raised the Irish regiment

de Leon

of Dillon which was to bring lustre to the exiled Irish. He had also taken a prominent part in the abortive rising in Ireland in 1641, and died in 1669, a Field Marshal of France.

Count Arthur Dillon (1670–1733) was already in France at the time of the siege of Limerick, a turning-point in Irish history, when 11,000 soldiers of Ireland's last great army sailed for France with most of their officers, while the Treaty which promised many reforms was "broken before the ink was dry". Arthur Dillon was a colonel in Dillon's Regiment, a regiment well-recorded in O Callaghan's *History of the Irish Brigade*, and in books about the Irish in France by Richard Hayes.

Count Arthur Dillon served for forty years with the French army, becoming a Field Marshal and, later, Governor of Toulon. He has been described as tall and handsome. His *Memoirs*, alas, were destroyed in the French Revolution. He had four daughters and five sons (four of whom served in the French army).

His fifth son, **Arthur Dillon** (b. 1721), a priest, had unexpected ecclesiastical honours bestowed on him, through royal favour. **Colonel James Dillon**, another of Arthur's five sons, commanded the Irish Brigade which drove back the English at the battle of Fontenoy. James was killed, but Louis XVI had seen the action and the following day he ordered that his brother Arthur, then a modest curé, be given the next vacant benefice. And so Arthur Dillon rapidly became Archbishop of Toulouse and Narbonne, and President of Languedoc, with an annual income of £40,000. He enjoyed his promotion to the full, setting up a courtly salon in Paris. His stables were envied by the King who once asked why he hunted while his clerics were forbidden the sport. "My vices are the vices of my ancestors, my priests' vices are their own", he explained. By 1788 his expenses far exceeded even his income. The revolution broke out with its anti-religious laws and Arthur, an inflexible loyalist, refused to take the oath, and fled to London where he died in 1806.

Count Arthur Dillon, the young nephew he had reared, not only became a revolutionary, but also a general of the Republic. He had even attempted to capture his uncle, the Archbishop, when he discovered he was hiding in Verdun!

Dillons were now leading citizens in Bordeaux. Of five brothers, sons of a Dublin banker who had emigrated to Bordeaux, two were priests, **Henry** and **Arthur**. Another was **Count Edward**, "le beau Dillon", a favourite of Marie Antoinette. (In fact he was accused of being one of her lovers, but this could have been an invention of her jealous courtiers.) A royalist Dillon, he was gentleman to the King's brother, the Duke of Artois. With his brothers, he tried to reform Dillon's Regiment to help restore the monarchy. Seeing little hope for the Bourbons, Count Edward journeyed to Ireland where, such are the twists of politics, he recruited an army for his Britannic majesty!

Dr Edward Dillon was Superior of the Irish College at Douai when it was closed by the French revolutionaries. On his return to Galway, he was made Bishop of Tuam. The United Irishmen were then spreading the gospel of the French Revolution. He had experienced it at first hand, and he preached against its principles so vehemently he was disliked and distrusted by his fellow countrymen.

Born in Dublin in 1745, **Count Theobald Dillon**, later a Field Marshal of France, had had an early military training with Washington in the American War of Independence. He was a colonel in Dillon's Regiment when the French Revolution broke out and all foreign legions in the army were abolished. The Dillon Regiment which had been commanded for

Count Theobald Dillon

101 years by successive members of the same family became a mere cipher—the 87th Regiment. Theobald, son of the 11th Viscount Dillon, became a general in the Cavalry Brigade, like a number of other Dillons now on the revolutionary side. His was a tragic end. When Napoleon was battling against Austria in 1792, Theobald was ordered to feign an attack on Tournai. The cavalry, misunderstanding him, turned on its own infantry with cries of "We have been betrayed" and massacred them. A bullet shattered Theobald's hip. Still thinking that "the aristocrat Dillon" had betrayed them, he was murdered by his own troops. Later, in an attempt to make amends, he was buried with honours in the prestigious Panthéon in Paris.

Arthur, Edward, Theobald and James were favourite names for Dillon sons, which must have been as confusing for the family as for the historian. **Colonel Arthur Dillon**, who had suffered the guillotine, left a daughter who was married to Count Bertrand. These two are remembered for their fidelity to the fallen Napoleon during his sad years at St Helena.

Until the close of the seventeenth century, the Dillons had been a distinctly martial family. In the eighteenth century they became politicians and scholars.

John Talbot Dillon (1740–1805) of Lismullen, County Meath, was Member of Parliament for Wicklow in 1771. In recognition of his services to Catholic interests in Parliament, Emperor Joseph II created him Baron of the Holy Roman Empire. A traveller, linguist and reporter, his objective memoirs give a contemporary view of the causes and effects of the French Revolution.

The 8th and last Baronet, and Baron of the Holy Roman Empire of that lineage, **Sir Robert**, formerly of Lismullen, died in Wicklow in 1982.

Captain Peter Dillon (1785–1874) was in the French navy. During his brief reign, the French King Charles X conferred the Legion of Honour on him, plus a substantial pension. In 1829, Peter Dillon published an account of his travels, particularly in the South Sea Islands.

John Blake Dillon (1816–66) from Mayo studied for the Bar at Trinity College, Dublin, having first tried the priesthood. He joined the Young Ireland Party with Thomas Davis, the poet, and other party nationalists impatient with Daniel O Connell, who abhorred violence. With Gavan Duffy, in 1842, he founded the *Nation* newspaper which helped ignite the abortive rising six years later. John Blake Dillon escaped to the obscurity of the Aran Islands until he could make his way to America. He practised in the New York courts until the amnesty of 1855 when he returned to Ireland. He became Member of Parliament for Tipperary, but he died from fever a year later.

His son, also **John Blake Dillon** (1851–1927), a non-practising surgeon, succeeded him to the Tipperary seat. This was the time of the rising star of Charles Stewart Parnell and the Land League, and John Blake Dillon, no less than many others, had his share of imprisonment.

A grandson, **James Dillon** of Roscommon (1902–86), twice held the post of Minister for Agriculture in the Irish government.

James Dillon's brother, **Myles Dillon** (1900–72), was a scholar of renown. He held many posts abroad, in America and England, and he lectured internationally. He was a Professor of Celtic Studies and director of the Celtic School at Dublin's Institute for Advanced Studies.

Through the centuries the Dillons have been very numerous and able, with their achievements being recorded internationally. There are many Dillons still in France, and in Paris their name is engraved on the Arc de Triomphe.

John Blake Dillon (1816–66)

Dillons have also settled in New Zealand, Canada and America. **Count Arthur Marie Dillon**, born in Paris in 1834, went to America where he was founder of the Commercial Cable Company. He is also credited with inventing the American-style election campaign!

Henri Patrice Dillon, born in San Francisco in 1851, became a noted lithographer in Paris.

Gerard Dillon (1916–71), a Belfast-born artisan, attained many skills before maturing as a painter and exhibiting at Dublin's Royal Hibernian Academy and other exhibition centres at home and abroad. A versatile artist who designed stage settings and wall hangings, wrote stories and recorded songs, he was obsessed with the theme of the clown, a prominent character in many of his paintings.

Eilís Dillon (1920–94), born in Galway, lived in America. She was a novelist, poet, playwright and author of many children's books.

Although Dillons may be found in the United Kingdom and, indeed, world-wide, they are almost certainly of the same family of de Leon which came from Brittany 800 years ago.

Clonbrock, built in 1785 near Ballinasloe, County Galway, was sold in 1976, and the accumulation of centuries of Dillon memorabilia and antiques was dispersed. The collection included an invaluable archive of photographs: from 1869, the 4th Lord Clonbrock and his wife recorded every aspect of nineteenth-century family life on their Galway estate.

The present representative of the Viscountcy, which was created in 1622, is **Henry**, 22nd Viscount of Costello-Galen and Count of France, who was born in 1973 and lives in London.

Doherty
ó Οοchartaigh

However you choose to spell Doherty, and there are at least half a dozen versions apart from with or without the O, it remains a Donegal name. It is believed to be one of the oldest hereditary surnames, and translated from the Irish it is thought to mean obstructive. Ranking fifteenth in the list of 100 most common Irish surnames, the motto on their coat of arms is *Ár nDúthcas* (for my inheritance).

According to the O Dogherty pedigree of 5 November 1770 in the Genealogical Office in Dublin, they are descended from one of the eight sons of Niall of the Nine Hostages, the legendary chieftain who was killed jousting in France in AD 405. Four of Niall's sons settled in Meath. The eldest, Laogarius, was Ireland's first Christian monarch, surely the very king who saw Patrick light his Pascal fire on the Hill of Slane?

Niall's four younger sons went north to Ulster and were known as the Hy Nialls. They reigned there for over 600 years until 1002, when Brian Boru assumed the high kingship.

The names of the descendants of Niall are renowned in Irish history. They were the O Neills who were princes and earls of Tir Eogan, the O Donnells, princes and earls of Tirconnell, and the O Melaghlins, kings and princes of Meath. The O Dohertys who descend from Niall owned the Inishowen Peninsula until, to quote their genealogical document, "the accession of King James I to the throne of England and Ireland in 1603, at which period six counties of Ulster were escheated to the Crown and granted to Scotch Planters".

From the eighth to the seventeenth centuries there was a constant power struggle between the clans and in the twelfth century, against the English invaders—few Normans penetrated as far as Ulster. For a while the O Dohertys maintained good relations with the English. Cunningly they used them to play O Neill against O Donnell. Many times they preserved their land, or their lives, by pretending allegiance to Henry VIII, or Elizabeth I. Thus they acquired their knighthoods.

Shane Mór O Doherty was knighted in 1541. His son, **Shane Óg**, who was knighted in 1585, was the father of Cahir, the most notorious of all the O Dohertys.

Cahir O Doherty (1587–1608) was only 14 when his father died and there were many family quarrels before Cahir was finally acknowledged as Lord of Inishowen. He has been described as extremely tall and handsome and very brave in battle. Still only in his teens, he was knighted by Mountjoy for military bravery and, in 1603, was invited to visit the Court in London. On his return to Ireland he was made an admiral of the new city of Derry. Intrigues enmeshed him and he was accused of treason, which provoked him, catastrophically, into the madness of attacking Derry, which he mercilessly burned. Retribution came swiftly; a strong Crown force was dispatched and he was killed, and his head was sent to Dublin to be exhibited. Cahir O Doherty earned himself the title "that audacious traitor" and his actions opened the floodgates for the plantation of Ulster and the tragedy which continues into the twentieth century.

Cahir's was the end of the O Doherty lordship of Inishowen. The year before his death, the northern earls had sailed away from Lough Swilly to spread their battered wings all around Europe. Cahir's brother **Seán O Doherty** soon followed, and his descendant, **Dr Ramón Salvador O Doherty**, who lives in Cadiz in Spain, is 11th in direct line from the

Dorrity

Dougharty

Mac Devitt

O Dogherty

51

Lords of Inishowen. In July 1990, he was ceremonially inaugurated as 37th O Doherty chieftain.

The Keep, all that remains of the fine castle built by the O Dohertys in 1430, still stands at Buncrana, in a ruggedly charming area of Donegal between Lough Swilly and Lough Foyle. A glance in the telephone directory will confirm that the O Dohertys continue to thrive around Inishmore. Across the sea in Scotland, where they fled to escape the persecutions following the plantations, there are also many of the O Doherty name.

Following the disaster of Derry, many of them went still further afield. **John Doherty** (also sometimes **Dougharty**) (1688–1755), settled in Worcester in England, where he had a school for over fifty years. Mathematics was his speciality and his many published works include *A Way of Finding Mean Times of the Moon's Phases and Eclipses*. A man of some distinction, he is buried in the cloisters of Worcester Cathedral.

Thomas Doherty (d. 1805) was a lowly countryman who went to England and found work clerking in a legal office. During his sixteen years there he studied law, and made an important collection of precedents and notes on legal cases which were so remarkable he was made a member of Gray's Inn, the legal institution in London. He devoted himself so obsessively to his vocation, and to editing a series of books on the duties of the Crown Court Assistant, that he utterly neglected his family, a nineteenth-century example of a man who died from overwork.

John Doherty (1783–1850) graduated from Trinity College, Dublin, and in the course of time reached the eminence of Chief Justice of Ireland. His reputation as a judge was surpassed by his performance in the House of Commons in London, where his impressive appearance and sharp Irish wit were much appreciated. So also was his connection, on the maternal side, with a former Prime Minister, George Canning. Although John Doherty and Daniel O Connell were in accord as regards the granting of Catholic emancipation, politically they frequently differed bitterly. When the House of Lords was almost within his grasp, over-optimistic investment in the railway industry lost him his fortune and closed his career.

Kevin Izod O Doherty (1823–1905), while studying medicine in Dublin, wrote articles for the *Nation*, mouthpiece of the Young Irelanders the protagonists of Home Rule. He was tried for treason and was deported to Van Dieman's Land (Tasmania). He was eventually pardoned and he returned to Dublin where he completed his medical studies. In 1862 he returned voluntarily to Brisbane, Australia, where he practised successfully for 23 years and was also a member of the Queensland legislative assembly. On a visit to Ireland he was so well received that he was elected Member of Parliament for North Meath, but when he returned to Brisbane three years later he found his medical practice had disappeared. He died a poor man.

William James O Doherty (1835–68) was a Dublin-born O Doherty who made a name as a sculptor in London. He had the good fortune to begin his studies in the Royal Dublin Society, with its government-sponsored school of art. He soon abandoned painting for sculpture and progressed so rapidly that by 1857 he was exhibiting in London's Royal Academy. He transformed his name to Dogherty, altering the spelling several times. His works were commissioned by the nobility and various institutions. He went to Rome to execute an important commission and to study but, alas, while on a visit to Berlin his promising career was cut short by an early death at the age of 33.

The Dohertys were certainly varied in their pursuits. At the beginning of this century, **Reggie** and **Laurie Doherty** were stylish tennis champions who graced the centre court at Wimbledon and wrote about the game.

The Dohertys also appear in Canadian records. **Charles Joseph Doherty** (1855–1931) of Montreal, lawyer and Minister of Justice, represented Canada at the League of Nations in 1920.

Among the many American Dohertys was **Henry Latham Doherty** (1870–1939), whose family emigrated to Columbus, Ohio, from Ireland. A public utility engineer, from his Philadelphia office he provided not only the engineering services but also the finance which ran the gas and electricity companies of thirty American cities. This engineer, who was said "to translate complex new techniques into goods and services by high pressure engineering methods", had his enterprise severely curbed by Roosevelt's New Deal.

Of course there were Dohertys in plenty in Europe. In the Bibliothèque Nationale in Paris there are numerous O Doherty papers. The Genealogical Office in Dublin describes the O Dohertys at various periods between 800 and 1845 as Lords of Inishowen in County Donegal, chiefs of the name, and Doherty of Newtown, County Leitrim; of Oldtown and Kedrah and Coolmoyne, of Bruis and Killimley and Outrath, Long Orchard and Cashel, of Ballydrehid and Moortown, all in County Tipperary.

No account of the O Dohertys—the O is being increasingly reclaimed—is complete without mention of the MacDevitts. In Irish, Mac Daibhed means son of David. This David was a chief of the Cinel Conaill (of the line of Niall), who was killed in 1208. From him descend many MacDevitts of Inishowen, who, as far back as the sack of Derry, were associates of the O Dohertys.

O Doherty's Keep, Buncrana, County Donegal

Doyle
ó ðúıll

Doyelle

Doyley

The Doyle name derives from a nickname and so never had an O or a Mac prefix. In Irish it is *dhubh-ghall*, a dark foreigner, signifying the Norsemen who, long before the Anglo-Normans, terrified the east coast of Ireland when they arrived in their longboats. They settled on the Leinster seaboard, mostly in the counties of Wicklow, Wexford and Carlow. Although there are pages of Doyles in the telephone directories of rural and urban Ireland, they do not spring from an identifiable forebear, nor are they necessarily related to each other. The name Dubhghaill—there was no sept—is occasionally recorded in the *Annals of the Four Masters*.

It was not until the eighteenth century that the Doyles began to make history. Then came a collection of remarkably able and talented Doyles.

The whimsically named Bramblestown, near the pretty village of Inistioge in County Kilkenny, nurtured a unique family. Between 1756 and 1856 came a dynasty of military men: a series of six major-generals, four of them baronets, and several Royal Navy officers. In 1911 a descendant, **Colonel Arthur Doyle**, did his utmost to sort them out in his book *A Hundred Years of Conflict, Being Some Records of the Services of Six Generals of the Doyle Family, 1756–1856*. The number of Doyle generals was too much for the *Dictionary of National Biography*, which, Colonel Arthur writes, "got them all mixed up", as also did the *Gentleman's Magazine*. In London, a Court official who was sending out invitations, remarked to the King, "I can never distinguish between them". Said the King, "Perhaps it's just as well that they have taken good care to distinguish themselves".

Colonel Arthur Doyle tells how, "Being Catholic they were bullied by James I, and bullied by Cromwell. Possibly they became Protestant by 1690 through marriage to a Scottish widow. Several were in King James's Irish army at the battle of the Boyne. Afterwards they were bullied again by William II who cut off a Doyle head and stuck it on the walls of Kilkenny Castle". They also served with the Irish Brigade in Europe where they were called Doyley and, in French, Doyelle. In the French army at that time, the Irish were at a disadvantage because of the vindictiveness of Sir Robert Walpole, the Whig Prime Minister, who made use of his friendship with a French cardinal to hold up the promotion of Irish officers.

Sir John Doyle (1756–1834), a general, was one of the four sons of **Charles Doyle** of Bramblestown. A graduate of Trinity College, Dublin, he served with the British army in the United States. When the Civil War ended there in 1784, he returned to Ireland where he was elected Member of Parliament for Mullingar and proved himself as eloquent a speaker as any in that talented, pre-Union, Irish House of Commons. Sir John raised the famous 87th Regiment in 1794 to serve in the Netherlands. At one time he was Private Secretary to the Prince of Wales. When he retired he was appointed Governor of Guernsey where his able administration, assisted by a nephew, also **John Doyle**, is commemorated by an impressive column.

Major Welbore-Ellis Doyle (1758–97) was in Philadelphia in 1788 where he founded a regiment from the Irish who were constantly deserting from the "enemy's" ranks. Called the Volunteers of Ireland, Doyle was its lieutenant-colonel. Unfortunately, the Irish, when they were displeased, had the habit of dashing back to the enemy's lines. A much-travelled soldier, Welbore was Military Envoy to Poland and Warsaw and died in Ceylon at the age of 39.

Lieutenant-General Sir Charles Doyle (1770–1842) was the soldier who introduced the "Ca Ira" cry into the British army during a deadly exchange with the French. He was sent to Spain to train the Spanish army and was made a Spanish lieutenant-general with the Doyle Triadores. He was Member of Parliament for Carlow from 1831 to 1852. He served in many European countries. In Portugal he became entangled in politics which led to him having some financial problems with the British army. However, his honour was vindicated by burial at Windsor.

A further three distinguished Doyles were **Major-General Sir Francis Doyle**, Baronet (1783–1839), **Major-General Charles Doyle** (1787–1848), and **Major-General Sir John Milley Doyle** (1781–1856). They all had enterprising army careers in Europe, Egypt, Canada, America and the West Indies. Several budding Doyle generals had seen action by the tender age of ten or fourteen, enticed into the army by enthusiastic fathers, brothers or uncles. Between battles they would return to Ireland to cultivate their land, become Members of Parliament or command the local militia. Eventually, they mostly left Ireland for England, though one Doyle baronet, formerly of the Royal Irish Fusiliers, remains in the Republic of Ireland.

James Warren Doyle (1786–1834) was born in New Ross, County Wexford. His father was a farmer and his mother a Quaker. He went to college in Coimbra, Portugal, but his clerical studies were rudely interrupted by the clash between the armies of Napoleon and Wellington (who annexed him as an interpreter with the English army). When Napoleon was defeated he was able to return home and begin his clerical ministry at Carlow College.

Probably marked by the rigours of war, his unorthodox battle-scarred appearance did not at first commend him to his pupils. They quickly discovered, however, that they had a knowledgeable teacher with a most original mind. He even dared express the hope of a possible union between the Established and the Catholic Churches!

He was a stern disciplinarian and wrote vehemently on the state of Ireland and its Church, using the initials J.K.L.—James, Bishop of Kildare and Leighlin. Three times he was asked to give evidence before a parliamentary committee in London, where they found him impressive. "You have been examining Dr Doyle", someone remarked to the Duke of Wellington. "No, but he has been examining us", replied the Duke.

Bishop Doyle renewed church discipline, built schools and the cathedral in Carlow where, worn out by overwork, he died and was buried at the age of 48.

John Doyle (1797–1868) was the forefather of a generation of Doyles who were to contribute greatly to the artistic and literary world. John first studied art in his native Dublin where he made a name painting horses. He went to London to try portrait painting, but, instead he was hugely successful as HB, the political cartoonist who brightened the pages of *Punch* magazine with his sketches of people in the public eye, from O Connell to Disraeli and Palmerston and many other famous characters. He never descended to coarseness or vulgarity unlike many of his contemporaries.

His son, **Richard Doyle** (1824–83), was taught by his father and at 19 he, too, was contributing to the newly-established humorous magazine, *Punch*. In fact it was Richard who designed its first, and famous, cover, which included among the images surrounding Mr Punch, his own dog, Toby. When *Punch* indulged in vicious cartooning of the Pope, Richard resigned. He illustrated many books by popular authors including Thackeray and Ruskin. On his death he was described as a "singularly

Sir John Doyle

sweet and noble type of English gentleman". A prime example of Irish adaptability!

His eldest brother, **Charles Altamont Doyle**, was also an illustrator. He had a high-born Irish wife, Mary Foley, and ten children. Charles, who did not enjoy his exile in Edinburgh as a civil servant, escaped by painting flowers, animals and fairies. Victorian critics later described his work as among the most imaginative of the period. Alas, in middle age he disappeared into the confines of a Scottish lunatic asylum. Only in 1978, when his sketch book, accidentally discovered in 1955, was published, did research reveal Charles not to be insane but merely an epileptic who was also overfond of burgundy. *The Last Great Conan Doyle Mystery*, written by Michael Baker, is beautifully illustrated with Doyle's sketches.

Charles was the father of **Sir Arthur Conan Doyle** (1859–1930), the Edinburgh-born medical doctor who gripped the reading public with his stories of Sherlock Holmes and Dr Watson and their cliff-hanging adventures in crime detection. Sir Arthur, who kept very quiet about his eccentric father, was as prolific a writer as his forebears had been artists and cartoonists.

This Doyle family has been described as the only one to have given, in the space of three generations, five separate entries to the *Dictionary of National Biography*, and that does not include the hapless Charles.

Henry Edward Doyle (1827–92), a Dublin painter, studied in London and Rome. In 1869 he was elected director of the National Gallery of Ireland. He was a member of the Royal Hibernian Academy and exhibited there frequently.

There were also some Doyle celebrities who were not born Doyles. One of these was "Martin Doyle", who was born William Hickey (1788–1875). A County Cork Protestant clergyman, he tried by his writings to encourage the peasantry to improve their farming methods. He helped establish an agricultural school at Barrow, and formed the South Wexford Agricultural Society, the first of its kind. He wrote copiously on practical issues, particularly landlordism and horticulture.

In the first half of this century, "Lyn C. Doyle" was a household name. It was the pen-name of a bank manager from Downpatrick, Alexander Montgomery (1873–1961), who wrote humorous plays and stories. He was the first writer to be appointed to the Irish Censorship Board.

Jack Doyle (1913–78), the "Gorgeous Gael", was born in Cork and left it to enlist in the Irish Guards. Spotting his potential, Dan Sullivan bought him out and trained him as a heavyweight boxer. He had many successes in the United States. He had style, good looks and he could also sing. Women adored Jack Doyle and followed him everywhere. He went into cabaret, did some wrestling, made films and married Movita, a film star. He was a charming playboy, until the champagne dried up when he went bankrupt and died in London.

During the Famine, many Doyles emigrated to America. Earlier, the family of **John Thomas Doyle** (1819–1906) had fled there after the rising of 1798. He was a lawyer who at one time was the general agent for the American Atlantic and Pacific Canal Company in Nicaragua (which failed to build the canal). He lived in California where he began to discover many facts regarding the possessions of the Roman Catholic missions during the Spanish occupancy. In fact the "Pious Fund", which he founded, recovered some of the money confiscated from the Church.

Richard Doyle, by Henry Edward Doyle (1827–92)

Duffy
ó ðußhthaigh

The Irish form of O Duffy—Ó Dubthaigh—is descriptive. It means black, but refers more probably to black hair rather than to skin or personality. With or without the O prefix the name is very numerous, especially around the original O Duffy homeland of County Monaghan. In the province of Ulster, where both English and Irish are pronounced differently to the south, it can be traced to Doohey or Dowey, whereas, in Munster, Duhig could be another form of O Duffy. Many O Duffys are recorded in the Church, especially in the eighth century, Ireland's golden age, when her scholars and monks had close ties with Europe. Some of the "Treasures of Early Irish Art" which have been on exhibition in the USA and parts of Europe in recent years were made around 1123 by an O Duffy craftsman to the order of the High King Turlough O Connor. The artistic skills of the O Duffys enriched many of the churches and monastic settlements, a vital Irish cultural heritage often plundered by the Norsemen.

Doohey

Dowey

Duhig

O Duffy

The clan must have been evenly distributed throughout the small island, for in the seventh century the patron saint of Raphoe, County Donegal, was Dubhtach, or Duffy.

At one period the number of O Duffy parish priests recorded in the diocese of Monaghan was remarkable. In 1175, King Roderick O Conor sent an **O Duffy**, Archbishop of Tuam, as his ambassador to Henry II of England.

Owen O Duffy lived in the sixteenth century and was an outstanding preacher. He boldly denounced the notorious Miler Magrath, the opportunist Bishop of Cashel who changed his religious allegiance as often as it was profitable, and also changed his wives.

Near Strokestown, County Roscommon, there were so many O Duffys that they gave their name to the town of Lissyduffy. In Leinster, they are thought to be connected with the two great families of Wicklow, the O Tooles and the O Byrnes.

In the eighteenth and nineteenth centuries, with their fellow countrymen, they served in the armies of Europe. Many Duffys also emigrated to Australia and America. **Father Francis P. Duffy**, Catholic chaplain to the 165th Infantry, wrote an account of the Irish-Americans in the First World War, *Father Duffy's Story: A Tale of Humour and Heroism, of Life and Death with the Fighting Sixty-Ninth*. It was published by George H. Doran & Co. in New York in 1919, and includes many Irish names.

James Duffy (1809–71), with little more than a hedge school education, made his way to the capital, Dublin, where, beginning as a bookseller, he saw a gap in the Irish publishing market and began a *Popular Sixpenny Library*, a series of books which both entertained and enlightened, particularly as regards the nationalist cause. This led to the publishing of more academic books. At his death in 1871, James Duffy & Company was employing 120 people, and it continues as one of Dublin's reputable publishing and printing companies.

Another **James Duffy**, following a family tradition of craftsmanship, was a Dublin silversmith and jeweller. **Patrick Duffy** (1832–1909), his son, a landscape painter, was a member of the Royal Hibernian Academy and exhibited in the Royal Academy in London.

Edward Duffy (1840–68), born in Ballaghadereen, County Roscommon, was a leading member of the military body known as the

Sir Charles Gavan Duffy

Fenians, later the Irish Republican Brotherhood. An active revolutionary, he was arrested several times. A sentence of fifteen years' imprisonment was too much for his poor health, and he died aged 28.

A Duffy family from County Monaghan made a long and outstanding contribution to politics, the law and education.

Sir Charles Gavan Duffy (1816–1903) adopted his widowed mother's name, Gavan, a gracious acknowledgement of her efforts to encourage him in his self-education, which he mostly achieved by omnivorous reading. He worked as a journalist in both Dublin and Belfast, and studied for a legal degree. With other patriots of his time he founded, edited and wrote for the weekly *Nation*, which became enormously popular. The authorities in Dublin Castle disliked its fiery, nationalistic ballads and it was suppressed. Meanwhile, Gavan Duffy had joined the Young Irelanders who had broken with Daniel O Connell's milder party. Their attempted uprising was ill-timed and poorly planned. Gavan Duffy was among those tried for sedition.

Surviving that experience he was elected Member of Parliament for New Ross, and fought in Parliament for land reform. He was disgusted when this failed. In poor health, seeing no outlet for his talents in Ireland, he emigrated to Australia in 1855. There he successfully combined both law and politics and, in 1871, was elected Premier of Victoria.

He retired in 1880 to Nice in the south of France, where he wrote on Australian law and Irish history, and his autobiography, *My Life in Two Hemispheres*. He married three times and had seven sons and five daughters.

Some of Sir Charles Gavan Duffy's Australian descendants were distinguished in their own right. Among his sons, **Sir Frank Gavan Duffy** (1852–1936) was Chief Justice of Australia from 1931 to 1936, and **Charles Gavan Duffy** (1855–1932) was assistant secretary to the Australasian Federal Convention of 1897, Clerk of the House of Representatives from 1901 to 1916, and Clerk of the Senate from 1917 to 1920. Sir Frank's eldest son, **Sir Charles Gavan Duffy** (1882–1961), was Justice of the Supreme Court of Victoria.

Sir Charles's fifth son, **George Gavan Duffy** (1882–1951), although he had a legal education in England, came to Ireland during the struggle for freedom. He defended the controversial Sir Roger Casement (1864–1916). Elected to the first Dáil, he was a strong nationalist and, as diplomatic envoy, he represented Ireland in Paris and, later, Rome. In 1931 he was a member of the Peace Delegation to London, while de Valera stayed at home. He was the last to sign the Treaty, which he did reluctantly. His views were not in accordance with the Free State government and he resigned as Minister for Foreign Affairs and gave up his seat in the first Dáil. Returning to his legal practice he had a very successful career.

George Gavan Duffy

Not one of Charles Gavan Duffy's five daughters married. **Louise Gavan Duffy** (1884–1969), who was born in France, went to university in Dublin. She became very interested in the Irish language and in the rising nationalist movement. A founder member of Cumann na mBan, a women's political society, she was a teacher in the school founded by Patrick Pearse. During the rising of Easter 1916 she worked in the kitchen in Dublin's General Post Office, in the thick of the fighting. After independence she founded Scoil Bhríde, a leading Irish language school in Dublin.

The life of **General Eoin O Duffy** (1892–1944) was as varied as it was erratic. Born in Castleblaney, County Monaghan, he was a military leader with Michael Collins. He was imprisoned in Belfast. During 1921 to 1922, at the formation of the Irish Free State, he was General Officer Commanding its forces. He was also Chief Commissioner of the Civic

Guards. When de Valera came to office, he was removed from these appointments. He began to found various opposition parties, including the notorious Blueshirts, similar to other fascist groups of the thirties. When his political career with the Fine Gael opposition party came to a close and the Blueshirts were disbanded, he began to look towards Europe. The Spanish Civil War provided him with a new crusade, and he organized an Irish Brigade to fight with Franco's nationalists. The Irish government was neutral, and it was with difficulty that O Duffy's Brigade recruited 700 men to go to Spain. They returned after six months and there were few volunteers for the second "crusade against communism". A documentary film made by Radio Telefís Éireann about this inglorious episode in Irish–Spanish history gives a vivid picture of the difficulties faced by the miniscule Irish Brigade.

Eimar O Duffy (1893–1935), son of a Dublin dentist, was himself a member of the profession, though he did not practise. Following a period of involvement in home politics—he did not favour the 1916 rising—he retreated to England where he developed his literary gifts. He wrote novels and satire, of which *King Goshawk and the Birds* is probably best known.

To many Irish children and their parents, Duffy means but one thing—Duffy's Circus. For three generations this circus has been travelling Ireland with its clowns, bareback riders and performing animals, all organized and directed by half a dozen Duffy brothers.

General Eoin O Duffy

The Cross of Cong

Egan
mac aoòhagáin

Keegan

Mac Egan

Through the generations the ancient Gaelic surname, Mac Aodhagáin, has been pared down to Egan. Mac Aodhagáin means son of Hugh, which in Irish is Aodh, a pagan fire deity. The Mac Aodhagáins, who were first recorded in the old Hy Many district of Galway and South Roscommon, later dispersed to Ormond, to the rich lands of counties Tipperary, Kilkenny and Offaly. They were hereditary ollaves, or lawyers, who advised in the administration of the old Irish Brehon law which was afterwards forcibly replaced by the English legal system. The MacEgans had been chief Brehons to, among others, O Conor Faly, King of Connacht. When the English law deprived them of their legal profession, many of the MacEgan ollaves found a new vocation in the Church.

Owen MacEgan (1570–1603) was appointed vicar apostolic of Ross, County Cork, by Pope Clement VIII. He persuaded Philip III of Spain to contribute money and men to help in the uprising against Elizabethan forces in Ireland, and, in June 1602 he landed near Kenmare. Six months after landing, the militant bishop was killed in a skirmish. A small cross marks his tomb in the convent at Timoleague, in his diocese of Ross.

Boetius MacEgan, a Franciscan friar, was Bishop of Ross in 1647. Three years later he was taken prisoner by Cromwell's army and executed.

Boetius Egan (1734–98) was Bishop of Tuam, County Galway. Far from supporting the rising of 1798, he is remembered in the annals for his outspoken opposition.

John Egan (*c.* 1750–1810) was the son of a clergyman in Charleville, County Cork. He studied law at Trinity College, Dublin, and embarked on a career as a barrister with a seat in the Irish House of Commons. The proposed legislative union of Great Britain and Ireland troubled his patriotism. Unfortunately, like a number of others, he quarrelled with the great orator Henry Grattan, which damaged his career. He was a notorious duellist.

Little is known about the Irish birthplace of **Pierce Egan** (1772–1849), but much is known about his writings. In 1821 his *Life in London*, illustrated by Cruikshank, was a best seller and won him praise from George IV and Thackeray. This book was possibly the inspiration for the *Pickwick Papers*. He also wrote guide books, including one about Dublin. Travelling every part of England, he reported races, prize fights, matches and amusements. His songs and witticisms were quoted freely and he originated the cartoon characters "Tom and Jerry". He was survived by a large family.

One of his sons, **Pierce Egan** (1814–80), although trained in art, turned to writing gothic novels which he illustrated himself. He is credited with being one of the pioneers of popular literature.

Darius Joseph MacEgan (1856–1939) was born in London. Although not authenticated among the officially recognized Irish chieftains, he styled himself The MacEgan. He was staff artist for both *Punch* and the *Illustrated London News*. He exhibited regularly at the Hibernian Academy, Dublin, and painted many portraits of Dublin's Lord Mayors and the Irish hierarchy.

William Egan and his sons were silversmiths and goldsmiths on St Patrick's Street in the city of Cork from the eighteenth century until recent times.

Michael Egan (1761–1814), a learned Franciscan, spoke many languages, probably acquired during his studies in Europe. He spent some time in Ireland before setting sail for America. He was Philadelphia's first Roman Catholic archbishop at a period when religion there was a most controversial issue. An unfortunate and bitter dispute between clergy and flock concerning the enlargement of the cathedral caused him such intense distress that he died less than four years after his appointment.

Patrick Egan (1841–1919) was born at Ballymahon, County Longford. At a very young age he became managing director of the North Dublin City Milling Company, one of Ireland's biggest companies. His compassion for the starving, landless peasants drove him into active politics. He was one of the founders of the Amnesty Association for the release of political prisoners. He campaigned with Parnell for Home Rule and his business experience was invaluable to the Land League. To avoid imprisonment without trial, the price for subversive activities, he fled to Paris. Eventually, in 1883, he was forced to sell his milling business and to emigrate to America. There he went into grain milling in Lincoln, Nebraska, and he soon had expanded into woollen mills and real estate. When he was granted his citizenship papers in 1888, he was able to take part in American politics as a Republican (he was a friend of James G. Blaine). He was sent as Minister to Chile and must have enjoyed his instructions—"to discourage British influence".

Many Egans went to earn their living in the United States of America. Among these was **Maurice Francis Egan** (1852–1924), who was born in Philadelphia of Irish–Scottish parents. His handsome father, **Maurice**, came to Philadelphia in 1825 from good Irish stock. Maurice junior first made a name for himself in journalism in New York. He was appointed Professor of English Literature at Notre Dame University, Indiana, and later at the Catholic University, Washington. He served in the diplomatic service and was "unofficial adviser" to Presidents McKinley and (Theodore) Roosevelt. From 1907 to 1918 he was Minister to Denmark and turned down an ambassadorship in Vienna. He has been described as "Dean of the Diplomatic Corps as well as its Prince Charming".

John Egan (c. 1750–1810)

During the Gaelic suppression, when the O and Mac prefixes had to be dropped, MacEgan was corrupted in some areas to Keegan. Today it is quite a common name, especially in counties Dublin and Wicklow, and also in counties Roscommon and Leitrim. Strangely, it does not appear in the former MacEgan territories.

A notable Keegan was **John Keegan** (1809–49), who was born in County Laois. His contributions to the *Irish Penny Journal* and the *Dublin University Magazine* made him the most popular of the "peasant poets".

In recent years there has been a revival of interest in Egan family history, and the numerous Egans held their first rally in August 1982 at Redwood Castle, near Lorrha in County Tipperary. The castle, built *c.* 1210 by the Normans, was captured in 1350 by the powerful local O Kennedy chieftains. They installed the MacEgans, and **Conly MacEgan** is on record as being there in 1640. Redwood Castle has been painstakingly restored by a Connacht lawyer, **Michael J. Egan** of Castlebar, who, aided by his family, has carried out all the restoration at his own expense.

A comprehensive history of clan MacEgan was co-authored in 1981 by **Dr Joseph** and **Dr Joan Egan** of Ann Arbor, Michigan, USA.

FitzGerald

mac geaRailt

Since they landed with the Anglo-Normans at Wexford in 1169, the FitzGeralds have played a major role in Irish political life. The FitzGeralds are regarded as Normans, although some think that they may have originated as the Gherardini of Florence before migrating across Europe to Wales, and thence to Ireland. FitzGerald means "son of Gerald', and this translated into Irish is Mac Gearailt. Like their Irish compatriots, they branched out, becoming separate families with various designations and settling in different parts of Ireland.

The Earls of Kildare who were later created Dukes of Leinster are the senior branch of this very extensive pedigree of FitzGeralds.

Richard Fitzgilbert de Clare, Earl of Pembroke, known as "Strongbow", who led the Norman invasion was accompanied by **Maurice FitzGerald**, Constable of Pembroke in Wales. Maurice was the progenitor of the FitzGerald lineage in Ireland. In 1176 the manor at Maynooth, County Kildare, was granted to him by Strongbow and he fortified it for protection from the native Irish.

Three centuries later, his descendant **Garret Mór FitzGerald** (d. 1513), 8th Earl of Kildare, built a college nearby. He lived through the reign of four kings of England. Edward IV appointed him Lord Deputy, an appointment he held through many turbulent years. Garret Mór manipulated his five daughters to consolidate his territories, marrying them to Burke of Clanricarde, Sir Piers Butler, later Earl of Ormond, Lord Slane and, flouting the Statutes of Kilkenny which forbade marriage with the Irish, to the chiefs MacCarthy Reagh of Muskerry and O Carroll of Ely. His sister was married to an O Neill of Tyrone.

In an unsuccessful attempt to oust the Tudors, Garret Mór supported the knavish Lambert Simnel who was crowned Edward VI of England and Ireland in Dublin in 1487. Such was his strength and popularity, Garret Mór managed to extricate himself from this blatant treachery.

Garret Mór FitzGerald was acknowledged by both the Irish and the English as the uncrowned king of Ireland. He ruled for forty years and has been described as "a mighty man of stature, full of honour and courage, open and plain, hardly able to rule himself when he was moved to anger, easily displeased and soon appeased, of the English well beloved, a good justiciar, a suppressor of rebels and a warrior incomparable".

In 1494 he went too far and displeased Henry VII who imprisoned him in the Tower of London for two years. When he was accused by the Archbishop of Cashel of burning down his cathedral he answered, "I would not have done it if I had not been told that my Lord Archbishop was inside". This delighted the King and, when someone exclaimed "All Ireland cannot govern this Earl", Henry rejoined, "Then let this Earl govern all Ireland". Garret Mór returned to Ireland to continue as Lord Deputy. He it was who introduced artillery to Ireland and, ironically, the Great Earl died from gunshot wounds received in a minor skirmish with the O Carrolls of Offaly.

Garret Mór's handsome son, **Gerald FitzGerald** (1487–1534), known as Garret Óg (the young), had his portrait painted by Hans Holbein. He had been reared at the English Court, a hostage for his father's loyalty. He returned to Ireland but he did not have his father's character. After a chequered career, he rebelled unsuccessfully against English rule and this inevitably led to his death in the Tower of London.

Garret Óg FitzGerald

Garret Óg's daughter, the **Lady Elizabeth FitzGerald**, was "The Fair Geraldine" immortalized by Walter Scott. She was a first cousin of Henry VIII and was brought up with the Princesses Mary and Elizabeth. She had two marriages; the first, when she was 15, to a 60-year-old widower. She lies beside her second husband, the Earl of Lincoln, in St George's Chapel, Windsor Castle. Her portrait is in Dublin's National Gallery.

The Fair Geraldine's brother, **Thomas FitzGerald**, 10th Earl of Kildare (dubbed "Silken Thomas" because of his liking for rich and colourful clothing), renounced his allegiance to Henry VIII, allying himself with the Irish lords, many of them his own cousins. Inevitably he, too, was imprisoned in the Tower. At the age of 24, with his five FitzGerald uncles, he was executed at Tyburn. On the walls of his prison may still be found the letters "Thomas FitzG"—the name was never completed.

Lady Elizabeth FitzGerald—"The Fair Geraldine"

Thomas was succeeded by his brother **Gerald**, 11th Earl of Kildare, at the age of ten. Realizing the determination of the Tudors to exterminate the FitzGeralds, he was smuggled abroad and was kept in hiding for many years by his blood relations, the O Conors, O Briens and MacCarthys. A scribe has written of him: "For the people conceite more to see a Geraldyn to reigne and triumphe, than to see God come amongst them". Gerald was educated in France with the Dauphin, and in Rome. When Elizabeth I came to the throne he converted to the Protestant religion and, in 1552, had his Kildare estates restored to him. But, once again a Kildare Earl was found to be treacherous, and he became the fourth generation of the Geraldines to suffer the Tower of London, where he died in 1585.

Robert, 19th Earl of Kildare, deciding Maynooth Castle was too dilapidated, bought the estate of Carton, also in Kildare. He had a magnificent mansion designed by the fashionable Richard Castle who, between 1728 and 1750, built houses for the Irish gentry. He did not live to enjoy it, for he died suddenly in 1744, aged 68.

There is an appealing FitzGerald story concerning the ape which is used in their armorial bearings. It seems that when John Fitzthomas, afterwards 1st Earl of Kildare, was an infant in their earlier castle of Woodstock in County Kildare, it caught fire. In the rush to escape, the baby was overlooked, but a pet ape, breaking its chains, grabbed the child and carried him to safety. Jonathan Swift, who quarrelled with the Earl of Kildare, filched the Kildare ape legend, using it in *Gulliver's Travels*. Gulliver is carried off and fed by the Brobdingnagian ape!

There is also a legend about the Earl of Kildare, known as "The Wizard Earl". According to County Kildare folklore, he sleeps there in the Rath of Mullaghmast from which he emerges occasionally to ride across the Curragh on a white horse shod with silver shoes. He is also supposed occasionally to haunt Kilkea Castle, a former FitzGerald fortress, now a hotel.

James, 20th Earl of Kildare (b. 1772), was created 1st Duke of Leinster. He laid the foundation of Leinster House, in south Dublin. When told that it was an unfashionable part of the city he retorted, "They will follow me wherever I go". Today, Leinster House in Kildare Street houses the Dáil, the seat of the Irish Parliament.

James married Emily Lennox, daughter of the 2nd Duke of Richmond. She was the guiding light in the splendid embellishment of Carton House. Her beauty was immortalized by Reynolds, the fashionable portrait painter. Her sister, Lady Louisa, married Speaker Thomas Connolly.

James and Emily had 22 children. Their twelfth child was **Lord Edward FitzGerald** (1764–98). "Eddie", wrote his doting mother, "carries a sword, the prettiest thing you ever saw, and is reading Marlboro's campaigns".

Eddie, who was educated in France, fought for the English in the American War of Independence. He remarked in later years he had fought on the wrong side!

He married Pamela, the adopted daughter of Madame de Genlis, and he brought his bride home to Frascati at Blackrock, Dublin. This once charming seaside retreat, now erased by supermarkets, was bought by his mother from Hely Hutchinson, Provost of Trinity College, Dublin.

Lord Edward had great personal magnetism. During one sojourn in Canada he was made honorary chief of the Bear Tribe. Back home he was welcomed as Member of Parliament for Athy, but, seeing little hope of constitutional change, he joined the United Irishmen, assuming their military leadership. A marked man, he was betrayed and died of his wounds.

Between 1326 and 1766 there were twenty Earls of Kildare, and their successors, the Dukes of Leinster, have contributed much to the nation's heritage. In 1795, the government founded St Patrick's College, Maynooth (built by Garret Mór) on the site of a former FitzGerald residence. By this magnanimous gesture it was hoped to win the loyalty of the Roman Catholic clergy, who, because of the French Revolution, could no longer be educated in France. In recent times Maynooth has become a constituent college of the National University and is open to students of both sexes.

The Earls of Desmond were head of the FitzGeralds in Munster. Between 1329 and early 1600, there were sixteen Earls of Desmond. In *The Twilight Lords*, Richard Berleth writes of their epic struggle against the Elizabethans. **James**, the Sugán (Straw) Earl was the last real leader of the Desmonds. With Irish, Spaniards and Italians, he was defeated at Smerwick by an English army which included Sir Walter Raleigh. Afterwards he was driven into ignominious rebellion and his territories were laid waste.

Catherine was a Munster FitzGerald who married a Kildare. She was the second wife of the 12th Earl of Kildare. Legends proliferate around her. In old age she was very poor and had a long walk to buy food. It is said that when she was 90 she trudged to market carrying her 60-year-old daughter on her back. In 1589 she met Sir Walter Raleigh. It is almost certain that she died in 1604, aged 100, not 140, and possibly not from falling out of a cherry tree according to local tradition! In Muckross House, Killarney, there is a copy of a portrait of this indomitable FitzGerald.

George Robert FitzGerald (1748–86) was of the Desmond blood, but was no credit to his family. His father was **Robert FitzGerald** of Turlough near Castlebar, County Mayo. His mother was Lady Mary Hervey, sister of the Earl of Bristol, and he was raised in English society. He did the Grand Tour, but did not benefit from it. His cheating at games, his duelling and quarrelling, lost him his wife, a sister of Thomas Conolly. He tortured his family, tying his father to a pet bear and locking him up for days. He kept a private army, the terror of County Mayo. Eventually he was arrested and condemned to death for killing a man. It is said that the rope snapped, giving him time on the gallows to repent.

In medieval times, **John FitzGerald**, Earl of Desmond, by virtue of his unquestioned powers as a Count Palatine, created his three sons hereditary knights: The Knight of Glin, the Knight of Kerry and the White Knight (the latter title is now extinct). According to the present Knight of Glin, these titles are likely to have arisen by usage and are more akin to a Gaelic chieftainship, an example of the Gaelicization of the Normans.

Desmond John Villiers FitzGerald is 29th Knight of Glin. His scholarship and sound business sense make a unique contribution to the

Lord Edward FitzGerald

historical knowledge and culture of his country. He has beautifully restored his castle at Glin on the Shannon estuary and it is open to the public in the summer. Walking through its richly furnished rooms studying portraits and relics of bygone FitzGeralds is a visual essay in Irish history.

The FitzGeralds have had continuous representation in Europe. In the eighteenth century they were prominent in the Irish Brigade. The Regiment of FitzGerald fought valiantly in the War of the Spanish Succession. When war became less of a preoccupation, the FitzGeralds distinguished themselves as scientists, surgeons, lawyers, politicians, writers and colonial statesmen. They were almost as numerous in the New World as in Ireland. **Francis Scott Fitzgerald** (1896–1940), author of *The Great Gatsby*, *This Side of Paradise*, and many other works, was an American of Irish descent.

Percy Hetherington FitzGerald (1834–1925) of County Louth studied law at Trinity College, Dublin. He was a writer and a sculptor whose works include the statues of Dr Johnson in the Strand in London, Dickens at Bath and Boswell at Lichfield.

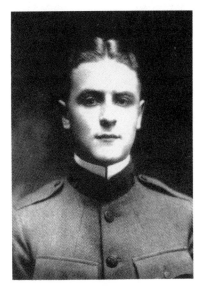

F. Scott Fitzgerald

A FitzGerald played his part in the achievement of Irish Independence. **Desmond FitzGerald**, whose parents were from Kerry, was born and educated in London and came to Kerry to study Irish. For thirty years before and after the Treaty (which he supported) he took a leading part in Irish politics. He was elected to three different parliaments: the first Dáil (an illegal body), the first Dáil under the Treaty, and the British House of Commons. Under the policy of abstention then in force, he did not take his seat at Westminster. Disturbed at the misrepresentation of Dáil Éireann by the British press, he instituted a Department of Publicity. He was a writer, poet and Abbey Theatre dramatist.

Whilst Minister for External Affairs, Desmond FitzGerald was head of a department set up to make a case for the removal of the border. During his tenure, the Irish Free State, as it was then, secured recognition by the League of Nations. He died in 1947, aged 58.

Garret FitzGerald, one of the four sons of Desmond FitzGerald, was born in Dublin in 1926, graduated from University College, Dublin, and was called to the Irish Bar. He wrote and lectured on political economy. A member of the Fine Gael party, he was Minister for Foreign Affairs, and he has been Taoiseach (Prime Minister) of a coalition government three times, including during the visit of President Reagan in 1984.

Cecil Woodham-Smith, the distinguished historical biographer, born a FitzGerald in England, felt passionately about Ireland and wrote a very successful book, *The Great Hunger*, a carefully researched account of the Famine of the mid 1800s.

In Tasmania, Melbourne and New South Wales, in engineering, medicine and the dynamic trio, brewing, religion and politics, the FitzGeralds frequently feature in Australian biographies.

Fitzpatrick

mac giolla phádraig

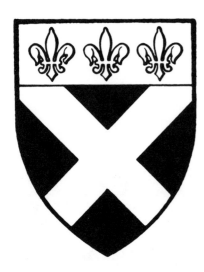

Kilpatrick

MacGillapatrick

Jerpoint Abbey, County Kilkenny

Fitz, the Norman-French prefix meaning "son of", is very common in Ireland—FitzGerald, Fitzgibbon, Fitzmaurice, etc. Fitzpatrick is the only Fitz name of pure Irish origin. In Irish it is Mac Giolla Phádraig (devotee of St Patrick). Fitzpatrick is a variation of this very old family name, a family whose members were Lords of Upper Ossory where they ruled like royalty in the counties of Leix (Laois) and Kilkenny.

They have pedigrees showing descent from King Heremon, who came from Spain in the fifth century—indeed some claim forebears as far back as *c.* 1383 BC!

The Cistercian Abbey of Jerpoint, County Kilkenny, one of the finest romantic ruins, was founded in 1158 by **Donagh MacGillapatrick**, known as the King of Ossory. In 1387, its abbot was fined for violating the Statutes of Kilkenny which forbade the admission of Irishmen as members of the community. Later the abbey was suppressed and its lands, as well as Gowran, once the seat of the Fitzpatrick Lords of Ossory, were taken by their enemies, the Butlers of Ormond.

Sir Barnaby Fitzpatrick (*c.* 1535–81), Lord of Upper Ossory, spent his childhood in England as a hostage for his father's loyalty. He must have been well thought of for he was a companion of the future King Edward VI and was educated in France where he was accepted in court circles. Alas, trouble began when he returned to Ireland. His loyalty was questioned by the Butlers, who abducted his wife and daughter. But Sir Barnaby Fitzpatrick, whose sept was one of the first to submit to Henry VIII, was knighted by him in 1558.

When the Cromwellians were ravaging the monasteries, the Vicar Apostolic of Ossory, **Brian Fitzpatrick** (1588–1652), who was also a poet, had the great *Book of the O Byrnes* transcribed, thus saving this valuable record from destruction, though not himself for he was murdered by the soldiers.

Although never outstanding, the Fitzpatricks are well-documented in the libraries of Ireland, France and the Vatican. Loyalty to the Stuarts caused the Fitzpatricks still further loss of power and territory, and many joined in the "Flight of the Wild Geese" to serve with distinction in the armies of France.

Some of them remained in Ireland, where **John Fitzpatrick** is recorded as of Castletown in the Queen's County (Laois). His son, **Richard** (d. 1727), commanded the *Richmond* in the Royal Navy in 1687 and was distinguished for action against the French in 1696 by a generous grant of land in Offaly. He was a Member of Parliament in the Irish House of Commons and was raised to the peerage as 1st Baron Gowran. His eldest son, **John Fitzpatrick**, succeeded to the Irish earldom of Upper Ossory in 1751.

John was father to **Richard Fitzpatrick** (1747–1813) who went to Westminster School and was a Member of Parliament. He has been described as "one of the best-known names in the history of the social life of the last half of the eighteenth century with the proud title of being the most intimate friend of Charles James Fox". Apart from leading a high life in London, he also managed to be in America with the army in 1777 at the battle of Brandywine, when he was promoted to general.

Until the late nineteenth century, the descendants of this family still possessed a good 22,000 acres of their Ossory lands.

The last Earl of Ossory's heir—a natural son—was **Bernard Fitzpatrick**, 2nd and last Lord Castletown of Granston Manor, Abbeyleix, County Laois. Lord Castletown, who died in 1937, combined Irish nationalism with an Irish belief in fairies. He extended Granston Manor, which passed to a nephew who assumed the Fitzpatrick name, but the ancestral home went out of the family and was burnt almost totally in 1977.

The Fitzpatricks were very versatile and great travellers. **Sir Jeremiah Fitzpatrick** of County Westmeath (born *c.* 1740) has received less credit than he deserves. Where he did his medical studies is not known. In England he was appointed Inspector of Health to the British army. Conditions for the men and their families were atrocious and Dr Fitzpatrick was well ahead of his time in his tireless efforts to improve them. In his earlier medical days in Ireland, he was sufficiently enlightened to recommend a diet for prisoners which included cereals and vegetables. He worried about the fate of the widows of Irish soldiers who were reduced to begging (and worse) in the West Indies. Although his work for prison reform equalled that of many well-known names, Fitzpatrick was a modest man who preferred to work in relative obscurity.

Thomas Fitzpatrick (*c.* 1799–1854) left County Cavan for America where, in 1824, he led the fur traders of Wyoming to new grounds and was credited with discovering the South Pass. To the Indians he was "Broken Hand" and "the greatest of the mountain men". In 1842, the first immigrant train to use the Oregon trail was piloted by Thomas Fitzpatrick.

Benjamin Fitzpatrick (1802–69) was born of immigrant parents in Greene County, Georgia. A planter and lawyer, he was Democratic Governor of Alabama. He reformed the state banking system in 1860. When he was US Senator for Alabama, he declined nomination for the Vice-Presidency.

John Bernard Fitzpatrick (1812–66) was the Roman Catholic Bishop of Boston who received the first wave of Irish immigrants escaping from the Famine.

William John Fitzpatrick (1830–95), a wealthy Dubliner, specialized in biography. He tried to prove that the Waverley novels were not written by Sir Walter but by his brother, Thomas Scott. He published biographies of famous romantic Irish characters of the eighteenth and nineteenth centuries.

Fitzpatricks left Ireland to play a variety of roles according to the country they found themselves in—and not always voluntarily! In Australia, the children of convicts turned to writing history, to politics or the reorganization of land administration. Of course, they were also prominent in the Church.

In South Africa, **Sir Percy Fitzpatrick** was in the legislative chamber with the Progressive Party which in 1905, tried to democratize the Boers in the Rand in Pretoria.

In the nineteenth century, there was a wave of emigration to South America, mainly to Argentina, where the Fitzpatrick name is now numerous. Many came from the County Meath area. They married compatriots and had large families.

In the twentieth century there are Fitzpatricks in exotic locations, such as Bridgetown, Barbados. A number of Fitzpatricks who have long since settled in the United Kingdom can be found in the highest ranks of the services.

There are many variations of this numerous name. Kilpatrick is more usually found in Ulster and may have come via Scotland.

Lady Geraldine Fitzpatrick, daughter of John William Fitzpatrick (d. 1809), Baron of Castletown and Upper Ossary

Healy

Ó hÉilidhe

Hely

Ó hEalaighthe

O Healihy

O Healy

Healy is a very widespread Gaelic name. There are at least 14,000 persons bearing some form of the Healy–Hely name and the O prefix is seldom used. They were chieftains who formed two distinct septs. The first of these derived its name, Ó hEilidhe from *eilidhe*, meaning claimant; their territory was around Lough Arrow in Sligo. Their seat was Ballyhely, one of several Ballyhelys. A fourteenth-century **Dermot O Healy** is described by the Four Masters (*see* Cleary) as "a princely farmer, the best of his time".

The other sept, Ó hEalaighthe (*ealadhach* means ingenious), were of Donoughmore in the barony of Muskerry, County Cork. They allied themselves with the MacCarthys, who were overlords of the whole district. By the end of the seventeenth century, the Cromwellians had dispossessed them of all their lands. In archives of that time they were recorded as O Healihy. MacLysaght mentions another variation, "the influential family of Hely d'Oissel of Normandy, ranked among the nobility of France, is descended from Peter O Hely, a Jacobite exile".

They were well-represented in the priesthood. **Patrick Healy** (d. 1579), a Franciscan, was educated in France and Spain. He was the last Bishop of Mayo before it was joined to the see of Tuam in Galway. A victim of the penal legislation of the time, he was executed at Kilmallock, County Limerick. Three centuries later, another Healy filled the archbishopric of Tuam: this was **John Healy** (1841–1918). A scholarly priest, he was a senator of the Royal and National Universities.

John Hely-Hutchinson (1724–94), a celebrated Provost of Trinity College, Dublin, was the son of **Francis Hely** of Gortmore, County Cork. In 1783, he married an heiress and assumed her family name, Hutchinson. In the same year she was raised to the peerage as Baroness Donoughmore of Knocklofty, County Tipperary. (Donoughmore, County Cork, was their original home). In his younger days John Hely was described as "an obstreperous patriot", while in later years he was "a man of unblushing venality". A graduate in law, he was not qualified for the exalted position of provost, but he intrigued his way into being elected. He proved a very efficient provost, although he outraged university sentiment, had constant disputes with the fellows and the students, and misused his powers for the advancement of his family. Trinity owes its Modern Language professorships to John Hely-Hutchinson. He supported Free Trade and Catholic reforms, unusual for a man of his position at that time.

He had six sons who distinguished themselves, mostly in England. One son, **Richard Hely-Hutchinson** (1756–1825), 1st Earl of Donoughmore, also championed Catholic reform in the House of Lords. He strenuously opposed every attempt to rule Ireland by purely coercive measures. **John Hely-Hutchinson** (1757–1832) was the 2nd Earl of Donoughmore and a soldier. In 1798, when the French, commanded by Humbert, landed in Killala Bay in County Mayo with 15,000 men, John Hely-Hutchinson was in command of the English at Castlebar. Alarmed by the size of Humbert's forces and their Irish pikemen, the militia under Generals Lake and Cornwallis fled. Despite this embarrassing débâcle, dubbed by the natives "the Races of Castlebar", Hely-Hutchinson retained his command. George IV sent him to Saint-Omer to offer an allowance of £50,000 a year to his crazy wife, Queen Caroline. The conditions were that she relinquish all British royal titles and never visit England again. She refused.

John Hely-Hutchinson (1757–1832)

The Hely-Hutchinsons built a splendid mansion, Knocklofty, overlooking the River Suir near Clonmel, County Tipperary. In June 1974, the present Earl and Countess of Donoughmore were abducted from their home by the IRA. They were found, unharmed, shortly afterwards. Knocklofty has since been sold and is now a hotel.

The artistic Healys were generations apart. Sadly, **Robert Healy** (1743–71) had a short life. His delightful pastels of Squire Tom Connolly's family and horses at Castletown, County Kildare, are his lasting memorial and have become very highly valued.

G.P.A. Healy (1813–94), although born in Boston, was the son of a sea captain of Irish origin. He was a successful portrait painter who studied in Paris, where he painted Louis Philippe and leading statesmen. On returning to America, he was commissioned to paint three of a series of United States Presidents: John Tyler, James Knox Polk and Zachary Taylor.

Father James Healy (1824–94) was one of 23 children born in Dublin. Long the parish priest of Little Bray, he was a most convivial man, a renowned wit whose company was sought at the dining tables of the gentry in his Wicklow neighbourhood.

Michael Healy (1873–1941), a Dubliner, was a stained glass artist. Richard Hayward, the Irish travel writer, described his work in the modern Dominican Holy Cross church in Tralee, Kerry, as "Exquisite… carried out in the most masterly style", and his genius as "traditional and reflective in spirit". He executed commissions for clients in America and New Zealand.

In the nineteenth century, from a combination of Healys and Sullivans of Bantry, came a remarkable family. **Timothy Healy** (1855–1931) was the son of **Maurice Healy**, a clerk. His mother's father, a Sullivan, was a schoolteacher. Her three brothers became Members of Parliament, as did her three sons, of which Tim Healy was the most outstanding. They were the foundation of a political grouping known as "the Bantry Band". While still in his teens, Tim Healy emigrated to London where, for a while, he worked as a railway clerk. T.D. Sullivan, his uncle, owned the *Nation* newspaper and he offered young Tim the post of parliamentary correspondent in London. Soon Tim knew all the Irish MPs at Westminster. He was invited to accompany Parnell as his secretary when he toured America and Canada. An audacious politician, he developed into a fearless and gripping speaker with a prodigious memory. He took an active part in the burning question of the day—the Land Movement. In 1884 he was called to the Irish Bar. When his party split over Parnell's involvement in the O Shea divorce, he turned against the leader and was expelled from the party. He received support from the Church, and also a cousin from Bantry, the powerful industrialist and newspaper proprietor, William Martin Murphy, and soon he was back in politics. He became a member of the English Bar and took on many cases of a political nature, including the defence of a number of the suffragettes. His wit and eloquence drew crowded houses. He supported Britain in the First World War, but the events following the rising of 1916 enticed him home. He had many opponents because he was against violence, but, following the Treaty—despite opposition—he became first Governor-General of the Irish Free State, a post he filled most happily from 1922 until 1927.

His brother, **Maurice Healy** (1887–1943), served in the First World War with the Royal Dublin Fusiliers. An eminent barrister in England and Ireland, he was a *bon viveur* and wit, and author of popular books about wine and the law, including *The Old Munster Circuit* and *Stay Me With Flagons*.

Timothy Healy

Joseph Healy (1889–1934), son of Tim Healy, also a barrister, served in the First World War and was with the British Naval Division at Gallipoli. A dedicated pioneer of motor cycling, on one occasion he rode the 320-mile round trip from Cork to Dublin every day for a week, and another time did the same between Dublin and Belfast, a 208-mile round trip! Until comparatively recently, family intermarriage seems to have been the custom. Tim Healy, for instance, married his double first cousin, while his daughter married her Sullivan uncle.

John Edward Healy (1872–1934) was born in Drogheda, County Louth, and won many prizes for literature at Trinity College, Dublin. A barrister and journalist, he edited the *Irish Times* for 27 years, from 1907.

Cahir Healy (1877–1970), born in Donegal, moved to Enniskillen, County Fermanagh, when very young. Like so many other leaders of that time, a rudimentary education was no obstacle to his progress towards taking his place as poet, journalist and littérateur. He was with Arthur Griffith in 1905 when he launched the Sinn Féin party, which favoured a dual monarchy. Although he tried to prevent partition, he sat at Westminster after the Treaty. Following the separation of the six counties, he was Nationalist member for South Fermanagh in the Stormont parliament. He has been described as one of the sanest and most far-seeing leaders of Northern nationalism. Working with the North Eastern Boundary Bureau, he tried to get a plebiscite for Tyrone and Fermanagh. His idea was that the border nationalists could choose whether to join the then Irish Free State, or remain with Britain. He sat in Westminster in the 1930s and again in the 1950s, but his political activities landed him in Brixton prison for nearly two years. His last years as a Nationalist Member of Parliament were darkened by the reappearance of the IRA and its concept of physical force, of which he disapproved.

Gerard Healy (1918–63) was born in Dublin, where he made a name as an actor at the Gate and Abbey Theatres, and on television. He wrote two plays, *Thy Dear Father* (1943) and *The Black Stranger* (1945), both of which drew big houses to Dublin's Abbey Theatre. He died while playing James Joyce, the leading role in Hugh Leonard's *Stephen D*, in London.

In the political upheavals in Ireland during the nineteenth century, many patriots were banished with the convicts to Australia. There were also emigrants from Ireland who played no small part in ameliorating the sorry state of their fellow countrymen who had made the long voyage in the convict ships. One of these was **Frederick Healy** (1794–1856) from County Tyrone, who became a successful farmer. In 1823 he was Principal Superintendent of Convicts in New South Wales, where he is recorded as being an efficient and sympathetic officer.

Hennessy

ó haonghusa

Henchy

Hensey

Seldom, if ever, is O now used to prefix Hennessy. In Irish it is Ó hAonghusa, which means descended from Aonghus or Angus (*aongus* means one choice). There were at least four Hennessy septs spread out over Leinster and Munster. In counties Clare, Cork and Kerry, there are a number of towns named Ballyhennessy.

The principal Hennessy family had its stronghold in north Offaly, near the hill of Croghan at Kilbeggan. The family shared its lordship with the O Holohans. Another branch of the Hennessys lived west of Dublin, where the Liffey flows between the counties of Meath and Dublin. The Norman invasion dispersed the Hennessys, who went south to counties Cork, Limerick and Tipperary where, today, most of the Hennessys are still entrenched. Hensey or Henchy are variants of the name.

It is in comparatively recent times that the Hennessys who remained in Ireland have come to the fore. They were, of course, very prominent abroad, especially in the service of France. **Maurice N. Hennessy** has written their history in *The Wild Geese: The Irish Soldiers in Exile*, published in 1975.

At Kilavullen, seven miles from Mallow, County Cork, Ballymacmoy House is on a cliff overhanging the Blackwater. This, from very early times until a few years ago, was the Hennessy family base. The Hennessy connection with brandy came about in 1740, when **Richard Hennessy** (1720–1800), third son of **Charles Hennessy** of Ballymacmoy, settled in France. He was an officer in Dillon's Regiment in the service of Louis XV. He fought at the battle of Fontenoy in 1745, and, as a wounded veteran, he decided to live in Cognac, because it was near to where his old comrades of the Irish Brigade were stationed. It was a lucky choice. Hearing that the local brandy had restorative powers, he tried it and sent some casks home to his Irish friends. Their response was hugely enthusiastic, which gave him the idea of going into the wine business. In 1765, he founded a company which was later re-formed by his son, James.

Although **James Hennessy** never became naturalized, he was accepted as a member of the French Chamber of Deputies and was a peer of France. He married into the brandy family of Martell.

Two Irish characteristics that the Hennessys brought with them to France were the appreciation of fine wines and good horses. They visited England frequently, and were among the first to sponsor a steeplechase there. The Hennessy Gold Cup still features in the racing calendar. Gainsborough, a horse from their stable, won the Triple Crown. In 1909 Hennessy's Lutteur II became the first French-owned horse to win the Grand National.

The Hennessy line of the French company remains unbroken, and, in the list of directors, the names Maurice, Patrick and Kilian testify to their adherence to ancestral roots. **Maurice** is head of the company, and his cousin, the Marquis de Geoffre de Chabrignac, is director. He has visited Ireland regularly with his son, Count Louis de Geoffre, the expected Hennessy heir.

A collateral branch of the Hennessys, based in England, retains strong links, by marriage, commerce or politics, with both France and Ireland. **George Richard James Hennessy**, 1st Baron Windlesham, was created a baronet in 1927 and a peer in 1937. He earned many distinctions in the First World War. He was also Minister for Labour and Vice-Chamberlain of the Household.

The 3rd Lord Windlesham, **David J. C. Hennessy** (b. 1932), was Minister for State in the Home Office and has held a number of appointments with English regional television companies.

Through the generations, Hennessys have filled many exalted ecclesiastical appointments. In the fifteenth century, **Nicholas Hennessy** was Bishop of Waterford and Lismore. In the nineteenth century, **John Hennessy** of Bulgaden, County Limerick, the eldest of eight children, went to America, where he was ordained at Carendalet, St Louis, Missouri. In 1866, as Bishop of Dubuque, he was appointed first archbishop of that state. He was a dedicated educationalist and died in his parish in 1900.

Sir John Pope-Hennessy (1834–91) was born in Cork, where he studied law. In 1859, he was Member of Parliament for Westmeath, the first Catholic Conservative member to hold an Irish seat. In 1867, he began his long series of colonial governorships: Labuan, the Gold Coast (where he took over Fort Elmina from the Dutch), the Windward Islands, Barbados, Hong Kong, Mauritius and the Bahamas. Although he was knighted in 1880, he was far from popular with his colleagues, because of his impulsive initiation of reforms. He sowed the seeds of colonial independence wherever he served. The worst his colleagues in the colonial service could say of him was: "His failure as a governor was due to want of tact and judgement, and his facility for initiating where he might conciliate".

In 1890, on retiring from the British colonial service, he bought Rostellan in Youghal, County Cork, a former property of Sir Walter Raleigh. He contested North Kilkenny as an anti-Parnellite Home Ruler. Despite Parnell's counter efforts, he held the seat. Ironically, the effort was too great for both men: they died in 1891 within a few hours of one another.

Sir John Pope-Hennessy (1913–94) was a descendant of this Youghal family. He held many posts in the international art world, including Consultant Chairman of European Paintings in the Metropolitan Museum, New York, and was Professor of Fine Art at New York University. Early in his career he was on the staff of the Victoria and Albert Museum in London. Specializing in Italian art, he won many awards for his books and articles.

His brother, **James Pope-Hennessy** (1916–74), served with the British Army Staff in Washington DC from 1944 to 1945. He was literary editor of the *Spectator* magazine, and published many successful books on politics and travel, as well as novels and biographies.

Henry Hennessy (1826–1901), a Cork-born scientist, was Professor of Engineering in the new Catholic University of Dublin. He was an outstanding mathematician and contributed many papers to learned societies. He was Professor of Applied Mathematics at the Royal College of Science, and vice-president of the Royal Irish Academy.

William Maunsell Hennessy (1829–89) was from Castlegregory, County Kerry. An Irish scholar and patriot, he was on the staff of the *Nation*, the newspaper founded by the Young Irelanders. He worked in the Public Records Office and edited many learned papers on Irish history, including *The Annals of Lough Cé*, a chronicle of events in Ireland from 1014 to 1590, which he translated in 1871. It was published in London in two volumes.

The parents of **William John Hennessy** (1839–1917) fled from their native Kilkenny to Canada, following the abortive rising of the Young Irelanders. They moved to New York, where William studied art, and his paintings were soon selling well. However, it was as an illustrator that he made his international reputation, illustrating books of poetry by Tennyson,

Longfellow, Whitton, Stedman and Browning. In 1863, he was elected an Academician, and, in England, he exhibited regularly at the Royal Academy.

William Hennessy went to America from Mitchelstown, County Cork, in 1842. In his *Dreamers of Dreams: Portraits of the Irish in America*, Donal O Donovan says that William was a drummer at the battle of Bull Run, Virginia, in 1861. His family, which settled in Boston, had to contend with the domination of the entrenched WASP community. Eventually, aided by the powerful weapon of education, the Hennessys breeched the ethnic barrier. His great-great-grandson **Edward L. Hennessy** became Chairman of the Board and Chief Executive of the automotive and aerospace business, Bendix Corporation, when it merged with Allied Corporation in 1983. He is an active member of many institutions for the promotion of education across the United States and visits Ireland regularly, where he has located his family roots.

Higgins
Ó hUigin

O Higgins

This name is a phonetic representation of the Irish Ó hUigin. *Uigin* means knowledge, skill or ingenuity, a more than apt description for this family which has produced an astonishing number of literary people. The O Higgins are a branch of the O Neills of County Westmeath. Today there are possibly 9,000 Higgins and fewer O Higgins, mostly in the west of Ireland. Higgins is a not uncommon name in Britain, the Commonwealth and the Americas. Some of the Higgins who have lived for generations in Ireland may well be descended from English settlers.

From the thirteenth to the seventeenth century, the family must surely have had a monopoly on the arts, especially poetry. **Tadhg Mór** (meaning big) **Ó hUigin** (d. 1315) was employed by the King of Connacht's brother, Manus O Conor, as his tutor and poet. His son, **Tadhg Óg** (young), addressed his poetry to the leading families of Connacht: O Connor Sligo, O Neill, MacWilliam Burke and O Kelly. He died in Galway 1448.

Tadhg Dall (blind) was the most famous of all the hereditary poets. His stylish poetry reflects Gaelic life in the fifteenth century. A quiet man, he urged fusion rather than faction between the clans. His prosperous homestead in Sligo was envied by the local O Haras, who plundered it; Tadhg's response was to write a satire about them. They retaliated by murdering Tadhg and his family in 1617.

Maolmuire, Tadhg's brother, studied abroad and joined the Franciscan Order. He lived for a while in Rome, where he wrote much of his poetry. The Pope appointed him Archbishop of Tuam, but he died in Antwerp *en route* home. Even if he had survived the trip home, his life expectation could well have been limited, as the fanatical Cromwellians had already martyred four of his Ó hUigin kinsmen.

In the seventeenth century, **Philip Bocht** (poor) had the distinction of being the first poet to be printed in the Irish language. The old Gaelic culture, which included the professors of poetry in its bardic schools, was eliminated by the end of that century. The O Higgin name did not feature again in literature for many generations.

Of the eminent Higgins who chose careers in medicine and the sciences, **John Higgins** (1670–1729) of Limerick was the most outstanding. After the defeat of the Jacobites, and the infamous Treaty of Limerick, he fled to France where he studied medicine at Montpelier. The Duke of Berwick, another defeated Jacobite and head of the French and Spanish forces, invited him to Spain to be chief medical officer in his army. There he saw active service with a number of regiments, including the Irish Brigade. Shortly after Philip V of Spain had appointed him his chief physician, the king had a serious illness of which he was cured by Dr John Higgins. He was rewarded by being made a Royal Councillor and was elected president of the Royal Academy of Medicine. He also successfully attended the French Ambassador in Madrid when he caught smallpox. John Higgins ended his days in Madrid, where he had gained the reputation of being "one of the best and most skilful physicians in Europe who is also capital company".

Few families are without their black sheep and **Revd Francis Higgins** (1669–1728), son of a Limerick apothecary, was one of these. A divinity graduate of Trinity College, Dublin, he proceeded to London where he preached sedition from the pulpit. His violent temper and low, unclerical tastes led to his eventual arrest. Newspapers described him as "a venal journalist, a corrupt magistrate and a proprietor of houses of ill repute".

Francis Higgins (1726–1802), another renegade, was born in poverty in County Down. He was reared in Dublin where he quickly saw the advantages which would open up to him by embracing Protestantism and the law. Marriage to a wealthy lady, who foolishly believed him to be of the landed gentry, did no harm to his prospects either. This deception led him to become known as "The Sham Squire". He amassed his wealth by manipulating gambling dens, under the cloak of respectability offered by his career as an attorney. He also joined the Dublin Castle establishment when he bought the *Freeman's Journal* newspaper and used it to attack Irish patriots, particularly the United Irishmen. It is also possible that he was implicated in the betrayal which led to the discovery and death of Lord Edward FitzGerald, for which his reward was £1,000.

Francis Higgins (from a caricature of the day)

Don Ambrosiano, Marquis de Osorno and Viceroy of Peru, was born **Ambrose O Higgins** (*c.* 1720–1801) in County Meath. He was dispatched to Spain to the care of his Jesuit uncle at Cadiz to follow in his footsteps, but he lacked a religious vocation. He sailed to South America where he earned his living for a while as a hawker outside the cathedral at Lima, Peru. It was when he joined the army that he found his true vocation and soon attained the rank of brigadier-general. At the age of 58, he fell in love with a very young Chilean girl, but for some reason, although a marriage was arranged, it never took place. They had a child, Bernardo, who was to become the first President of Chile.

Bernardo O Higgins (1778–1842) was born in Chile and sent by his father to be educated in England. As the son of the Viceroy of Peru he met George III and Prime Minister Pitt and also a group of young revolutionaries who were intent on freeing Chile from Spain. His father disowned him when he heard of these activities. After his father's death in 1801, he became active as a revolutionary in Chile. In 1814 he was defeated by the Spanish and fled to Argentina. He returned to Chile several years later to lead a successful rising which ensured independence for Chile in 1818. Bernardo O Higgins was elected as the country's first President and ruled as a virtual dictator. He introduced many reforms, even attempting to restrict gambling and bullfighting. Like those other former Irishmen, Commodore Barry of the USA, and Admiral Browne of Argentina, he, too, understood the might of the sea and founded the Chilean navy, whose first flagship was the *O Higgins*. An inland province of Chile with an area of 2,746 square miles was also named O Higgins. He divided up the large estates, granted freedom to the Indians and made concessions to the Protestants. His reforms were too radical for the right wing, represented by the Church and the estate owners, who vigorously opposed his socialism. Eventually he had to concede defeat. "As Chile no longer needs me I must resign" he said, and retired to Peru where he lived for the remaining nineteen years of his life. Like his father, he never married. He is still revered in South America and ranks among the great liberators of that continent.

Bernardo O Higgins

Dr Bryan Higgins (1741–1818) emigrated from Collooney, County Sligo, to study medicine at the University of Leiden in the Netherlands, as the penal laws forbade him to study or work in Ireland. Ironically, he chose to settle in London where he opened a school of practical chemistry. He carried out experiments and wrote many papers on his findings, including the discovery of a new type of cement. He achieved widespread fame and the Empress Catherine invited him to Russia. He also spent several years in Jamaica, helping to upgrade the sugar and rum industries.

His nephew, **William Higgins** (1763–1825), also from Collooney, joined his uncle in England. He studied chemistry at Oxford University and was one of the first scientists to attempt to explain chemical phenomena through the use of the atomic theory. He was, ahead of John Dalton, the greatest of the English chemists at the time. He returned to Ireland where he worked very fruitfully for the new Apothecaries Hall and the Irish Linen Board. He was Professor of Chemistry at the Royal Dublin Society at the time of another brilliant chemist, Richard Kirwan. He died in Dublin, in his Grafton Street home.

Henry Bourne Higgins (1851–1924), son of a Methodist Minister of Newtownards, County Down, was one of the numerous O Higgins who emigrated to Australia. He was awarded a scholarship to Melbourne University, where he obtained a legal degree and had to conquer a frustrating stutter before he could become a successful barrister. He sat in the Geelong Parliament and was Attorney-General and Judge of the High Court. Like many of the O Higgins, he had a literary side. He encouraged Australian poets to write about their own country and founded a poetry scholarship. He visited Ireland once and was a great supporter of Home Rule.

Harvey Jerrold O Higgins (1876–1929), born in London, Ontario, in Canada, was a novelist and journalist. He is regarded as having introduced the literary use of the psychoanalytic method in the writing of detective stories. One of the founders of the Authors' League, he was affectionately described as the poet laureate of the commonplace man.

In the twentieth century, while the outstanding Higgins have primarily been literary, the exception was a politician. **Kevin O Higgins** (1892–1927) was born at Stradbally, County Laois and, in 1918, while a law student at University College, Dublin, he joined Sinn Féin and was interned. Following the granting of independence, he held three ministerial posts in the government. When the Civil War broke out he took active measures to restore law and order, and defended the execution of 77 Republicans between 1922 and 1923. His father was shot dead by Republicans in 1923. Kevin O Higgins founded the Civic Guard which later became the Gárda Síochána, Ireland's police force. He was an advocate of an independent and united Ireland within the British Commonwealth. He was assassinated, in 1927, on his way to mass near his home in County Dublin.

Frederick Robert Higgins (1896–1941) was born in Foxford, County Mayo, and reared in County Meath. He began his literary career by contributing articles on a wide range of subjects to a variety of journals. W. B. Yeats asked him to write for a series of broadsheets published by his sisters at the Cuala Press. Frederick directed and managed Dublin's famous Abbey Theatre and, in 1937, toured with it in America. His was the inspiration for the Irish Academy of Letters. He wrote plays and poetry, and *The Gap of Brightness* is considered to be his most memorable work.

Aiden Higgins was born in Celbridge, County Kildare, in 1927. He has travelled and worked in a variety of countries, including South Africa, Spain and England. His short stories and novels have been translated into almost a dozen languages. *Langrishe Go Down* is probably his best-known novel so far.

Alex Higgins, who was born in Belfast in 1950, won his first World Snooker Championship in 1972. Known as "Hurricane Higgins", he shot to stardom as a brilliant though controversial player in a game which has since become universally popular and is accorded hours of viewing time on television.

Kevin O Higgins

Joyce
seoígh

Since they landed off the west coast of Ireland towards the end of the twelfth century, the Joyces have integrated with the Gaels and are still to be found mainly in Connacht. Father Woulfe, an authority on the origin of Irish names, considers the name Joyce to have originated from Joie (Joy), a Norman personal name. James Hardiman's comprehensive *History of Galway*, published in the last century, contains many facts, and a few fantasies, concerning the Joyces.

He wrote that **Thomas Joyes** sailed from Wales in the reign of Edward I (1239–1307) and arrived with his fleet at Thomond, probably at the mouth of the Shannon. He married Onorah, daughter of O Brien, Prince of Thomond. During a voyage to Connacht, Onorah gave birth to a son who was named **Mac Mara** (Son of the sea). Mac Mara married a daughter of O Flaherty, Prince of Iar Connacht, from whom descends the Joyce family in Ireland.

For a while the Joyces were a tributary of the O Flahertys, but in time they developed into a powerful clan in their own right, owning a vast acreage in the barony of Ross, which is still known as "Joyce's Country". The Joyces were numbered among those prosperous merchants called, somewhat derisively, "The Fourteen Tribes of Galway", and several Joyces filled the important role of Mayor of Galway.

In early ecclesiastical manuscripts there are records of **Walter Jorse**, or Jorz, or Joyce, brother of **Thomas**, Cardinal of Sabine and Archbishop of Armagh until 1311. Thomas was succeeded by his brother, **Roland**.

Theobald na Caisleán (of the castles) was the nickname of a Joyce who was a chieftain from 1570 to 1600. He earned this name because of the number of strongholds he built around Galway: Doon Castle by the sea near Clifden, Castle Kirk on an island in Lough Corrib, Clonbur on the eastern boundary of Joyce's Country and, probably, the nearby abbey of Ross Hill. Theobald lived in Renvyle Castle, once an O Halloran stronghold. Grace O Malley, the pirate queen, made an unsuccessful attempt to capture it. Renvyle, which commands the entrance to Killary Harbour, is a historic house which was later owned by the Blakes, and the famous doctor, poet and wit, Oliver St John Gogarty. It is now a hotel.

During the crusades, **William Joyce**, who was married to Agnes Morris of Galway, was travelling through Italy to Greece when he was captured by the Saracens. It was seven years before he escaped to Spain where, according to Hardiman, an eagle indicated a place of buried treasure to him. He returned to Galway with this wealth and used it to build the city walls and to found churches and other public edifices. He was buried in the Franciscan friary and left three sons, **James**, **Henry** and **Robert**.

William's granddaughter, **Margaret Joyce**, nicknamed Margaret na Drehide (of the bridges), married Domingo de Rona, one of the wealthy Spanish merchants who traded with Galway. He died in Spain, leaving her an immense fortune. She then married Oliver Óg Ffrench, who was Mayor of Galway in 1596. While he was abroad, she occupied herself with building bridges all over Connacht at her own expense. There is a legend that one day while she was watching the men at work on a bridge, an eagle dropped a gold ring into her bosom. It was adorned with a brilliant stone, a gem to which no one could put a name. Considering the part eagles have played in the story of the Joyces, it seems appropriate that their coat of arms should display two eagles.

Jorse

Joyes

Between the fourteenth and seventeenth centuries, Joyce prelates were numerous. There were two bishops of Armagh between 1307 and 1324, and **William Joyce** was Archbishop of Tuam from 1487 to 1501. In the seventeenth century, two Joyces of the Dominican Order contributed to the establishment of the University of Louvain in Belgium, a centre for Irish theologians for many centuries.

Despite his victory at the battle of the Boyne, the Joyces had reason to be grateful to "King Billy", William III. Among the British subjects William released from slavery in Algeria was a Joyce of Galway. During his fourteen years in captivity, he had become a skilled gold and silversmith. When he returned to Galway this skill enabled him to become a rich man. He bought an estate at Rahoon from a Cromwellian, which his three daughters inherited. Some of Joyce's marked silver can still be found. This **William Joyce** is, probably, the originator of the famous Claddagh ring which incorporates two hands clasping a heart.

The Joyces, many of whom had been active in the various attempts to free their country from colonial domination, suffered the loss of their properties and were forced to flee abroad. In France, **Walter Joyce**, Chevalier de St Louis, was with the Regiment of Berwick from 1774 to 1785. There were also Joyces in the Irish-American Brigades.

The Turkish baths in Dublin were popular with the eighteenth-century bucks. The baths were managed by one Dr Achmet Borumborad, assumed to be a genuine Turk. He was later revealed to be no Levantine practitioner, but a **Patrick Joyce** from Kilkenny who had put his childhood upbringing in the Levant to rewarding use!

Robert Dwyer Joyce (1830–83), born in Glenosheen, County Limerick, had to overcome the misery of famine and a minimal education in his youth. He took over the post of principal teacher at Clonmel Model School from his brother. Resigning from schoolteaching, he set himself the daunting task of studying medicine at Queen's College, Cork. To earn his fees he contributed articles, poems, stories and ballads to local magazines and newspapers. He graduated after eight years, and then, strangely enough, took a post as Professor of English Literature at the Catholic University College, Dublin! Unhappy with the political situation at home, he emigrated to Boston where he became a successful writer. His books sold well; *Deirdre* sold over 10,000 copies in a single week. He also lectured at Harvard Medical School. Even in America, he never abandoned his Fenian allegiance, and he died on his first visit home to Ireland.

His older brother, **Patrick Weston Joyce** (1827–1914), was also self-educated, a historian and scholar who specialized in teaching and preserving the Irish language. His book, *The Origin and History of Irish Names of Places*, is a classic. He also pioneered the collecting of Irish music and was a member of the Royal Irish Academy.

Another of the family, **Weston St John Joyce** (1858–1939), rambled, cycled and climbed the Dublin mountains and wrote articles, which he illustrated himself with drawings or photographs. His articles were published in the *Evening Telegraph* and the *Weekly Irish Times*. He gained such an extensive knowledge of Dublin that, in 1912, M.H. Gill the Dublin publishers brought out his book, *Neighbourhood of Dublin*, a work which has been reprinted many times.

James Augustine Joyce (1882–1941) was the Dublin-born poet, novelist and playwright who brought international fame to the Joyce name. He was sent to one of Ireland's premier boarding schools for boys, the Jesuit Clongowes Wood College, but because of his father's financial instability, he was soon removed from it. He continued his education with the Jesuits as a day boy in Dublin's Belvedere College. On graduating from University College, Dublin, he began a chequered life, trying a number of commercial ventures while writing all the time. Following some peregrinations around Europe, he settled at Trieste with Nora Barnacle from Galway, who became his life's companion and finally, at the urging of his children, his wife. Always in financial difficulties, he received much generous help, especially from mature women friends who recognized his genius. His masterpiece, *Ulysses*, which was published in Paris, caused a world-wide sensation and was banned in the USA and Great Britain, though, extraordinarily, not in Ireland. His earlier books, *Dubliners* and *Portrait of the Artist as a Young Man*, were so well received that he was encouraged to spend seventeen years writing his great *Ulysses*, despite innumerable operations to save his eyesight. *Ulysses*, which relates the incidents of one day in the life of a variety of people in Dublin, has had a profound effect on many writers and has provided an industry for critics. One of the first novelists to use the "stream of consciousness technique", Joyce immortalized Dublin, incidentally making a welcome contribution to tourism. He never returned to live in the city that he knew so well in his mind, but settled with his wife and children in Zurich, where he is buried. He said of his writing that he tried "to forge in the smithy of my soul the uncreated conscience of my race".

James Joyce, drawn by Augustus John

His brother, **Stanislaus Joyce** (1884–1955), joined him in Trieste, taught in the Berlitz School there and was a professor in the University of Trieste. Before the Second World War, Stanislaus was expelled from Italy for his opposition to Fascism. He wrote several books, including recollections of his famous brother, *My Brother's Keeper*.

The notorious **William Joyce** (*c.* 1906–46) was something of a mystery man who brought no credit to the Joyce name. He was born in Brooklyn, USA, of an English mother and Irish father. From 1914 to 1922 he went to school in Galway, and then went to England with his family. For a time he was active in Sir Oswald Mosley's British Union of Fascists before setting up a similar organization of his own. In August 1939 he went to Germany to offer his services to Joseph Goebbels' Nazi propoganda ministry. During the Second World War his spine-chilling radio propaganda talks, prefaced by the phrase "Germany calling" in a fruity British accent, made him more a target for allied comedians than an enemy to be feared. He was dubbed "Lord Haw Haw". At the end of the War, despite disguising his identity, his distinct voice gave him away. He was captured and convicted of treason at the Old Bailey in London and hanged.

Mervue, near Galway city, though now dilapidated, was once a splendid house built by a Joyce merchant banker as his family home, in about 1777. **Pierce Joyce** kept a private pack of hounds there. His grandson, **Lieutenant Pierce Joyce**, sold Mervue to Royal Tara Ltd., which uses part of the house as offices for its china manufactory.

The Corrib Country, published in 1947, contains tales of the Joyces which the author Richard Hayward picked up from local people while travelling in Connemara. "The tall, outrageous Joyces", one man recalled them. "Wasn't it a lifelong regret of Frederick the Great that he could never get a Joyce for that Regiment of Giants that was his chief pride. And I believe he tried everything fair and foul to come by that desire." Edward Blake, in his *Letters from the Irish Highlands* (1823), described a **Ned Joyce**, one of a large family of tall men, as "being between six and seven feet in height and large in proportion".

Kavanagh

caomhánach

Cavanagh

MacMurrough

To get to the Kavanagh roots it is necessary to go back to the kings of Leinster, the MacMurroughs. Their various descendants branched out to form several new clans: Davis, O Morchoe (Murphy) and Kinsella. The Kavanaghs descend from that unpopular Irish king, **Dermot MacMurrough** (1110–71). His son, **Donal**, acquired the Kavanagh agnomen when he was sent, as was the custom, to be fostered near Gorey, County Wexford, by the monks at Kilcavan, which in Irish is Cill Caomhán or St Kevin's Church. Possibly to distinguish him from other Donals, he was nicknamed Caomhánach (of Kevin), which was Anglicized to Kavanagh. The surname may sometimes be written as Cavanagh, but it is never prefixed with O or Mac, which signifies son or grandson, as the monks were strictly celibate!

Dermot MacMurrough, styled Lord of Hy Kinsella, King of Leinster and the Foreigners, was a major figure at that crossroads of Irish history marked by the departure of most of the Norsemen and the arrival, in 1169, of the Normans accompanied by the English. The endless feuding with the other high kings was squeezing him out of his Leinster kingdom. His enemies were led by Rory O Conor, King of Connacht, and his ally, Tiernan O Rourke, Prince of Breifne. O Rourke was Dermot's lifelong rival. There was probably more of revenge than of romance in Dermot's brief abduction of O Rourke's wife, Devorgilla, when he was 42 and she was 44 and not unwilling! He later scornfully returned her to O Rourke. When he lost his only ally, the most powerful king in Ireland at that time, Murtough MacLochlainn of Aileach in the north, the defeated Dermot travelled to France to seek help from Henry II (1133–89). Henry was willing to go to Ireland and sought the blessing of the Pope, Adrian IV, the only Englishman so far to sit on the papal throne. He encouraged Henry in the undertaking, because he wanted him to discipline the Irish Church which was much in need of religious reform.

Meanwhile, Dermot had recruited one of the prominent Norman leaders in Wales, Richard Fitzgilbert de Clare, Earl of Pembroke, popularly known as "Strongbow". The Earl was persuaded to go to Ireland, but only on condition that Dermot gave him his eldest daughter, Aoife (Eva), in marriage, and the right of succession to his kingdom.

The invaders arrived off the coast of Wexford in May 1169, followed in August by Strongbow and his troops who landed further west at Waterford. The Norse together with the Irish fought bravely, but were mercilessly defeated by the technically superior Normans. In the midst of the terrible carnage, Aoife was married to Strongbow. Shortly afterwards the Anglo-Normans went north to take their main objective, the capital city, Dublin. The following year Dermot died and Strongbow was left to deal with the rival Irish kings.

Finally, Henry II arrived to check that there would be no rival to his throne from the Norman barons. And so began the 800-year occupation of Ireland. Although Dermot MacMurrough was partly responsible, it has since been recognized that his aims were not entirely self-centred. He was seeking help from Europe to create order out of the chaos and end the rivalries to which his country had sunk. He was a man of many parts, a patron of religion and learning. Although he sacked abbeys, he also founded them. The ruins of his castle at Ferns, County Wexford, testify to its vast magnificence. He kept one of the great books of Irish literature, the *Book*

Dermot MacMurrough

of Leinster. Tradition says that Dermot is buried in Vallis Salutis, the Cistercian Abbey he founded in Baltinglass, County Wicklow.

Irish kingship was not hereditary, hence the intense rivalry, often leading to the maiming of potential successors, sometimes by gouging out their eyes. Although **Donal Kavanagh** was Dermot's favourite son, he was not appointed king. He did, however, inherit vast territories in counties Wexford and Carlow, where the Kavanaghs, one of the most numerous of Irish names, are still rooted.

Art MacMurrough (1357–1417), who styled himself Kavanagh, reigned for a record 42 years. In the same period England had eight kings, some of whom had been deposed or had died violently, including Richard II who, in 1394, had come to Ireland with his mighty army. He overcame all resistance and forced the great Art MacMurrough Kavanagh, with many of the other kings and chieftains, to submit—which they did with great pomp and ceremony. But not for long! No sooner had Richard departed than war broke out again and, when he returned to Ireland to quell it, his throne was seized by Henry IV (1367–1413), who, on his return, quietly had him murdered.

Art Óg (young) **MacMurrough Kavanagh**, a direct descendant of Dermot MacMurrough, is regarded as one of the great kings of Leinster. He was succeeded by his son, **Donough**, who was followed in the kingship by his nephew, **Donal Reagh** (swarthy).

In medieval times when the Gaelic poets were held in high esteem, **Eileen**, daughter of a Kavanagh chieftain, is said to have inspired the great thirteenth-century poet Carol O Daly, who composed the hauntingly sweet love song, "Eileen Aroon".

From St Mullins by the banks of the Barrow, bordering counties Wexford and Carlow, came **Cahir MacArt Kavanagh**. St Mullin was a patron of the Kavanaghs, and for centuries the abbey was the burial place of the kings of Leinster. In 1541, Cahir, The MacMurrough of Borris, was induced by the English Deputy, Sir Anthony St Leger, to renounce the MacMurrough prefix and to promise that "in future no one should be elected chief but they would obey the king's law and hold their lands by knight-service and accept such rules as the king should appoint". For this he was created Baron. In 1544 he is recorded as providing Irish soldiers to serve at the siege of Boulogne. Having exchanged his kingdom for a barony, he assumed the style, or title, MacMurrough which, he knew, would mean far more to his own people.

The MacMurrough territory extended from Carlow in the north to Enniscorthy in the south. The very full account of the family given in *Irish Family Records* states that they were elected kings up to the reign of King Henry VIII, and that their chiefs were acknowledged as The MacMurrough by the English.

Kavanaghs, a branch of the MacMurroughs, joined the exodus from Ireland following the breaking of the Treaty of Limerick in 1697. They were officers in the Irish Brigade in the French army. **Brian Kavanagh** is remembered particularly because he was the tallest man in King James's army. **Charles Kavanagh** was also very tall and one of the numerous Kavanaghs in the service of Austria. He became a general in the Austrian army and was Governor of Prague in 1766.

Nothing good can be said about **Joseph Kavanagh**, who behaved savagely during the French Revolution. A bootmaker by trade, he joined the citizens who looted the Tuileries, seized the guns and attacked the Bastille. Appointed a police inspector in 1792, he was part of the brutal gang who murdered 1,500 helpless men and women at the prison of La Force.

During the reign of terror he raided royalist houses, helping to send many to the guillotine.

The Kavanaghs do not seem to have made much of an impact on the New World. One who did was **Edward Kavanagh** (1795–1844), who was born in Maine of Irish parents who had emigrated to Boston in about 1780 and set up a store and a milling industry. They went on to become shipbuilders and prosperous land-owning merchants. Edward, who went to Europe and developed a gift for languages, was a non-practising barrister and held a number of public offices. His was a Catholic family, which may have prompted his petition to divert some of the tax paid to non-Catholic ministers of religion to the building of Catholic churches. He took his action to the Supreme Court which, in 1801, ruled that "the Constitution obliged everyone to support Protestant ministers" and reminded Kavanagh that "Papists must expect nothing more than toleration". Nonetheless, he was appointed chargé d'affaires to Portugal, where he spent six years. He sat on the Boundary Commission for Maine and became Governor of Maine in 1843, dying the following year.

Morgan Kavanagh, an eccentric, was born about 1800 in Tipperary. An assiduous, if uninspired, writer, he produced novels and poetry. **Julia Kavanagh** (1824–77), his daughter, far surpassed her father. She lived in London and Paris and wrote many popular novels of her day. Like Lady Blessington, she was among the earliest of women travel writers. In the nineteenth century, two other Kavanagh women authors wrote mostly poetry. They were **Ethna Kavanagh** and **Rose Kavanagh** of County Tyrone, who was born in 1859 at Killadry.

Arthur MacMurrough Kavanagh (1831–89), thirteenth child of **Thomas MacMurrough Kavanagh** and **Lady Harriet Kavanagh**, was born at Borris House. When his mother saw his tiny body with only a vestige of arms and legs, she exclaimed "Thank God he was born to me and not to anyone else". Through her rigid discipline and the co-operation of her highly intelligent son, she helped him to grow into one of the most able and physically active of men. He astounded his tutor with his ability to absorb Latin, Greek, zoology, astronomy and advanced mathematics (the latter led him to the study of navigation). Archery, water colours, poetry—he successfully tried them all. With his chair strapped to his horse he hunted, shot and fished. When Lady Harriet discovered him wooing a local girl in the woods, she thought it time to widen his horizons and sent him, his tutor and his two elder brothers on a world tour. He was in Russia at 18, and travelled on horseback all over the Middle East and India, encountering many hair-raising adventures, and suffering illness and often a lack of money. Once he had to earn a living as a dispatch rider. By the time he made his way home to Borris, his tutor and his two brothers had died, and Arthur had become The MacMurrough Kavanagh.

When Borris was ravaged by the Famine, Arthur set up industries to combat poverty. He married a cousin and reared seven children. He was a Member of Parliament at 35. Finding the journey to and from Westminster too tedious, he sailed his yacht from St Mullins and tied it up on the Thames beside the House of Commons.

For thirteen years he was an MP, looked up to and loved by his peasantry. During the Fenian rising, his people turned against him and he had the bitter blow of losing his seat in Parliament. Still active and, as always, cheerful, he lived only a few more years, dying in London in his Chelsea townhouse. Many books have been written about this amazing man.

It was from Borris House that Eleanor Butler (1745–1829), who was staying with her sister, Lady Susanna, wife of **Thomas MacMurrough**

Julia Kavanagh

Kavanagh, eloped to Wales with her close friend, Sarah Ponsonby. There they settled down together and became known as the famous "Ladies of Llangollen".

Thomas Henry Kavanagh, who was born in Mullingar, County Westmeath, in 1820, won his Victoria Cross (Britain's highest military honour) in India. There is a photograph of him in *The History of the Victoria Cross*, published in London in 1904. His medal was presented by his son to the museum at Lucknow, India. He died in Gibraltar in the house of his friend, Lord Napier of Magdala.

Poetry flows through the Kavanaghs, surfacing in unexpected places. The twentieth century produced the quirky Monaghan poet, **Patrick Kavanagh** (1906–67). He grew up on his father's small farm at Iniskeen and his poetry springs from the old Gaelic tradition. Although in maturer years he disapproved of his most popular poem, "The Great Hunger", written in 1942, it is highly thought of, as are his novels *The Green Fool* and *Tarry Flynn*. His work is represented in major anthologies.

Patrick Kavanagh

The castle at Enniscorthy, once the stronghold of the Wexford Kavanaghs, has passed through many owners and is now a folk museum. Many Kavanagh-built abbeys enrich the southern Irish countryside, especially in counties Carlow, Wicklow and Wexford. The Kavanagh drinking horn, made of ivory and ornamented with gilt metal plates and bands, and standing sixteen inches high, is preserved in the National Museum, Dublin.

Today Borris House is once again lived in by a MacMurrough Kavanagh. **Andrew MacMurrough Kavanagh**, a descendant of Cahir MacMurrough Kavanagh, and of the intrepid nineteenth-century Arthur, assumed his mother's name by deed poll. Borris is a palatial mansion, which was built by the renowned Irish architects Richard and Vitruvius Morrison on the site of an older castle. With his wife and growing family, Andrew is striving to restore it to something of its former glory by developing the potential of its land and buildings.

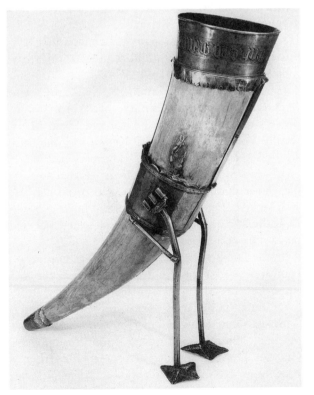

The Kavanagh drinking horn

Keane

ó catháin

Kane

MacCloskey

O Cahan

O Kane

O Keane

Sir Robert John Kane

The Keanes and Kanes are somewhat confusing genealogically. Originally from two different septs of Ó Catháin, Anglicized to O Cahan, they became in modern times Keane and Kane, making it simpler to distinguish their topographical origins. The Kanes, sometimes O Kanes, were Lords of Keenaght and Coleraine, in County Derry in the twelfth century. They drove the O Connors from Dungiven and were themselves dispersed following the plantations of Ulster. From 1170 they began to be recorded in the *Annals of the Four Masters*. Kane is still essentially an Ulster surname, while Keane is the Munster and Connacht form of the name, although this could have been a minor branch of the Ó Catháins of Ulster.

Bloskey O Kane's claim to fame is that, in 1196, he killed Murtough Mac Lochlainn, heir to the northern high kingship. The MacCloskeys of Derry descend from him. In the nineteenth century the family could boast of **Dr MacCloskey**, Archbishop of New York who, in 1875, was made a cardinal.

Domnel Ballagh O Cahan (Kane) was their last chieftain. At one time he joined forces with Hugh O Neill, Earl of Tyrone, against the English. Later, he joined the English forces, although he paid the price for this, losing most of his land, but was repaid with a knighthood by James I. This did not save him from dying in the Tower of London in 1617, after many years of imprisonment without trial.

Richard Kane (1667–1736) from County Down had a versatile military career. He reached the rank of brigadier-general in the British army. He fought in France and took part in the defeat of Louis XIV's army at the battle of Blenheim. He transferred to the French army and was a lieutenant-colonel at the victory of the French at the battle of Malplaquet in 1709. Two years later he was in Canada with the Regiment of Irish Foot. He was the military governor of Gibraltar in 1720, during the dispute with Spain. With this background of international service, he wrote widely on military strategy.

The Thomond O Cahans or O Keanes, mostly of Connacht and Munster, particularly County Waterford, provided many distinguished officers for the armies of France and Spain in the seventeenth and eighteenth centuries. **Eugene O Keane** was one of fourteen brothers, four of whom served in France's wars. He was killed in action there in 1693.

Music was one of the few Irish arts that survived the suppression of the old Gaelic culture. A musician who could play the harp was welcome and well looked after in the homes of the humble as well as the mighty. **Echlin O Kane** (1720–90) was an accomplished performer who was invited to play in the courts of Europe.

In the Dublin Genealogical Office, and in the archives of other European countries, particularly England and France, the pedigrees of the Keanes are amply recorded. In the nineteenth century they were recorded for their involvement in the army, as well as the theatre, science and technology,

Sir Robert John Kane (1809–90) was one of the leading scientists of his time. The son of a Dublin manufacturing chemist, he studied at Trinity College, Dublin, and in Paris. He held many professorships, including Professor of Natural Philosophy with the Royal Dublin Society. He brought his scientific mind to bear on potential sources of wealth that Ireland could harness to develop its industries. In 1845, he was a member of the commission set up to investigate the potato blight and to help relieve the terrible distress during the Famine which followed the failure of that crop. He was the first president of University College, Cork and, later, vice-chancellor of the newly created University College, Dublin.

Edmund Kean (1787–1833) was born in London. His father was Irish and his mother, an actress, is reputed to have been a natural daughter of the Marquis of Halifax. Despite being deserted by his father and abandoned in a Soho doorway by his flighty mother, Kean survived to reach eminence, and merit eight and a half pages in the *Dictionary of National Biography*. He became the leading actor of his time, in spite of the handicaps of being deaf, lame, small and eccentric. It was his Uncle Moses, a mimic and ventriloquist, who inspired him to study Shakespeare, whose tragic characters suited him admirably. At London's Drury Lane Theatre, his Shylock mesmerized the audience. Coleridge, the leading critic of the day, wrote, "To see Kean is like reading Shakespeare by flashes". Kean toured the USA in 1820. A few years later, his divorce case shattered his nerves and his career. While playing Othello to his son Charles's Iago, he had a seizure and died shortly afterwards, burned out at 46.

Edmund Kean

Charles John Kean (1811–68), his second son, was born in Waterford, the home of his mother, Mary Chambers. Charles had a far more privileged upbringing than his father. He went to Eton until the age of 16, when his parents' marriage broke up. He was bright enough to be offered a cadetship in the East India Company's service, which he could have accepted if his father had agreed to settle an income of £400 on his mother. However, Edmund Kean refused to do this. The stage was inescapably in Charles's blood and he began acting at Drury Lane, albeit in a humble role.

Although always in his famous father's shadow and never as brilliant, or as dissolute, he fared well enough. After a separation of some years, father and son were reunited, and acted together. Charles toured abroad and, for ten years, was director of Queen Victoria's theatricals at Windsor Castle. He revolutionized lighting techniques, and managed the Princess' Theatre in London. He spent a period in Melbourne, where he was praised for helping to raise the social standing of actors and the theatre in Australia. In 1842, he married an actress Ellen Tree (1805–80) in St Thomas's Church in Dublin. That same evening she played Juliet to his Romeo in a performance of *The Honeymoon*. Charles died in Chelsea, London, a year after his retirement.

Michael Kean (d. 1823) was born in Dublin. He studied art before going to London, where he soon made his name as a miniaturist and exhibited at the Royal Academy between 1780 and 1790. He was taken into partnership by the owner of the famous Derby China factory. When the owner died, Michael Kean married his widow and became owner of the factory whose reputation was greatly enhanced by his artistry. But his quick temper drove his wife away and eventually led to the sale of the business. Their only son followed a different career, he was a naval captain.

Joseph B. Keane (d. 1859), one of Ireland's nineteenth-century architects, was educated at the Dublin Office of Works and produced such outstanding work that he was made a Fellow of the Royal Institute of Architects of Ireland. He designed churches, and Queen's College, Galway, was also built to his design. A very fashionable architect, some of his handsome Irish country mansions are still standing: Barmeath Castle, Dunleer, County Louth; Camolin in County Donegal; Castle Irvine in County Fermanagh; Edermine, near Enniscorthy in County Wexford, which he designed, in 1839, in the Italianate style for the Powers of whiskey distillery fame. He also designed Glendalough House at

Annamoe, County Wicklow, for the Childers family, one of whose sons, Erskine, was President of Ireland until his sudden death in 1974.

Paul Kane (1810–71), who was born in Mallow, County Cork, went to Canada with his parents in around 1818. He left school to work in a furniture factory. While in his early twenties, he travelled south to the USA and then to France and Italy where he studied painting. Returning to Canada ten years later, he began to record the native Indians' lifestyle, travelling the country by canoe, horseback and even snowshoe. The resulting series of paintings are of rare historical value and can be seen in the Royal Ontario Museum, Toronto, as well as in the Parliament Buildings in Ottawa. Paul Kane left a written record of his travels in his book *Wanderings*.

August Henry Keane (1833–1912) of Cork was educated in Dublin and studied for the priesthood in Rome. He did not have a vocation, however, and instead devoted his life's work to anthropology, working on geographical and ethnological research and languages. He developed his own system of ethnology. He published many books and was Professor of Hindustani at University College, London, until 1885.

John Thomas Keane (1854–1937) took a calculated risk travelling as Haj Mohammed Amin on the pilgrimage to Mecca in 1877. This seems to have passed off well for he went on other pilgrimages, accompanied by a wealthy Moslem friend. He followed up his success with the books *Six Months in Mecca*, *My Journey to Medina* and *Blue Water*. He died in Australia.

The Keane dynasty of Cappoquin, County Waterford, apart from serving abroad in many capacities, has contributed much to its native land. **Sir John Keane** (1781–1882), 1st Baronet, was a Member of Parliament at home and served with the British fleet in the Middle East. Sir John's second son commanded a brigade in the Peninsular war under Wellington. Later he took a division to America to serve under General Pakenham. He was wounded at the battle of New Orleans, became Governor of Jamaica and later Commander-in-Chief in India, where he commanded the British army in the First Afghan War when the Afghans surrendered after the capture of the town of Ghuznee. For his service he was made **Lord Keane of Ghuznee** and held the rank of lieutenant-general. **Sir John Keane** (1872–1960), 5th Baronet, was a barrister and for twelve years was a member of the first Irish government's Senate and a director of the Bank of Ireland. His son, **Sir Richard Keane** (b. 1909), 6th Baronet, is a writer and farmer at Cappoquin. In the Keane family home there are many portraits and historic relics of Sir Richard's distinguished antecedents.

Edward Vivien Keane, also of Cappoquin, was a civil engineer and, in 1886, built the railway running from Perth to Guildford in Western Australia. He was rewarded with a gift of 80,000 Australian acres and also became Lord Mayor of Perth.

John Joseph Keane (1839–1918) was an Irish-American bishop, who, in 1900, was appointed Bishop of Dubuque in Iowa, one of a remarkable number of Irishmen to fill that post. During the Famine of the mid-1880s, he emigrated with his parents from Ballyshannon, County Donegal. He worked in a store, while also studying avidly, so that when he obtained a place at college, at the age of 20, he was able to complete his theological course in three years instead of the usual six. He was the first rector of Washington University. Pope Leo XIII appointed him to serve in two important consultative posts in the Vatican in 1897.

James John Keane (1857–1929) had a fairly similar background to Bishop John Keane, and also became Bishop of Dubuque. An energetic diocesan administrator in his American parishes, he was also, in 1920, a member of the Peace Commission on Ireland. He was a supporter of the League of Nations, created in 1920 to preserve peace and settle disputes by arbitration or conciliation, which had its headquarters in Geneva. In 1946 its role was taken over by the United Nations.

Although she was born a Skrine, in County Cork in 1904, to omit **Molly Keane**, would leave an unforgivable gap in the Keane history. Before the Second World War, under the pseudonym M.J. Farrell, she wrote novels and plays which were a dazzling success in London's West End theatres. When her husband died she stopped writing. In the 1980s, in her eighties, she made a come-back with a best-selling novel, *Good Behaviour,* a black comedy about the impoverished Anglo-Irish. This was followed by *Time After Time.* Both novels have been adapted for television by the BBC.

Marie Kean (1922–93), who was born in Dublin went on the stage when she was ten. For generations she was one of Ireland's most popular actresses, frequently appearing at Dublin's Abbey Theatre and winning international awards.

John B. Keane (b. 1928) of Listowel, County Kerry, is a playwright and publican. He gathered his material while working in London as a roadsweeper and barman before returning to Listowel in 1953 to buy his own bar. With no theatrical experience, but an inexhaustible reserve of native literature in his blood, he wrote his very popular series of plays, beginning in 1959 with *Sive.* This was a great success and led to the production of many of his subsequent plays in Dublin's Abbey Theatre, as well as in London and the USA.

John B. Keane

87

Kennedy
ó cinnéide

O Kennedy

There are very many Kennedys in all parts of Ireland and abroad. In the twentieth century, Kennedys far outnumber O Kennedys or Ó Cinnéides. Kennedy is also an important name in Scotland, although it is possible that the Scottish and Irish Kennedys originate from the same stock in the distant past. In Ireland they are descended from **Dunchaun**, brother of the mighty King Brian Boru. Their name comes from his father, **Ceann Éidig**, meaning helmet head. They were Dalcassians, belonging to the same sept as the O Briens of Thomond in the south-west. For generations they lived around the valley of Glenomra near Killaloe in County Clare, now an inland cruising centre on the River Shannon where it flows out of Lough Derg. It is a county redolent of history. Nearby is Beal Boru, from which Brian Boru took his title and where he had his palace at Kincora. Killaloe was the royal seat of the Dalcassian kings. Killokennedy preserves the name of one of its most important families.

The arms of the O Kennedys have three helmets, which historians of heraldry suspect may be a pun on Ceann Éidig, as *éidig* means helmet. Like most true Gaels, the O Kennedys had their own banshee, a fairy woman whose wailing was said to forecast death or disaster.

A mournful Gaelic poet wrote of the O Kennedys, "…who reddens the javelin over the wide smooth Glean Omra. The race of our Dunchaun who through valour, obtained the lands without dispute".

When quarrels with the O Briens and the MacNamaras drove them from their territory, the Kennedys crossed the Shannon and went south to the rich lands of counties Tipperary and Kilkenny. From the eleventh to the fifteenth centuries they were Lords of Ormond, and the clan grew immense and divided into three branches, their chiefs being designated Donn (brown), Fionn (fair) and Rua (red) (the colour of the hair was a distinguishing feature for the ancient Irish). Close to the banks of the Shannon they built the castles of Annagh and Dunally. There were also O Kennedys of Galway who were of the Hy Many sept (*see* O Kelly).

The Kennedys dealt with the various conquests and confiscations better than many other Gaelic families. In 1185 Theobald Walter, founder of the powerful line of the Butlers, arrived in the wake of the Normans and was granted the Kennedy territory and the titles of Ormond, together with their lands around Nenagh. However, the Kennedys stood firm and won back their territory including, for a while, the fine castle built by the Normans at Nenagh. Nearby, the Kennedys founded a Franciscan Abbey. From 1231 to 1252 **Daniel O Kennedy** was Bishop of Killaloe. The cathedral there is still a place of Christian worship. At Lackun near Lorrha in County Tipperary, one of their chieftains, **O Kennedy Fionnan**, emulating the Normans, built himself a fortress of stone.

In the National Library of Ireland, the Ormond deeds record the interplay between the O Kennedys and the Butlers. A seal of 1579 for **Awley O Kennedy** shows the impression of a mermaid with a comb in one hand and a mirror in the other. During his visit to Ireland in 1963, the government, in its enthusiasm, presented President John F. Kennedy with one of these irreplaceable documents, to the delight of the transient president no doubt, but to the dismay of Irish archivists.

Until 1746, the O Kennedys still owned over 20,000 acres, despite losses to the Butlers, to Cromwell and to the plantations. Many of the

O Kennedy castles were destroyed in the wars. Newtownmountkennedy House, the large mansion which they built in Wicklow in 1670 and which was burned in the Williamite wars, was rebuilt, but the Kennedys departed from it following the death of **Sir Richard Kennedy** in a duel in 1710. In his book, *Irish Homes and Castles*, Desmond Guinness praises the house for being "today, in such good repair".

By the seventeenth century, their day was over and the Kennedys began to follow the emigrant trail. In the Irish Brigades in France there were many Kennedy officers and men. Those who went to Spain had their name transformed to Quenedy.

Matthew Kennedy (1652–1735), who went to France following the defeat at the battle of the Boyne, settled in Paris where he was a notable literary figure. His *Dissertation on the Royal Family of the Stuarts* is just one of his many writings in several languages, including Irish.

A strange case came before the Irish courts in 1779, when two **Miss Kennedys**, daughters of a wealthy County Waterford family, were abducted. It was not altogether unheard-of in those days for daring young men of high fashion but no means or morals, to attempt to improve their finances in this desperate fashion.

John Pitt Kennedy (1796–1879) was born in County Donegal. He studied at the Royal Military Academy in Woolwich and, in 1815, he was commissioned in the Corps of Engineers. After service abroad he returned home and began to pioneer the study and development of agriculture. Despite his efforts to establish a model farm and training centre in County Dublin for the practical organization of agriculture, he met with little response from the establishment. His potential was recognized in 1849 when the commander in charge of India, Sir Charles Napier, invited him to build the great military road stretching across the frontier from Simla to Tibet. For this mammoth engineering feat the road was given his name. He retired to London where he was on the board of the Bombay, Baroda & Central Indian Railway.

Patrick Kennedy (1801–73) of Wexford had his early education taken care of by the Carew family. He began his career in Dublin as a teacher. Later he opened a bookshop in Anglesea Place. He both sold books and wrote them, specializing in Celtic mythology and folklore.

Sir Arthur Edward Kennedy (1801–83) was of the Kennedys who established themselves in Cultra, County Down, in the seventeenth century. Graduating from Trinity College, Dublin, he bought an army commission and spent some years soldiering in Canada before returning to Ireland. He spent the famine years working as a poor law commissioner in County Clare. Afterwards he joined the colonial service, where he was successively Governor of The Gambia, Sierra Leone and Western Australia. During his seven years in Australia, the economy expanded, as did the population, because of the influx of convicts. Arthur Kennedy used convicts to build roads and drain swamps around Perth. He also cleaned up the police force before he left Australia in 1862, to become Governor of Vancouver Island, Canada. He was Governor-in-Chief of the West African Settlement, and Governor of Hong Kong before returning once again to Queensland. He brought with him his Chinese domestic staff, which greatly incensed some Australians who felt he was doing them out of work. A strong-minded man, Arthur Kennedy survived many a political storm, and died, in his 80s, in Aden on the voyage home.

A kinsman of Sir Arthur's from Cultra, **Hugh Kennedy** (1829–82), was a registrar of Balliol College, Oxford, before emigrating in 1852 to become secretary of the University of Sydney, where he remained for the rest of his life. Although described by some as more ornamental than useful, and gravely distressed towards the end of his life by unfortunate land speculation, the records he compiled, often in Latin, form the basis of the University of Sydney's official archives.

Evory Kennedy (1806–86) was born in County Derry. He studied medicine in all the best places—Dublin, Edinburgh, London and Paris—before settling down to practise in Dublin, where he was very popular and held many important posts. He was Master of the Rotunda, the world's second-oldest maternity hospital. He was less successful in politics however, failing to secure a seat in Parliament for Donegal.

The Kennedys can boast an admiral in the family, **Sir William R. Kennedy** (b. 1838). He was also the author of many rollicking sea shanties and adventure stories.

When the Irish Free State, as it was then called, came into being in 1922, **Hugh Kennedy** (1879–1936) was its first Chief Justice. It was four generations later before Ireland appointed the first woman District Justice, **Eileen Kennedy** (1914–1983), who for many years presided over the Juvenile Court in Dublin.

Jimmy Kennedy achieved fame in the USA as a songwriter. His classic, *Red Sails in the Sunset*, brought him a fortune in royalties. He retired to live in County Wicklow and, in 1983, aged 80, went to live in the sunnier climate of Gibraltar, but died there the following year.

The tragic Kennedy family of America, whose sons dominated American politics for a decade at least, came originally from a County Wexford farming family. **President John Fitzgerald Kennedy** (1917–63) visited Ireland only five months before his assassination, and spent a while in the ancestral cottage at Dunganstown, taking tea with his Kennedy kinsmen. The promise and vitality of his brief presidency brought a reflected glory to Ireland, where his violent death, coupled with that of his sister and brothers, was very keenly felt.

For over thirty years **William Kennedy**, an Irish-American journalist of New York, was a failed novelist. Suddenly, in 1984, when he was 54, his novels about the people of Albany were discovered and published by Viking and Penguin. *Ironweed* won him the Pulitzer Prize and a host of other literary awards.

The Kennedy surname is widely distributed in Ireland and is very common—possibly numbering in the region of 20,000, and maybe twice that number in America.

Jean Kennedy Smith, sister of John Fitzgerald Kennedy, was appointed US Ambassador to Ireland by President Clinton in 1993.

Keogh

mac eochaidh

Keogh is a quintessentially Gaelic surname. Kee–Oh would be a good approximation of its proper pronunciation by a native Irish speaker. It originates from Eochaidh, a popular personal name, and the family is said to descend from an **Eochaidh O Kelly**. The family divided into three septs. One was at Ballymackeogh in County Tipperary. The Lords of Magh Finn (Moyfinn) were near Athlone in the midlands and Roscommon in Connacht, where until comparatively recent times there was an area known as Keoghville. The third and predominant sept were the MacKeoghs of Leinster who came from the same stock as the O Byrnes, for whom they were also hereditary bards. In medieval times, following the Anglo-Norman invasion, they moved, with the O Byrnes and the O Tooles, across the plains of Kildare to the protection of the wooded Wicklow mountains, and also south to the coast at Wexford.

In 1534, **Maolmuire MacKeogh** was described in the *Annals of the Four Masters* as the chief professor of poetry in Leinster. In this century, Douglas Hyde mentions several poets of the name in his *Literary History of Ireland*. The **Reverend John Keogh**, born in 1653 at Cloondeagh, County Limerick, had his property confiscated during the Cromwellian usurpations. His strange mathematical demonstrations of religious problems were admired by Sir Isaac Newton. Though he wrote obsessively, nothing of his was ever published. His eldest son, also **John** (1681–1754), was a botanist and zoologist.

John Keogh (1746–1817) was a pioneer of Catholic emancipation. Although he did not live to see it, he laid the foundation for Daniel O Connell's proudest achievement. John Keogh was not born into any great wealth, but he worked his way up to become a comfortable Dublin merchant whose country house at Mount Jerome, outside Dublin, was the constant meeting place for all those who were sincerely concerned with overcoming the laws grievously restricting those who practised the Catholic faith.

Seeing no hope of making headway in Ireland, he went with a committee to London where he spent three months laying these injustices before the appropriate ministry. He was favourably received on the whole, but when he returned home his challenge was to spread his enthusiasm to the Catholics and rouse them from their lethargy. In London he had met with the approval of that great fellow-Irishman, Edmund Burke, and it was said of him that "when Keogh returned he laid aside his court wig, court manner and only retained his Irish feelings".

He had sympathy with the aims of the United Irishmen, but strove to prevent Catholics from being compromised by their inclination towards violence. The greatest triumph of his life came with the Relief Act of 1793. Wolfe Tone often visited his home, and it was suspected that John Keogh knew about the plans for the 1798 rising and was even arrested and imprisoned for a few days. He was so deeply upset by the repercussions following the rising that he retired to the seclusion of his home, a broken man. He lived just long enough to see the beginning of the fruitful agitation for Catholic emancipation. To Daniel O Connell he had once boasted that he had made men of the Catholics who had sunk into apathy and despair.

William Keogh (1817–78) was born at Keoghville, County Roscommon, and became one of the most controversial figures at the Irish

Haughey

Hoy

Kehoe

Mac Keogh

O Hoey

Bar. He studied law at Trinity College, Dublin, and built up a very successful practice. He went into politics and was Member of Parliament for Athlone. He was one of the founders of the Catholic Defence Association, which was pressing for Catholic emancipation. He was also concerned with the other burning injustice that held the people of Ireland in its iron grip—the lack of tenants' rights. He was made Attorney-General in 1855, and, the following year, a judge. Although born a Catholic, he did not practise his religion and his advocacy of the Tenants' Rights League waned as his prosperity grew. He became a *bon viveur* and his wit is said to have been second only to Father James Healy, his close friend and neighbour, near Bray, County Wicklow.

He was an impartial judge, but when he unseated the popular Home Rule candidate, J. P. Nolan, following the 1865 trial of the Fenian prisoners Luby, O Leary and O Donovan Rossa, he was reviled. In his summing up before the jury, he had accused the Catholic clergy of "undue influence on their behalf". His severe judgement was greatly resented and for the remainder of his life he was constantly in danger of attack, his effigy was burned and he found a drawing of a coffin under his plate. Eventually, broken in body and mind, he went abroad to Bingen on the Rhine, where he had a stroke which ended his life.

A branch of the family who spelled their name K'eogh lived for generations in County Limerick. Although Catholic, they remained landed gentry with their seat at Castletroy. **Colonel K'eogh** served in the British army. Another member of the family, **Edmond K'eogh**, who lived at Kilbride House, had property in Holland as well as a villa in Lausanne, Switzerland. During the Famine of 1847 to 1848, he distributed food from Kilbride. But he too fell ill and died not long afterwards in Rotterdam. Kilbride was taken over by the Land Commission and divided into small farms.

Myles W. Keogh (1848–76) was born in Orchard House, near Leighlinbridge, County Carlow, and took part in three wars during his short life. The last of these has become part of American folk history and inspired a number of film sagas. He first enlisted in the army of Pope Pius IX, where he was appointed second lieutenant in the Battalion of St Patrick, a unit of the Irish Volunteers who went to defend the Papal State in 1860. Myles Keogh was a member of the garrison that surrendered at Ancona. Although the Irish were given the option of being repatriated, Keogh, who had distinguished himself with the army, remained in Italy until the end of that war.

A tall, good-looking young man, he went to America to take part in the Civil War and was a brevet lieutenant-colonel, aged 26, when it ended. Much of America had yet to be explored, and the West, said to be the largest undeveloped area left on earth, was being opened up. Railroads, telegraph systems and roads were all being built by labourers, many of whom were from Ireland. This was Indian country and they were quite naturally upset by much of this development.

Myles Keogh met his counterpart in the flamboyant George Armstrong Custer, just a year his senior. They headed the 7th US Cavalry campaign launched in 1876 to contain the Indians in Montana and South Dakota, where Chief Sitting Bull of the Sioux had 20,000 Indians under the command of the 32-year-old Crazy Horse. A surprise attack by the Sioux, in a stream called the Little Big Horn, trapped 600 cavalrymen. The Indians annihilated them, scalping every single American. The only living creature remaining on the battlefield was Keogh's horse, Comanche. He was rescued and revered for twenty years. When he died he was stuffed and displayed in the Museum of the University of Kansas. Myles Keogh was buried in New

Myles W. Keogh

York and there is a memorial window to him in St Joseph's Church at Tinryland, Carlow.

The family of Keogh which was Anglicized to O Hoey and Hoy was of the same stock as the MacDonlevys and were kings of Ulster up to the twelfth century. From that sept came **John Cashel Hoey** (1823–93), who edited the *Nation*, the revolutionary Fenian publication founded in 1842 by the Young Ireland Party.

During the First World War, **Sir Alfred Keogh** was director general of the Army Medical Services. On the Eastern Front he became interested in the cause and cure of malaria, which had so greatly afflicted the troops. In Britain he set up special malaria hospitals and, with Sir Ronald Ross, promoted the use of quinine for its control.

Mary Una Keogh (1903–89) was one of the eleven children of **Joseph Keogh**, a Dublin stockbroker. Following a liberal education she was invited by her father to join his stockbroking company. At the age of 22 she shocked the very conservative, and all-male, Dublin Stock Exchange by applying for membership. Since the Irish Constitution ensures equal opportunity to every citizen over 21, she had to be admitted. Further proof of her ability was provided when she became the first woman in forty years to be admitted to membership of the London Stock Exchange. She married the Russian architect, Bayan Giltsoft, and they lived with their four children in the Wicklow village that he had designed.

Kirwan

Ó Ciardubháin

Kirovani

Kyrewain

Kyrvan

Kyrwan

Quirovan

The Anglicized version of this name has never had an O or Mac prefix, while in Irish it is Ó Ciardubháin. Their sept seems to have settled in County Louth before they moved to County Galway. They claim descent from **Heremon**, a son of the King of Spain who conquered Ireland in the sixth century BC.

Little mention is made of the Kirwans in the history books until they settled in Galway and became prosperous men of affairs and leading members of "The Fourteen Tribes of Galway". **John Kirwan** was the only Catholic Mayor of Galway between 1654 and the granting of Catholic emancipation in 1829.

The Kirwan family has had both Catholic and Protestant bishops. **Reverend Stephen Kirwan** (c. 1530), born at Clonfert, County Galway, and educated at Oxford and Paris, converted and became first Protestant Bishop of Kilmacduagh in County Galway. He combined missionary fire with the sword, for he was also one of the commissioners of martial affairs in Connacht.

Walter Blake Kirwan (1754–1805) was ordained as a Jesuit, but converted and became a Protestant preacher of such eloquence that, when he appealed for charity, not only did thousands of pounds overflow from the collection plates, but also jewellery and gold watches. During his very last sermon he made such an impassioned appeal that there was enough on the plates to found a children's home in Dublin, which still commemorates his name. His son, **Anthony La Touche Kirwan**, followed his clerical father, becoming Dean of Limerick.

On the Catholic side there was **Francis Kirwan** (1588–1661), a colourful Bishop of Killala who ended his days abroad, a refugee from Gaelic politics. His early education was at Galway, at the classical school belonging to his uncle, Reverend John Lynch. After his ordination he went to Lisbon and, later, taught in Irish colleges in France. He had a radiant personality and included St Vincent de Paul among his many friends. In France his ordination was a very splendid occasion. There were thirteen bishops, fifteen abbots and thirty Doctors of the Sorbonne in attendance at the church of St Lazaire in Paris. His voyage back to Ireland was marred when pirates relieved him of all his books and personal goods. Ireland was in the final throes of the struggle between the old Gaelic order and the new English imposition. Curiously, the Confederate Catholics had adopted the motto "Ireland United for God, King and Country", which is very similar to the wording on the Kirwan coat of arms, which displays three black choughs, or red-legged crows.

Francis Kirwan was a friend of the Italian papal nuncio, Rinuccini who, finding the Irish issue too difficult and confusing, returned to Rome. Kirwan was banished to the wilds of Connacht where, following years of great hardship, he had to flee to Brittany, a haven for many Irish exiles. It was a sad ending for a man whose good humour and holiness were legendary. A story is told of his counselling a man who had left his wife. The bishop urged him to take her back on pain of eternal damnation. "I could bear the flames of hell better than my wife's company", said the husband. The bishop told him to try it by putting his hand in the candle flame. The cauterization duly restored the marriage. Bishop Francis Kirwan is buried at Rennes.

Little is recorded of the female line. As was considered suitable, Kirwan girls married their fellow Galway tribesmen. In the 1620s, **Julia** and **Emily Kirwan** married into the Martyn family of Ballinahinch.

The national libraries in London and Paris hold papers relating to the well-travelled Kirwans. To follow their progress it helps to know that, apart from the Irish Ó Ciardhubháin, the name might also appear as Kyrwan, Kirovani, Kyrvan, Kyrewain, or even Quirovan. The British Museum in London has a warrant of Viscount Wentworth granting a pardon to **Martin Kirovani** of Galway "for leaving the kingdom without a licence on 26th September 1637". In contrast, the Salisbury Mss record a request from **Peter Kyrewain** (*c.* 1600) "for a licence to transport forty tons of beer without custom to Galway where there is a garrison of sixteen hundred soldiers and the country all round is waste".

Richard Kirwan of Cregg Castle, Corundulla, Galway, was a military man of 6 feet 4 inches in height. He went to France and was with Dillon's Regiment at the battle of Fontenoy. He was rewarded by Louis XV who presented him with a watch inlaid with diamonds and pearls. An over-fondness for duelling led to his dismissal from France, so he entered the imperial service of Austria. He retired to his Connemara home with the jewelled watch, which is said to be still in Kirwan hands, although whose is not common knowledge.

In the late eighteenth century, **Edward Kirwan** lived in Bordeaux, where many Irish military families founded businesses, particularly in the wine trade. The articles he wrote for *The Spectator*, which he also edited, led to his accusal as a royalist and subsequent imprisonment by the revolutionary authorities for being far too right-wing.

There were several Kirwans practising medicine in France, including a **Dr James Kirwan** who was physician to the king in 1756. In the late eighteenth and early nineteenth centuries, a Kirwan *émigré* is mentioned as being a member of the nobility of Dauphiny in south-east France, while another, **Charles de Kirwan**, is in the records as being Sub-Inspector of Forests.

Most enduring of this Galway family's alliance with France is its Château Kirwan vineyard in the Gironde. The Kirwan appellation may still be found in the wine merchants' lists, although the name of the present proprietors is Schroder and Schyler.

Owen Kirwan, a humble Dublin tailor, conspired with Robert Emmet to manufacture ammunition. He exploded the rocket that precipitated the insurrection of 1803, and was executed at the same time as Emmet.

Richard Kirwan (1733–1812), a nephew of Richard (the tall swordsman) of Cregg Castle, is the most distinguished Kirwan. Chemist, natural philosopher, musician, linguist, scientist and much more, he was one of the happier Irish eccentrics. Educated abroad and ordained as a Jesuit priest, he left the Church in favour of the family estates at Galway. He married a penniless but aristocratic Blake girl of Menlo, County Galway, and spent his honeymoon in jail for her debts! He did not hold this against her, but she died young and he went to Dublin and then London to immerse himself in various studies, particularly the law. Catherine of Russia and the radical John Horne Tooke were numbered among his diverse admirers. Ill health drove him back to Dublin, but, crossing the Irish sea, his library was stolen by an American privateer. It would be interesting to know in whose library it now reposes.

He was soon absorbed into the brilliant company of the Royal Dublin Society. A member of many learned institutions, he was the first president of the Royal Irish Academy. Honorary degrees were showered upon him,

Richard Kirwan (1733–1812)

but he declined a baronetcy, preferring the title of Inspector-General of His Majesty's Mines in Ireland. He was never parted from his huge sheltering hat—whether in his house or a guest at Dublin Castle. Irrespective of the season, he received his friends prone on a couch before a blazing fire. He dined alone and always on ham and milk. He was terrified of flies, and kept six large dogs and an eagle. He died of malnutrition, not because of poverty but, it is said, because of his overly-severe efforts to starve a cold. His friends described him as a good landlord who was indifferent to money.

In the nineteenth century the family was shocked by **William Bourke Kirwan** (*c.* 1814), who was accused of murdering his wife. A Dublin miniature painter and water colourist, he exhibited at the Royal Hibernian Academy. He also did anatomical drawings for surgeons. In a famous trial in Dublin, he was sentenced to death, in 1852, for the murder of his wife. During the trial it was revealed that he had a mistress by whom he had eight children. He did not hang, but was transported for life, probably to Australia, where he would have encountered many of his fellow Irishmen.

The Kirwan pedigree is long and interesting; they were great travellers. Over fifty years ago a very good family tree was compiled by **Lieutenant Commander Denis A.R. Kirwan** and **Sir John Waters Kirwan**, both of whom feature in *Burke's Landed Gentry of Ireland*. The Kirwans were soldiers, merchants, clerics, lawyers, scientists and administrators. Their name crops up as explorers from the Polar ice caps to the Australian outback, with the pyramids of Egypt in between.

An offshoot of the Cregg Castle lineage is mentioned in *Who's Who* as: "**Sir Archibald Laurence (Patrick) Kirwan**, KCMG, CMG, TD, B. Litt, OXON, Director and Secretary, Royal Geographical Society since 1945, explorer, editor, archaeologist, excavations historical, political geography, traveller", a good example of the peripatetic Kirwans.

Unlike many prominent families, the Kirwans did not build outstanding castles. They captured Castlehacket in County Galway from the Norman Hacket family and it has been rebuilt several times. It is now a Georgian mansion with windows looking towards Cnoch Ma, reputed to be the mountain home of King Finbarre and his Connacht fairies, the legendary protectors of the Kirwans of Castlehacket. It was inherited by a scholarly Kirwan descendant, Percy Paley, who died in 1985. He built up a vast library with special emphasis on genealogy. When the house was sold in 1986 there was an auction lasting several days.

Though the Kirwan family has spread throughout the world, their mainspring has always been County Galway. In Galway city, close to the Great Southern Hotel in Eyre Square, there is a government office which was once a Kirwan house, on which their arms are carved in grey limestone. A tomb at Killanin, near Ross just outside Galway, bears the arms of the Martins of Ross and the Kirwan family, signifying a union long ago within the Fourteen Tribes of the port of Galway which once traded with all Europe.

de Lacy

de Léis

The de Lacys sailed from Lasy in Normandy with William I to conquer England at the battle of Hastings in 1066. They then crossed to Ireland where their military prowess was richly rewarded by King Henry II. He granted **Hugh de Lacy** (d. 1186) 800,000 acres, which belonged to the O Melaghlins and covered almost the whole of the Irish midlands. He made him a lord and viceroy of Ireland.

Hugh de Lacy got on well with the Irish and his second marriage was to Rose, daughter of King Roderick O Conor of Connacht. Henry II soon began to suspect him of royal ambitions, which he put a stop to by sending over his son, Prince John. Hugh built many castles, including the magnificent Trim Castle by the River Boyne. Today it is a dramatic ruin enclosed by a 500-yard outer wall, inside which there is a collection of fascinating buildings. The castle is a focal point for Anglo-Irish history: it was where the army of Edward Bruce halted on its retreat from Munster and where Richard II imprisoned the youth who was later to become Henry V. When Hugh de Lacy demolished the venerated abbey at Durrow to build a castle for himself, his head was chopped off by an outraged Gael.

Hugh was succeeded by his eldest son, **Walter de Lacy** (d. 1241), and his second son, **Hugh de Lacy**, drove one of the earlier Norman conquerors, John de Courci, from Downpatrick in Ulster and acquired all his lands. Hugh was made Earl of Ulster, the first honorary title that the English created in Ireland. There was constant war between the de Lacys and the king's men and eventually King John expelled Walter from Meath, and he went to Scotland, followed by Hugh. The brothers are believed to have met up again in a monastery, where for a while they did manual labour before joining a crusade against the heretical Albigensians in France. Hugh later managed to sneak back to Ireland to join up with O Neill and together they laid waste much of Leinster. When Hugh died he was buried at Carrickfergus and his grand Ulster title reverted to the Crown. This most turbulent man left no male heirs—they had all been killed in battle.

There were some prominent de Lacy clerics, such as **Thomas Lacy**, who was a Prior of Kells in County Meath in about 1507 and **Reverend Hugh Lacy** (d. 1581), who was Bishop of Limerick from 1557 to 1571, when he was imprisoned by Queen Elizabeth, but, in the main, they were men of the sword. **Pierce Lacy** was executed in 1607 because of his activities against the Elizabethan usurpers. Because of his membership of the Supreme Council of the Confederate Catholics, **Colonel John Lacy** was excluded from the amnesty granted following William III's decisive siege of Limerick in 1691.

Among the numerous Lacy papers of that period is a charter of **Walter de Lasci**, "remitting to the citizens of Chester the customary two pence paid by them over a cargo of white corn in his land in Ireland, with liberty to the said citizens to enter and lease his part of Drochda, free of duty".

The history of the de Lacys, from their arrival in Ireland in the twelfth century right up to the eighteenth century, is a predominantly military one. Following the Treaty of Limerick, an estimated 19,000 men-at-arms joined the "Wild Geese" in their flight to Europe where their military genius earned them lasting fame.

Count Peter Lacy (1678–1751) of Killedy, County Limerick, was only twelve when, with other members of his family, he fought against the Williamite army at the siege of Limerick. Following the capitulation he

Lacey

Lacy

de Lasci

Ó Laitheasa

Count Peter Lacy

sailed with Sarsfield's troops to France to join the Irish Brigade. His father and his two older brothers were killed, and, in 1697, when the peace of Ryswick disbanded the Athlone Regiment of the Irish Brigade, Peter Lacy went into service with Peter the Great, Czar of Russia. The Czar selected him to train his Grand Musketeers, 100 Russian nobles equipped at their own expense.

He reorganized the Russian army and instilled it with a spirit of discipline and duty, which may well have enabled the Russians to defeat the King of Sweden's invading army. He served under five eighteenth-century sovereigns and much of his success was owed to never involving himself in Court intrigue. After fifty years of campaigning, fighting on land and sea, he retired, aged 73, to his estates at Segewold, close to Riga on the Baltic coast, where he had once been governor. He had five daughters and two sons. Described as the most famous military man in Europe, he is credited with having converted the Russian military force from one of the worst in Europe to one of the best. As recently as 1891, a division was named after him in Russia.

His son, **Count Franz Moritz Lacy** (1725–1801), was born at St Petersburgh and received a military education in Germany. His father entrusted him to the care of a distant kinsman, Count Maximilian Browne, an Austrian Field Marshal. He served in the War of the Austrian Succession and, at the age of 25, he was a full colonel. He saw service in the Seven Years' War. The Empress of Austria, Marie Theresa, regarded him very highly and so too did her son and heir, Joseph II. Lacy reached the peak of his career when, in 1766, he was made a Field Marshal and president of the Court War Council. He resigned in 1774, but continued for many more years to work a fourteen hour day. In *The Irish Sword* (vol. XII, No. 45), Christopher Duffy describes him as "undisputed master of the military machine". When the Emperor Leopold was installed, Lacy's interest waned. His temperament could not cope with the violence of the 1790s. He had many interests, and on his estate in the Vienna Woods he planned what was probably the first European garden based on an English style of landscaping. A liberal man, he was well ahead of his time in that his park was open to the public.

Count Franz Moritz Lacy

Francis Anthony Lacy (1731–92) was the son of an Irish officer who had gone to Spain with the Duke of Berwick, James II's natural son. Lacy served in the Irish infantry in the Regiment of Ultonia and he commanded the artillery at the siege of Gibraltar in 1779. His imposing personality, fortified by a ready wit, were the credentials that sent him as Spanish minister and plenipotentiary to the courts of Stockholm and St Petersburgh. He was highly thought of in Spain, and was employed in responsible military posts. In 1789, he was appointed Governor and Count General of Catalonia.

General Count Maurice de Lacy (1740–1820), a member of the same family as Count Peter Lacy, was born in Limerick during the great frost of 1740, which killed an estimated 400,000 people. No doubt it was family influence that got him a commission in the Russian army where he took part in Turkish and French campaigns. He had reached the rank of general when he visited Limerick between 1792 and 1793, and made provision for his immediate family, to whom he is said to have left a fortune. Following his death at his palace at Augustowek, a chancery suit was begun and continued until 1847, in a vain effort to recover the bequest.

Count Maurice's sister, **Mary de Lacy**, married Terence O Brien in Ireland. Their son, Patrick O Brien (1790–1870), went to Russia to join his uncle as the adoptive heir of the Russian de Lacys. He became **Patrick**

Count O Brien de Lacy. His title was recognized by the Russian government.

The ancestral estates at Ballingarry, Bruff and Bruree in County Limerick were divided, mostly among the many de Lacy heiresses.

There are still de Lacys in Russia. The Hermitage Museum in St Petersburg contains two portraits of Count Peter Lacy which are much in need of restoration.

Patrick Count O Brien de Lacy's descendants are numerous and prominent in Poland, where they participated in Poland's wars of liberation. The Polish de Lacys lost all their property in the Second World War. Some have remained in Poland, while another part of the family is living in Argentina.

In County Wexford, a Gaelic name, Ó Flaithgheasa (*flaith* meaning prince), which changed to Ó Laitheasa, was Anglicized to Lacy. It is possible that this was the family of **Brigadier–General Denis Lacy** of Tipperary, who fought as a Republican in the Civil War in Ireland in 1920 and was killed in action.

The Lacys are still very numerous in Ireland, particularly around Dublin and the south. If they did emigrate to the Americas or Australia, they have yet to gain prominence there.

Maurice Count O Brien Lacy, Princess Droutschkaia and family in Poland in 1925. The Count was a descendant of Patrick Count O Brien de Lacy

Lynch
ó loingsigh

Blosse Lynch

de Lench

Linch

Longseach

Lynchehan

Ó Loingseacháin

O Lynch

Lynch was not always the short, simple Irish surname that it is today. First there was the legendary **Labradh Longseach**, monarch of Ireland for eighteen years from 541 BC. Undoubtedly a sea-warrior—*longseach* means mariner—his name lingers on in a variety of spellings: Ó Loingsigh, Linch, Ó Loingseacháin, Lynchehan. A number of distinct clans with lands in almost every province of Ireland bear the name.

The Lynches stem from two totally separate roots. The foremost bearers of this numerous name were originally called de Lench, and arrived 800 years ago with the Normans. Some believe that they came from the city of Lintz in Austria, and that they might have had Charlemagne as an ancestor. The lynx on their crest—a sharp-sighted animal—signifies the vigilance of a forebear, a Governor of Lintz who put up a strong defence when that city was under siege.

In the fifteenth century these Norman Lynches became one of the most powerful of "The Fourteen Tribes of Galway". These prominent families were cultured, prosperous merchants who traded with Europe and kept their territories secure by intermarriage. Galway was once a walled town. In medieval times it was impossible for a man of means to exist without fortifications; he had the choice between a walled town or a castle. **Sir Robert Lynch**, 4th Baronet (*c.* 1691), owned Corundalla Castle, and **Nicholas Lynch** (*c.* 1673) owned nearby Annaghdown Castle. Connacht is rich in castles, for they were a necessity in the west of Ireland far longer than in the rest of Europe.

One of the finest surviving Lynch castles is in narrow Shop Street in Galway, where it has been converted into a branch of the Allied Irish Bank. There are Lynch memorials everywhere in this small city, on ancient stone doorways and on tombstones, and especially in the Collegiate Church of St Nicholas, which the Lynch family built in 1320. On an outside wall there is a Lynch memorial window and it is near here, in 1493, that **Major James Lynch Fitzstephens** is supposed to have hung his son Walter who, in a jealous rage, had killed a visiting Spaniard.

From 1484, when **Dominic Lynch** was given the city's first charter by Richard III of England, until 1654, when Roman Catholics were declared outcasts, there were 84 mayors of Galway named Lynch.

In 1566, **Dominic Lynch** founded the free school at Galway. It was here that a kinsman, **Alexander Lynch**, gathered together 1,200 scholars from all over Ireland, developing a great school of classical and Irish learning. Here, too, his son **John Lynch** (1599–1673), a historian, received "the beginnings of his erudition". Ordained a Jesuit, John was compelled to become a fugitive priest until the rebellion of 1641 which temporarily eased religious intolerance. He was appointed Archdeacon of Tuam, but was soon forced to escape to France. He translated Keating's *History*, and wrote *Cambrensis Eversus*, a valuable work on Irish history designed to correct the calumnies written about Ireland by Giraldus Cambrensis (*see* Barry), a French cleric who came with the Normans.

In the Middle Ages the port of Galway conducted a flourishing trade with Spain and France. Many Lynches were educated abroad, some entering the priesthood, others the services or government, but these records are not as well-preserved as religious records.

Richard Lynch, who was born in Galway in the early 1600s, went to Santiago de Compostella in Spain where he studied for the Jesuit order.

He became rector of the Irish College in Seville in 1637. An outstanding theologian, he published many important works and died in 1676, in Salamanca.

Dr Dominic Lynch, also of Galway, joined the Dominican order at Seville and, from 1674, was Professor of Theology there. Later he presided over the Dominicans in Rome. In Paris he published a large collection of works on philosophy and died there in 1697.

Despite imprisonment and poverty, **James Lynch** (*c.* 1608–1713), Archbishop of Tuam, managed to administer his diocese, sometimes from abroad. He was, at different times, chaplain to Charles II of Spain and to James II of England. He died in the Irish College in Paris at the age of 105. He and other highly intellectual people, forced to follow careers outside their own country, serve as a reminder of what was lost to Irish culture during the years of religious and national suppression.

A Lynch family, originally from Galway, settled in Mayo and, through marriage, added Blosse to their Lynch patronymic. In the nineteenth century, several of the eleven sons of **Henry Blosse Lynch** achieved lasting recognition as explorers. **Captain Henry Blosse Lynch** (1807–73) of Partry House, Ballinrobe, joined the Indian navy at sixteen. He had an aptitude for languages which helped towards his rapid promotion and appointment as second in command to Colonel F. R. Chesney of County Down. After Chesney's return to England, Blosse Lynch went on to explore the River Tigris in Persia and was the first to navigate it as far as Baghdad. He was a commodore in the Indian navy before retiring to make his home in Paris. For his help in negotiating peace following the Persian war in 1857, the Shah awarded him the highest class of the Order of the Lion and Sun.

Thomas Kerr Lynch, a graduate of Trinity College, Dublin, joined his older brother, Captain Henry Lynch, in a second expedition along the River Euphrates. Thomas founded a business in Baghdad and developed a popular River Tigris steamer service. For generations the Blosse Lynch family have been extensive landowners in County Mayo. Their Partry home was sold in 1990.

Quite distinct from the Norman Lynches of County Galway, the Gaelic Ó Loingsigh, also Lynch, come from a number of septs, mostly in counties Clare, Sligo and Limerick, though some branched north to County Donegal and south to County Cork.

Through the centuries there were many distinguished prelates from all branches of the Lynch family. **Alan O Lynch** (*c.* 1411), the Dominican Prior of Killaloe, came from County Sligo, and the linguist and Gaelic scholar **Patrick Lynch** (1757–1818) came from County Clare. **Dr John Joseph Lynch** (1816–88) from Clones, County Monaghan, emigrated to Canada and became Bishop of Toronto, while another Lynch, also from Clones, emigrated at the age of one with his parents and became Bishop of Charleston, South Carolina. During the American Civil War he suffered many disasters and at one time had to minister to 10,000 Catholic refugees. In 1863 Dr Lynch went to Rome with a letter from Jefferson Dane expressing the desire of the Confederacy for peace, but returning from Rome he found his diocese in ruins. He went north to collect alms to promote reconciliation between north and south, and was known as the ambassador of goodwill.

Driven out by the Cromwellians, many Lynches went to Europe, mostly to France, to join the services, the legal and medical professions, or to enter commerce. **Count Jean Baptiste Lynch** (1749–1835), a descendant of Irish *émigrés*, was Mayor of Bordeaux and a Jacobite, and lost much

Count Jean Baptiste Lynch

of his property during the French Revolution. However, he managed to retrieve his inheritance and founded a wine business. This is no longer in the family, but the claret bottled at Château Lynch-Bages near Bordeaux is appreciated by wine connoisseurs. Although his family were royalists, **Isidore Lynch** (1755–1841) joined the republicans and fought in the Napoleonic wars, commanding the infantry at the first battle of Valmy when they defeated the Prussians.

As a result of the mass emigration following the Famine of 1846 to 1848, an Irish colony grew up in Argentina where, mostly in Buenos Aires, there were Browns, Dillons, Sheridans, Lynches and a host of others of Irish origin. **Patrick Lynch** (1824–86), like many another Irish youth, left his home to join the British army. He eventually settled into a new career in South America, where in time he was transformed to "Patricio Lynch the foremost Chilian naval hero."

That notorious Irish courtesan, **Madame Elizabeth Lynch**, was the wife of Francisco Lopez II of Paraquay, son of a hereditary dictator. During the twelve years before her father-in-law's death, she lived like royalty in Asunción and showed every hospitality to visitors from Europe. The wars between Paraquay, Argentina and Brazil brought an end to the good life, and her husband and young sons were killed. Elizabeth Lynch escaped and ended her days in England.

A descendant of the expatriate Argentinian Lynches was none other than the Cuban Communist revolutionary, **Ernesto "Che" Lynch Guevara** (1928–67). He was executed in Bolivia.

Innumerable Lynches found new homes in the United States of America. **Colonel Charles Lynch** (1736–96), whose family had been in the United States for several generations, was a descendant of the chiefs of Dalriada in north Antrim. He was an administrator of such rough justice to those under his command that he gave his name to the phrase "lynch law". **Thomas Lynch** (1749–79), whose family was three generations removed from Ireland and were rich plantation owners, was the youngest of the signatories of the Declaration of Independence.

Dominic Lynch (d. 1837) was of the lineage that had given 84 mayors to Galway. His father, a merchant of Galway also called **Dominic**, opened a commercial house in Bruges to send flax seed back to Galway, and in 1785 he sailed to America, where he prospered. He sent his son to Ireland and France for his education. The younger Dominic Lynch went into the wine importing business, introducing château-bottled wines from France. He was a gourmet and an elegant man who raised the social standards of New York. He had a home in Greenwich and a mansion in Westchester which he inherited from his father. His interest in music made his home a focal point for American society and he introduced grand opera to the United States. He travelled to Europe to select an opera company and made sure that they were well looked after on tour. He also helped many musicians and actors, including Fanny Kemble. He died in Paris and was mourned in America as "the greatest swell and beau New York had ever known".

The Lynches were among the many Irish people who made the long voyage south to Australia, not always of their own free will. **John Lynch** (*c.* 1841) was a stonemason who probably landed in Australia on a convict ship. He became an opponent of assisted migrants, convict labour for public works, and the importation of coolies. He was active in Catholic lay affairs and was an important figure in the operatives' political movement in the 1840s. "One of the few manual workers capable of speaking for the workman", one newspaper journalist wrote of John Lynch.

The house of Dominic Lynch in Galway

Arthur Lynch (1861–1934) had a Scottish mother and an Irish father who fought at the Eureka Stockade. He had a wide-ranging education, graduating from the University of Melbourne in the arts, civil engineering and also acquiring a degree in medicine. He studied science and psychology in Berlin and then got into journalism in London. He next tried his hand at politics in Ireland, where, in 1892, he was unsuccessful as a Parnellite candidate.

From journalism in Paris he went on to South Africa where, as Colonel Lynch, he organized a troop of Irishmen to fight with the Boers. In his absence, in 1901, he was elected a nationalist candidate in Ireland. Returning home via London he was arrested, tried for treason and narrowly escaped hanging. An extraordinarily versatile man, in 1909 he became a Member of Parliament for West Clare in the British House of Commons. He was reinstated to the rank of colonel and sent by the British government to Ireland to seek recruits for the allied cause in the First World War. This was one of his failures.

He retired to London where he practised medicine and wrote an astonishing variety of books, from poetry to a refutation of Einstein's theory of relativity. Little wonder that Arthur Lynch has been described as having a touch of Don Quixote.

In Ireland, one of the more prominent Lynches of the nineteenth century was an outstanding Dublin woman, Hannah Lynch (1862–1904). She played a large part, while still very young, in the Ladies Land League, which had been formed to counter the evictions resulting from the Land War of the 1880s. Hannah's activities led to her having to flee to France. She took with her the metal type for her Land League publications, which she continued printing from Paris. She settled in France and wrote many novels and travel books.

Liam Lynch (1890–1923) took part in the 1916 rising and was a divisional commander. He was chief of staff in the Republican army during the Civil War and was killed in action.

Stanislaus Lynch (1907–83) was born in County Cavan and wrote authoritatively on hunting and the Irish horse. His work has been translated into many languages and he has received Olympic Diplomas for Literature.

In the twentieth century, the arts and politics have been illuminated by three Lynches from Cork. Patricia Lynch (1897–1972) was a leading writer of children's stories; Charles Lynch (d. 1984) was a doyen of Irish concert pianists; Jack Lynch (b. 1917), winner of six All-Ireland medals—five for hurling and one for Gaelic football—was leader of the Fianna Fáil party and was Taoiseach (Prime Minister) for two terms in the 1970s.

Château Lynch wine label

MacCabe
mac cába

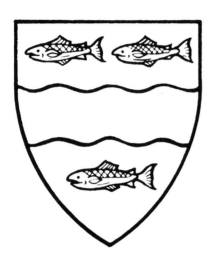

In medieval Ireland few chieftains would have considered themselves secure without the protection of Scottish fighting men, and, until the sixteenth century, they were the strong arm of Irish warfare. These mercenaries, or gallowglasses, as the Irish called them, came from the Hebrides. The MacCabes came from Inis Gall—Isle of the Norsemen—as captains of gallowglasses to the O Rourkes and the O Reillys of Breifne, now the counties of Leitrim and Cavan. They may have been a branch of the Scottish MacLeods and they have earned frequent mention in the *Annals of the Four Masters*. Today the MacCabes are a numerous family and are still predominant in the north-west counties of Ireland. In Irish the name is Mac Cába—*cába* meaning a cap or a hood—and it was probably this distinctive headdress, as depicted on a tomb in Roscommon Abbey, which gave rise to the MacCabe name.

Cathaoir MacCabe (d. 1740), who was born at Mullagh in County Cavan, was a very popular bard. His great friend, the blind Turlough O Carolan (1670–1738), the most renowned of Irish harpists, was not only a musician but also a composer and poet. Some of his manuscripts are preserved in the British Museum Library. When O Carolan died, Cathaoir MacCabe, who survived him by only two years, wrote a most beautiful lament. Coincidentally, O Carolan had himself once written an elegy for Cathaoir, having been hoaxed into believing him dead.

Thomas MacCabe, born in the eighteenth century in Belfast, was a watchmaker as well as part-owner of a cotton mill. He was also a humanitarian and was largely responsible for stopping greedy Belfast merchants fitting out their ships for the lucrative slave trade.

His son, **William Putnam MacCabe** (1776–1821), is the best-recorded of all the MacCabes. Born in Belfast, he was an active member of the United Irishmen leading up to the time of the 1798 rising. He is supposed to have been one of Lord Edward FitzGerald's bodyguards. His aptitude for disguise and mimicry helped him evade the law. A Wexford gentleman who knew him well testified that he could never recognize William until he revealed his identity. Following the 1798 rising he was captured, but managed to persuade the Scottish soldiers who guarded him that he was their fellow countryman. Thinking that they had wrongly arrested him, he was released! However, now that Lord Edward FitzGerald was dead and the United Irishmen had been defeated, he had no future in Ireland. He went to France where, using knowledge inherited from his father, he established a cotton mill near Rouen in Normandy. He died in Paris aged only 45.

Edward MacCabe (1816–85), who was Dublin-born, studied for the priesthood at Maynooth College. The vast granite church off the main street in Dun Laoghaire, County Dublin, is a monument to his parochial activity. It was accidentally burned down in 1965, but has been handsomely rebuilt in the modern idiom. Edward MacCabe became Archbishop of Dublin in 1879 and, three years later, a cardinal. He was something of a thorn in the side of patriots who were agitating for the removal of the restrictive laws regarding ownership of land. It has been said of him that he failed to appreciate the importance of the issue.

Many nineteenth-century romances flowed from the pen of **William Bernard MacCabe** (1801–91), a Dublin journalist. **Charles Caldwell MacCabe** (1836–1906), grandson of a County Tyrone immigrant to

America, became a Protestant bishop nicknamed "Chaplain MacCabe" during the Civil War.

Alasdair Mac Cába (1886–1972), born in County Sligo, was principal of a Sligo school when he was elected a member of the supreme council of the Irish Republican Brotherhood in 1914. He played an active part in the struggle for independence and, afterwards, in the Civil War. He gave up politics and, in 1935, with £500 and the support of his fellow teachers, founded the still flourishing Educational Building Society, of which he was the first managing director.

Eugene MacCabe (b. 1920) successfully combines farming in Clones, County Monaghan, with playwriting. He is the author of many Abbey Theatre plays. *The King of the Castle* was the most popular production of the 1954 Dublin Theatre Festival, and it has been followed by several more successes.

The distinctive cap or hood that gave rise to the MacCabe name is depicted on a tomb in Roscommon Abbey

MacCarthy

mac cárthaigh

Cotty

Macartie

MacCartney

Of all the Irish surnames with the prefix Mac, the most numerous is MacCarthy, especially in counties Tipperary, Cork and Kerry. As well as being an ancient name, it is also an eminent one. The MacCarthys claim ancestry back to the third century, to Oilioll Olum, King of Munster, who had three sons: Cormac Cas, Eoghan and Cian. The descendants of Eoghan became the rulers of South Munster and were known as the Eoghanacht. One of their lords was **Cárthach**, meaning the loving one, although the Lonergans who set fire to his house in 1045 and burned him alive inside it must have thought otherwise! From this time on his offspring were known as MacCarthy, which means the son of Cárthach. As time went by, this name developed as many as twenty variations, from Macartie in France to Cotty in Ireland.

Muiredach Mac Cárthaig (1012–*c.* 1092), King of Munster, was succeeded by his son **Cormac** (d. 1138), who was not only King of Munster, but also a bishop. For centuries, until the arrival of St Patrick, the spectacular Rock of Cashel had been the seat of the Munster kings. In 1101, King Murtagh O Brien granted it to the Church. Here, between 1122 and 1138, Cormac built what is known to this day as Cormac's chapel. Its design demonstrates Irish awareness of Continental trends.

When Cormac died he was buried at Cashel. A century ago, when his tomb was opened, the ancient crozier of Lismore, which is thought to have been Cormac's, was found. It is now in the National Museum. The London Museum has a rare Elizabethan transcript of a charter granted to **King Dermod**, son of Cormac MacCarthy. These princely MacCarthys built splendid castles all over their Munster territory, at Muckross, Macroom, Killaha, Mourne, Timoleague, Srugrena, Kanturk and many more.

Four personal names stand out in the MacCarthy lineage, Saorbhreathach which became Justin, Fineen Anglicized to Florence, Donal and Cormac. In about 1446, one of these Cormac MacCarthys, **Cormac Laidir** (the strong), Lord of Muskerry, built the enduring Blarney Castle. Although he fought with the English against the local FitzGeralds, **Cormac MacDermot MacCarthy** struggled to preserve his own territory. He put off Queen Elizabeth's demands for his allegiance with what she described as "fair words and soft speech"—pleasant talk intended to deceive without offending, which is how the Blarney stone acquired its reputation for imparting eloquence to those who succeed in kissing it.

A family tradition holds that the Blarney stone is a piece of the "Stone of Destiny"—the inauguration stone of the kings of Scotland, sent by King Robert Bruce to the MacCarthy kings of Desmond. They were to give it to Robert's brother, Edward, who attempted to become High King of Ireland by driving out the English.

In the early 1600s, the fierce **MacDonagh MacCarthy**, Lord of Duhallow, was building an enormously strong castle at Kanturk, County Cork. There is a tradition in the area that MacDonagh forced wayfarers to work on this castle until they dropped dead, and that he even had their blood mixed with the mortar. Whatever the truth of this, the castle was certainly considered to be cursed. When MacDonagh asked his stepbrother, **Macauliffe**, who had the gift of second sight, to prophesy its future, the seer replied, "It is too good for the crows to live in. It will never be finished". The local English settlers, feeling it to be a threat, had the building stopped. In a terrible rage MacDonagh MacCarthy smashed in the glass tiled roof, an innovation for its time. Today the shell remains as an eerie reminder of bygone times.

In 1565, **Donal MacCarthy Mór** (died *c.* 1596) of the senior branch of the family, was created Earl of Clancarthy by Queen Elizabeth, despite the fact that the MacCarthys were engaged in continuous fighting for land and power, sometimes with the English but more often against them.

Little has been recorded of the MacCarthy women, although a **Lady Eleanor MacCarthy** is revered because she protected Gerald FitzGerald following the murder of his five uncles by Henry VIII in the Tower of London in 1537.

Florence (Fineen) MacCarthy Reagh (1562–1640), Lord of Carbery in Munster, was rewarded by Elizabeth for serving the Crown against his neighbours, the FitzGeralds of Desmond. Florence caused suspicion, however, by secretly marrying his kinswoman the Lady Ellen, the daughter and sole heiress of Donal MacCarthy Mór, at a midnight ceremony in Muckross Abbey. Deeming this union between the two main branches of the Clan Carthy to be a threat to her Munster sovereignty, the Queen committed Florence to the Tower of London. She trumped up a treason charge against him, accusing him of connivance with the Spanish, so that Florence was in and out of the Tower of London for the next 37 years. He has been described as a man of heroic stature and benevolent aspect. Fortunately he was also a scholar, and during his incarcerations he wrote a learned history of Ireland, though it had to wait 200 years for publication. In his later years he had little affection for the Lady Ellen who had borne him four sons, so much then for their romantic midnight marriage!

From the twelfth to the sixteenth century the MacCarthys ruled as Princes of Desmond, South Munster. The grand titles bestowed on them by Elizabeth were forfeited for their part in the later Jacobite wars, and they were driven out to put their military skills to use in Europe, Africa and America.

Justin MacCarthy (d. 1694) was the third son of **Donal MacCarthy**, 1st Earl of Clancarthy, and Lady Eleanor Butler, a sister of James, Duke of Ormond. Justin served in Louis XIV's campaigns, but, following the English Restoration, he returned to Ireland to join James II in his attempt to oust the Williamites. James created him Viscount Mountcashel in 1689 and subsequently Duke of Clancarthy. Louis XIV lured him back to France, where he formed the Irish Brigade. Justin was wounded many times in the wars both in Ireland and France and, in 1694, he retired to the Pyrenees to recuperate, but died there. Lacking an heir, Justin had adopted his cousin, **Florence Callaghan MacCarthy** of the Carrignavar sept.

The 3rd Duc de Clancarthy, **Callaghan MacCarthy**, was an officer in the Irish Brigade and a Knight of the Order of St Louis. He fell at the battle of Fontenoy in 1745. The 7th Duc de Clancarthy, **Pol MacCarthy**, served with Napoleon III as a lieutenant in the Franco-Prussian war of 1870. He was created a Knight of the Royal Order of Christ of Portugal. He left no male heirs.

Governing came naturally to the MacCarthys. **Charles MacCarthy** (d. 1792), who commanded a regiment in the service of the King of Portugal, was appointed Governor of Miranda in 1790. **Charlotte MacCarthy** was descended from the Lords of Cashmany who had fled to France with James II. In 1764 she married Jean Gabriel Gueroult. **Sir Charles MacCarthy** (d. 1824), her eldest son, was adopted by his uncle, **Charles Thaddeus MacCarthy**, whose name he assumed.

Justin MacCarthy (d. 1694)

Sir Charles served in the Berwick Regiment in the Irish Brigade until the French Revolution, when he transferred to the English service. In 1812 he was appointed Lieutenant-Governor of Sierra Leone and Governor in Chief of Senegal. He was promoted to brigadier-general of the West Coast of Africa but was killed a few years later by the Ashanti. He had worked wholeheartedly against the injustice of slavery and is commemorated by an island named after him off the West African coast.

In the eighteenth century a MacCarthy was Governor of Madras and in the nineteenth century **Sir Charles Justin MacCarthy** was Governor of Ceylon.

In France the MacCarthys distinguished themselves in the army and in the Church. The **Abbé Nicholas Tuite MacCarthy**, who died in Annecy in 1833, was a magnificent preacher. **Count Justine MacCarthy** (d. 1812) of Tipperary, who settled in Toulouse, was renowned for his library, which was said to have been worthy of a sovereign.

Not until 1896 did a MacCarthy attain beatification. This was **Blessed Thaddeus MacCarthy**, Bishop of Cork and Cloyne, who died in 1492 after a long and hopeless struggle against religious and political intrigue in Ireland. His body lies under the high altar in the Cathedral of Ivrea, Italy, where he died on his way home.

Diarmuid MacCarthy (c. 1630–1715) of Cork was probably a graduate of the famous Blarney Academy of Poetry of which he later became president. Alas, these were cruel times for the arts. The "Wild Geese" had fled and there was little money or regard for poets. When Diarmuid's horse died, there was no patron to pay for replacing it and so he was prevented from travelling. He wrote a tragic poem about his fate, a fate shared by all of the hereditary poets at the end of the Gaelic era, including his kinsman **Eoghan MacCarthy** (1691–1756), also of Cork, a prolific poet in both Irish and English. In more recent times, **Denis Florence MacCarthy** (d. 1882) was born in Dublin and held the chair of English Literature and Poetry at the Catholic University of Ireland.

Justin MacCarthy (1830–1912) came from a poverty-stricken family near Cork. He became a journalist, working in Cork, Liverpool and London. His early novels and biographies were reasonably successful and he eventually made history his speciality. He served in the Irish Party under Parnell and was Member of Parliament for County Longford. Overwork in both politics and literature wrecked his health and ruined his eyesight. He had to use dictation for the last fifteen years of his life.

Having been prolific builders in earlier days, it is not surprising that the MacCarthys should have produced a leading architect of the nineteenth century. **J.J. MacCarthy**, who designed St Patrick's Church in Armagh and many others throughout the country, has been described as the Irish Pugin. He also designed some fine country mansions, including Cahirmoyle in Limerick and, for the Earls of Granard, Castle Forbes in County Longford.

In the 1950s, after a determined search lasting over a century, a branch of the MacCarthy Reagh family was traced to Montreal, Canada. **D'Alton McCarthy** (1836–98) emigrated to Canada from Blackrock, County Dublin, with his parents in 1845. He made his reputation as a barrister and Queen's Counsel. He left the Conservative party and became an independent over the issue of the Jesuits' Estate Act. He was a supporter of the Equal Rights movement in Toronto.

For generations innumerable MacCarthys have emigrated to the USA, including many lawyers, priests and missionaries. **Charles MacCarthy** (1873–1921) was a political scientist, publicist and educationalist. He

Justin MacCarthy (1830–1912)

trained to become an outstanding inter-collegiate football player, while graduating in political science from the University of Wisconsin. He worked fruitfully with a succession of American presidents.

Colonel Daniel E. MacCarthy was the first American soldier to set foot in France in 1917. When he landed there he found a letter of welcome from Pol MacCarthy, 7th and last Duc de Clancarthy.

Eugene McCarthy was Senator for Minnesota from 1958 to 1970. Munster ancestry could well be claimed by **Senator Joseph MacCarthy** (1909–57), the investigator of Communists, and **Mary MacCarthy** (1912–89) the writer.

Australia undoubtedly harbours many a MacCarthy. **Denis McCarthy** sailed for Sydney in 1800 on the *Friendship*, following his capture during the 1798 rebellion. When he drowned in mysterious circumstances twenty years later, the *Hobart Town Gazette* described him as "a man with a speculative turn who had been the owner of three vessels and had acquired considerable land and other property".

Some MacCarthys travelled no further across the sea than England. In the eighteenth century, conditions for the seamen aboard Royal Navy ships were not good. In 1798, during the Napoleonic wars, **John MacCarthy** led the mutiny aboard HMS *Inflexible*, leaving the fleet no option other than to sail into enemy ports in France and Spain. King George III intervened, and thereafter conditions improved aboard the ships.

Lillah MacCarthy (1875–1960) was for decades a popular dramatic actress. Bernard Shaw was one of her patrons. She gave a speech at the opening of the Shakespeare Memorial Theatre at Stratford-on-Avon, and wrote her memoirs, entitled *Myself and My Friends*.

Sir Desmond MacCarthy (1877–1952) was one of London's most formidable drama critics. He wrote for *The Sunday Times* from 1928 until his death.

Timothy MacCarthy had the exhausting experience of accompanying the explorer Sir Ernest Shackleton (1874–1922) in Antarctica. When the *Endurance* sank, he escaped with Shackleton in open boats and sailed 800 miles in icy seas to the relative safety of South Georgia Island.

McCartney and MacCartney are both variants of MacCarthy, the Scottish family founded by **Donal**, a grandson of **Cormac Fionn MacCarthy Mór**, King of Desmond (d. 1246).

Liverpool is a second home for many generations of Irish and Ireland could well claim a share in the fame of **Paul McCartney** of the famous pop group The Beatles, who was born there in 1942. In the twentieth century, Britain continues to honour worthy people of Irish extraction. In recognition of his services to industrial relations, Sir Harold Wilson conferred a peerage, in 1975, on **"Baron Bill" McCarthy** of Hedington. He was born in 1925, left school at 14, and is a research fellow at Nuffield College, Oxford.

In war and marriage the MacCarthys have been allied to most of the great Irish families. The beautiful Muckross estate of MacCarthy Mór at Killarney is now in the care of the State and is a splendid centre for the history and folk arts of Kerry. It is in a beautiful setting by the lakes of Killarney, close to the Abbey where Florence secretly married his kinswoman, the Lady Ellen.

Terence MacCarthy, who was born in Belfast in 1957 has been recognized by the Irish Genealogical Office as a chieftain of the MacCarthys and uses the designation MacCarthy Mór.

MacDermot
mac διαρμαδα

Dermody

Kermode

MacDermot-Roe

Mac Diarmuid

Mulrooney

The MacDermot lineage can be traced back to the seventh century, to **Muiredach Mullethan**, King of Connacht from AD 697 to 702. A descendant of his, **Conchobhar**, King of Connacht (d. 971), was a forebear of the O Conors, one of Ireland's most important royal families. His brother, **Maelruanaidh Mór**, Anglicized to Mulrooney, is described in the ancient annals as Prince of Moylurg. He was an independent warrior who established his own principality in the territory of Moylurg, in the present-day County Roscommon, which in due course expanded and became the patrimony of the MacDermots.

For five generations Mulrooney's descendants used the surname O Mulrooney. One of them, **Dermot**, King of Moylurg from 1124 to 1159, became sufficiently eminent for his descendants to adopt the surname MacDermot. Dermot or Diarmuid derives from *di* (meaning without) and *airmit* (meaning injunction), in other words a free man. When Dermot died in 1159, his son, styled MacDermot, handed on this enduring name to the powerful MacDermot family who, for centuries, owned so much territory in counties Roscommon and Sligo it became known as "MacDermot's Country".

The ancient Cistercian abbey of Boyle, founded in 1161, now a handsome ruin, was under the patronage of the MacDermots for a long time. The *Annals of the Four Masters* recorded thirteen heads of the family as having been buried there. Until its dissolution in the second half of the sixteenth century, it was the foremost religious establishment in Connacht.

Conor succeeded Dermot, and was in turn succeeded by **Tomaltach na Carraige** (Timothy of the rock). The rock on Lough Cé where Tomaltach built his fortress in 1204 is a place of legend. The fairy king, Cé, from whom the lake gets its name, was known as Nuadha of the Silver Arm and lived here in druidic times. He was king of the Tuatha de Danaan warriors and legend has it that he was drowned when the waters of Lough Cé burst forth from the earth.

In 1585, **Brian MacDermot**, Prince of Moylurg and a vigorous warrior in his youth, became chief of his name. Brian was patron and collaborator with the scribes who compiled the famous *Annals of Lough Cé*, a chronicle of Irish events from 1014 to 1590, now in Trinity College, Dublin. Brian married Maev, daughter of O Conor Sligo. Over the centuries the MacDermots married into the aristocratic Gaelic families of Connacht, including the three principal Norman families, the Burkes of Clanrickard, the MacWilliam Burkes of Mayo and the Burkes of Glinsk.

When Brian died in 1592, the inheritance of his son, also **Brian**, was put into wardship, as the boy was under age. In the Patent Rolls of 1606, in the reign of the Catholic James I, Brian is described as "Chief of his Name". In 1616 he is acknowledged legally to be lord of his various estates in Sligo, including his castle in the barony of Boyle, since renamed Rockingham. The patent setting out these possessions is a colourful work, covering sixteen parchment skins. Brian's marriage to Margaret Burke of Dermalcahny, County Galway, is recorded in a priceless document which is in the care of the head of the MacDermot family of Coolavin at Monasteraden, County Sligo.

In 1599, in the Curlew Mountains overlooking Boyle in the heart of MacDermot country, and on the main route linking Connacht with Donegal, Irish troops led by **Conor Óg MacDermot** and Brian Óg

O Rourke routed an English force under Sir Conyers Clifford. Guerrilla encounters excepted, this was the last defeat in battle of the English in Ireland. Sir Conyers Clifford, one of Queen Elizabeth's famous generals, is buried on Trinity Island, one of the many islands on Lough Cé, or Lough Key as it is known today.

Charles MacDermot, styled Cathal Roe (Charles the red) and Prince of Moylurg, was born when the powerful Gaelic families were being dispossessed by Elizabethan "adventurers". Because he favoured the Catholic Stuarts, Charles forfeited most of his properties, including his fortress on Lough Cé. He removed to Coolavin (Cuil O Finn, meaning refuge of the O Finns) on the shores of Lough Gara. It was Cathal's sister, Una, whose tragic love for Thomas Costello was immortalized in Douglas Hyde's *Love Songs of Connacht*. Thomas was heir to the Costellos, with whom the MacDermots were constantly at war. Her brother imprisoned Una on his island fortress to keep her away from Thomas. She fell into a deep sleep from which it seemed only Thomas could have aroused her. He tried to reach her, but was driven away. Time and again he tried to swim to her while she was dying, but eventually he drowned and they were buried together on the island.

The accession of King James II also meant the restoration to the MacDermots of their ancient territories. To show his gratitude, **Hugh Charles MacDermot** garrisoned Sligo town at his own expense. But by then James had led the Irish to defeat at the battle of the Boyne, where 4,000 Irish and 2,000 of King William of Orange's men were killed, and the following year at the battle of Aughrim in County Galway. Hugh was captured and was driven from Roscommon.

The MacDermots of Connacht are one of the rare septs to have been authenticated by the Irish Genealogical Office so that they can use the designation MacDermot, chief of the name. They are the only family in Ireland to have the added courtesy title of prince.

Hugh Hyacinth O Rorke MacDermot, Prince of Coolavin (1834–1904), was Solicitor General for Ireland, and Attorney-General and a member of the Privy Council in 1892. He had twelve children. His eighth son, **Frank MacDermot** (1886–1975), was a distinguished writer. Called to the English Bar in 1911, he campaigned for Home Rule, and fought in France during the First World War. Afterwards he won a seat for Roscommon and sat in the Dáil. He formed the National Centre Party, whose aim was to ease the strife between northern and southern Ireland and to work for unity through improving relations with Britain. He resigned when General Eoin O Duffy, who had fascist inclinations, took over the party leadership. In 1938, de Valera made him a Senator. By then he had turned to writing and was correspondent for *The Sunday Times*. Frustration with the censorship in neutral Ireland during the Second World War drove him to New York, and later to Paris. His biography of Wolfe Tone, published in 1939, has become a classic.

Frank MacDermot's nephew, **Charles John**, succeeded as MacDermot, Prince of Coolavin. He managed a rubber estate in Malaya and was a prisoner of the Japanese during the War. He died in 1979 and was succeeded by his brother, **Sir Dermot**, Prince of Coolavin (1906–89), whose knighthood was conferred on him when he was an ambassador in the British Diplomatic Service. He exemplified the numerous Irish who have attained high rank in the service of England without sacrificing an Irish identity and who retire to live in Ireland. His son **Niall** (b. 1935) is currently MacDermot, Prince of Coolavin.

Apart from the MacDermots who descend from the O Conor kings of Connacht, there were other septs, of which the principle one was MacDermott-Roe, chief of Tir-Tuathail, whose seat was Alderford in County Roscommon.

In 1605, **Conor MacDermott-Roe** had to surrender his lands of Camagh and Kilmactrany to the English king who claimed sovereignity over all the land of Ireland. To ensure his loyalty, the king returned these lands to Conor. Several decades later Conor's grandson, **Henry MacDermott-Roe,** or Henry Bachach (meaning lame), of Kilronan, County Roscommon, received a similar favour from Charles II. It was this family that changed the name of its castle at Ballyfarnan, near Boyle, from Camagh to Alderford. **Mrs MacDermott-Roe** is remembered because of her patronage of Turlough O Carolan, the last of the line of royal harpists. When he was blinded by smallpox at the age of 14, she took him into her household, looked after his education and gave him a home until he died in 1738. He is buried in the family vault at Kilronan.

The last MacDermott-Roe of Alderford died without a male heir early in this century and was buried in France, in Monte Carlo, where he had lived for many years. While the designation MacDermott-Roe is therefore now dormant, the surname is far from uncommon in Ireland.

Many of the family went far afield and, in earlier times, **Henry MacDermott** (1798–1848), of the sept that converted to the Protestant religion, made his career in Australia. His father was an officer in the British army and Henry went there with the 39th Regiment in 1827 and settled in Sydney. He started a business and was active in politics and municipal affairs. He was Mayor of Sydney in 1845 and was ahead of his time in his recognition of the importance of the labour movement.

The MacDermots spell their name in diverse ways. There is MacDermottroe, MacDiarmuid, MacDermot, Dermody and even Kermode, which comes from the aspirated Irish version of the name in Connacht. MacDermott is the most usual spelling in the USA. As they spread from the west of Ireland it is difficult to distinguish the identity of the various branches of the family, especially in the eighteenth century, when very many of them went to serve with the Irish regiments in France. Some went to England, and their names are recorded in army and navy lists in many areas of the developing British empire. The MacDermotts of Ramore, County Galway, had sons in both the armies of Austria and England. Archives in London, Paris and other European cities contain accounts of the MacDermots as well as some of their correspondence.

During the late nineteenth and early twentieth century there was an outburst of minor MacDermot poets, balladeers and writers, both at home and abroad. In America, **Peter Rowe MacDermot** fought in and wrote about the American Civil War. In 1920, in London, **Norman MacDermott** opened the famous Everyman Theatre in Hampstead, where worthwhile plays were given short runs so that young actors could have the valuable experience of acting in plays that had little hope of becoming expensive West End productions. The Everyman is now a cinema. In Ireland, **Ruari MacDiarmuda**, known as "Rory of the Hill", wrote in the romantic nationalistic vein popular in the 1920s.

In his youth, **Martin MacDermot** (1823–1905) was an ardent Young Irelander and contributed poems to the *Nation*. He became an architect and was commissioned by the Egyptian government to help with the rebuilding of Alexandria after the battle of Tel-el-Kebir in 1882.

A Dublin street is named after a famous twentieth-century MacDermot, a hero of the fight for independence. **Seán Mac Diarmada** (1884–1916)

Seán Mac Diarmada

112

was only 16 when he left his native Kiltyclogher, County Leitrim, for Glasgow and worked for a while on the electric trams before going on to Belfast. He mastered the Irish language and, when he returned home, became active in promoting the Republican movement. At 28 he was crippled by polio, but carried on with his propaganda and was on the military council that planned the 1916 rising. He was one of the seven signatories of the Proclamation of the Republic. He was involved in the fighting in the General Post Office in Dublin and was one of the fifteen who were cruelly executed between 3 and 12 May 1916.

Today the legendary Lough Key, once a MacDermot stronghold, is a popular recreation area. The estate, which had been acquired by the Stafford King Harmon family, was sold some years ago when their magnificent house was destroyed by an accidental fire. There is a Forest Park and a Wildlife Centre and boats for hire on the lake.

Rockingham Castle, Lough Key

MacGrath

ᵯᴀᴄ ᴄʀᴀɪᴛʜ

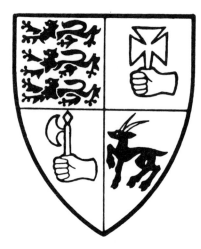

McGraw

Magrath

Magraw

MacGrath can be spelled in a variety of ways, although the pronunciation remains much the same. The Gaelic version is Mac Craith, meaning son of Raith, *raith* signifying either grace, or prosperity. The MacGraths are one of the 100 most numerous families and there could well be over 10,000 today in Ireland.

They spring from two distinct septs. The first is from counties Donegal and Fermanagh where its chiefs were the hereditary guardians of the monastery of St Daveog at Lough Derg. This sept's sixteenth century Castle Magrath is at nearby Pettigo.

The second sept comes from around Clare, in an area once known as Thomond—O Brien country. For centuries, these MacGraths were poets attached to the powerful O Briens and were responsible for recording their pedigrees as well as their battles. In the eleventh century, **John Mac Craith**, who wrote *The Wars of Turlough*, was their historian. **Andrew MacGrath** (d. 1790) was regarded highly as a poet, but his creativity was blunted by a fragile character and a wild nature. For many generations the MacGraths presided over the bardic school at Cahir.

Between 1391 and 1463, the diocese of Killaloe in County Clare had a succession of four McGrath bishops. Two centuries later a Magrath of the Donegal branch, gave the Magrath name lasting notoriety. **Miler Magrath** (*c.* 1523–1622), a Franciscan friar, was caught in the crossfire of the Reformation. He converted and became Anglican Archbishop of Cashel. Shortly after Elizabeth's death he held four bishoprics—Protestant as well as Catholic—and seventy livings and was twice married. He was an avaricious man and probably a paid informer for the English. He did not care about his numerous and dispersed flock. So shrewd an intriguer was Miler Magrath that no one dared censure him. He lived to be 100 and was buried in Cashel Cathedral.

Edmund Magrath, his grandson, acted as a spy from the beginning of the Irish Rebellion. For this he obtained a special letter of dispensation from Cromwell preventing transplantation from his lands and, in 1657, had orders to have his estate (in Ballymore), "not exceeding 800 acres Plantation measure", restored to him. Not thirty years after the death of the notorious Archbishop of Cashel, a very different and esteemed **Miler Magrath**, a Franciscan friar, died a martyr's death in 1650.

In *The Irish and Anglo-Irish Landed Gentry*, O Hart lists many Magraths whose lands were confiscated during Cromwell's plundering. There is the remains of a MacGrath castle just outside Waterford town where many of the family had settled.

The MacGraths were among the thousands who fled from the troubles in Ireland to find a new and more promising life in Europe—or further afield. In the National Library, Dublin, there are intriguingly brief references that throw some light on their social history. Archives in Paris contain receipts for pension payments and certificates of Catholicity, dated between 1752 and 1767, for **Françoise Thérèse MacGrath**, daughter of **Lieutenant-Colonel François MacGrath**.

Marsh's Library, Dublin, has extracts from a "Warrant of the Lord Deputy" granting a baronetcy to **J. Magrath** of Allevollan, County Tipperary, in 1629. There are also allegations in a suit for separation for adultery and cruelty brought by **Lady Ellen Magrath** (daughter of Lord Kinsale) against **Sir J. Magrath**, in 1701.

Joseph McGrath (1877–1966)

Some Magraths were neither lords nor ladies. In the archives, a petition from **Mary Magrah** asks for £40 due for linen she had washed for the late Lord Kingston, and there is a laundry bill, *c.* 1793, from **Bridget MacGrath** to Sir Skeffington Smith.

It was in the nineteenth century that the MacGraths began emigrating to North America. Following in the wake of the disastrous rising of 1798, **John Magrath** went to the USA. His son, **Andrew Condon Magrath** (1813–93), a Confederate and a veteran of the Civil War, became a judge and Governor of South Carolina.

James McGrath (1835–98) left Tipperary for Canada in 1856 and worked as a missionary before going south to the USA, where he built many churches and was elected the first Provincial of the Oblate Fathers in America. **John Harte McGraw** (1850–1910) was Governor of Washington, and **Matthew J. McGrath** (1876–1941) from Tipperary was a police officer in the USA and an outstanding athlete.

From its inception, the Irish community in America were enthusiastic baseball players. **John Magraw** was manager of the New York Giants baseball team during their "golden age".

The MacGraths are numbered among the many Irish who sailed from Waterford to establish themselves in Newfoundland. **Sir Patrick Thomas MacGrath** (1868–1929), who was born in St John's, was owner-editor of a daily newspaper. He was president of the Upper House of the Newfoundland Legislature, and his wide knowledge of history influenced Newfoundland's gaining control of mainland territory following the Labrador dispute.

In the twentieth century, Dublin-born **Joseph McGrath** (1877–1966) fought in the 1916 rising and was jailed in England. In 1922 he was the new Irish government's first Minister for Labour, and also Minister for Industry and Commerce. Disillusioned by politics, he went into business and contributed greatly towards Ireland's economic progress. He was prominent in the founding of the Irish Hospitals Sweepstakes. He led the field in breeding and racing horses and one of his horses won the Epsom Derby in 1951. In the 1950s he was one of the patriotic group which revived the old Waterford Crystal industry which had been dormant for 100 years. His son, **Patrick McGrath**, followed in his footsteps and was a director of many companies.

On a Waterford roadside, a stone monument commemorates the most famous McGrath since Miler of the two religions and the four bishoprics. This was "Master McGrath", the great Waterford greyhound who won the Waterloo Cup three times between 1866 and 1871 and was beaten only once in the 37 courses he ran in public. As a pup he was a weakling and was given to a lad named McGrath who was instructed to drown him. Instead the boy kept the dog and reared him to become a world champion!

John Magraw, manager of the New York Giants

MacGuinness

mac aonghusa

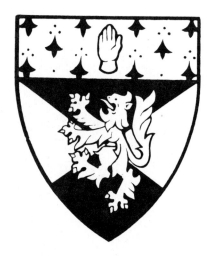

Guinness

MacInnes

Magennis

One way of spelling Guinness in Irish is Mac Aonghusa, or son of Aonghus (*aongus* meaning one choice). The family dates back to the fifth century, the time of St Patrick, and is descended from Saran, chief of Dal Araidhe. Since those far-off days the name has had many different forms. While sixteen variations are given in the *Special Report on Surnames in Ireland* published in 1894, two dozen might be a more accurate estimate. In Scotland, the name is recognized as MacInnes, while Angus is the equivalent of Aonghus. Early records of Irish life are comparatively scant, yet there is no doubt that from the twelfth century on the Magennises were the principle territorial lords of Iveagh in County Down. **Art Magennis**, the Lord of Iveagh, is mentioned in public records at a very early period, with, of course, various spellings of his name.

The family's principle stronghold at Rathfriland near Newry was known as "Gap of the North". This was destroyed in the wars of 1641. Another of their fortresses, Dundrum (Ridge Fort), built in the twelfth century on the site of a prehistoric fort, is still visible. In 1588, **Felix Magennis** built himself a new castle, but the only trace of it today is the name of the town—Newcastle.

The continual struggle for power between the Magennises and their local rivals turned to the defensive when the Anglo-Normans began their infiltration, followed by the Bruce invasion from Scotland in 1315. In Tudor times the Magennises prudently trimmed their sails and, it is recorded, remained "loyal to Queen Elizabeth". Writing in 1582, Sir Henry Bagenal mentions, "Magennis liveth very civilly and English-like in his house, and every festival day weareth English garments amongst his own followers". A Magennis, however, was uncivil enough to be on the winning side at the great Irish victory at the battle of the Yellow Ford in 1598, when Hugh O Neill led an Irish army that routed the English.

Then came the tragic reversal at Kinsale in 1601, when what had promised to be a triumph turned out to be a disaster. Somehow the Magennises were among the lucky few, and for a period had their 22,000 acres in County Down restored to them, while **Magennis of Iveagh** was created a Viscount by James I. But, with the arrival of Cromwell's army, the old Ulster landowners were deprived of their properties and titles.

There were no longer any coronation ceremonies at Coisleac Aonghus (the footstone of Aengus), the rock bearing a footprint at Warrenpoint, County Down, where the Magennises were inaugurated Kings of Ulster long ago. In *Leabhair na hUidhre* (Book of the Dun Cow) there is an account of the feasting at Dun Rudhraidhe (Rory's Fort) enjoyed by Bricriu of the Venomous Tongue, King Conor MacNessa and the Red Branch Knights. This legendary fort was taken from the Magennises in 1509 and was finally dismantled by Oliver Cromwell. And so the Magennis warriors melt into the Celtic twilight.

In the sixteenth century they had indulged in exceptionally savage behaviour. **Sir Conn Magennis** ransacked Newry and cruelly ill-treated, or barbarously murdered, its Protestant inhabitants. His wickedness was matched by that of his wife, the **Viscountess of Iveagh**, who is reported to have been as cruel to the English and Scottish inhabitants of the town.

The Magennis name appears in exalted places. **Arthur Magennis** was made Bishop of Dromore by Pope Paul III in 1534, but changed his allegiance to Henry VIII, while managing to retain his bishopric in the reformed Church. **Hugo Magennis** (d. 1640), a relative of Viscount Iveagh, was Franciscan Bishop of Down and Connor until his death in 1640.

The Magennises were leaders in the desperate rising of 1641, when they fought side by side with the Ulster leaders, O Neill, Maguire and MacMahon. The strife was continuous and, in the following generations, laid the foundation for some of the bitterness that afflicts that province to the present day.

In 1689, while Derry was under siege, James II summoned 46 peers, 228 commoners and 7 Protestant bishops to Dublin. This assembly of the Irish Estates was called "The Patriot Parliament". One of the viscounts was a **Magennis of Iveagh**. This was a historic occasion, the last legislative assembly of the Irish race until 1922, and the last at which the Roman Catholic faith was represented. A year later came the fateful battle of the Boyne, after which the Gaelic peers, including Iveagh, vanished from Ireland. They went to Europe with the "Wild Geese" and put their swords at the disposal of those countries that gave them refuge.

The 2nd Viscount Iveagh, **Brian Magennis**, a colonel in Iveagh's Regiment in the Austrian army, was killed in action in 1703. His brother **Roger**, the 3rd Viscount, fought in France and Spain. Later some went further afield, to America, where **John R. MacGuinness**, who was born in Dublin in 1840, was a general in the US army.

Charles Donagh Magennis (1867–1955) was born in Derry and studied architecture in Dublin. He emigrated to America where he built churches, schools and colleges across that continent. He designed the famous bronze doors of St Patrick's Cathedral in New York City.

The only Victoria Cross to be won by an Ulsterman in the Second World War was awarded to **Leading Seaman James Joseph Magennis**. It was sold in London in 1986 for £5,000.

In Ireland, the Iveagh title was revived in the nineteenth century by the Guinnesses. They were thought to have been originally Gennys who were in Cornwall in the 1650s. The Guinness name has become synonymous with wealth and the largest brewery in the world. The St James's Gate brewery was founded in 1759 beside one of the old walls of the city of Dublin. Very soon **Arthur Guinness**, known affectionately as "Uncle Arthur" because of his philanthropy, was brewing the stout, a strong black porter with a creamy head, which became popular in Dublin and worldwide. Since then the 4-acre site has expanded to 66 acres. In the two hundred or so years since its foundation, the company has maintained unbroken family connections down to today's sixth chairman.

Sir Benjamin Lee Guinness (1798–1868) was Lord Mayor of Dublin and restored St Patrick's Cathedral. **Sir Arthur Edward Guinness**, Baron Ardilaun (1840–1915), restored Marsh's Library, originally built in about 1702. He donated St Stephen's Green, a park of more than twenty acres, to the city of Dublin, and a statue there commemorates him. **Edward Cecil Guinness** (1847–1927), 1st Earl of Iveagh in the new creation, launched the family business as a public company. His contributions to hospitals and housing in the capital city were immense.

Rupert Edward Cecil Lee (1874–1967), 2nd Lord Iveagh, who won the Diamond Sculls at Henley Regatta, was with the Irish Hospital Corps in the Boer War. His only son, **Viscount Elveden**, was killed in 1945. In 1939, **Lord Iveagh** presented his palatial home, Iveagh House at St Stephen's Green, to the government for use as the headquarters of the Department of Foreign Affairs, and his extensive gardens to the nearby University College, Dublin.

Joseph McGuinness, a member of the Sinn Féin executive in 1917 and one of the patriots who fought for Irish independence

Arthur Guinness

The Guinness family has long achieved an equilibrium between working and living in Ireland as well as England. They set up a brewery at Park Royal, London, in 1934. More recently, breweries have also been established in Nigeria and Malaysia. A tour of Guinness's brewery beside the River Liffey is mandatory for visitors to Ireland. The *Guinness Book of Records*, issued annually, and many other brilliant advertising ideas, have kept their singular product to the forefront internationally. So, too, have the activities of the many wealthy members of the family whose matrimonial entanglements make a continuing saga.

The Honourable Desmond Guinness (b. 1931) is the second son of the 2nd Baron Moyne, **Brian Guinness**. His mother is Diana Mitford, whose second marriage was to Sir Oswald Mosley, the British fascist leader. Desmond Guinness, art historian, writer and conservationist, is one of the founders of the revived Irish Georgian Society, whose headquarters are at Leixlip Castle, County Kildare. He was instrumental in saving Thomas Connolly's former home, Castletown in County Kildare. It is now a foundation and is open to the public, a centre for a wide variety of entertainments.

The Guinness brewery in the early nineteenth century

MacGuire
mag uidhir

McGuire

Maguire

By the close of the twelfth century, the Maguires were rulers of County Fermanagh in Ulster. The Mag Uidhir (*uidhir* meaning pale), had their fortress strategically placed at the gateway to Ulster, between Upper and Lower Lough Erne. It has since passed through many hands and is still well preserved.

The Maguires have been prominent in Fermanagh since at least AD 956 and are closely connected with the O Neill kings of Ulster and with the O Donnells. Although the princely Maguires have long since vanished, the summit of Cuilceagh Mountain, near Swanlinbar, and the hill of Cornashee, near Lisnaskea, are still associated with the ceremonial inaugurations which were held there for their chieftains.

Towards the close of the thirteenth century, with the installation of **Donn Maguire**, the family began to feature in the records. **Cathal MacManus Maguire** (1439–98), a chief of the MacManus sept of the Maguires, was both a learned historian and a bishop. He was born on an island in Lough Erne, and, according to the Four Masters, he compiled *The Invaluable Annals of Munster* which preceded their own great work.

Nicholas Maguire (1460–1512), born in County Cavan, was another outstanding bishop and historian. He was educated at Oxford and was renowned for his sermons and his hospitality.

Hugh Maguire, Lord of Fermanagh, succeeded his father, **Cuconnaught**, who died in 1589. Hugh inherited the vast estates that had been in the family since 1302. He played the usual game of his time, wooing and then repulsing the English. He and his followers fought many fierce battles around Lough Erne and in nearby Cavan, which he laid waste. He was the hero of a rare Irish victory, when a small English force was beaten at the Ford of the Biscuits near Enniskillen. It was he who stirred the northern chiefs to rise against the encroaching English. He led them to victory in 1598, when he commanded the cavalry at the battle of the Yellow Ford, driving the remnants of the English army back to Antrim. In 1600 he killed Warham St Leger, an important settler in Ireland, and Provost Master of Munster, but died of wounds himself a few hours later.

Hugh is praised fulsomely in the *Annals of the Four Masters*. After his death, and the departure of his son to Genoa, almost the whole of Fermanagh was confiscated and planted with English settlers. Hugh's brother **Cuconnaught**, who succeeded him, is thought to have arranged the ship on which he and Hugh's son set sail with the famous "Flight of the Earls" to Europe in 1607, the beginning of the Irish diaspora.

Conor Maguire (1616–45), Baron of Enniskillen and son of an O Neill mother, was a rakish youth who dissipated much of his inheritance. He was dismally unsuccessful in the fateful year of 1641, when the Gaels made their final effort to oust the colonizers. Conor Maguire plotted with the Ulster nobles in an attempt to capture Dublin Castle, the seat of English power. He was a poor organizer, his scheme was discovered and he was imprisoned in the Tower of London until his execution.

Following the devastations by the armies of Cromwell and William of Orange, the Irish landed aristocracy, including the majority of the Maguires, fled, in 1691, with the "Wild Geese" to France and Austria. A regiment of infantry in James II's army had been commanded by a Maguire, **Baron of Enniskillen**. James II also paid £2,190 a year "for our secret service" to **Dominick Maguire**.

The Maguire titles, which died out in about 1795, were acceptable to the French court to which they had given their allegiance while serving in the many Irish regiments. Maguires appear in the archives of Europe's capitals, from Paris to Copenhagen and from Madrid to London. A journal was kept by **Rochfort Maguire**, who commanded HMS *Plover* on the Bering Straits Arctic Expedition from 1852 to 1854, which included a journey to the Sandwich Islands.

At Tempo Manor, near Enniskillen, there are the remains of an old Maguire castle. There, early in the nineteenth century, **Constantine Maguire** was succeeded as chieftain by his brother, **Captain Bryan Maguire**. But Bryan was dissolute, and his duelling and eccentricities led to poverty. He died in Dublin in 1835 and his only son went to sea and was never seen again. Strangely, about a century ago the historian John O Donovan identified sailors working on the British and Irish cross-channel service to be direct descendants of the great seventeenth-century Hugh Maguire.

Captain Bryan Maguire

Father Tom Maguire (1792–1847), son of the Maguire gentry of Knockninny in County Cavan, was, for a while, curate to his uncle, **Dr Patrick Maguire**, a bishop. When Father Tom became a parish priest he proved to be a most contentious character. He was involved in a marathon theological discussion which went on for nine days. His love of sport, combined with a taste for high living, may have upset his housekeeper, who is suspected of poisoning him!

Another **Thomas Maguire** (1831–89) was born in Mauritius where his father was a magistrate. He was sent to Trinity College, Dublin, at the age of 15. He proved to be a brilliant scholar and, in 1880, he was the first Catholic to be made a fellow and was Professor of Moral Philosophy.

John Francis Maguire (1815–72), the son of a Cork merchant, was called to the Irish Bar in 1843. He founded the still popular *Cork Examiner* newspaper and played a major part in politics, using his writing to campaign for tenants' rights. He declined all English honours and, in 1857, when the Princess Royal was married he criticized her allowance, which he thought excessive. A businessman and philanthropist, he was Mayor of Cork four times. He went abroad regularly, becoming a good friend of Pope Pious IX, and travelled through Canada and the USA, writing extensively about Irish-Americans.

Many of the Maguires found their way to the New World. **Charles Bonaventure Maguire** (1768–1833) was a Franciscan. Having suffered the horrors of the French Revolution and its antipathy to Christianity, he afterwards volunteered for the less arduous American mission. A highly educated, cosmopolitan priest, he became a very active and able pastor in the Pittsburgh diocese.

Yet another priest, **Thomas Maguire** (1776–1854), who was born in Philadelphia, died in Quebec in Canada, where he had become famous for his dedication to the expansion of the French language.

The less numerous Connacht branch of the family, who spelled their name McGuire, or MacGuire, was prominent in Virginia. **Hunter Holmes McGuire** (1835–1900) was a surgeon, a Confederate Medical Officer and chief surgeon to Stonewall Jackson. Following Jackson's death he continued as army medical director. From 1865 to 1878 he was Professor of Surgery at Virginia Medical College and helped set up the College of Physicians and Surgeons at Richmond, Virginia.

In a pedigree in Dublin's Genealogical Office there are records of the McGuires of Kentucky and of Kansas City, Missouri. Actress **Dorothy McGuire** (b. 1918) was a film star in America.

Conor Maguire (1889–1971) was born in Cong, County Mayo, son of a native Irish speaker and teacher. He promoted the language all through his life. He studied law and was a judge and Attorney-General in the early days of Home Rule. In recognition of his work for the Red Cross he was honoured by both France and Spain.

The violinist **Hugh Maguire** was born in Dublin in 1927 and was educated at Belvedere College. He has been lead violinist in a number of Britain's orchestras, including the London Symphony Orchestra and the British Broadcasting Symphony Orchestra, and has performed all over the world. He is Professor at the Royal Academy of Music in London and artistic director of the Irish Youth Orchestra, as well as violin tutor to the National Youth Orchestra of Great Britain.

Edward McGuire (1932–86) was the son of **Senator Edward McGuire**. Dublin-born, his distinctive style brought him fame as a portrait and still-life painter.

Terence Maguire was born in Belfast and lives in Dublin. Since 1991 he has been recognized as the Maguire, Chief of the Name. He is devoted to a quest for the Maguire chalices. For three centuries the Maguire nobility gifted chalices to their local churches. In turbulent times these chalices became scattered as far apart as Scotland and Canada. Terence Maguire has set himself the task of recovering these important Irish artefacts.

The original castle built by Maguires in the fifteenth century at Enniskillen in County Fermanagh was later incorporated into the 'Watergate' built by planters in the seventeenth.

MacKenna

mac cionnaith

The MacKennas are a branch of the southern Uí Neills who, for generations, have been largely concentrated in Ulster. At Trough, in north Monaghan, they were lords of Truagh, as it was formerly spelled. Despite the ban on the Gaelic O or Mac prefix, the MacKennas never dropped the Mac from their name. In Irish it was Mac Cionaoda (now Mac Cionnaith), meaning son of Cionaoid. Little is known of the MacKennas in earlier times, and it is not until the eighteenth century that a variety of McKenna writers began to emerge.

Niall MacKenna (flourished *c.* 1700), a poet and harpist, was born in the The Fews, County Armagh, but settled in County Louth. He is remembered best for his pretty song "Little Celia Connellan".

Theobald MacKenna (d. 1808) was secretary, in 1791, to the Catholic Committee, a moderate group eager for parliamentary reform and Catholic emancipation. Deeply disturbed by Wolfe Tone's republicanism and the anti-religious gospel of the French Revolution, he resigned. He favoured the linking of Ireland's parliament with that of Britain, but when the Act of Union was passed he was bitterly disillusioned by all its broken pledges. He wrote many scathing pamphlets expressing his disgust. In his writings he also promoted the idea of raising the Catholic Church in Ireland to the establishment status enjoyed by the Protestant Church.

Father Charles MacKenna, a parish priest, left his native Trough to be a chaplain with the Irish Brigade in France and fought at the battle of Fontenoy in 1745. John O Hart's *Irish Landed Gentry* lists a number of high-ranking MacKenna officers who served with these Irish Brigades.

John (Juan) MacKenna (1771–1814) was born at Clogher, County Tyrone. His great-great-grandfather, **John**, a Jacobite High Sheriff in County Monaghan, had been killed by the Williamites shortly before the battle of the Boyne. A kinsman Alexander O Reilly, a general in the Spanish army who had been Governor of Louisiana from 1767 to 1769, took the young John MacKenna to Spain in 1784 and had him enrolled in the Royal Academy of Mathematics at Barcelona. From there he graduated to the Irish corps of engineers in the Spanish army where he served under Alexander O Reilly. Promotion was not fast enough for him and, in 1796, John MacKenna set sail for Peru with an introduction to a fellow Irishman, the Viceroy Ambrosio O Higgins. His engineering training had been thorough, and was of great benefit to Chile, where he became Governor of Osorno. A most skilled engineer, he was given the job of building fortifications along the coast when an invasion from France was threatened.

In 1810 he joined the revolutionary party led by Carrera, but they soon fell out and MacKenna was banished, only to be recalled and promoted to brigadier-general in order to fight the Spanish. When Bernardo, son of Ambrosio O Higgins supplanted Carrera, MacKenna joined him. He became caught up in the power struggle between these two rival dictators and, in a duel in Buenos Aires, was killed by Carrera's brother. He had married a Chilean lady whose name was Vicuna, and his son, **Benjamina Vicuna MacKenna** (1831–86), far from following in the family military career, became a very distinguished Chilean writer and historian.

The stream of MacKenna writers continued in Ireland with no less than three Stephen MacKennas. Two were novelists who wrote in the mid-1880s. The third, **Stephen MacKenna** (1872–1934), is famous for his translation of Plotinus. He started off inauspiciously enough, working in a Dublin bank, and then went into journalism in London. When he moved to Paris he met many of the leaders of the Irish literary renaissance. He joined the international brigade fighting for Greece when it was attacked by Turkey. This adventure began his enduring love of Greek literature. He travelled extensively and worked as a journalist in the world's capitals. He abandoned a lucrative job with a New York newspaper, disliking its yellow journalism, to return to Dublin to work for the Irish language revival. He took no active part in the 1916 rising because of poor health. Between 1917 and 1930 he concentrated on his major work, the translation of the *Enneads* of the great Greek philosopher, Plotinus.

Father Lambert McKenna (1870–1953), a Jesuit priest born in Dublin, studied in Europe. He collected and edited religious and folk poetry in the Irish language. Working with the Irish Texts Society, he edited the famous *Contention of the Bards* (*see* Cleary) and many anthologies of Irish bardic poetry and historical works, which had for long been neglected.

Siobhán McKenna (1923–86) was born in Belfast and brought up in Galway, where her father, **Owen McKenna**, was a professor at University College, Galway. Her mother was an O Reilly. Graduating from university with degrees in Irish and French, she studied acting and became Ireland's leading actress, known particularly for her performances in Shaw's *St Joan* and as Molly Bloom in James Joyce's *Ulysses*.

The actor-director **Thomas Patrick McKenna** (b. 1929) of Mullagh, County Cavan, is more usually known by his initials, T.P. He has been a member of the Abbey Theatre and has made many stage, screen and television appearances in England.

Many MacKennas emigrated. **Charles Hyacinth McKenna**, a Dominican priest who was born in Ireland in 1835, went to the United States in 1851. He became a powerful preacher and writer in Jacksonville, Florida.

Joseph McKenna, whose parents were Irish, was born in Philadelphia, Pennsylvania, in 1840. He became a legislator, congressman and Supreme Court jurist in California. At one time he was suspected of bias towards promoting the railroads. His record on the bench was praised for sound judgement spiced with social vision.

Martin McKenna (1832–1907) belonged to a farming family that emigrated to Australia. He was born in Kilkenny to **Patrick McKenna** and Anastasia Feehan. In 1845, when the Great Famine was threatening, he emigrated with his cousin, Michael, to Victoria. He worked in the mines before going into business with his cousin and another friend. Together they built up the very successful Campaspe Brewery in Kyneton. They branched out into farming and had between four and five thousand acres. He was Mayor of Kyneton and was elected to the Legislative Assembly. There were eleven McKenna children born in Kyneton.

It is recorded in *Burke's Guide to Country Houses* that, in 1874, the great Marshal McMahon, President of France, sold his Castle Ardo, near Ardmore, Waterford, to **Sir Joseph McKenna** of the National Bank, uncle of the politician **Reginald McKenna.** As it was more a folly than a home for living in, the McKennas abandoned it in 1918 and *Burke's* describes it as "a crazy ruin". Reginald McKenna was a British politician and an expert on taxation during the first quarter of this century.

Stephen MacKenna

MacMahon

mac mathúna

Mac Mathghamhna

Mohan

Vaughan

MacMahon—in contemporary Irish, Mac Mathúna—means son of a bear. **Mahon** was the son of Murtagh Mór, an O Brien king of Ireland who died in AD 119. The MacMahons are a lively people distinguished by many clerics and very many military men, especially in France. Historians almost all agree that Mahon is not usually the same name as MacMahon, although they will concede that Mohan, or even Vaughan, could, in some cases, be a variation of MacMahon.

There are two distinct MacMahon septs, one whose territory, Corcabaskin, was adjacent to the O Briens of Thomond in County Clare, and the other whose chiefs were lords of Oriel in counties Louth and Monaghan. They are a most numerous clan, around 10,000 today in Ireland, and still very much at home in their ancestral territories.

The Corcabaskin MacMahons' last chieftain died after the battle of Kinsale, accidentally killed by his own son. Also at Kinsale was **Brian MacMahon**, who turned traitor and informed the enemy of the Irish plans of attack.

The last chieftain of the Ulster MacMahons of Oriel, **Hugh Óg MacMahon** (1606–44), was a lieutenant-colonel in the Spanish army. He inherited a rich estate in County Monaghan and when he returned home in 1641 he became involved with Conor Maguire in the conspiracy to capture Dublin Castle. They were betrayed by Owen O Connolly who had won their confidence. For several years they were imprisoned in the Tower of London. Making a brief escape, they were discovered hiding in Drury Lane and were charged with high treason and executed in 1644.

Hugh Óg's cousin, **Heber MacMahon** (1600–50), who was born in Monaghan and ordained in Louvain, was Bishop of Down and Connor. He was also deeply involved in politics and was a leading member of the Catholic Confederation that met at Kilkenny. Owen Roe O Neill of Ulster was his trusted friend and, when he died mysteriously in 1650, Bishop Heber MacMahon was made a general. Although he was not expected to demonstrate any military prowess, he took part enthusiastically in some small bloodthirsty battles, which led to his capture and execution. Bishop Heber MacMahon has been absorbed into Irish folklore as a martyr.

In the seventeenth and eighteenth centuries, the MacMahons kept the highest ecclesiastical office in the land very much in the family. Three MacMahons were appointed Bishop of Armagh: **Bernard MacMahon** (1680–1747), his uncle, **Hugh MacMahon** (d. 1737) and his brother, **Ross Roe MacMahon** (1698–1748).

An **Abbé MacMahon**, a soldier-priest, served with the Irish Brigade. He was a chaplain at the Bastille when it fell to the Paris mob at the beginning of the French Revolution.

Probably the most colourful character in the annals of the MacMahons was a woman, **Maire Rua** (*rua* meaning red), daughter of **Turlough MacMahon**. She was notorious for the number and variety of her husbands and lovers. Contemporary historians have purged her reputation and it seems she had but three husbands. Born in about 1615 in County Clare to an O Brien mother, she was married in her teens to Daniel Neylon, who died young. Next she chose Conor O Brien and together they built the still handsome, though ruined castle of Lemaneagh at the edge of the Burren district in County Clare. When he was killed in the Cromwellian wars, Maire, to protect her eleven children and her property, married a

Maire Rua MacMahon

Cromwellian soldier and raised one of her sons a Protestant. She was indicted for murder but was pardoned. As a strong-minded woman of the west of Ireland, reminiscent of Grace O Malley, it is easy to see how she, too, entered the realms of folklore.

The remains of Carrigaholt Castle dominate the harbour at Loop Head in County Clare. **Teige MacMahon** (d. 1601), the last of the lords of Corcabaskin, lived here and must have witnessed the ships of the Spanish Armada pause here in 1588. Later, Carrigaholt fell to Sir William Penn, father of the Quaker founder of Pennsylvania.

When there was no longer any point in fighting at home for their own land, the MacMahons fled abroad. In the lists of the Irish Brigade in France their name constitutes a litany of high-ranking officers.

In 1763, Louis XV wished to ennoble **John Baptiste MacMahon** (1715–80), but John had to verify his descent from King Brian Boru before he could be titled Marquis d'Eguilly! His son, **Maurice Francis MacMahon**, suffered greatly for his royalist allegiance during the French Revolution. He died in 1831 leaving seventeen children. One of these was **Edmonde Patrice MacMahon** (1808–93), who was to become a Field Marshal and President of the Republic of France. Like his ancestors in Ireland, and later France, he was a professional soldier. It was General MacMahon who led the victorious French at Sebastopol. When he captured the Malakoff fortress and was told to leave it (it was mined) he retorted, "J'y suis, j'y reste" (here I am and here I stay). He was the hero of the day and was created Duke of Magenta. During his six-year presidency, his royalist feelings made it difficult for him to control the rabidly republican French of the 1870s. At Ardmore in County Waterford there is the ruin of a gingerbread castle known as Ardo or Ardogena which was inherited by General MacMahon. Having little use for it, he sold it in 1874 to the McKennas.

The palatial Château de Sully near Bordeaux, home of **Philippe MacMahon**, 4th Duke of Magenta and direct descendant of the nineteenth-century President of France, is by no means a ruin. The Duke proudly shows visitors the 18-carat gold sword presented to his ancestor by the people of Ireland in 1860. Both he and his wife have a deep interest in Ireland and attended a ceremony held in Limerick commemorating the scattering of the "Wild Geese".

When there was no hope of defeating the English conquerors, many MacMahons crossed the Irish sea to earn a living, and often achieved high office, in the service of England. **John MacMahon** (d. 1817) was typical of the many who, fleeing from the intolerable English in Ireland, found that the English in their own country placed no obstacle to the advancement of their careers! Born in Limerick, John MacMahon integrated well, and rose to be George IV's private secretary and keeper of the privy purse, a job which must have needed incomparable diplomacy and may have earned him his baronetcy.

As he lacked an heir, the title went to his half-brother **Sir Thomas MacMahon** (1779–1860), who served in the Portuguese army and was Adjutant-General to Her Majesty's Forces in India. His son, **Sir Thomas Westropp MacMahon** (d. 1892), served in the Crimea. This line of military MacMahons based in England continues to the present day, to the 8th Baronet.

Still more MacMahons are to be found in *Burke's Peerage 1970*. **Sir William MacMahon** (1776–1837), another member of the Limerick family, ensured his acceptance by the establishment in Ireland by converting to Protestantism. At the age of 38, he was appointed Master of the Rolls

Edmonde Patrice MacMahon

and acquired a baronetcy. One of his seven sons, **Sir Charles MacMahon** (1824–91), who was born in Omagh, County Tyrone, served in the army in Canada and India. In 1853, he went to Australia and was soon Melbourne's Chief Commissioner of Police. At one time his remarkably successful business deals were called into question, but he survived the accusations and was elected a member of the Legislative Assembly and was knighted in 1875.

The MacMahons proliferated in Australia. **Gregan McMahon** (1874–1941), son of Irish parents, was born in Sydney and was a brilliant student. He forsook a legal career for acting and producing. The Gregan McMahon Players staged many of the classics and toured Australia. **Sir William McMahon** (b. 1908) was Prime Minister of Australia from 1971 to 1972.

Scholars have reached the conclusion that the notorious **Charles Patrick Mahon** (1800–91) who called himself "The O Gorman Mahon" was of the Clare MacMahons. A flamboyant soldier and politician he quarrelled with Daniel O Connell. Spurning a career in law, he embarked on one which took him all over the world. He became an intimate of Louis Philippe and Talleyrand in France. The Czar of Russia appointed him to his bodyguard. He soldiered in the Far East, South America, was an admiral in the Chilean navy, a colonel in Brazil's army and a colonel in Napoleon III's regiment. He re-entered politics in Ireland as a supporter of Parnell. He unwittingly led to the downfall of Parnell by introducing him to Katherine O Shea. The hero of thirteen duels, many of them fatal to his opponents, he died in London at the age of 91, vigorous to the last, although it is not possible to authenticate all his adventures.

The MacMahons are almost as widespread in the United States as they are in Ireland. **Bernard MacMahon** (d. 1816) was driven there by the state of Irish politics. He settled in Philadelphia, where he made his name in the cultivation of rare plants. Helped by his Irish wife he built up one of the biggest seed businesses in the United States and had the evergreen shrub, *Berberis mahonia*, named after him.

John Van Lear McMahon (1800–71), son of an Irish Presbyterian father and a Maryland mother, graduated from Princeton University as a lawyer. A lack of social graces hampered his progress, but his determination overcame this disadvantage. He was elected to the Maryland House of Delegates and became a successful lawyer. He was active in the construction of the Baltimore and Ohio Railroad, as were many other Irish emigrants, although the bulk of these were employed as labourers—the pick-and-shovel men.

In the twentieth century, a Connecticut senator, **Brien McMahon**, introduced the Atomic Energy Act and promoted the peaceful use of atomic energy, for which he has been commemorated by a postage stamp.

Back in the homeland, **Bryan MacMahon** (b. 1909) of Listowel, County Kerry, is one of Ireland's leading short story writers and has had his plays produced at Dublin's Abbey Theatre.

MacNamara

mac conmara

Half a century before America was discovered, **John Macmiccon MacNamara**, Lord of Clancullen and High Chieftain of the Dalcassians, completed the building of Bunratty Castle begun by his father, Sioda, and planned his dream castle at Knappogue. These two splendid County Clare castles have survived the depredations of war and poverty over the past five centuries. Today visitors from home and abroad (Shannon airport is nearby) flock to the medieval banquets and entertainments that are held regularly in these magnificent relics of the past.

The MacNamaras took their patronymic, Mac Conmara (meaning son of the hound of the sea), from the Atlantic Ocean which pounds the high cliffs off the County Clare coast. The MacNamaras were the second most powerful clan after the O Briens, Lords of Thomond, and were descended from Cas, ancestor of all the Dalcassians, an ancient Irish chieftaincy. As hereditary marshals of Thomond, the MacNamaras had the right to inaugurate the chief of the O Briens, who very often was a king, and there was frequent intermarriage between these two strong families.

As was common, they eventually divided into two septs, the chief of Clancullen West being described as MacNamara Fionn (fair) and the chief of Clancullen East being MacNamara Reagh (swarthy). They earned a reputation as builders and are recorded as having built 42 castles, 15 fortresses and several friaries. **Macmiccon MacNamara Fionn** received a papal bull authorizing him to install Friars Minor in Quin Abbey, near Ennis, which he built in 1402. Many of the family lie buried in the shadow of the now roofless abbey.

Like their ancient fortresses, the MacNamara seats are all in County Clare. From the woods around Cratloe Castle, built in 1610, came the oaks for London's old Westminster Hall and the royal palace in Amsterdam.

In the seventeenth century, having lost most of their power and possessions to the Cromwellian confiscations, many MacNamaras dispersed to Europe and, in later years, to America, Canada and Australia, where their name still features, often prominently.

Given the meaning of their name, it is not surprising that the MacNamara men usually opted for a naval rather than a military career and that they boast many admirals. At the outbreak of the French Revolution there was a **Count MacNamara** who was commodore of the French fleet in the Far East; previously he had played a useful role there as a diplomat. In September 1790, he put into the Indian port of Ile de France, but was assassinated by colonizers and soldiers of the French garrison who had heard of his hostility to the principles of the revolution.

James MacNamara (1768–1826) from County Clare was in the British navy where he saw much service up to the Peace of Amiens. In a duel provoked by a fight between two dogs, he killed his opponent and, in 1803, was tried for murder. At his trial, Nelson, Hood and other distinguished officers testified to his character and service, so that he was acquitted. In 1814 he was appointed an admiral. As recently as the Second World War there was a **Rear Admiral Sir Patrick MacNamara** (1886–1957).

Genealogical papers relating to the MacNamara family are widespread. Some are in the Bibliothèque Nationale in Paris. In the British Museum there is a letter in French from Queen Mary II to the Abbess of Ronchery at Angers in France, thanking her for helping a **Miss MacNamara** whose father had served as a major in the King's Troop.

Donnchadha Ruadh Mac Conmara, who was born in East Clare in about 1715, was educated in Rome for the priesthood. His character was not in accord with that discipline and he was expelled, whereupon he turned to writing poetry. He was a competitor at the Court of Poetry held by Piaras MacGearailt in Cork in 1743. Donnchadha earned his living for a while as a schoolmaster in Waterford and it is possible that he emigrated to Newfoundland from there. Whether he did or not is uncertain, yet he wrote a poem, "The Adventures of a Luckless Fellow", which, as an account of an emigrant's voyage, would seem to be authentic, especially as there was constant traffic between Waterford and Newfoundland at that time. Whether he made it to Newfoundland or not he must have returned, for there are accounts of his career in Ireland as a schoolteacher and of his dismissal for being drunk. To qualify for various other jobs that might be available to him, he converted from Catholic to Protestant and back again. He seems to have travelled in Europe, which may have given him the inspiration for that famous poem of rich nostalgia, "Bán Chnoic Éireann Oigh", (The Fair Hills of Ireland), which sounds infinitely more mellifluous in Irish. His "Song of Repentance", written towards the close of his days, is considered to be far superior to the sentimental poetry of the eighteenth century. He lived to be 95 and died in his native Waterford.

"Fireball" MacNamara brought no honour to the name. He shot his way around France and, returning to his native County Clare, continued his aggressive ways, robbing and killing. Despite all this he was a popular villian. In 1836, he ended on the scaffold and is buried beside one of his victims in the abbey at Quin built by his ancestor.

Francis MacNamara (d. 1945), once of Doolin and of Ennistymon House (now the Falls Hotel), was a poet and an eccentric. He is best known as the father of two daughters, Caitlín, who married the great Welsh poet, Dylan Thomas, and Nicolette Devas, later Shepard, artist and author of *Two Flamboyant Fathers*. The second of Francis's three wives, Edie McNeill, was a sister of Augustus John's wife, Dorelia, and brought Francis and his daughters into the commune presided over by this robust painter.

The popular ballad with the rousing tune, *MacNamara the Leader of the Band*, was written at the beginning of this century by **Patrick MacNamara** from Limerick.

Michael MacNamara was the regimental sergeant major of the Munster Fusiliers in the First World War, while **Thomas MacNamara**, who also served with the British army, was the man who, in 1920, helped to smuggle Eamon de Valera to the United States.

In the US, **Robert MacNamara** was president of the World Bank from 1968 to 1981. Born in San Francisco, he lists among his many appointments general manager of the Ford Motor Company and US Secretary of Defense, from 1961 to 1968.

In Canada, **Arthur James MacNamara** (1885–1962) was Deputy Minister for Labour. In Australia, **Francis MacNamara** (1894–1961) of Melbourne was air vice-marshal of the Australian Flying Corps. In *Burke's Irish Family Records*, published in 1976, there is a comprehensive account of the MacNamara pedigrees.

Francis MacNamara, painted by Augustus John

MacSweeney

mac suibhne

The Sweeneys trace their ancestry from Niall of the Nine Hostages, the fifth-century High King of Ireland, through the eleventh-century King of Aileach in Donegal who was Flaherty of the Pilgrim's Staff. Following a family dispute over the succession of the Aileach kingship, Flaherty's grandson, Anrathan, sailed across the sea to Scotland. There, according to a sixteenth-century family history preserved in the Royal Irish Academy, he acquired extensive lands in Argyll and married a daughter of the King of Scotland. The Sweeney (Suibhne) from whom the family name derives was a great-grandson of Anrathan who built Castle Sween in Knapdale, reputedly the oldest stone castle in Scotland.

Suibhne is undoubtedly an Irish name. In the fifth century there was a high king of Ireland called Suibune. There was a Suibhne Abbot of Lismore, County Waterford, and another of Clonmacnoise, County Offaly. A Saint Suibhne is recorded as dwelling on the penitential Skellig Michael, a rock island off the Kerry coast. These were first names and there are not necessarily any family relationships.

It was not until the coming of the Normans in the twelfth century that Suibhne was adopted as a surname by a senior branch of the Ua Niall clan in Scotland. There too the name Loughlin originated, which survives to the present day as a first name in the Sweeney family.

During their long stay in Scotland the Sweeneys maintained their Irish links. **Maolmhuire MacSweeney** married Beanmhidhe O Conor (d. 1269), granddaughter of King Rory O Conor of Connacht.

The Sweeney family remained in Scotland until the fourteenth century, when they returned to Ireland having lost their lands in Argyll to Robert Bruce whom they had opposed at the battle of Bannockburn in 1314.

After the battle of Bannockburn there is no further mention of the Sweeney family in Scottish history. The Sweeneys of Skipness had moved to Northumberland and the Sweeneys of Castle Sween had returned to Ireland, where the senior branch returned to Rathmullan, almost in sight of the ancient (c. 1700 BC) stone fort, the Grianan of Aileach, from which they had departed for Scotland over 200 years previously.

They divided into three branches: Mac Suibhne Fanad, Mac Suibhne na d'Tuatha and Mac Suibhne Banagh. Rathmullan was the seat of MacSweeney Fanad for the next 400 years, during which time their influence extended from Donegal into Connacht and Munster. In Donegal their principle seats were Doe Castle and Rahan Castle near Killybegs.

In Scotland the inauguration of the Mac Suibhne chiefs had taken place at Iona, where they were also buried. In Ireland they were inaugurated in Kilmacrenan, County Donegal, where Mac Suibhne Fanad had the privilege of sitting at the right hand side of The O Donnell, Prince of Tirconnell.

Rory Mac Suibhne (1472–1515), 10th Lord of Fanad, was one of the most renowned of his clan. His wife, Maire, styled Princess of Fanad, commissioned the *Leabhair Chlainne Suibhne* (The Book of the Clan Sweeney). This manuscript, now in the Royal Irish Academy, is a book of personal prayers and a family history. There is also a section dealing with the diseases and characteristics of that most important member of the medieval household, the horse.

At the beginning of the seventeenth century, in common with many of the old Irish nobility of Ulster, the MacSweeneys lost most of their lands in

Mac Swiney

Sweeney

Sweeny

the plantation of the province. Their fine Castle Doe went to the Brook family. The Carmelite monastery of Rathmullan, built by **Ruadhri Mac Suibhne** and his wife, Maire ÓMaille, in 1516 to commemorate the untimely death of their son, was taken by Bishop Knox who used it as his residence.

Following the expulsion of the Sweeneys from Donegal in the seventeenth century, a copy of the clan book was preserved by the Roddy family of Leitrim. In the eighteenth century the penal laws prevented the official recording of Catholic families—including the Sweeneys who remained Catholic. Some are recorded in Spain and France, but, unlike the earls in Ulster, the Sweeney family did not escape to Europe. In fact, MacSweeney Fanad opposed the "Flight of the Earls" from Rathmullan.

Today, the acknowledged senior member of the Fanad family is the **Chevalier Loughlin Sweeney**, a Dublin bank manager and consultant, whose family moved from Donegal to the midlands in the seventeenth century. Part of a copy of *The Book of the Clan Sweeney* was in their possession until early in the nineteenth century. It was lost when the family was expelled from their property, Sweeney's Hill near Emo Park, by the Earl of Portarlington who wanted to extend his Monasterevan estate.

The present representative of the Sweeney family in Spain, living in Madrid, is **Doña Mary de Navascues**, Marquisa de Casacagal, whose Sweeney forebears were governors of Cuba.

In Germany the family was represented by the **Marquis MacSwiney** of Mashanaglass, who died in 1986. This family is of the Doe Castle branch, and lived in Cork for generations. The first Marquis was a Papal Chamberlain who returned to Ireland in the 1920s to assist with the establishment of its diplomatic service.

Terence MacSwiney

In the nineteenth century, many Sweeneys emigrated to Canada and the United States. **John Sweeney** (1821–1901) of Clones was Catholic Bishop of St John's, New Brunswick, Canada. **James Fielding Sweeny** (1857–1940), born in London, was Anglican Archbishop of Toronto, Canada. **General Thomas William Sweeney** fought with the Union forces during the American Civil War in the 1860s. He became involved with the Fenians who tried unsuccessfully to establish an Irish Republic in Canada. Today the Sweeney clan in Canada is represented by **Captain Richard Mingo Sweeney**, whose family, descendants of Sweeney Banagh, emigrated from County Tipperary in 1830. **Peter Barr Sweeney** (1825–1911), a New York lawyer and politician and a City Chamberlain, was reputed to be the guiding intelligence of the "Tweed Ring" in New York city before Tammany Hall was cleaned up by "Honest John" Kelly.

The tragic death by hunger strike of **Terence MacSwiney** (1879–1920) is still deeply felt in Ireland. Born in Cork, a poet and a revolutionary, he was the first West Cork member to be elected to Dáil Éireann. In 1920, when Lord Mayor of Cork, he was arrested by the military and sentenced to two years imprisonment. He went on hunger strike and, despite worldwide efforts to effect his release, he died on the 74th day of his fast.

James Johnson Sweeney (1900–86), of Irish ancestry, was one of the world's most celebrated art historians and administrators. Among the many important posts he held was Director of Painting and Sculpture in the New York Museum of Modern Art. He received many honorary degrees, including an honorary LL D from Trinity College, Dublin.

At their clan rally in 1979, mass was celebrated for the first time since the reformation in the ruins of the Priory at Rathmullan. The arms of the principal families have been erected at Doe Castle.

Malone
ó maoileoin

Malone—in Irish Ó Maoil Eoin—means servant of St John. Eoin is the Irish name for John. In the early Middle Ages, Clonmacnoise, the great centre of Christian scholarship by the River Shannon, had a number of Malone abbots and bishops.

From the sixteenth century, the Malones rose to prominence both in Church and State. They owned much of the land surrounding their seats in the midlands. They were also kinsmen of the kingly O Conors of Connacht.

Because of the ecclesiastical focus on Rome, priests and monks travelled continuously to and from Europe, where there were many monasteries.

Reverend William Malone (1586–1656), a superior of the Jesuit Mission to Ireland, was driven abroad by the penal laws. He became president of the Irish College in Paris.

Malones sat in the Irish Parliament and three Malones served with the army of King James II. Following the army's defeat at the battle of the Boyne, eight Malones lost their properties and their civil rights. Many of them were forced to seek refuge in Europe, where they are frequently recorded in the archives of Spain and France.

A branch of the Malone family converted to the Protestant religion, and so were able to remain on their Irish estates and to achieve high office in the State and in the legal profession. Of this family, **Richard Malone** of Ballynacargy, County Westmeath, was a diplomat in Holland. His son, **Anthony Malone** (1700–76), was an able lawyer and a Chancellor of the Exchequer. As a Member of Parliament for his county he was fearless in his criticism of the English Crown's annexation of revenues collected in Ireland, and its intolerance of Roman Catholics.

He left his estates to his nephew, **Richard Malone** (1738–1816), who was the first and last Lord Sunderlin. Richard built the great house of Baronston at Ballynacargy, County Westmeath. Following many vicissitudes, it was demolished in 1929. In the nearby graveyard at Kilbixey lie the remains of his nephew, the most renowned of all the Malones. He was **Edmund Malone** (1741–1812), an outstanding Shakespearean critic. He graduated in law from Trinity College, Dublin, and, on inheriting a modest income, was able to settle in London where he was soon accepted into the literary and artistic life of the city. He made his name as a scholar and writer, unravelling the sequence of Shakespeare's plays. It was Malone who exposed the forger, William Ireland, who claimed he had discovered original Shakespearean manuscripts.

Edmund Malone met Dr Johnson and helped Boswell with the revision of his famous *Life* of this remarkable man. Malone's friends included many of the leading artists and politicians of the day, including Horace Walpole, Edmund Burke, George Canning and the Irish Lord Charlemont. He was painted by Sir Joshua Reynolds.

In the eighteenth century, one of Dublin's legendary street characters was "Molly Malone" who, in the words of the old ballad, "Wheeled her wheelbarrow through streets broad and narrow, singing cockles and mussels, alive, alive oh!" According to the song, "She died of a fever [probably typhoid] from which no one could save her, and that was the end of sweet Molly Malone".

Reverend Sylvester Malone (1822–1906) of County Clare was ordained at Maynooth, County Kildare. His *Church History of Ireland* became a standard reference book. He worked for the revival of the Irish language and left a bequest for an essay prize of £100 which, on one occasion, was won by the great Irish scholar, Dr Douglas Hyde who, in 1938, became the first President of Ireland.

The numerous Malones have spread throughout Ireland. Some of those who emigrated to America are featured prominently in the *Dictionary of American Biography*. In fact, **Dumas Malone** (b. 1892), a Professor of History at the University of Virginia, was its editor for ten years.

Further outstanding kinsmen include **Sylvester Malone** (1821–99), a Catholic priest who left his native County Meath for America, where he selflessly cared for immigrant Irish famine victims in Brooklyn. **Walter Malone** (1866–1915), a pioneer of racial and religious freedom, who is lauded for his epic poem about the Mississippi River, a saga of the feuding between the Spanish invaders and the native Indians. **Thomas Frazer Malone** (b. 1917) of Sioux City has been recognized internationally for his contribution to the study of geophysics.

Edmund Malone (1741–1812), etching by Sir Joshua Reynolds

Martin

O Mártain

Martin, although not uniquely Gaelic, is as widespread a name in Ireland as it is in England. One of the Martin families of Connacht claims descent from **Olyver Martin**, who was a Crusader under Richard II (1367–1400). **Giolla Earnáin Ó Mártain**, who died in 1218, was a bard and a chief brehon; there were several bishops of that sept in the fifteenth century. The Martins who came with the Anglo-Normans were one of the group of families known as "The Fourteen Tribes" who ruled Galway.

Gilmartin

Kilmartyn

Martyn

Francis Martin (1652–1722) of Galway, an Augustinian, studied at Louvain. There was much religious dissension in Europe and he sided with the Pope in the controversy over papal infallibility. Foreseeing defeat ahead for King James II, he drew up plans for the assassination of William of Orange, using this as a thesis for his doctorate in theology! Despite some protests, the University of Louvain awarded him his doctorate. Nor did his later attack on St Augustine cause him any setback. He entered the religious arena again when he wrote to the Protestant Archbishop of Tuam, suggesting a union between the two faiths, which quite impressed the archbishop. A remarkable priest for his time, he ended his days in Bruges.

Richard Martin (*c*. 1660), a lawyer, was dubbed "Nimble Dick", because he exploited his profession to his own advantage. During the Williamite conquests, realizing his estates would be confiscated, he rushed to the English king to tell him how he had saved the Galway Protestants, and so was granted the patent that protected the Martin estates for many generations. By the time of Richard's death he owned one of the biggest tracts of land in the British Isles, much of it seized from the native O Flahertys with the blessing of Charles II.

Succeeding Martins were wild, tempestuous, Connemara gentry given to duelling and gambling. They remained Catholic, but, when they were no longer permitted to own land, **Robert Martin** (1714–94) turned Protestant so that his son would be eligible to become a member of the English Parliament where he could fight for civil rights for the Irish Catholics. His son, **Richard Martin** (1754–1834), was one of Ireland's famed eccentrics—and benefactors—who ruled his 200,000 acres in Connemara with feudal abandon. An inveterate duellist, he was dubbed "Hairtrigger Dick". Ironically, as High Sheriff for Galway, it was he who had to pass sentence of death on "fighting FitzGerald", with whom he had had several affrays. He would not tolerate ill-treatment of animals, and anyone found guilty of abusing dogs, horses, cattle or birds would be rowed across the lake to Richard's small island keep, where he exercised his patent to hold court, and there they suffered imprisonment until they repented.

Richard had taken his seat in Parliament at the age of 22, and had followed in his father's footsteps, advocating Catholic emancipation. He also played an active role in abolishing the death penalty for forgery. Despite ridicule, he succeeded in having Parliament pass the first Act ever to prevent cruelty to animals. In 1824, he became one of the founders of the Royal Society for the Prevention of Cruelty to Animals. This had already earned him a new name, "Humanity Dick", bestowed on him by his friend the Prince Regent. His love for animals is a monument to human progress, although his obsession with this work almost lost him his Irish possessions, and his son **Thomas** had to mortgage the land to pay his debts and help towards some restoration.

Richard Martin (1754–1834)

Thomas Martin's daughter was the beautiful **Mary Letitia** (1815–50), known as the Princess of Connemara. To reach her home at Ballynahinch Castle, an avenue stretching for thirty miles had to be negotiated. Although she was a great success in London society, she thought only of the welfare of her father's tenants. When devastating famine came to Galway in 1847, Letitia and her father Thomas spent all they had on relief work. He caught the fever and died while helping the sick. The castle and its lands were taken over by an insurance company, and Mary Letitia had to go abroad. She wrote a few novels, married, and died in childbirth aboard ship *en route* to America. *Julia Howard*, published the year of her death, is an autobiographical account of the famine in Connemara. Ballynahinch Castle is now a hotel.

The various branches of the Martin family spread throughout Connemara. **Violet Martin** (1862–1915) was the other half of the cousinly duo known as Somerville and Ross who wrote the classic *Experiences of an Irish RM* and the television success, *The Real Charlotte*. Her cousin, Edith Somerville, was from County Cork, and Violet had taken her pen name from Ross, the Martin house outside Galway. Together they wrote many humorous novels about Anglo-Irish country life. When Violet died, Edith carried on as if they were still together, always using their two names.

Edward Martyn

Edward Martyn (1859–1923) of Tulira Castle, County Galway, was educated in Dublin and Oxford. He was both musical and literary and founded the Feis Ceoil, the annual Irish musical festival. With Yeats and Lady Gregory, he helped found the Irish Literary Theatre, which later developed into the famous Abbey Theatre in Dublin. He wrote a number of plays, took an active part in the Irish language revival and in the improvement of church music. His celebrated feuding with his fellow writer and Galway colleague, George Moore, was spiked with wit and affectionate malice. From 1904 to 1908 he was president of Sinn Féin, the party campaigning for Home Rule. Despite his many eccentricities, Edward Martyn did much to vitalize Irish culture. He did not marry and eventually became a recluse in his Tulira Castle, which fell into decay.

In the 1960s, Tulira Castle was inherited by his relatives **Lord** and **Lady Hemphill**, who restored it and turned its 248 acres into a Connemara Pony stud farm of international repute. Overcome by the recession of the 1980s they had to put it on the market. They sold the contents and lived on the estate until 1986, when a businessman from Washington DC bought Tulira Castle for £1 million.

There are many Martins from both at home and abroad. **Robert Montgomery Martin** (1803–68) was from County Tyrone in Ulster. When still in his teens he went to Ceylon, now Sri Lanka. It was the beginning of his world travels, which produced a steady flow of books. His *History of the British Colonies* brought him to the notice of George IV. He wielded his pen for the improvement of British rule abroad, not least in his native country. In Hong Kong, in 1845, he disapproved of the governor raising revenue from the sale of opium, and resigned his office.

John Martin (1813–75), yet another Ulster Martin, this time from County Down, was the son of a Presbyterian minister and was educated at Trinity College, Dublin, where he became involved in the politics of the Repeal Association. His brother-in-law was the patriot John Mitchel. When Mitchel was deported to Tasmania for advocating land reform, John Martin founded a revolutionary paper, the *Irish Felon*, which resulted in his own deportation to Tasmania. Returning to Ireland in 1856, he established the National League and was a Home Rule Member of Parliament for Meath. He was known everywhere as "Honest John Martin".

134

Other Irish people went to the Antipodes voluntarily. **Sir James Martin** (1815–86) was born in Fermoy, County Cork. He was a small boy when his family emigrated to Australia. In Sydney he was a journalist and a solicitor prior to becoming Attorney-General. He was Prime Minister on three occasions.

There are descendants of Irish Martins in Canada, Australia and America. **Henry Newall Martin** (1848–96), born in Newry, County Down, one of a dozen children of a Congregational minister, was taken to America at an early age. A brilliant mind overcame a minimal education and, while studying at the Medical School of London University, he won a scholarship to Cambridge. He was the first to hold the chair of Biology at the newly founded Johns Hopkins University in Baltimore, where he was described as having put "physiology in its proper relation to the science and art of medicine".

Mother Mary Martin (1892–1975) was one of the most outstanding of the many sparkling Martin women. She was born in County Dublin, the eldest of twelve children of the owner of a large construction company. During the First World War she served as a Voluntary Aid nurse in France and Malta. After the War she did her maternity nursing training in Dublin. Bishop Joseph Shanahan, an African missioner, sent her to work in Calabar, Nigeria. Conditions for women were so bad there that she was inspired to form a religious order of women to set up hospitals in Africa. However, for years she was frustrated by ill health and obtuse male prejudice against religious women taking an active part in medical maternity work. It was not until 1934 that Pope Pius XI gave permission for women to play their part in every branch of medicine.

Two years later, Mary Martin founded the Medical Missionaries of Mary in southern Nigeria. In 1938, although again very ill, she was professed a nun. She returned to Ireland to found a novitiate in County Dublin and a maternity hospital in Drogheda, County Louth. The Archbishop of Boston, Cardinal Cushing, was her great supporter. Cardinal Montini, later to be Pope Paul VI, was among the guests at the 25th anniversary celebrations in Drogheda. In 1963 the Red Cross awarded her the Florence Nightingale Medal, and in 1966 she was made an honorary fellow of the Royal College of Surgeons in Ireland—the first woman to be so honoured. Now there are Medical Missionary hospitals throughout Africa, the USA, Italy and Spain, thanks to this determined woman who breached the medieval gender barriers of the medical and religious professions.

F. X. Martin (b. 1922), a priest of the Augustinian Order and a distinguished academic, is Professor of Medieval History at University College, Dublin. In the 1970s, when archaeologists were excavating the ninth-century site of Viking Dublin, Father Martin led a crusade to save it from Dublin Corporation, who wanted to bulldoze the site and build modern offices there. Despite the protests of thousands of citizens, the preservationists lost the site, but, because of the crusade, more than two million artefacts were excavated by archaeologists and are now in the National Museum in Dublin. Father Martin was to be fined £200,000, plus legal costs, by the Corporation, which was reduced by a High Court decision to £89,000. Father Martin accepted the High Court decision, but commented that, as a "mendicant friar", he had no personal money or property to meet the decision.

Moore

ó mórdha

O More

T oday it would be impossible to differentiate between the ancient Gaelic O Mores and the Norman Moores who came to Ireland 700 years ago. Moore is also a very common name in Britain. The English name, of course, means a mountainy heath, whereas the Gaelic *mórdha* means noble. This may have been because the **Ó Mórdha** who originated the name was 21st in descent from Conal Cearnach, an outstanding member of the legendary Knights of the Red Branch.

The Ó Mórdhas were chieftains of County Leix (now Laois), and the town of Abbeyleix got its name from the Cistercian Abbey founded there in 1183 by **Conor O More**. In the Abbeyleix estate of the de Vescis there is a tomb with a carved effigy of **Malachi O More**, said to be the last of their chieftains.

Six miles from Abbeyleix, a local man with a sense of history calls his garage "The Pass of the Plumes", to commemorate the spot where the O Mores, in 1599, are said to have slaughtered 500 of the Earl of Essex's soldiers, whose plumed helmets were strewn all around after the battle.

Rory is a traditional O More name, and a **Rory O More** was leader of the Irish who fought long and valiantly against the Tudors. His son, **Owney Macrory O More**, retrieved some of his inheritance. In 1599 he also imprisoned Thomas Butler, Duke of Ormond, General of the Irish royalist army and Lord Lieutenant, and subsequently released him with a millstone around his neck! It was an O More who, in 1513, shot dead Garret Mór, the FitzGerald known as the "uncrowned king of Ireland". Patrick Sarsfield, one of Ireland's greatest soldiers, had an O More mother.

In County Laois, four miles from Portlaoise, a dramatic ruin on the Rock of Dunamase stands silhouetted on the otherwise flat landscape—all that the Cromwellians left of the Dunamase stronghold of the O Mores. Early in the eighteenth century, the O Mores of County Laois joined the Irish exodus to Europe. Many were officers in the Irish Brigade in France. One family who left Ireland in 1691 (before the battle of the Boyne) ranked in France's aristocracy as Lords of Valmont.

In the 400 years since its foundation, Trinity College, Dublin, had only one Catholic provost until 1990. That was the **Reverend Michael Moore** (1640–1726), who received his appointment from King James II. It was he who, with the librarian, a MacCarthy, saved the library when a fire broke out. Although he was a most able provost, his tenure was short, owing to a terrible indiscretion. Preaching in the presence of James II, he took as his text, "If the blind lead the blind both shall fall into the ditch". James had a Jesuit confessor whose sight was exceedingly poor and he took this personally. Moore was banished abroad, first to Rome, then to Paris, where he became rector to the University there. Ironically, he lost his sight, and the fine library he intended to bequeath to the Irish College in Paris had all but vanished by the time he died, pilfered by a servant who took advantage of his disability.

Arthur Moore (1666–1730) was one of the very earliest economists. Born in Monaghan, he made his home, and also his money, in England. He was an early advocate of free trade and in 1712 he promoted the Treaty of Commerce with France and Spain.

Henry Moore (1751–1844) left Dublin for London to work as a woodcarver. Instead he became the devoted servant of John Wesley, who appointed him as one of his literary executors. He wrote a life of Wesley and, despite many opportunities for improvement, he adhered to the austere life of a travelling preacher.

Thomas Moore (1779–1852) was the first of the Moore celebrities. The son of a Dublin grocer and wine merchant, he went to Trinity College after it had been opened to Catholics in 1793. There he met all the leading revolutionaries, but his mother restrained him from joining in their subversive activities. He went to London to study law and rapidly made a reputation as a poet. He had much charm but no money, and patrons got him a government appointment in Bermuda to ensure him an income. Given his poetic talents, he found the work far from congenial and appointed a deputy so that he could tour the Americas before returning to London. He fell in love, married, and wrote poetry, satire, plays and operas. When it was discovered that his deputy in Bermuda had absconded, leaving Moore with a debt of £6,000, he had to travel abroad to escape a debtor's prison. He met Lord Byron, who was so impressed with him that he gave Moore his autobiography, not to be published until his death. Byron died soon afterwards and Moore sold the book, but was persuaded by the Byron family to withdraw it. He gave back the money but, alas, burned the book. Later he wrote his own life of Byron. *Moore's Melodies*, his nostalgic songs about Ireland, were very popular and brought him fame and fortune. Despite Daniel O Connell's best efforts, he would take no part in Irish politics. Trinity College has commemorated him handsomely with a statue at the front gate.

Thomas Moore

There are no less than seven Moore mansions scattered throughout the four provinces. In Connacht, Moore Hall was built in 1795 by **George Moore**, whose antecedents had fled to Europe with the "Wild Geese". George had done well in the wine trade in Spain and was able to return home to build his mansion at Ballyglass in County Mayo.

George's son, **John Moore**, joined the United Irishmen and, when the French General Humbert landed at Killala in 1798 and declared Connacht a republic, he made John Moore its first, and last, president. The rising was quelled by the English and John, a gentle man, was jailed in Waterford where he died. The book, *The Year of the French*, is based on this episode.

John's brother, **George Henry Moore**, is best remembered because he owned the horse, Croagh Patrick, which won the Stewart's Cup at Goodwood. **George Augustus Moore** (1852–1933), the novelist, was George's eldest son. He was educated in England and went to France to study art, but turned to writing. His first novels broke new ground by being outspoken regarding sex, greatly shocking the Victorians. He was a serious writer and *Esther Waters*, written in 1894, made his reputation and has been filmed. He and his neighbour in Connemara, Edward Martyn, were sparring partners and both contributed to the foundation of the Abbey Theatre. George Moore was an irascible man with a biting wit. He had a fierce love-hate relationship with Ireland and the latter part of his life was spent in Ebury Street, Chelsea; he found that London suited him best.

His younger brother, **Colonel Maurice Moore**, looked after the estate at Moore Hall, but, when he was made a Senator in the newly-established Irish Free State, the anti-Treaty IRA vindictively burnt Moore Hall, ignoring the fact that the Moores had always been exemplary landlords.

Mooresfort, near Lattin in County Tipperary, was owned by a different branch of the Moore family. **Charles Moore**, a Member of Parliament, remodelled it in the 1850s. His son, **Arthur Moore** (1849–1904), was created a papal count and founded Mount St Joseph's Cistercian Abbey at Mount Heaton, County Offaly, close to his family home.

George Augustus Moore (1852–1933)

Robert Ross Rowan Moore (1811–64) of Dublin was the eldest son of William Moore of the Rowallane family which settled in Ulster in 1610. He was a political economist and a close friend of the patriot, Thomas Davis. He was a member of the Irish anti-slavery society, and in 1841 in Limerick he put a stop to a scheme for the exportation of apprentices to the West Indies. Like an earlier Moore, Arthur Moore (possibly an ancestor), he was a campaigner for free trade.

Temple Lushington Moore (1856–1920) of Tullamore studied architecture in Glasgow. He designed many churches, including the cathedral in Nairobi. He was highly regarded as an architect in England. His only son was drowned when the *SS Leinster* sank off the Irish coast in 1918.

Brian Moore is a novelist with an international reputation. Born in Belfast in 1921, he had a variety of odd jobs before writing *The Lonely Passion of Judith Hearne*, which became a best seller and has been followed by a regular flow of original works, including *The Luck of Ginger Coffey* and *Catholics*, which have been filmed. He lives mainly in America, but visits Ireland occasionally.

The Viscounts of Drogheda, whose family name is Moore, descend from a soldier who came from Kent with the Tudors. They had their estates in Mellifont in County Louth. **Sir Garret Moore** became so firm a friend of Hugh O Neill, Earl of Tyrone, the great rebel, that in 1607 before he fled to the Continent O Neill stayed with him. When taking his leave, O Neill wept bitterly, never revealing that he was leaving Ireland for ever. The descendants of these Moores later moved to Moore Abbey, County Kildare, a major Irish country house built in 1767 by **Field Marshal Sir Charles Moore**, 6th Earl and 1st Marquis of Drogheda. In the 1920s, Moore Abbey was rented by Count John McCormack, the celebrated Irish tenor. The 10th Earl of Drogheda sold the house to the Sisters of Charity who have a hospital there.

Moores are widespread and numerous in Ireland today. Many have returned to the O prefix, while a few have reverted to the Irish Ó Mórdha.

Murphy
ó murchú

Maccamore

MacMurrough

Ó Morchoe

Ó Murchadha

Murphy—Ó Murchadha or Ó Murchú in Irish—means sea warrior. It is the most common and widely dispersed name in Ireland. It takes up more than 48 pages in the combined Irish telephone directories, and there have been notable Murphy families in all four provinces.

One sept were chiefs of Siol Aodha in County Tyrone. Another sept originated from the Uí Fiachrach, who were chiefs around Sligo Bay until they were driven out by the Anglo-Normans. A third sept, who were chiefs of Uí Feilme, were prominent in County Wexford and later spread to County Cork.

The Wexford Murphys were directly descended from the kings of Leinster. In the thirteenth century a descendant, **Dermot MacMurrough**, the warring King of Leinster, opened the floodgates to the Anglo-Normans. The Murphys descend from Dermot's brother Murrough. One of the few authentic surviving chiefdoms, The Ó Morchoe is a designation held by **David Nial Creagh Ó Morchoe** of Gorey, County Wexford (a retired brigadier in the British army), who farms there. Oulartleigh, the mansion occupied by his family until the 1850s when his great-grandfather ran out of money, is nearby. It is close to the area where the Ó Morchoe, known also as the Murroughs, or Maccamores, were most concentrated.

In most Irish families a definite thread runs through the generations. In the innumerable Murphys there is a whole skein to be unravelled. Murphys figured largely in the lists of the Irish Brigades in Europe. In the nineteenth century, for instance, there were **Marshal le Baron O Murphy**, Commandant of the Légion d'Honneur; **Colonel le Chevalier O Murphy** and **l'Abbé Charles** of the 3rd Regiment of Cuirassiers.

Seán Ó Murchadha na Raithíneach ("na Raithíneach" after the Cork village of his birth), or John Murphy, born about 1700, was the last recognized head of the Blarney bards. Before him there was **Daithi Ó Murchú**, or David Murphy, the blind harpist who entertained Grace O Malley, known as Granuaile the pirate queen.

Arthur Murphy (1727–1805) of Clonquin, County Roscommon, was educated in France, as was customary for those who could afford it. Not liking the commercial work offered him on his return to Ireland, he went to London. Lack of money turned him to acting and he made his début in Covent Garden as Othello. This gave him an entrée to London literary life, and soon essays, verse, translations, periodicals and plays were pouring from his pen. In 1761, with Garrick playing one of the principal parts, his play, *The Way to Keep Him*, was a great success at Drury Lane. It was produced in Dublin as recently as 1977.

Arthur Murphy wanted to study law but entrance to the Bar was forbidden to actors. His influential friends, however, had this ban removed, enabling him to qualify and to practise law. It was said that his literary talent was more given to adaptation than to originality. All his life he worked hard and lived well, but was never out of debt.

His elder brother James had adopted their mother's name, French, and, as **James Murphy French** (1725–59), he shared with Arthur the legal and literary life of London.

John Murphy (1740–1820) of Cork went to London to study engraving. In time he became a master of the mezzotint and was commissioned to make plates for the nobility and the family of George III.

Arthur Murphy

Because of his allegiance to the United Irishmen, **Denis Brownell Murphy** was forced to leave Dublin in 1798. Safe in London he made a name as a miniaturist, even being appointed by royalty. His fame was surpassed by his daughter, Anna Brownell James, who was one of the early art historians.

James Cavanagh Murphy (1750–1814) of Cork began work as a bricklayer, followed by study in a Dublin art school. He lived for a long while in Spain and Portugal, becoming an eminent authority on Iberian architecture. His advice was sought when London's House of Commons was being extended.

Three Cork men have been successful sculptors. **Thomas J. Murphy**, born in 1881, son of **John Murphy**, also a sculptor, went to London where he had a very successful career. **Seamus Murphy** (1907–75), born near Mallow, County Cork, became a stone carver at 14 and later studied at the Cork School of Art, where he won a scholarship to Paris. He specialized in portrait heads and sculpted many leading Irishmen. He was Professor of Sculpture at the Royal Hibernian Academy and his book, *Stone Mad*, published in 1950, has been made into a play.

The Murphys have had a remarkable number of ecclesiastics. In the eighteenth century **Edward Murphy** was Archbishop of Dublin. **John Murphy** (1772–1848), Bishop of Cork, was a scholar who collected the largest private library in Ireland (the Murphys were given to book collecting). He sold most of this in London, except for 120 Irish manuscripts which he left to Maynooth College in County Kildare. **Francis Murphy** (1795–1858) from Navan, County Meath, went to Australia where he became Bishop of Adelaide. **Reverend Canon Jeremiah Murphy** (1840–1915) of Cork, who was ordained at Maynooth College, was an Irish speaker, traveller and writer. When he died, his library, which was sold in Cork, weighed fifteen tons.

The most remarkable of the many ecclesiastics was **John Murphy** (1796–1883) of the Cork distilling family. His youth was spent chasing rainbows, as midshipman, traveller in China and financier in London. In North America his work with the Hudson Bay Company brought him close to the Indians who made him an Indian Chief and named him "Black Eagle of the North". During a severe illness he had a vision and, as a result, went to the Beda College in Rome to study for the priesthood. Back again in his native Cork, Father John Murphy commissioned the fashionable architect Pugin, with generous contributions from Murphy's distilleries, to design the church of St Peter and St Paul of which he was made an Archdeacon.

His brother **Francis Stack Murphy** (1807–60) was a lawyer, a Member of Parliament for Cork and a scholar. He helped Francis Sylvester Mahony with literary contributions. His first cousin, **Jeremiah Daniel Murphy** (1806–24), a boy genius, mastered seven languages, wrote verse in various languages and contributed to intellectual magazines, but died very young.

Two revered Murphys are the patriot priests, **Father John Murphy** and **Father Michael Murphy**. Father John (*c.*1753–98) of Ferns, County Wexford, was a leader in the rising of 1798. He had been educated in Spain and was parish priest of Boolavogue. At first a loyalist, he became outraged by the savagery of the army and led his people in revolt. He was killed in action, as was his colleague, Father Michael.

James Gracey Murphy (1808–96) of County Down, a Presbyterian minister, compiled Latin and Hebrew grammars and many biblical and philosophical studies. **Reverend James E. P. Murphy** of Cork (b. 1850), a Protestant, translated the four gospels into Irish. **Reverend Hugh Davis**

Murphy (b. 1848), also of the Protestant faith, came from County Antrim and was chaplain to the Lord Lieutenant of Ireland.

The most notable woman bearing the Murphy name was the famous courtesan **Marie Louise O Murphy** (1737–1814), fifth daughter of an Irish soldier who had taken up shoemaking in Rouen, France. After his death, their mother brought the family to Paris where she traded in old clothes while finding her daughters work as actresses or models. Marie Louise posed for Boucher, a painter at court. He painted her so attractively that she came to the notice of Louis XV, who soon appointed her his mistress. Their child is supposed to have been General de Beaufranchet. She married three times and was divorced by her third husband, who was thirty years her junior. For a period during the reign of terror, she suffered imprisonment because of her royal connections.

Patrick Murphy (b. 1834) of County Down achieved physical notoriety as the tallest man in Europe at eight feet and one inch. He was exhibited internationally, but died at the early age of 28. His embalmed remains were returned to County Down, to medical practitioners.

A branch of the Murphy family, originally from County Wexford, moved to County Tipperary when their lands were confiscated by Cromwell. A member of the family who saved the life of one of William III's entourage was granted a lease of lands at Ballymore, Cashel, County Tipperary, in 1689. Succeeding generations lived there until it was sold in 1848.

Another branch of the Murphy family of Cork lists about seventeen family seats in the Cork city area. **Jeremiah James** (b. 1795) of Lota Park died in 1851, at Pisa during a tour of Italy. The Neapolitan sailors refused to carry his coffin, fearing it would bring them bad luck, so the resourceful Murphys had the body shipped home from Naples inside an upright piano. He was buried in this in County Cork, three months later.

The Murphys of Cork have been as famed for their alcohol as for their priests. In 1825, **James Murphy** of Ringmahon, Blackrock, County Cork, a Justice of the Peace, founded with his brothers the prosperous firm of James Murphy and Company, Distillers, while in 1854, **James Jeremiah Murphy** of Bellevue, Passage West, County Cork, and his brothers founded the firm of James J. Murphy, Brewers of Cork.

In 1867, the James Murphy company merged with the Midleton and four neighbouring distillers to form Cork Distillers Ltd. In 1966, in another big merger, with Powers and Jamesons, they became Irish Distillers Ltd., now the biggest whiskey distillers in Ireland, with headquarters at Midleton, County Cork. The Murphy family is still represented on the board.

This family has been prominent, too, in the world of sport. **Frank Murphy**, who won the Grand National riding Reynoldstown, was killed in the Second World War. **Flora Murphy** (b. 1932) was an international tennis champion. **Patricia Ann** (b. 1943) was a British ski champion.

William Martin Murphy (1844–1921) of Bantry, County Cork, was one of Ireland's first business tycoons. He established railways, tramways and large department stores in Ireland, Britain and Africa. He founded the Irish Independent Group of newspapers. He was a Member of Parliament, but refused a knighthood offered him by Edward VII during his visit to Ireland in 1907. In the 1913 general strike in Dublin he led the employers, earning the obloquy of the workers, but he was not without philanthropic concern for the poor, of which there were many in Dublin.

Thomas Murphy (b. 1935) of County Galway trained as a teacher, and is one of Ireland's leading playwrights. He was a recent director of Dublin's national theatre, The Abbey, and his play, *The Gigli Concert*, made a great impact.

The Murphys are well represented in Australia, especially in law and medicine. **Francis Murphy** (1809–91) of Cork went to Sydney as a colonial surgeon. He settled there and took up farming and politics. He was knighted in 1860.

In the United States of America there are probably more Murphys than in Ireland. **Henry Cruse Murphy** (1810–82) was the grandson of an Irish doctor who had emigrated to the New World. He practised law in Brooklyn and was its mayor for many years. He served in the state senate, and besides being a progressive promoter of such developments as railways and the Brooklyn Bridge, he was also a scholar and collected a fine library.

John Murphy (1812–80) of Omagh, County Tyrone, was brought to the United States as a child. He too had that remarkable feeling for books typical of so many of the Murphys, and became a publisher. Murphy and Company specialized in publishing theological books at their headquarters in Baltimore, Maryland. (The original Baltimore is in County Cork.)

John Benjamin Murphy (1857–1916) was of Irish parentage. He became one of the leading professors of surgery in Chicago, and invented the famous Murphy Button which simplified abdominal operations.

It was a different Murphy sept who were to advance the progress of temperance reform. **Francis Murphy** (1836–1907) of County Wexford arrived penniless in New York at the age of 16. For many years he led a dissipated life until a term in prison brought him into contact with a reformer, which led to his taking a pledge of total abstinence. He developed into a dynamic preacher in the cause of temperance, drawing thousands to his meetings and, it is said, causing the closure of 500 saloons in Allegheny and the adjoining counties. He carried his reform campaign to Canada, Australia and other countries.

Tammany Hall, the New York headquarters of the Democratic Party, reached its peak under the leadership of **Charles Francis Murphy** (1858–1924). The son of poor Irish immigrants, he spent his childhood in East Side, New York. A man who could handle men, he worked his way up from the dockyards to become a successful politician and master of diplomacy. He made his fortune from real estate, and was held in esteem because of his remarkable aloofness from the various corrupting influences then prevalent.

The father of **Frank Murphy** had emigrated to America and was jailed for his part in the Fenian attack on Canada. In 1933, Frank Murphy, who had studied law in Dublin and London, was Governor General of the Philippines, in 1936 he was Governor of his native Michigan, and in 1939 he was US Attorney-General. He died in 1949.

Audie Murphy, who was born in Texas in 1924, earned more decorations than any other US soldier in the Second World War. Afterwards he became a star in films including *Beyond Glory* and *To Hell and Back*. He died in a plane crash in 1971.

Michael Charles Murphy, who was born in Massachusetts of Irish parents, coached the US Olympic teams in the 1900s, and introduced the crouching start for athletes which is now used by sprinters everywhere. Priests, publicans, politicians and police are among Ireland's contributions to the New World. Two of New York's most able police commissioners have been Murphys. **Thomas Murphy**, a police commissioner of New York City in 1951, was afterwards a federal judge, and prosecutor at the Hiss trials. **Michael J. Murphy**, also a New York City police commissioner, led the drive against corruption in the 1960s.

Charles Francis Murphy

Nolan

ó nuallám

Nowlan

O Nolan

Nuall, the diminutive of this ancient surname, is said in Irish to mean either noble or famous. The head of the family was styled Prince of Foharta, now known as Forth, in County Carlow. To this day it remains the heart of the Nolan homeland. Under the kings of Leinster, the Prince of Foharta had the hereditary task of inaugurating the MacMurrough king, whose ancient seat in County Carlow is the palatial Borris House, still occupied by a descendant. With the arrival of the Anglo-Normans in the twelfth century, there were no more Irish kings.

In the sixteenth century, the Nolans spread to counties Mayo and Galway where they prospered and possessed much land. In 1585, **Thomas Nolan** of Ballinrobe, County Mayo, was given a grant of land in return for acting as a Clerk for that county. He was also one of the first English-style innkeepers in Connacht. These inns succeeded the old Irish *biatach*, or house of hospitality. In 1616, Thomas Nolan was licensed to keep taverns and sell wines and spirits throughout most of Connacht and Westmeath, a benefit enjoyed by succeeding Nolans.

There were at least three high-ranking Nolans in the Irish army that battled with the all-conquering Cromwellians in 1649. Following that ruthless suppression of Gaelic Ireland, the Nolan name begins to feature in the European archives. **Don Diego Nolan** was a captain in the Spanish Netherlands in 1660, and there were Nolan officers and men in other European military services.

Recruits for the Irish Brigade in France sailed from the Irish coast in boats which had smuggled wine, laces and silks from France. On the return journey to France their cargoes were contraband wool and recruits entered on the ships' books as "Wild Geese", the name they came to be referred to by the cautious country people.

In 1726, **Captain Moses Nolan** of Carlow was hanged at St Stephen's Green, Dublin. The charge was that he had "shipped off 200 men these two months past, and had 100 more to go for the night he was arrested". He was caught red-handed by the troops at Bulloch Harbour in Dalkey, County Dublin.

A much more notorious character, **Philip Nolan** (*c.* 1771–1801), claimed to have been born in Belfast, but it is more likely that he was born in America and reared in the family of General James Wilkinson, the army adventurer who fought in the American War of Independence and, later, conspired with Spain in an attempt to overcome Spanish Mexico. In all of this he was ably assisted by Philip Nolan, a contraband trader in horses who was also Wilkinson's agent for his tobacco dealings in New Orleans. Nolan was killed in a fracas near San Antonio. An obituary in a local newspaper described him as having "a magnetic personality, though lacking in education".

Michael Nolan, (d. 1827) was a legal writer and an attorney of the Court of Exchange in 1787. He was called to the Bar at Lincoln's Inn, London, where he introduced important Poor Law Reform Bills.

Frederick Nolan (1784–1864) was one of a number of Nolans who managed to retain their property and profession by embracing the Established Church. He was born in County Dublin in Old Rathmines Castle, the seat of his grandfather. An evangelist, he earned a reputation, both at home and in England, as a theologian and linguist. The last of his line, he was buried in Navan in the ancestral vault.

There were Nolans listed among the many who fought in the Irish American Brigade during the Civil War, in the 1860s. There were also Nolans in the British army.

Lewis Edward Nolan, son of **Major Babington Nolan** who wrote about cavalry, was a captain in the 15th Hussars. He was killed in 1854 at Balaclava in the Crimea during the foolhardy Charge of the Light Brigade which caused General Bosquet to remark, "C'est magnifique, mais ne c'est pas la guerre". (It is magnificent, but it is not war.)

Through the generations, a Nolan family had their seat at Ballinrobe Castle in County Mayo. In 1589 it was attacked by their neighbours, the Burkes, who were repulsed but who retaliated by burning everything around them. The Nolans also owned Iskerone Castle and several other properties in County Sligo.

Gregory Nolan of this family was High Sheriff of County Mayo and was elected agent for the county to the Catholic Confederation of Kilkenny, which met in 1642. Although their lands were confiscated by Cromwell and they suffered transplantation, they managed to recover 5,600 acres at Ballinderry. As wealthy land-owning gentlemen, they married into the powerful Galway families of Browne, Martin and French.

The last of this Nolan family to be recorded in *Burke's Landed Gentry of Ireland* was in the 1912 issue. He was **Philip Nolan** (1844–1902) and he was in the élitist Indian Civil Service. His family motto was *Cor Unam Via Una* (one heart, one way).

Brian O Nolan, alias Flann O Brien, who wrote the "Myles na gCopaleen" column in the *Irish Times* between 1941 and his death in 1966, gathered a multitude of followers who delighted in his send-up of the "Irishry". He was a graduate of Celtic studies at University College, Dublin, and his satiric humour flowed through a series of novels and comedy fantasy plays.

Brian O Nolan (Flann O Brien)

A most distinguished Nolan, who has been very generous to the home of his ancestors, was **Sir Sidney Nolan** (1917–92), the Australian painter, poet and theatrical designer who launched Australia onto the international art scene. A series of his paintings are centred on two heroic, crazy Irishmen, the bushranger Ned Kelly and John O Hara Burke, who, with Wills, were the first white men to cross Australia from south to north. Sir Sidney Nolan's paintings sell for upwards of £100,000 and in 1986 he donated fifty of them to Ireland.

The most extraordinary and poignant of the Nolans is **Christopher Nolan**, who was born in Mullingar, County Westmeath, in 1965. Brain-damaged, physically crippled and totally silent from birth, he was taught by his mother to type with a device attached to his forehead. The result has been astounding, a release of highly sophisticated language which, in 1981, was published in a book entitled *Damburst of Dreams*. His autobiography, *Under the Eye of the Clock*, won the Whitbread Book Prize in 1988 and became an immediate best seller.

In West Cork, a sept who spelled their name Ó hUalⅼacháin are presumed to have used a variant of the Ó Nualláin spelling, which is usually Anglicized to Nolan. Nolan is a very common name in every province, with the exception of Ulster. A rare variant is Nowlan, of which an outstanding representative is **Kevin B. Nowlan** (b. 1921), Professor of Modern History at University College, Dublin, and author of historical works.

Nugent
núınnseann

Gilsenan

Greville Nugent

Mac Giolla Seanáin

Uinnseadun

Winsedan

de Wynchester

Hugh de Nugent who, with Hugh de Lacy and his cousins Gilbert and Richard, came to Ireland with the Normans, could trace his lineage back eleven generations to Albert, Comte de Perches of Normandy. The family took their name from Nugent Le Rotrou near Chartres in France, from whence they came. In Ireland they were given generous grants of land and were created Barons of Delvin, and Lords of Westmeath, the county in which they mainly settled. As with Irish families, they divided into septs.

To preserve their Nugent patrimony one branch of the family married a Greville. There is a Greville Nugent family mausoleum at Fore, County Westmeath, that ancient site where St Fechin had his holy well and many Nugents are buried.

Nearby is Delvin, a pretty village from which the heads of the Nugent family, who were barons of Delvin, took their title and where they built Clonyn Castle.

The Nugents are now numerous in the United Kingdom as well as in Ireland. In the past some of the English Nugents must have crossed over to Ireland, where their name was transformed variously into Uinnseadun or Winsedan or even de Wynchester, which might indicate that they came from that cathedral city. They settled in Cork where they formed their own clan based in Aghavarton Castle near Carrigaline. Between 1444 and 1862, twelve sons of this family served in various armies.

The Norman Nugents soon identified themselves with the native Irish. There is an account of **Andrew Nugent** of Donore, County Westmeath, who, in 1641, was a captain in the Irish army that defended Kilsoglin against the English. For this, both he and his son were dispossessed. In the wake of the disasters which followed the 1641 rising, many Nugents left Ireland and their records are in the archives of Austria, Belgium, France, Spain and Italy. In fact, manuscripts relating to their activities are remarkably plentiful.

For example, in 1622 **Francis Nugent**, a Capuchin friar, wrote to Rome, complaining about a book written by Philip O Sullivan. In the Stuart Archives in Paris there is a warrant of 1704 in which James III (1460–88) admits **Ann Nugent** to be a Woman of the Bedchamber to his sister, the Princess. These archives also contain an account of allowances being made to the women of the Irish regiments to rejoin their husbands in Italy, possibly referring to the Nugents' Regiment of Horse.

County Westmeath is rich in former Nugent mansions, although they are now mostly in ruins or in other hands. Accounts of the powerful families which built them occupy no less than eighteen pages in the *British Dictionary of National Biography*, a factual account of life in Ireland in the sixteenth to nineteenth centuries.

The Nugents have a long and chequered history. **Sir Richard Nugent** (d. 1460), 10th Baron of Delvin, inherited through his mother. He waged constant war against the native Irish, for which he was well rewarded. He wielded much power as Lord Deputy of Ireland.

Another **Sir Richard Nugent**, 12th Baron (d. 1538), was also loyal to the English Crown. He sided with Gerald, 8th Earl of Kildare, against Clanricarde who led the Irish chiefs. Richard became Lord Deputy and governed for a while. In a dispute over a pension due to Brian O Conor which was withheld by Richard, O Conor took him hostage, only releasing him after much bloodshed and on payment of the pension. In his zeal to protect the English Pale, Richard pursued Brian O Conor to Offaly where he razed his castle at Dangan, but was himself killed.

Christopher is one of the most popular names in the Nugent family. **Sir Christopher Nugent** (1544–1602), 14th Baron of Delvin, was educated at Cambridge under the eye of Queen Elizabeth. He even wrote *A Primer of the Irish Language* especially for her, to help her to learn the language and thus understand her subjects! Nevertheless, he spent his life constantly suspected of treason and ended it imprisoned in the dreaded Dublin Castle. A moderate man, he lived in extreme times.

Richard Nugent (1583–1642), 15th Baron of Delvin and 1st Earl of Westmeath, was unjustly dispossessed of land on which he had spent a fortune. He joined the anti-government conspiracy of 1606 which misfired, and he was imprisoned in Dublin Castle. He escaped and went into hiding for several years. Eventually he won back King James's favour. In 1641 his refusal to join his fellow Irish gentry in the revolt against the English led to his assassination.

His grandson, **Richard Nugent** (d. 1684), 2nd Earl of Westmeath, wholeheartedly supported James II. He is said to have burned his castle before Cromwell could get to it! At the time of the Restoration, after many vicissitudes, most of his estates were restored to him. It was he who, possibly in thanksgiving, rebuilt the chapel at Fore where he and many of his descendants are buried.

Christopher Nugent (d. 1742)

Thomas Nugent (d. 1715), a second son of Richard who styled himself Baron of Riverstown, was Chief Justice of Ireland. He was not a good lawyer and was considered to be over-zealous in reversing the severe laws enacted against his Catholic countrymen. Unfortunately, he was divided in his political loyalties and he earned the scorn of the Irish by not participating in the battle of Kinsale.

Major-General John Nugent (d. 1754), 5th Earl of Westmeath, fought in practically every battle in Europe. He married an Italian countess, and their son Thomas, 6th Earl, was the first of the Westmeath line to conform to the established Protestant religion.

Christopher Nugent (d. 1731) of Dardistown, County Meath, elected to take his sword abroad after the siege of Limerick. He changed the name of the Regiment of Sheldon to that of Nugent, but was deprived of it because he followed the Old Pretender to Scotland. Another **Christopher Nugent** (d. 1742) entered the service of the Republic of Venice and attained the rank of general.

The aggressively self-centred activities of **Robert Nugent** (1702–88) of Carlanstown, County Westmeath, engendered the coining of a new verb—to nugentize. A politician as well as a poet, he trimmed his sails to suit every wind: he amassed a fortune by marrying, in succession, a trio of widows all well-endowed by previous husbands. They were described as being "nugentized". In London he could command the company of the literary world, including Johnson, Walpole and Goldsmith, as well as royalty. He was controller of the Prince of Wales's household. The Prince borrowed heavily from him but could not pay his debts. George III compensated Nugent with "palaces, pensions and peerages". Titles were important coinage and he was raised to the Irish peerage as Viscount Clare and Baron Nugent and, later, Earl Nugent. Religious denomination was socially vital and Robert changed from Catholicism to Protestantism, but, when he was dying, he reverted to Catholicism.

George Nugent (1757–1849), natural son of a Westmeath Nugent, died at the age of 92 in his Berkshire manor, a baronet and a retired Field

Marshal. He was a graduate of the Royal Military Academy at Woolwich and served with many British regiments of foot. He was in America for the expedition up the Hudson, and the storming of Forts Montgomery and Clinton. He returned occasionally to Ireland where he commanded at Belfast, and, at another time, was Member of Parliament for Charleville, County Cork.

In Britain and in Europe, the soldierly Nugents served on many battlefields and were distinguished with innumerable foreign orders. **Sir John Nugent** (d. 1779) of Ballynacor, County Westmeath, joined his uncle, **Major Francis Nugent**, in the French service. He distinguished himself at the battle of Fontenoy in 1745 when he was made a Knight of St Louis. His participation in the defeat of the English at Fontenoy did not inhibit Sir John from marrying an English lady, nor her from returning with him to his Irish estate.

Count Michael Anthony Nugent (d. 1812) concluded his military career as Governor of Prague in Czechoslovakia. His nephew **Laval**, Prince and Count Nugent (1777–1862), Senior Field Marshal in Austria of His Apostolic Majesty's Armies, Knight of the Golden Fleece and Grand Prior of Ireland in the Sovereign Order of St John, was from Ballynacor, County Westmeath. He died with these impressive titles and was buried in Frangipani Castle, his former home near Fiume, now Rijeka at Susak, in the former Yugoslavia. Today, Nugent Hall commemorates his sons, who were upholders of Croatian rights against the encroachments of Habsburgs and Magyars.

This same Laval Nugent had graduated from the Military School in Vienna into the Austrian service where his uncle, **Oliver Count Nugent**, was a colonel. Laval fought at Marengo and was a major-general at 32. Such was the flexibility of a military career in those days that he also filled in as a diplomat and was a lieutenant-general in the British army. He fought against the French and conducted Pope Pius VII back to Rome from his French exile. At the age of 83, astride his horse and attired in full Field Marshal's uniform, he saw to the removal of the dead and wounded after the defeat of the Austrians by Napoleon at Solferino.

Christopher Nugent (d. 1775) of County Meath was one of the few Nugents who did not follow an army career. He studied medicine in France and practised in Bath, England. His contribution to medicine was a notable advancement in the treatment of hydrophobia. His daughter was married to the great Edmund Burke.

Many different septs of the Nugent family are included in the biographies of the Irish landed gentry and the peerage. However distantly connected, they may be recognized by their remarkable coat of arms and crest, which invariably features a cockatrice, or basilisk, the mythical reptile hatched by a serpent from a cock's egg, which can blast with its evil eye! In a book published in 1978 by the Meath Archaeological and Historical Society, *The Green Cockatrice*, the author, who calls himself Basiliske, suggests that it was **William Nugent**, elder brother of Sir Christopher Nugent (1544–1602), who wrote the plays attributed to William Shakespeare! "Shakespeare", he insists, "travelled nowhere compared to the Nugents who had connections everywhere, and were related by blood or fosterage to the leading families in Ireland, England, not forgetting the Medicis in Italy".

Originally Ballinlough Castle, Clonmellon in County Westmeath was the stronghold of the very much older Celtic family of O Reilly. The Nugents acquired it quite peacefully in 1812 when Hugh O Reilly changed his name to Nugent as part of a marriage settlement. **Sir Hugh Nugent** (1904–83) saved Ballinlough in the 1930s when, as a result of the

Wyndham Land Act, the estate was broken up and the house was scheduled for demolition. Sir Hugh, who was later sadly blinded in a car accident, replanted the estate so that the lough is framed by splendid trees. With **Lady Nugent** he restored the house, which is an archive of O Reilly mementoes, including many portraits. Sir Hugh was a Count of the Holy Roman Empire, a title conferred on his ancestor Andrew O Reilly by Maria Theresa of Austria. He was probably the first Nugent in hundreds of years to serve in the Irish army; he was a captain in the Irish Free State army, and also an officer in the Royal Air Force during the Second World War.

Many Nugents left Ireland to set up new branches of the family in Canada, Australia and America. There are also some who are not Norman Nugents. In earlier times, when spelling was far from exact, the old Gaelic name Mac Giolla Seanáin, which was Anglicized to Gilsenan in some cases, was also transformed to Nugent!

Delvin Castle in County Westmeath, ancestral home of the Nugents

O Brien

Ó BRIAIN

O Brian

Brian Boru (925–1014), High King of Munster for 38 years, came nearer than anyone to uniting Ireland. In Armagh in 1001 he proclaimed himself High King and Emperor of the Irish. By winning over Malachy, a royal rival, he began to drive away the marauding Vikings. He also rebuilt the ruined monasteries and sent envoys overseas to replace their lost books. He is credited with having originated surnames, although they did not come into use until years after he died. Brian appears also to have limited royal succession to male heirs, thus depriving Irish history of a balancing factor. He may have been adversely influenced by the notorious Gormflath. She was beautiful and she was certainly power hungry. She became wife first to the Norseman Olaf, then to the High King, Malachy. When Malachy rejected her she turned to Brian. Then, ambitious to put Sitric, her son by Olaf, on the throne, she transferred her affections to Sigurd, Earl of Orkney, which encouraged him and his Irish and Scottish allies to do battle in Dublin Bay on Good Friday, 23 April 1014.

Brian's forces won the most resounding of all Irish victories, the battle of Clontarf. Brian, supposedly now an incredible 89, watched unguarded in his tent and was slain by an escaping Norseman. Sigurd and many of his allies were killed too. No more is heard of Gormflath, but **Donough**, her son by Brian, began the lineage of the O Briens who, with the O Neills and the O Conors have been for centuries the leading Gaelic aristocratic families.

Following Brian's death, his royal family began to use the O Brien surname, Brian meaning raven. The Viking departure led to the inevitable power struggle between the aspirants to the high kingship. There was enmity between Brian's sons and the various chieftains. Donough achieved the kingship, but only of Munster.

A grandson of Brian's, **Donal Mór O Brian** (d. 1194), who was married to Dermot MacMurrough's daughter, was for years locked in battle for that elusive goal, rule of all Ireland. In the twelfth century, the contenders for the high kingship, apart from the O Briens, were the Mac Lochlainns of Aileach in Ulster and the O Conors of Connacht. The story of Donal Mór, King of Munster, is a saga of ruthless battles, blinding of rivals and abandoning of hostages. But Donal Mór had also to contend with the arrival of the Normans. He managed to keep them out of his kingdom of Thomond beyond the Shannon. This gave him peace, which allowed him to build Cistercian abbeys at Kilcooley, Holycross and Corcomroe, and cathedrals at Killaloe, Cashel and Limerick where Conor, last High King of Munster, lies in his tomb.

Murrough O Brien (d. 1551), finding he could not defeat Henry VIII, led the Gaelic chiefs in acknowledging Saxon sovereignty. He adopted the Protestant religion, dropped his royal title and was rewarded by being created 1st Earl of Thomond in 1543.

Donough O Brien (d. 1624), 4th Earl of Thomond, was Governor of Clare and Thomond. Known as "The Great Earl", he was one of those Irish heirs who were cunningly nurtured at Queen Elizabeth's court with the intention of winning them away from their intransigent Irish kinsmen. In 1599, at the head of a large army of the Queen's troops, he toured his Irish domains and found them ravaged, whereupon he inflicted terrible retaliation, hanging the entire garrison of Castle Dunbeg on the nearby trees.

Donough O Brien, 4th Earl of Thomond

149

Murrough O Brien, 1st Earl of Inchiquin

Murrough O Brien (1614–74), 1st Earl of Inchiquin, studied the art of war with the Spanish army in Italy. He fought on the English side in the rebellion of 1642. He was married to the daughter of the Lord President of Ireland, William St Leger. With the Cromwellians he sacked and burned towns, earning the nickname "Murrough of the Burnings". He savagely drove the Catholics from Cork, Youghal and Kinsale. When the monarchy was restored in England, he sided with Charles II. This did not help him, for he was now regarded as a traitor by both the Irish and English. He went to Rome to seek pardon from the Pope for his atrocities and passed his remaining fifteen years doing severe penance.

Conor O Brien, who, with his wife, the famous Maire Rua MacMahon, in 1643 built Lemenagh Castle in County Clare, headquarters of the Inchiquin O Briens, was killed by the Cromwellians. It was about this time that the O Briens moved to Dromoland Castle, which various members of the family have improved over the years. Incorporated in the walled garden is an old gateway from Lemenagh. In 1962, Dromoland was bought by Irish-Americans and is now a hotel with a sumptuous conference centre. **Sir Donough**, 16th Baron Inchiquin (1897–1968), built Thomond House on a hill overlooking Dromoland. The 18th Baron, his nephew **Conor Myles John O Brien**, now runs it as a hotel.

There are many branches of the O Brien family, and a multitude of grand and very confusing titles. **Daniel O Brien** (1577–1663) was the 1st Viscount Clare and a member of the Supreme Council of the Catholic Confederation. A kinsman, **William O Brien**, 2nd Earl of Inchiquin, was on King William's side at the battle of the Boyne in 1690. So, incongruously, though not in person, was the Pope—a fact ignored by the Orangemen of Ulster!

It was the 3rd Viscount Clare, also **Daniel O Brien** (d. 1690), who raised Clare's Dragoons, one of the many Irish regiments which went to France. He forfeited his title by following James II.

In 1706, the 5th Viscount Clare, **Charles O Brien**, who commanded Clare's Dragoons, was killed in action at Ramilles. The 6th Viscount Clare, also **Charles O Brien** (1699–1771), was an outstanding military commander at the battles of Dettingen and Fontenoy and was made Marshal of France. A present-day descendant is **Monsieur Henri le Marquis Henri-Francais le Tonnelier de Breteuil**, who lives in France.

Many O Briens joined the exodus that followed the Treaty of Limerick, and from these descend the Spanish and French O Briens. The Dutch O Briens had left Ireland in the sixteenth century. In many instances the name was somewhat transformed.

There was, of course, an imposing list of distinguished churchmen in the family. **Tighearnagh** (d. 1088), one of the rare O Briens of Connacht, was Abbot of Clonmacnoise, the great Irish seat of religion and learning which the warlike O Briens plundered several times. Tighearnagh wrote his *Annals*, in Latin, and copies of his writings are in the Bodleian Library, the British Museum and Trinity College, Dublin.

Terence O Brien (b. 1600) was ordained in Toledo, Spain. He was Provincial of the Dominicans in Ireland before being made Bishop of Emly in County Tipperary.

John O Brien, a Bishop of the Cork diocese in the 1740s, was an eminent scholar who wrote an Irish-English dictionary and many historical works. Succeeding O Brien churchmen have produced many useful and scholarly works in the Irish language.

The O Briens multiplied and spread, mostly south into Munster, and began to play a part in political and cultural affairs. There were a number of admirals in the family, including **James O Brien** (b. 1769), a very able mariner who achieved seniority rapidly. By 1847 he was a full admiral. The previous year, on the death of his brother, he had become 3rd Marquis of Thomond. Despite three marriages he had no heirs, and with his death the Marquisate of Thomond and the Earldom of Inchiquin became extinct.

Sir Lucius O Brien (d. 1795), an energetic parliamentarian, pressed for legislative independence for Ireland. His tragically early death at the age of 32 ended a promising career. His grandson, born at Dromoland Castle, was **William Smith O Brien** (1803–64). At first he followed the pattern of many aristocratic landowning families: school in Harrow, university at Cambridge and Conservative Member of Parliament for Ennis in County Clare. As his views became more nationalist he veered towards the Young Irelanders, who wanted to see the Union with Britain repealed. Daniel O Connell, the "Liberator" who won Catholic emancipation, said of him: "He now occupies his natural position, the position which centuries ago was occupied by his ancestor, Brian Boru". Smith O Brien became a leader of the Young Irelanders and, hoping for aid from France in 1848, the year the French monarchy fell, he took up arms at Ballingarry in County Tipperary with other landowners. As a revolution it was a dismal failure.

William Smith O Brien

Following State trials, he and other leaders spent some years in Australian jails. He was pardoned in 1854 and, in his last speech in the British House of Commons, on the very day of the Chartist demonstrations led by another O Brien, James Bronterre, warned that if his country "were not allowed her own legislature they would have to encounter the chance of a republic in Ireland"—prophetic words which became fact less than a century later.

Charlotte Grace O Brien (1845–1909), youngest of William Smith O Brien's seven children, was greatly moved by the conditions she had witnessed on board the "coffin ships", on which Irish emigrants sailed to America. She did much philanthropic work on their behalf and wrote several books about the great exodus. She was an ardent member of the Gaelic League set up for the restoration of the Irish language. **Dillon O Brien** of Roscommon, who had also experienced conditions on the emigrant ships after the Famine of 1846, covered this period in his novels of American life.

James "Bronterre" O Brien (1805–64) of Longford was a colourful lawyer who joined the Chartist movement in London. He wrote seditious articles, signed "Bronterre", which led to a period of imprisonment. **Peter O Brien** (1842–1914) of Clare was the Lord Chief Justice who became known as "Peter The Packer", because of his ability to pack juries who would favour his case.

There were three William O Brien patriots, all writing at about the same period. **William O Brien** (1852–1928) of Mallow, County Cork, edited the militant *United Ireland Journal*. The Plan of Campaign to reduce high land rents was started by him. This was achieved with the Wyndham Land Act in 1903. Then he worked for agreement between unionists and nationalists with the All for Ireland League. He also wrote several novels and reminiscences.

William O Brien (1881–1968), also of Cork, was a member of the Irish Socialist Republican Party from an early age, and an intimate of the revolutionary trade union leaders, James Connolly and James Larkin. He helped establish the biggest trade union in Ireland, the Irish Transport and General Workers Union, and took part in many socialist upheavals and strikes.

Liam Ó Briain (1888–1974), a patriot scholar, studied in France and Germany and fought in the Easter Rising. For a while he played a part in

151

politics. He was Professor of Romance Languages at University College, Galway, translated European classics into Irish and was a regular broadcaster.

In the twentieth century the O Briens have had two outstanding women writers. **Kate O Brien** (1897–1974) of Limerick wrote many successful plays and novels. During her most fruitful years she suffered the fate of many leading writers of the time, the banning of her books by the Irish Censorship Board. She is now acclaimed as "the Jane Austen of Limerick". **Edna O Brien** (b. 1932), a convent girl from County Clare, had a sensational success with her first novel, *The Country Girls*, which she has followed with a series of novels and plays.

The name **Vincent O Brien** is synonymous with horses, both in Ireland and internationally. Some of Ireland's most successful thoroughbreds come from his training stables at Cashel, County Tipperary. He trained the unbeaten two-year-old Danzatore, which, in 1983 was sold to a New Zealand stud for £4 million.

Edward Conor Marshall O Brien (1880–1952), a grandson of William Smith O Brien, was an author, an outstanding yachtsman and, *inter alia*, an architect. A committed nationalist, he landed German arms for the Irish volunteers in his yacht *Kelpie*. He joined the British navy in the First World War. After the War he built the ketch *Saoirse* to his own design, and was the first Irishman to sail around the world in his own yacht. In 1927, in another of his yachts, *Ilen*, he sailed to the Falkland Islands. *Across Three Oceans*, an account of his voyages, was followed by a dozen books and novels about sailing. In the Second World War he went to sea again and sailed small boats between the United States of America and British ports for the Allies.

Another of William Smith O Brien's talented grandsons was **Dermod O Brien** (1865–1945), of Foynes, County Limerick, who became a distinguished portrait painter and president of the Royal Hibernian Academy and the United Arts Club.

Marchese Guglielmo Marconi, the Italian pioneer of wireless telegraphy, met and married his first wife, **Beatrice O Brien** of Dromoland Castle, when he was working in Ireland. She died in Rome in 1976.

Conor Cruise O Brien (b. 1917) has had a versatile career. He served in the Irish Diplomatic Service and with the United Nations in the Congo. He was Chancellor of Ghana University, and served as a minister in a coalition government in Ireland. He writes political commentary for newspapers and periodicals at home and abroad. He has recently completed a book on the eighteenth-century statesman, Edmund Burke.

The O Brien name is conspicuous in American history. In the eighteenth century, **Maurice O Brien** of County Cork emigrated to America with his wife and five sons, and settled in Machias on the coast of Maine. One of his sons was **Captain Jeremiah O Brien**, and, when the navy arrived to load timber for the British army, Captain Jeremiah and his brothers captured several of their ships, an incident which has since been recognized as the first naval engagement of the American Revolution. In 1900, the American navy commemorated the O Brien action by naming one of their battleships *Jeremiah O Brien*.

Matthew O Brien, born in 1804 in County Tipperary, was Provincial of the Dominicans in America in 1850.

William O Brien (1826–78) left the family farm in County Offaly for America, where he found an opening in mining and amassed a huge fortune, although he did not live to enjoy it.

Fitzjames O Brien, born in 1828 in Limerick, developed his literary talents by contributing to leading American periodicals, writing short stories and poems. He was with the Northern army in the Civil War, in which he was fatally injured.

Larry O Brien (b. 1917) was John F. Kennedy's political organizer and was Postmaster of the USA from 1965 to 1968.

In England there have been very many O Briens, spanning several generations. **Leslie Kenneth O Brien** (b. 1908) had the distinction of being a governor of the Bank of England. Now Lord O Brien of Lothbury, he has had a distinguished career in the international world of commerce and the arts, to which he has given his especial patronage.

The painter, **George O Brien** (1821–88) of Dromoland Castle, County Clare, was the fifth son of **Admiral Robert O Brien** (1766–1838). He went to Australia in about 1837, but settled in Dunedin, New Zealand, where an exhibition of his paintings was held in 1968.

In 1949 **Donough O Brien** published *History of the O Briens from Brian Boroimhe—AD 1000–1945*, which gives a thorough account of this ancient Irish family.

Bunratty Castle in County Clare, once a fortress of the O Brien Kings of Thomond

O Byrne

Ó BROIN

Byrne

O Beirne

Until the arrival of Cromwell and his armies, the O Byrnes had been among the most powerful and prominent Gaelic families. They traced their ancestry from King Milesius, who came to Ireland from Spain in 558 BC, and his son, Heremon, and from the two great warriors, Ugane Mór and Cathir Mór.

The O Byrne surname (in Irish Ó Broin) derives from **Bran** (meaning raven), who was son of Maolmordha, King of Leinster, who died in Cologne in the year 1052. With or without the O prefix, it is still one of the more numerous Leinster names, though it has spread throughout the country.

Originally, the O Byrnes' patrimony was in north Kildare. Like so many other septs, they were driven out by the invading Anglo-Normans, and they sought refuge in the nearby Wicklow Mountains. Here the O Byrnes became very powerful and waged continuous guerrilla warfare on the invaders for three centuries. The O Byrne country, called Crioch Bhranach, included the present Newcastle, Arklow and Ballinacor, all in County Wicklow.

A junior branch of the clan surpassed the more senior O Byrnes in power and wealth, acquiring large tracts of land. Their stronghold was at Ballinacor in the Glenmalure valley, deep in the Wicklow Mountains. On the death of the head of the senior O Byrnes, **Fiach MacHugh O Byrne** succeeded to the chieftaincy and became one of the most formidable Irish warriors during the reign of Elizabeth I. He immediately joined forces with his neighbour Lord Baltinglass (James Eustace) and together they defeated Lord Grey in a fierce battle at Glenmalure. Afterwards, Fiach MacHugh O Byrne held out at Ballinacor for a number of years. From time to time he rallied his forces to wreak havoc on the foreigners inside the Pale, or on those he considered his natural enemies, not necessarily foreigners. He surrendered with other chiefs at Christ Church in Dublin, but, as was suspected, this was a mere formality.

When Red Hugh O Donnell and Art O Neill, the young sons of Sir Hugh O Donnell, chief of Tirconnell, and the rebel Shane O Neill, escaped from their long imprisonment in Dublin Castle after Christmas 1591, it was across the snow-covered Wicklow Mountains to Ballinacor that they made their perilous journey. Young Art O Neill died from exposure, but the O Byrnes sent O Donnell safely on his way home to Fermanagh.

Rose O Toole, a sister of the O Toole chieftain of Castlekevin, was the second wife of Fiach MacHugh O Byrne. She must have been an outstanding woman as women are rarely mentioned in the chronicles. At one time when Fiach could not be present at a parley held by the great Hugh O Neill, he wrote to ask her to represent her husband. He also arranged for her safe conduct. In the *Leabhar Branach*, the book of the O Byrnes, the poets are unusually fulsome in their praise of her beauty and wisdom.

In 1597 Fiach MacHugh O Byrne was finally captured by the forces of the Queen's Lord Deputy. His head was cut off and impaled on the gates of Dublin Castle. His son, **Phelim**, was confirmed as his successor by Queen Elizabeth I. Because of the perjury common to the courtly adventurers of those times, charges trumped up against Phelim, although they were disproved, deprived him of his inheritance, and so the O Byrnes of Wicklow lost nearly all their property. It is recorded that in 1628 "Phelim, Chief of the O Byrnes, was turned out upon the world a beggar"!

He was by no means the only Irishman to be thrown upon the mercy of the world in those harsh times. There was another O Byrne, **Daniel Byrne** of Timogue in the "Queen's County" (Laois), who was not too proud to turn his hand to trade when Cromwell dispossessed him of his estates. He went into the tailoring business, making uniforms because he knew that the army at least would pay regularly. So successful was he that at the Restoration his son, Gregory, was made a baronet in May 1671. A story is told that as father and son were walking together in Dublin, Sir Gregory said, "Father, you ought to walk on the left of me, I being a knight and you but a private individual". "No, you puppy", said Daniel. "I have the precedence in three ways. First, I am your senior, secondly, I am your father, and thirdly, I am the son of a gentleman and you are but the son of a poor lousy tailor!" Gregory's descendants married into the English aristocracy and, through various profitable settlements, assumed the now extinct titles of nobility of Leicester, de Tabley and Warren.

Charles Byrne achieved a brief notoriety even though he was not a member of the nobility. Byrne, who had an Irish father and Scottish mother, was known throughout Britain as the Irish Giant. Although both his parents were of normal stature, their son was eight feet four inches tall. He travelled the country exhibiting himself at shows. In 1782, he created a sensation in a pantomime at the Haymarket in London. He died while still only 20, from drink and vexation after gambling away £750. His skeleton is in the Museum of the College of Surgeons in Lincoln's Inn, London.

The O Byrnes, because of their adherence to the Stuart cause, were losers in their own country. They went abroad, mostly to France, where many of them rose again to their former rank. Among the leading Irish citizens of Bordeaux were **Gregory**, **Daniel**, **John** and **Emily O Byrne**, formerly of Cabinteely, County Dublin, descendants of the gentleman tailor.

Gregory O Byrne was a captain in Berwick's Irish Regiment and **John O Byrne** was a wine merchant in Bordeaux, where he had extensive vineyards. He was granted letters of nobility by Louis XVI in 1770 and was styled the Chevalier O Byrne of Macon La Hourange, Bordeaux. He was succeeded by his son **Richard**, who died in 1803.

During the revolution in France there was hardship for all, including the Irish refugees. The **Abbé O Byrne** suffered imprisonment. **Madame Florence O Byrne**, a royalist and mother of three sons who were active with the Vendean anti-republicans, was guillotined. **Patrick James O Byrne**, Doctor of the Sorbonne, Superior of the Irish College in Paris, escaped to Ireland and became president of Maynooth College. **John O Byrne** fought in the 92nd Regiment of the revolutionary army—the former Regiment of Walsh.

Miles Byrne (1780–1862) was born on a Wexford farm. In 1796 he agreed to join the despised yeomanry, on condition that he would obtain the renewal of a lease of land for his mother. However, because of his brother's death, he was absolved from serving and thus never wore a red coat. Instead, he carried a pike and fought at Vinegar Hill in 1798 with the United Irishmen. Some years after that defeat, he was sent by Robert Emmet to Paris, to his brother Thomas Addis Emmet, the agent of the United Irishmen. From Bordeaux he sent a report on the state of Ireland to Napoleon who, in 1803, decreed the formation of the Irish Legion in the service of France. Because of the collapse of Emmet's conspiracy, Miles Byrne remained in France where he was commissioned and served in Napoleon's campaigns. After the revolution of 1830, he received the Legion of Honour from Louis Philippe. A monument to his memory was erected in Montmartre. His three-volume *Memoires*, published in Paris in

Charles Byrne

1863, are highly thought of. No ballad commemorates Miles Byrnes' bravery at Vinegar Hill; perhaps because he went abroad he was soon forgotten at home.

William Richard O Byrne (1823–96) was High Sheriff of Wicklow and a Home Rule Member of Parliament for that county. He succeeded to the family estates at Cabinteely, County Dublin. He is remembered because he wrote *The Naval Biography 1849–1854*, a valuable work for which he was given a substantial testimonial from the Board of the Admiralty and many naval officers.

Andrew Byrne (1802–62) left Navan, County Meath, for America where he was the first Bishop of Little Rock. He had been ordained in North Carolina and for ten years carried out the arduous task of missionary priest to the Indians. He was sent back to Ireland twice to recruit nuns and priests for his mission.

John Byrne (1825–1902) was a pioneer of electric surgery. He adapted the electric cautery knife to operate on malignant diseases of the uterus. He practised in Ireland during the Famine before emigrating to New York, where he had to graduate again from the New York Medical College.

Brian Oswald Donn Byrne (1889–1928) the novelist (sometimes known as Brien O Beirne), was born in New York County of parents from Forkhill, County Armagh. The family returned home and he spent his childhood in the Glens of Antrim. At University College, Dublin, he learned to speak Irish. Dr Douglas Hyde, folklorist and founder of the Gaelic League, aroused his interest in Irish history and literature. He went abroad to study for a diplomatic career, but was diverted by a love affair with an Irish girl. He followed her to New York and they married in 1911. He had high hopes of becoming a serious poet, but was forced to accept less congenial work in New York, contributing to encyclopaedias and dictionaries. Joyce Kilmer, the poet, helped him return to literary work and he began a series of novels which had immense popularity at that time; *Messer Marco Polo* is probably his best-known novel. He was drowned, while still only 39, when his car ran into the sea in County Kerry, where he had chosen to live. A headstone under a quicken tree at Rathclaren, County Cork, commemorates this Irish-American novelist.

A much-loved Dubliner was **Alderman Alfred Byrne** (1882–1956). He reared most of his family in the handsome Lord Mayor's house in Dawson Street in the years preceding the Second World War, when he was Lord Mayor for ten years. A new Lord Mayor is now elected every year.

León Ó Broin of Dublin (b. 1902) was a member of the Sinn Féin and Fianna Éireann nationalist organizations. While still a schoolboy he was imprisoned and when released he joined the Irish Volunteers. Following the granting of independence he entered the Civil Service and was also called to the Bar. He has written many short stories, plays, histories and biographies in Irish and English.

In the world of the media, **Gay Byrne** has successfully hosted Radio Telefís Éireann's top-rated live television programme, *The Late Late Show*, since 1962, six months after the station opened.

The O Byrne family formerly of Cabinteely, County Dublin, have a curious crest atop their armorial bearings: a mermaid holds a mirror in her right hand and a comb in her left. Their motto is *Certavi et Vici* (I fought and I won).

Gay Byrne

O Callaghan
ó ceallacháin

In direct line from **Ceallachán**, King of Munster from AD 935 until his death in 954, comes the widespread family of O Callaghan. Ceallachán was also Chief of the Eoghanact tribe which included the most powerful families in Munster, including the MacCarthys. Ceallachán became a folk hero and is the ancestor of many of the families which are still in the County Cork area. Even further back than Ceallachán's time, there is a manuscript in Dublin's Genealogical Office showing the tree of posterity of Milo, *c.* 1400 BC, which includes the progenitors of the O Callaghans and continues up to AD 1614! There is also a manuscript that records a pedigree of the O Callaghan chiefs and their vast territories, from AD 900 up to 1933. They were settled in County Cork until about 1670 when, as with so many Gaelic families, they were driven to Connacht.

Genealogists believe the name Ceallachán is derived from the word strife. This is certainly appropriate for King Ceallachán who, in the heat of his youth led his warriors to ravage counties Meath, Kilkenny and Waterford, not even hesitating before plundering the monastic settlement at Clonmacnoise. He it was who defeated Cinneide, father of the great Brian Boru, who was to drive the Norsemen from Ireland and give his name to the O Briens.

From the seventeenth century when the family dispersed, two distinct lines emerge. One fled to Spain and have long since become Spanish citizens, while the other lived for centuries at Lismehane, their mansion near the village of O Callaghan's Mills in County Clare. It was through intermarriage with related Westropps that they consolidated their properties and acquired the additional surname.

Don Juan O Callaghan (b. 1934), the O Callaghan Chief of the Name, is a lawyer in Barcelona, Spain. Don Juan is in the direct line from Ceallachán who was the 42nd Christian King of Munster.

In 1641, just before Cromwell's army forced many of the Gaelic landowners to flee abroad, **Colonel Donogh O Callaghan** was a member of the Supreme Council of the Irish Confederation of Kilkenny. Following the rebellion of that year, he lost his property, and was outlawed. Another member of his family had preceded him abroad, this was the **Abbé John O Callaghan** (1605–54), a notorious Jansenist.

Cornelius O Callaghan (1742–97) of Shanbally Castle, Clogheen, County Tipperary, was created Baron Lismore in 1785. His son was known as the 1st Viscount Lismore and his daughter was the mother of one of the Dukes of Devonshire, whose family owns Lismore Castle.

Father Jeremiah O Callaghan (1780–1861) blazed a trail through Paris and Rome, preaching vehemently against usury, rack-renting and capitalism. When he went to London he was actively supported by William Cobbett, a reformer and journalist. Eventually Jeremiah was found a congenial clerical post in North America, where he earned the name "Apostle of Vermont", befriending both the French Canadians and the immigrant Irish.

Edmund Bailey O Callaghan (1797–1880) of Mallow, County Cork, studied medicine in Dublin, Paris and Quebec. He dabbled in politics in Canada, which led to his having to escape to Albany, New York, where he settled and practised medicine. He studied the records of the Dutch founders of New York and wrote the first published history of the city. There was no financial profit from this huge labour, yet with his own

Callaghan

Kealachan

O Callaghan Westropp

O Kelaghan

money he published a second volume. He produced eleven quarto volumes of *State Records or Documentary History of the State of New York, 1849–51*, plus an astonishing variety of other publications.

One of the first Roman Catholics to be admitted to the legal profession in Ireland since the penal laws were repealed was **John Cornelius O Callaghan** (1805–83). He was a Young Irelander and was on the staff of the *Nation* newspaper. His great work of 25 years, *History of the Irish Brigades in the Service of France from the Revolution in Great Britain under James II, to the Revolution in France under Louis XVI* was published in Glasgow in 1869 in eight volumes. He declaimed, "I love, not the entremets of literature, but the strong meat and drink of sedition—I make a daily meal on the smoked carcass of Irish history".

Sir George Astley O Callaghan (1852–1920), a London-born O Callaghan who was the son of an army captain, was the admiral who commanded the frigate that entered Peking in 1900 during the rising of the "Harmonious Fists", commonly known as the Boxer rebellion.

The O Callaghan name is recorded extensively in the archives of Spain. In Germany, **James O Callaghan** and his brother, **Louis**, filled the post of Baron and Grand Veneur (agent) to the Margrave of Baden-Baden. Their elder brother, **John**, was a captain in O Brien's Regiment in the French army. Their youngest brother, **Cornelius** (d. 1741), was a captain in the Ultonian Regiment in Spain where he died at Oran, leaving an O Callaghan son. There were Callahans who fought at Bunker Hill in the American Revolution.

Genealogists give scant recognition to women. To be recorded they have to be an heiress, or have some special talent (or notoriety). In America there was **Trixie Friganza Delia O Callaghan** (1870–1955) who was an actress and singer. **Rose Mary O Callaghan Westropp** of the Lismehane branch is mentioned in *Burke's Irish Family Records* as having painted the great jockey Pat Taafe on that most loved of Irish racehorses, Arkle.

Colonel George O Callaghan (1864–1944) added the surname Westropp to comply with the will of his maternal uncle. He was aide-de-camp to three of Britain's kings: Edward VII, George V and Edward VIII. He was president of the Irish Farmer's Union and a member of the first Irish Senate. His son, **Conor John O Callaghan Westropp** (d. 1986), inherited Lismehane, but demolished it and built a small house nearby.

In the 8th Olympic Games in Amsterdam in 1928, **Dr Pat O Callaghan** of Kanturk, County Cork, won Ireland's first gold medal as an independent nation in the 16-pound hammer event. He subsequently practised for many years as a medical doctor in Clonmel, County Tipperary.

A very English Callaghan of Irish origin is **James Callaghan** (b. 1912), son of a chief petty officer in the navy. A member of the British Labour Party, in 1976 he became Prime Minister of Britain upon the unexpected retirement of Sir Harold Wilson.

According to Dr Edward MacLysaght, a former Chief Herald of Ireland, the Ulster O Callaghans of counties Armagh and Monaghan are a different sept from those who sprang from King Ceallachán. He suggests their name was probably originally O Kelaghan or Kealahan.

The O Callaghans are obviously still jealous of their ancient lineage to judge from the clarification which appeared in an Irish newspaper in 1978: "Aubrey W. O Callaghan has not announced his engagement. The announcement by Aubrey E. O Callaghan is that of his grandfather".

O Connell

ó conaill

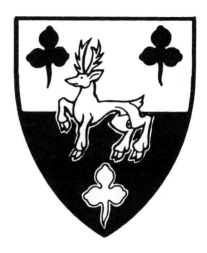

Connell

I n very early records there is mention of Magunihy, a chieftain in East Kerry whose second name was Conghal, meaning son of Connell. He was not necessarily Irish for there are other versions of Connell. In Wales it is Cynvall, in Britain Cunovalos, while the Celts spelled it Kunovalos.

The O Connells of Kerry were an ancient, landed gentry with a distinctively European outlook. In west Kerry they were for generations hereditary Constables of Ballycarbery Castle near Cahirciveen, under the Gaelic rulers of South West Munster, the MacCarthy Mór sept. In 1650, Ballycarbery was taken apart by the Cromwellians though its remains are still visible.

Around the rugged coastline of County Kerry a confusion of O Connells came forth to distinguish the name at home but particularly in Europe and various other parts of the world. Their ancestral home, Derrynane, has been well preserved and is open to the public.

John O Connell was seneschal of the mighty Duke of Ormond (*see* Butler). When the Duke was laying out the 1,752 acres of the Phoenix Park in the 1600s, O Connell was granted 200 acres in payment for his building the wall around the Park and supplying the stone from his own quarry. In the Phoenix Park, a popular recreation area for Dublin city, is the Vice Regal Lodge, once the residence of the English Viceroys and now the official residence of the President of Ireland, known as Aras an Uachtaráin. The American embassy also has its residence there. John O Connell's medieval Ashtown Castle, greatly restored, is now a museum and visitor centre.

Muircheartach O Connell (1738–1830) entered the Austrian service as a young man. He changed his first name to Moritz, "being better suited", he said, "to German orthography". Following service in various battlefields he returned to Ireland where he attacked the soldiery and killed many and was eventually killed by them. His body was drawn by a ship from Kenmare estuary to Cork city where, according to the historian Professor Maurice O Connell, "his head is said to have graced the city gates".

In the mid-eighteenth century **Count Daniel O Connell** began a promising career in the Austrian army. He caught the approving eye of the Empress of Austria, Maria Theresa (1717–80), which resulted in his being given the office of Imperial Chamberlain, or Master of Ceremonies at the Court of Vienna. In the army he held the rank of general and he was created a baron by Maria Theresa. He married an Austrian lady and their only child became a canoness.

Another Count Daniel O Connell, **Daniel Charles** (1745–1833) entered the Swedish regiment in 1761, transferring to Clare's, after it became Berwick's Regiment in the Irish Brigade. His was a distinguished army career spread over various battlegrounds. Following the revolution in France he retreated, for a time, to England. After the Restoration he returned to France where he was appointed a Peer of France. He died at the Chateau Madon, near Blois. He was one of the youngest of 22 children. Inscribed on the family tombstone is an appreciation of this fertile O Connell mother: "A model for wives and mothers to admire and to imitate"!

Mrs. Morgan John O Connell in 1892 published two volumes on the history of the Count, *The Last Colonel of the Irish Brigade.*

Sir Maurice Charles Philip O Connell (1766–1848) served as a captain in the French army under the Duke of Berwick in the early stages of the French Revolution. He went on to command the British legion in

Spain in the Spanish Civil War at that time. This Legion was partly organized by "The Liberator", Daniel O Connell. Sir Maurice continued his military career in Australia, where he married a daughter of the notorious Captain (later Vice-Admiral) William Bligh of HMS *Bounty*. Long before being knighted he was described as "the tall and dashing O Connell, a strict disciplinarian whose chief pleasures were war, duels, steeplechasing, horse racing and women". In his last ten years he was head of the Queensland Freemasons.

His nephew was **Daniel O Connell** (1775–1847) of Cahirciveen, County Kerry, the towering figure of nineteenth-century Ireland. He was fostered out at birth until the age of four, an honourable and ancient custom of the Gaelic upper classes. He was adopted by his wealthy, childless uncle, **Maurice O Connell** (1727–1825), nicknamed Hunting Cap, who made him his heir and sent him to school in Saint-Omer in France where a number of the O Connells were educated because Catholics in Ireland were deprived of an education at that time. Daniel had to leave when the French Revolution broke out. Witnessing its bloody excesses left him with an abhorrence of violence for political ends, however just. He studied for the Bar in London, then built up a successful practice at home in the turbulent years from 1798 to 1800. He was a forceful orator who spoke out fearlessly against the approaching Act of Union. When it was passed, he roused the people to demand emancipation from the penal laws suffered by Catholics both in Ireland and in England. His oratory made him an international figure and the French novelist Balzac said of him that he "incarnated a whole people". Despite taunting the Irish to shake off their servile lethargy, he became their idol. He was elected Member of Parliament for Clare in 1828. When he took his seat in the House of Commons, which hitherto no Roman Catholic had been permitted to do, he forced through the granting of Catholic emancipation in 1828.

Daniel O Connell

In 1832 he was elected a Member of Parliament for Dublin. Economically and politically the Union was proving as adverse for Ireland as he had foreseen. In an attempt to reverse this, O Connell founded the Repeal Association in 1840. He began to hold his famous "monster meetings" in every town and village. With his forceful personality he combined the passions of religion and nationalism. At one time he was imprisoned for sedition, but the House of Lords had him released after a few months.

"The Liberator" was less revered by the younger generation, because he always sought to achieve sovereignty by non-violent means. The Young Irelanders insisted on guns above strategy. As an ageing man, broken in health and spirit and foreseeing the terrible famine to come, O Connell struggled without hope, both in Ireland and in the House of Commons. On a pilgrimage to Rome, he travelled only as far as Genoa, where he died. He was one of the few Irishmen to change the attitudes of his fellow Irishmen, encouraging them to believe that united they could achieve at least some of their legitimate aims.

The Liberator had a serene home life. He had married his cousin, **Mary**, and they had a large family. Their former home in Dublin's Merrion Square is still standing. Of his four sons, **Maurice** (1803–52) and **John** (1810–58) were both politicians and lawyers. **Morgan** (1804–85) followed the family profession and went into the services. On a wave of popular feeling, he went to the aid of Simón Bolívar in South America. Subsequently, he served for some years in the Austrian army. He tried Irish politics for a while, but disagreed with his father on the subject close to his heart, repeal.

Ireland has never ceased to be grateful to Daniel O Connell, who won Catholic emancipation. He was a big man in all respects, which makes it fitting that he is commemorated by John Foley's impressive statue in Dublin's widest street, formerly Sackville Street, now O Connell Street. Daniel O Connell is buried in Glasnevin cemetery, his monument an enormously high round tower. The present representative of the family, **Sir Morgan O Connell**, 6th Baronet, lives at Lakeview House, Killarney. The family chronicler, **Basil O Connell**, has done sound genealogical research on this very interesting family.

The O Connell name is rarely encountered in the ancient annals, although it is known that from earliest times there were bishops and scholars of the name. **Peter O Connell** (1775–1826) kept a school in his native County Clare. He tried to win Daniel O Connell's patronage for his Irish-English dictionary, but, although The Liberator spoke the language fluently as a youth, he had no feeling for the ancient tongue. The manuscript of Peter O Connell's work is in the British Museum. It was rescued by that great scholar, Eugene O Curry, after its creator had been forced to pawn it!

Frederick O Connell (1876–1925) was also a scholar. He was educated at Trinity College, Dublin and was, for a period, a pastor of the Church of Ireland. Born in Connemara, he was a fluent Irish speaker and, when his wife died, he devoted himself completely to linguistics and, in particular, to Irish. He was known to his colleagues as Conall Cearnagh, meaning Connell the Square, and was one of the first directors of Radio Éireann.

Father Daniel O Connell's (b. 1896) family can trace their lineage back to the seventh century. Although he is of the same sept as The Liberator, he was not named after him. Daniel is as traditional to the family as Garret is to FitzGerald and Justin to MacCarthy. This Daniel O Connell was born in Rugby in England. His parents died when he was young and he came to Ireland and began his clerical studies at 17. He won international repute as both astronomer and seismologist. From 1938 to 1953 he was director of the Jesuit observatory at Riverview, New South Wales, Australia. He left there to become director of the Vatican Observatory in Castelgandolfo, near Rome, where he remained for eighteen years until his retirement in 1970.

Professor Maurice O Connell, a great, great grandson of The Liberator, Daniel, has kept the family flame alight. He has written books and edited numerous volumes of O Connell correspondence. He is one of the founders of DOCAL, the Daniel O Connell Association Limited which holds regular O Connell heritage workshops in Caherdaniel, County Kerry. He was formerly Professor of History at Fordham University, U.S.A.

MacConnell is a different surname from O Connell. It comes from the Irish Mac Dhomhnaill meaning son of Daniel, and is very numerous in Ulster, in counties Antrim, Down and Tyrone.

O Connor

ó conchúir

Conner

Connor

Ó Conchobhair

O Conor

In Ireland's history the O Connors are so numerous, eminent and varied that an encyclopaedia would scarcely do them justice. *The Dictionary of National Biography* lists nineteen O Connors. It is believed that few families can trace their descent through so many generations of ancestors. Many of their pedigrees and records are stored in the Irish Genealogical Office, and in France, Spain and Austria. The O Connors are outstanding in Irish history, highlighting its triumphs and its tragedies.

O Connor—in Irish Ó Conchobhair or Ó Conchúir—comes from a personal name meaning champion. The name is shared by six distinct septs in various parts of the country, several of which are now extinct.

O Connor of Corcomroe in north Clare, close to the Atlantic, descended from a **Conchobhar** who died in 1002. O Connor Faly, meaning of Offaly, boasted a pedigree going back to the second century, to Cathaoir Mór who was King of Ireland. Their territory ranged from the hills of Cavan to the lakes of Westmeath and the boglands of Offaly, where Dangan was the headquarters of their chieftain. Their name comes from **Conchobhar** (d. 979), son of Fionn, lord of Offaly.

O Connor Kerry, chief of the O Connors of Munster up to the Norman invasion, commanded an extensive area in County Kerry known as Iraghticonor. Their stronghold was Carrigafoyle Castle. The O Connors are still very numerous in Kerry.

There was also a strong sept in Ulster known as O Connor Keenaght. Although they were largely wiped out in battle with the O Kanes, there are still many O Connors in Ulster. It is thought that they were descended from the famous third century King of Munster, Oilioll Olum, eponymous ancestor of many Gaelic families.

The royal O Conors of Connacht eventually separated into three distinct septs: O Conor Roe, O Conor Sligo and O Conor Don. The first two have faded out. The family headed by O Conor Don remains a uniquely Gaelic family, the most eminent of all the O Connors.

The Connacht O Conors derive their name from **Conchobhar** (d. 971), King of Connacht. Conchobhar was of a long line of Connacht kings when kings needed to be champions to maintain their supremacy. Two high kings, who were monarchs of all Ireland, descend from him.

Conchobhar had to submit to the mighty Brian Boru (*see* O Brien), King of Munster, who assumed the chief sovereignty and gave Ireland a unity she has not since known. Later the O Conors contended with neighbouring chieftains, particularly the powerful O Rourkes.

In 1119, **Turlough Mór O Conor** was High King of Ireland. He was not so much a warrior as a statesman. He tried to centralize his government, he built stone bridges and castles and had a fleet of boats on the Shannon and on the Atlantic. He maintained a mint to coin silver money. He also plundered every part of the country, as was the custom. His three marriages endowed him with twenty children.

His son, **Roderic**, succeeded to the high kingship. His reign coincided with the invasion by the Anglo-Normans which led to the Treaty of Windsor in 1175, when Roderic (or Rory) pledged himself to recognize Henry II of England as his overlord. Kings of England now became Lords of Ireland, which meant that Rory held his kingdom of Connacht only as a vassal of English royalty. Like a number of the O Conor kings, after a life of much strife he retired to monastic seclusion in the Augustinian abbey of

Cong. In 1198 he died, the last of the Irish kings, and was buried in Clonmacnoise in County Offaly, the most celebrated of Ireland's holy places. He lies near the high altar where his father, Turlough Mór, was buried in 1156. Thus ended the royal Gaelic leadership.

When Roderic abdicated, he was succeeded by his brother, **Cathal Crobhdhearg** (meaning of the red hand). Cathal had close contact with two kings of England, King John and King Henry III. The family archives contain letters written by him in Latin. The annals record that he died in 1224, having become a monk in one of the monasteries he had founded. Historians cannot agree as to the exact monastery, Knockmoy in Galway, or Ballintubber, which Cathal had founded in 1216. The three main branches of the O Conors of Connacht: O Conor Roe, O Conor Sligo and O Conor Don descend from Turlough.

Clonalis is the family seat, near Castlerea in County Roscommon. In the seventeenth century, when the penal laws drove the majority of the Gaelic families abroad, the O Conors remained with their people and were not persuaded to revoke their Roman Catholicism. They also accumulated a treasure house of family archives, dating back to the sixth century. In 1977, Janet and Gareth Dunleavy of the University of Wisconsin, who had spent six summers working at Clonalis, completed the arrangement of the 100,000 documents from the various O Conor seats. When they published *The O Conor Papers* they included a surname register to help people who have Irish names and are searching for some clue to their origins.

Clonalis was built early in the eighteenth century and it contains many portraits and relics of this great family. Despite the inability of the government to ease the financial burden, the O Conor family is striving to preserve Clonalis. It is the only house open to the public that is wholly of the old Irish, as distinct from most other families who arrived in the wake of the Anglo-Norman invasion.

Not a trace remains of Belenagare, their ancient seat, from which the O Conors moved to Clonalis. Belenagare was the birthplace of four remarkable O Conor scholars.

Charles O Conor (1710–91), the antiquarian scholar, succeeded to Belenagare in 1749. As a Catholic, he was debarred from many of the aspirations natural to a country gentleman. He had received a classical education from a Franciscan friar, which may also have inspired him to start collecting Irish manuscripts. The blind harpist, Turlough O Carolan, the last of the bards, often stayed in his house, and his harp remains at Clonalis. There are also many letters from Charles O Conor to distinguished scholars of his day, including Dr Samuel Johnson.

Charles O Conor (1710–91)

His two grandsons were also scholars. The **Reverend Charles O Conor** (1767–1828) was educated in Rome and, after a short time as a pastor in Roscommon, left to be chaplain and librarian to the Marchioness of Buckingham, who invited him to arrange and translate the collection of manuscripts at Stowe. There he worked intensively and, encouraged by financial help from the Buckinghams, he catalogued important Irish manuscripts and published a learned four-volume work in Latin. Many of these manuscripts, including the famous *Stowe Missal*, are now in the Royal Irish Academy. Tragically, he suffered a mental illness and returned to die at Belenagare. His brother, **Matthew O Conor** (1773–1844), was also educated for the priesthood in Rome, but transferred to law. He used family documents to research many historical works.

Charles Owen O Conor Don (1838–1905) was educated at Downside in England, and was Member of Parliament for Roscommon until he was defeated by the Parnellites. He sat on many royal commissions and, in 1881,

Arthur O Connor

was president of the Royal Irish Academy. He wrote a family history, *The O Conors of Connacht.*

Arthur O Connor (1765–1852) was of the Conner family of Manch House, Ballineen, County Cork. He changed his name to O Connor. He went from Trinity College, Dublin, to the Bar, practised in Dublin and was a Member of Parliament. When he joined the United Irishmen he was arrested, tried for high treason, imprisoned several times and, in 1803, deported to France. He became a general in Napoleon's army and married Elisa de Condorcet, daughter of the French philosopher and statesman, the Marquis de Condorcet. He was known as General Condorcet O Connor of the French Service. His wife was a niece of the Marshal de Grouchy who commanded an abortive invasion of Ireland between 1796 and 1797.

Arthur's elder brother, **Roger O Connor** (1763–1834), was a barrister and was also a member of the United Irishmen, which led to him serving a term of imprisonment in Fort George, Scotland. His home, Dangan Castle, burned down following a suspiciously heavy insurance cover. He eloped with a married woman. He was tried for robbing the Galway mail train and claimed that he "had but wanted to obtain from it some letters incriminating a friend". He was outrageously eccentric and took to writing imaginary annals and foolish books.

Of the many politicians in this O Connor family, the most flamboyant was **Feargus O Connor** (1794–1859), a son of Roger, the eccentric, and a nephew of Arthur, the Napoleonic general. Feargus, a Protestant Irishman with a lot of energy and the gift of the gab, was born at Connerville, County Cork. He was a barrister and a supporter of the Reform Bill. Although elected as a Member of Parliament, he was unseated for lack of the required property qualifications. He founded a committee of radical unions in England, which led to the setting up of the "physical force" Chartists. He was imprisoned for seditious libels. Later he became a Member of Parliament for Nottingham. He began to deteriorate mentally and, in 1852, he was declared insane and was put in a home. It is said that when he was buried at Kensal Green in London, 50,000 people attended his funeral.

The O Connor name has been remarkably prominent in painting and sculpture. **James Arthur O Connor** (1792–1841) was born in Dublin and was at first an engraver, like his father. Finding this insufficiently creative, he transferred to landscape painting, and went to London where his pictures were exhibited at the Royal Academy. They were recognized as possessing extraordinary merit, but he died a poor man. He had worked for some time in Mayo, at Westport House, seat of the Marquess of Sligo of the Browne family. Many fine O Connor paintings can be seen there. Today an Arthur O Connor painting commands a high price.

John O Connor (1830–89) of Derry began his career as a call boy in a Dublin theatre, then progressed to painting scenery. Soon he transferred to London where he worked at Drury Lane and other leading theatres. He revolutionized nineteenth-century English theatre with his stage design and scene painting. The scenery for all the leading Shakespearean plays and Greek drama revivals at Cambridge were his inspiration. He was also much in demand with the nobility as a portrait painter.

Andrew O Connor (1874–1941) is the progenitor of a succession of international O Connors who have been remarkably talented artists. Andrew's father (also called Andrew) had taken his family to the USA where he fought in the Civil War and was afterwards commissioned in New England to design Civil War monuments. For a while he was a designer for Tiffany's in New York. Andrew, his eldest son, also a sculptor, worked and exhibited internationally and was a pupil of Rodin. A major commission of his was the Vanderbilt Memorial bronze doors for St Bartholomew's Church in New York. In the USA he also sculpted many of the leading military and political heroes. The Christopher Columbus statue at Genoa is his and so is the magnificent Daniel O Connell in the Bank of Ireland in Dublin's College Green. In Ireland his ecclesiastical sculpture was not in tune with the ideas of the hierarchy: his Triple Cross monument, which they commissioned, was hidden for many years and has only recently been erected at Dun Laoghaire Harbour in County Dublin.

His son, **Patrick O Connor** (1909–63), served in the Second World War with the 69th Regiment of New York, the "Fighting Irish". He was a painter and sculptor and, later, curator of the Municipal Gallery of Modern Art in Dublin. In his youth he was a boxer and wrestler and represented the USA in swimming at the Tailteann Games in Dublin in 1932.

His son, **Andrew O Connor** (b. 1943), has been a conservator at the National Gallery of Ireland since 1974. He was one of the Executive Committee for his grandfather's Centenary Exhibition in Dublin in 1974.

Jerome Connor (1876–1943) was taken to Massachusetts when he was very young. He ran away from home at 13 and worked at many trades until he found his vocation in sculpture. He held his first exhibition in Philadelphia. He sculpted the Walt Whitman Memorial and the monument to Archbishop Carroll. A cast of his statue of the Irish patriot, Robert Emmet, stands in Dublin's St Stephen's Green. He was moved by the Irish rising which began in 1916. He was commissioned to do a memorial to those who died when the Germans torpedoed the *Lusitania* off Kinsale in 1915. Working on this for fourteen years, he spent much time in Ireland where he also executed designs for the Irish coinage and did relief portraits of the members of the first Irish cabinet. In later years he suffered many frustrations and was afflicted by alcoholism and poverty.

William Conor (1884–1968) studied art in his native Belfast and saved every penny that he earned from manual labour until he was able to further his art studies in Dublin and Paris. He recorded the workers in the mills and shipyards of his native Belfast. Towards the end of his life he was honoured with an OBE and an honorary MA from Queen's University, Belfast. There is a Conor Room at the Ulster Folk Museum. When asked why he spelled his name with only one N, he would say it was because he "could never make Ns meet!"

As was customary with the Irish, the O Connors served in the military, administrative, medical and diplomatic services of many countries. From the Kerry O Connors came **Bernard Connor** (*c.* 1666–98). He studied medicine in France and Germany and afterwards travelled through Europe, gaining much experience taking care of the medical needs of important politicians and royalty. For a year he was court physician to Jan Sobieski, King of Poland. In 1694 he went to England where he was so highly regarded that he was made a licentiate of London's College of Physicians, and a member of the prestigious French Academy. But he could not cure the fever of which he died when only 32.

General Luke Smythe O Connor (1806–73) of Dublin served in both the East and West Indies and was Governor of The Gambia in 1852. **Colonel Charles O Connor** of the Irish Brigade was an officer in the royalist army in France. **Sir Luke O Connor** (1832–1915) of Elphin, County Roscommon, enlisted in the ranks of the Royal Welsh Fusiliers and won a Victoria Cross and a commission for his bravery at Alma when the Russians were defeated by the Franco-British armies in 1854. **General Gerard O Connor** raised a regiment at his own expense to fight for independence in South America. He fought in the campaigns in Venezuela and New Granada and accompanied Bolívar to Peru where he served as his Chief of Staff.

Charles O Conor (1804–84), who was born in New York City, was senior counsel for Jefferson Davis in his indictment for treason.

Among the many O Connor ecclesiastics were two brothers of the O Connor Kerry sept, **Michael** (1819–72) and **James O Connor** (1823–90), who were both bishops in the USA.

In Britain the O Connors followed a diversity of callings. **Sir Nicholas Robert O Conor** (1843–1908) of Roscommon entered the British Diplomatic Service. He was minister at Peking from 1892 to 1895. As ambassador at St Petersburg he represented Queen Victoria at the coronation of Czar Nicholas. From 1898 until his death he was ambassador to the Sultan of Turkey.

Thomas Power O Connor (1848–1929) of Athlone graduated from University College, Galway, and went to London to work as a reporter. From 1880 to 1885 he was a Nationalist Member of Parliament for Galway. In 1924 he was "father" of the House of Commons in London (the member with the longest continuous service). He made his name in the publishing world as "T. P." O Connor and founded and edited many newspapers, including the *Star*.

John O Connor (1850–1928) had a rudimentary education followed by work as a van driver and commercial traveller. He was both a Fenian leader and a Member of Parliament, but he sacrificed his seat by remaining faithful to the fallen idol, Parnell. Under the Coercion Act he suffered imprisonment a number of times. He applied himself to the law and, perhaps ironically, was called to the English Bar in 1893.

James Charles O Connor (1853–1928) was from Cork. He studied at Trinity College, Dublin, and then went on to Germany. He had the unique distinction of being a pioneer of the Esperanto movement in the English-speaking world. He translated the Gospel of St John into Esperanto and wrote many standard works on the subject.

Sir James O Connor (1872–1930), a lawyer, came from Wexford. According to *The Times* he had "a career which was, we believe, without precedent in England or in Ireland. Starting as a solicitor, he was called to the Irish Bar, became successively Law Officer, Judge and Lord Justice, and after retirement most unusually he was re-admitted as a solicitor".

Roderic O Conor (1860–1940) was one of the Roscommon O Conors. He studied painting in Dublin and Antwerp. Inheriting his family's estates enabled him to live on his income and paint in France for the rest of his life. His contemporaries were Van Gogh and Toulouse-Lautrec. Gaugin was a particular friend. A film and a biography are a testament to his increasing reputation.

Peter O Connor of Thurles won a gold medal in the Hop, Step and Jump at the Olympic Games in Athens in 1896. When the Union Jack was hoisted at the presentation of the medal he climbed the flagstaff and replaced it with the flag of his native land! This first Irish flag to be flown for an Olympic victory was there to proclaim he had won for Ireland, rather than for Britain. In 1906 he set a world record for the long jump.

Frank O Connor (1903–66) the short story writer was not an O Connor at all. He was born an O Donovan (q.v.).

Terry O Connor (d. 1983) advanced music appreciation in Ireland. Her first job was in a cinema playing six hours a day, seven days a week, for £1.25! When Radio Éireann came on the air she was appointed leader of a trio which developed into the Radio Éireann Orchestra. She founded

Thomas Power ("T.P.") O Connor

the Dublin String Orchestra and introduced modern composers such as Britten, Bartok and Schoenberg to Ireland.

Cardinal John O Connor was born in Philadelphia in 1920, one of seven children. His antecedents had connections in counties Cork and Roscommon. His father (b. 1883), a gold leafer in Philadelphia, was the only member of his family not to have been born in Ireland. His mother was of Bavarian origin.

He was ordained in the diocese of Philadelphia in 1945 and served as chaplain with the US naval forces in the Caribbean, Europe and the USA. He was awarded several decorations and was appointed Chief Naval Chaplain in 1975. He retired in 1979 with the title of Rear Admiral and was appointed to the Military Vicariate in New York where he was Auxiliary Bishop, and later, Bishop of Scranton, Pennsylvania. Upon the death of Cardinal Cook, he was appointed Bishop of New York and was made a cardinal in Rome by Pope John Paul II. He was on the committee of five bishops who drafted the US pastoral letter on War and Peace in 1983.

Cardinal John O Connor

John O Conor of Dublin (b. 1947) is one of a number of accomplished musicians who have come to the fore in Ireland in recent years. He studied in Dublin and Vienna and became known abroad when he won the International Beethoven Piano Competition in Vienna in 1973. He tours extensively throughout the world and fills the National Concert Hall and the Royal Dublin Society's hall when he plays in his native city.

The O Connors are leaders in Ireland's golfing community. In July 1985, at the Royal St George course in Sandwich, **Christy O Connor Jr** shot a first round of 64, the record set in 1934 by the great Henry Cotton.

O Donnell

ó dónaill

Ó Domhnaill

O Donel

Niall of the Nine Hostages, forefather of the O Neills of Ulster, was making raids on Britain and France towards the end of the fourth century when the Romans were returning home. From **Conall Gulban**, a son of Niall, descend the O Donnells of Tirconnell (meaning Conall's territory). They take their name from Domhnaill (meaning world mighty) an ancient and very popular Irish personal name. In time Tirconnell became known as Donegal, the area in Ulster where this powerful family was established for many generations.

Their chiefs were inaugurated at Kilmacrenan, north of Letterkenny in County Donegal, first in a religious ceremony and then on the Rock of Doon, in a civil ceremony. It was here, in 1200, that **Eignechan** was made the first Chief of the O Donnell clan. Like many of the ruling families at that time, they occupied themselves in tribal conflict, mostly attacking their kinsmen, the O Neills.

The various septs bearing the O Donnell name, of which Tirconnell of Donegal was the largest and best known, held lands in Corcabaskin in west Clare and in Hy Many in County Galway. Although they have since spread south to Munster, to this day the O Donnells are most numerous in Donegal. From **Niall Garbh** (d. 1439) descend the O Donnells of Ross and Newport, Larkfield and Grayfield, Castlebar, and the branches who settled in Spain and Austria.

St Colmcille (521–597), one of the three patron saints of Ireland, who was born at Garton, County Donegal, was a kinsman of the O Donnells. He was the monastic scribe responsible for the *Cathach*, the famous Latin manuscript of the psalms which was the battle book of the O Donnell warriors. The book, which survived much rough handling at home and abroad, is now in the Royal Irish Academy, while its elaborate silver shrine is in Dublin's National Museum. A very full account of the book is given by Rupert J. Ó Cochlain in Volume 32 of *The Irish Sword*, the journal of the Military History Society of Ireland.

The O Donnells were predominantly warriors. Accounts of the deeds of their heroes reflect the early military history of Ireland and the Continent. **Chief Hugh Roe O Donnell** (1461–1505) built a castle and monastery at Donegal which in the sixteenth century was the stronghold of **Manus O Donnell** (d. 1563), Lord of Tirconnell. In 1527, his predecessor had built Lifford Castle to keep out the O Neills. Manus was a flamboyant man who dressed like Henry VIII, married five times and had nineteen children. With O Neill, Manus attacked the Pale in an effort to overthrow the establishment in Dublin Castle. They failed and had to submit to the Lord Deputy. Manus was deprived of his lordship and was taken prisoner by his own son, **Calvagh**, who held him at his castle in Lifford.

It is believed that Calvagh (d. 1566) had quarrelled with his father because he was jealous of the influence **Hugh Dubh**, his half-brother, had with Manus. In 1554 Calvagh went to Scotland hoping to entice Sorley Boy MacDonnell's brother, James, a kinsman on his mother's side, to help him in his struggle with the O Neills on the coast of Antrim. Meanwhile, his half-brother, Hugh Dubh, enlisted Shane O Neill's help. This enraged Calvagh, whose sister was married to Shane O Neill, who treated her abominably. Calvagh and his wife were captured near Lough Swilly. He was horribly tortured while Shane took his wife as a mistress. When released in 1564, Calvagh fled to England to demand justice from

Elizabeth I. In return for his loyalty he was restored to his "country", but died shortly afterwards.

Since Calvagh's son **Con** was in prison, the despised half-brother, Hugh Dubh, was inaugurated O Donnell, Lord of Tirconnell. The ceremony took place at the Rock of Doon when a long white rod, *an slath bán*, was presented to him. The inaugural address exhorted him to, "Accept this auspicious symbol of your dignity and remember to imitate in your government the whiteness, straightness and unknottedness of this rod: that no evil tongue may find cause to asperse the candour of your actions with blackness; nor any kind of corruption, or ties of friendship, be able to prevent your justice; therefore in a lucky hour take the government of this people to exercise the power given you in freedom and security".

Hugh's son was the famous **Chief Red Hugh O Donnell** (1571–1602), whose youthful abduction was a poignant episode in Irish history. The English Deputy, Sir John Perrot, in order to check the rising power of the O Donnells and their alliance with the Hebridean Scots, plotted to kidnap the O Donnell heir. A ship with a cargo of Spanish wine came into Lough Swilly, and the 17-year-old Red Hugh and two companions were invited on board. The hatches were closed and the ship sailed for Dublin, where they were incarcerated in the dreaded Castle.

It was not until three years later, on the eve of the Epiphany (January) 1582, that Red Hugh and two young sons of Shane O Neill, Henry and Art, escaped (for the second time). On a three-day trek across the snow–covered Wicklow Mountains to Glenmalure they suffered intense hardship and Henry O Neill was separated from the others. Art O Neill died of exposure, but Red Hugh, helped by the O Byrnes and O Tooles of Wicklow, eventually reached his father's castle at Ballyshannon in Donegal. Hugh had to suffer the loss of his two big toes which had been frostbitten. His father handed the chieftainship over to Hugh, and, in 1598, he joined with Hugh O Neill in the decisive battle of the Yellow Ford, when the English were heavily defeated. But a few years later came defeat at Kinsale, after which Red Hugh was sent to Spain for help. There Philip III received him well, but Hugh, in 1602, fell suddenly ill and died at Simancas. It was suspected that he was poisoned by a spy, James Blake of Galway, but modern research inclines to the belief that he died from natural causes. His life was a brief 31 years and he left no children.

Rory O Donnell (1575–1608), who had fought with his brother, Red Hugh, at Kinsale, assumed the chieftainship when Red Hugh left for Spain. Together with O Conor Sligo he tried to restore Irish power to Connacht by guerrilla tactics. In 1602 both O Conor and O Donnell had to submit to the Crown. In exchange, Rory was knighted and given the English title of Earl of Tirconnell. He was not pleased with the lands allowed him and, correctly, suspected that the government was planning to break the power of the Gaelic lords. Together with Tyrone and Maguire he took part in a mismanaged plot to seize Dublin Castle. The plans were leaked and he and Tyrone were lucky to escape to Rome, where he died aged only 33.

Rory had married Bridget, a daughter of the 12th Earl of Kildare. Their daughter **Mary O Donnell** (1608–49) was born in England after her father's escape to Rome. James I gave her the royal name of Stuart and she was known as Mary Stuart O Donnell. She was reared by Lady Kildare, her grandmother, who also chose a husband for her but, unfortunately, he was not to the liking of Mary Stuart. Both she and her maid adopted male disguise and, accompanied by a manservant, planned their escape to Ireland. Whenever her disguise aroused any suspicion, she allayed it by making passionate love to a girl, or offering to fight a duel! She went to

Brussels, continued on to Genoa and married an O Gallagher. When she was expecting her second child she wrote in great distress to Cardinal Barberini. The last heard of this remarkable woman was that she was a widow living in Prague.

Sir Niall Garbh (1569–1626), Calvagh's grandson, had vehemently opposed his cousin Red Hugh's election as chief. He captured the O Donnell fortress at Lifford and also Donegal Abbey, and installed himself as chieftain at Kilmacrenan. He was implicated in Cahir O Doherty's catastrophic rebellion at Derry in 1608 and was sent to the Tower of London, where he spent 27 miserable years.

Hugh O Donnell (d. 1704) was known as Balldearg O Donnell because of a red birthmark, a feature found in several members of the family. Born in Donegal, he joined the Spanish army and became a brigadier. He returned to serve James II, but reached Ireland when the battle of the Boyne was lost. In a romantic bid to fulfil a prophecy that Ireland would be saved by an O Donnell with a red spot, he rallied 10,000 men to his side in Ulster. History repeated itself and soon there was inter-tribal jealousy and his army fell apart.

In what has been described as an age of reason rather than patriotism, Balldearg joined William III's forces and demanded the Earldom of Tirconnell, plus suitable compensation for the loss of the brigadier rank he had held in Spain. He ravaged Connacht before setting off on a number of military missions on the Continent. In 1697 he returned to Spain and died a major-general.

The O Donnells who sailed for Europe with the "Wild Geese" were not slow to establish themselves in the military hierarchy. **Major-General Henry Count O Donnell** (a descendant of Calvagh, Chief of Tirconnell) was the founder of the Austrian branch of the family. With his O Donnell cousins from Larkfield, County Leitrim, he went to Austria to join his uncle, General Count Hamilton. Henry's eldest son, **Count Joseph O Donnell** (1755–1810), was the skilful Finance Minister who steered Austria through the economic disaster following the Napoleonic invasion. Joseph's son, **Field Marshal Count Maurice O Donnell**, born in Vienna in 1780, was the father of the famous **Major-General Maximilian Count O Donnell** who, as aide-de-camp to the Austrian Emperor, Franz Josef, saved him from assassination in 1853. The lineage of the Counts O Donnell von Tirconnell in Austria is a continuing one.

Henry's brother, **Lieutenant-General Joseph O Donnell** (1722–87), lived in Spain, where the Irish always received the same opportunities for promotion as the native Spanish. He had six sons and two daughters. His eldest daughter, **Beatrix**, married Count Manuel de Pombo, Colombia's national hero. Her many descendants are still in South America.

Carlos O Donnell (1773–1830) was the second son of General Joseph O Donnell. Carlos's son was **Leopoldo O Donnell** (1809–67), the most outstanding of the Spanish O Donnells. Following the successful Moroccan campaign, he was created Duke of Tetuan in 1860. He was Governor of Cuba for a while and was Prime Minister of Spain in 1858. Leopoldo's nephew, **Lieutenant Carlos O Donnell** (d. 1903), was Chamberlain, Minister for State and ambassador at the courts of Brussels, Vienna and Lisbon. Carlos's son, **Juan** (1864–1928), presided at the Irish Race Convention held in 1919. The delegates endeavoured to gain the support of President Wilson of America for Ireland's claim to nationhood, but their efforts ended in failure. In 1956, the National University of Ireland conferred an honorary degree on his descendant, **Leopoldo, Duke of Tetuan** (b. 1915).

Leopoldo O Donnell (1809–67), Duke of Tetuan

It is impossible to visit Madrid today without recognizing the influence of the O Donnells. One of its principal streets bears the name, as do many shops, commercial houses and garages. There is one family of thirteen O Donnell brothers and in the telephone directory they are numerous. The present Duke of Tetuan of the Spanish O Donnells has five brothers, all married.

After the battle of the Boyne in 1690, **Daniel O Donel** was one of the family who went to France, taking with him the *Cathach*. It was deposited in a monastery where it was discovered by a priest in the 1880s. **Sir Nial O Donnell** of the Newport, County Mayo, family claimed it as the badge of their chieftaincy. This was disputed by the other branches of the family. Finally the *Cathach* reached the neutral haven of the Royal Irish Academy, where it was placed by **Sir Richard Annesley O Donnell**, 4th Baronet of Newport House (now a first class hotel).

James Louis O Donnell (1738–1811) left his Tipperary home to study in Rome and in Prague, where he was ordained a Franciscan friar before returning to Ireland. In the eighteenth century, there was much contact by sea between Newfoundland and the port of Waterford, where he was Prior to the Franciscan house. Newfoundland merchants asked for him to be sent to their country. He arrived in 1796, aged 58, and made such a valuable contribution to the religious and political life of this new land that he was dubbed the "Apostle of Newfoundland".

John Francis O Donnell (1837–74) was the son of a Limerick shopkeeper. At 17 he was a reporter for the *Munster News*. He went to London to work for a number of journals. Charles Dickens took an interest in him. In 1826, when A.M. Sullivan was editing the Young Ireland revolutionary newspaper, the *Nation*, John Francis returned to Dublin to work for him. Whether living in Dublin or London, he championed the nationalist movement. He had a great love of poetry and a promising literary career was cut short by his early death in London.

The O Donnells have that rare enough distinction, especially in Ireland, of having had a cardinal in the family. **Patrick O Donnell** (1856–1927) was born in Kilraine, County Donegal. At 24 he was the youngest bishop in the world at the time, and became a cardinal in 1915. He was instrumental in building churches and schools. He showed particular concern for the restoration of the Irish language, and with healing the nationalist rift following the death of Parnell. He was one of the founder members of the National University of Ireland.

The best-known O Donnell writer is **Peader O Donnell** (1893–1986), who was born in Donegal into a family of eleven children. He moved from teaching to trade unionism, and involved himself in the problems of small farmers and labourers. He fought in the Civil War in Ireland. Later he joined various left-wing movements in Europe. In the 1930s he wrote plays, short stories and novels, including the much admired *Islanders*. He edited *The Bell*, one of Ireland's finest literary magazines, in its final years. He encouraged young writers, including the irascible genius, Patrick Kavanagh.

All the Irish branches of the O Donnells are extinct in the male line except Larkfield. The sole surviving member is The O Donnell of Tirconnell, **Father Aedh O Donel** (b. 1940), who is a Franciscan missionary in Zimbabwe. The headship of the clan will pass from him to his Spanish cousins, represented by the Dukes of Tetuan.

John Francis O Donnell

O Donoghue
ó ðonnchú

Donahue

Donoghue

Donohoe

Dunphy

O Donjou

Ó Donnchadha

Because of the Anglicization of Irish names there are a number of versions of this very common Gaelic name. It is particularly common in south-west Cork and Tipperary. It is formed from the personal name Donagh, meaning brown warrior.

As well as variations in the spelling there are several distinct families. It was Anglicized to Dunphy by the Ossory branch, who were of the same stock as the Fitzpatricks who founded the Cistercian Abbey of Jerpoint in County Kilkenny in 1158 when Donagh MacGillapatrick was King of Ossory. Surnames were coming into general use at about this time.

In 1387, the Abbot of Jerpoint was fined for a violation of the Statutes of Kilkenny, which prohibited the admission of Irishmen as members of the community. In 1540, the abbey was suppressed and its lands were given to the Butlers. It is one of the finest of the many monastic ruins in Ireland.

The O Donoghues of Cashel, County Tipperary, though related to the all-powerful MacCarthys, were frequently in territorial conflict with them, which led to the eventual decline of this particular sept. The O Donoghues of Desmond were kinsmen of the O Mahonys, descendants of the kings of Munster. They were among the many prominent families which fought at the battle of Clontarf in 1014.

By the fourteenth century, the O Donoghues had been driven out of their territories by the MacCarthys and the O Mahonys. They settled in Kerry where they became lords of all the land around Killarney. Here they separated into two clans whose chieftains were O Donoghue Mór and O Donoghue of the Glens.

Ross Castle, by the lakes of Killarney, was the headquarters of the O Donoghue Mór family. In the reign of Elizabeth I their properties were confiscated and were subsequently acquired by Sir Valentine Browne. A succeeding Valentine Browne was granted "the lakes of Killarney, with all the islands of or in the same, and the fisheries of the said lakes, and the soil and bottom thereof". The Browne titles, which included Earl of Kenmare and Viscount Castlerosse, are now extinct and Ross Castle is an imposing ruin by the lake.

In ancient times an O Donoghue of the Glens was supposed to have gone over to the fairies. According to the legend, on May Day he used to glide over the lakes of Killarney on a white horse accompanied by the sound of unearthly music and attended by troops of spirits scattering flowers. (It would be nice to think that it was this unearthly connection which helped the O Donoghues of the Glens to retain their considerable property until comparatively recently.) **Geoffrey O Donoghue of the Glens** (1655–98) was one of the foremost poets and scholars of the seventeenth century.

Following the battle of the Boyne in 1690, O Donoghues begin to appear in European and South American history. O Donoghues exiled in Spain transformed the name to O Donjou. **Juan O Donjou** (1751–1821) was the last Spanish ruler of Mexico. The O Donoghues were high-ranking officers in the military lists of France, Spain and Austria.

Those who managed to survive the turbulent seventeenth century in their native Cavan, Galway, Kerry and Cork became active in politics. **Daniel O Donoghue of the Glens** (1833–89) of County Kerry was educated at Stoneyhurst in England. He was Member of Parliament for Tipperary and became a prominent figure in national politics, and was regarded by Charles Gavan Duffy as an extreme nationalist. He was challenged to a duel by Sir Robert Peel, the Conservative Prime Minister who repealed the Corn Laws. Peel had called O Donoghue "a Mannikin traitor". His political career ended in bankruptcy in 1870.

Patrick O Donoghue, another patriot O Donoghue of that time, was tried at the Clonmel Assizes with Smith O Brien, Meagher and MacManus and was sentenced to death, which was reduced to transportation for life to Van Dieman's Land, now Tasmania. **Francis Joseph O Donoghue** (1875–1911) of Dublin studied painting in Paris and was an exhibitor at the Royal Hibernian Academy in 1899. An early victim of the motor car, he was knocked down and killed on Morehampton Road in Dublin.

John O Donoghue (d. 1893), a lawyer and a Kerry journalist, became editor of the *Freeman's Journal* in 1871, and wrote *The Historical Memoirs of the O Briens*. **David James O Donoghue** (1886–1917) was born in Chelsea, London, of Cork parentage. He returned to Dublin and became a successful bookseller. He edited, among other publications, *Poets of Ireland*, a useful reference book of the time.

John O Donoghue (1900–64), son of a small farmer, tried life from many angles: policeman, monk, labourer in England and, finally, writer. His reminiscences, *In a Quiet Land*, were rejected many times before becoming a Book Society choice and bringing him fame.

Newburgh, New York, on the Hudson River, was the birthplace of **T. Donoghue** and his two sons **Tim** and **J. F. Donoghue** who, each in his turn, rated as the fastest skater in the world. J. F. Donoghue won every event at the International Championship Meeting at Amsterdam in 1981.

The Irish played a leading part in the growth of San Francisco, opting for business rather than the hazardous Californian gold-fields. One immigrant, **Peter Donahue**, established the city's street lighting system and its first iron foundry. He operated a steamboat line and organized a railroad company. His brothers-in-law made fortunes in urban development.

Patrick Donohoe (1811–1901), a journalist, founded and edited the *Boston Pilot*, a newspaper for the Irish who made up half the population of south Boston.

The present O Donoghue of the Glens, **Paul Vincent O Donoghue**, lives in County Offaly. The family seat, Ballinahown Court, was sold in 1965.

Ballet-dancing does not feature as one of the great Irish arts, although the famous ballerina Dame Ninette de Valois was born in Ireland. So, too, was **Deirdre O Donohoe**, who began her career dancing with Dame Margot Fonteyn in *The Sleeping Beauty*—as the mouse! After graduating from the Royal Ballet School in London, she won several scholarships and travelled abroad. In 1974 a back strain put an end to her dancing, but she began a very successful teaching career and even worked with the late, great Rudolf Nureyev.

Daniel O Donoghue of the Glens

O Donovan
ó ðonnaБháin

Donovan

O Donoven

In his useful book, *Irish Names and Surnames*, Father Woulfe says that the O Donovans belong to the royal race of Munster and that they were originally chiefs of Carbery, a district lying along the River Maigue in Limerick. Their principal stronghold was at Bruree (Brugh Riogh), the royal residence. Donnabháin is a combination of *donn* (brown) and *dubhán* (a derivative of *dubh*, meaning black).

Around 1178, following the arrival of the Normans, the O Donovans were driven from Carbery. They found refuge in south-west Cork where, aided by their trusted allies the O Mahonys, they settled.

Few Gaelic families are as well recorded as the O Donovans. Until the end of the Jacobite wars they had considerable power and extensive possessions. Some O Donovans moved to Kilkenny, while another branch settled in Waterford. In Munster, particularly in the Cork area, they are still very numerous.

The official Chief of the Name is **Morgan Gerald Daniel O Donovan** of Hollybrook House, Skibbereen, County Cork. At one time the family fortress was Crom Castle on the River Maigue, while their Donovan Castle was in the hills near Drimoleague in County Cork. This O Donovan family is one of the most ancient in Ireland, with a pedigree which can be traced back to Ceallachán, King of Munster in AD 964. Ceallachán's son **Donovan** ruled as chief in AD 977, and it was from him that the family took its name.

Crom O Donovan, who owned Crom Castle, was seventh in descent from him. All the O Donovan families descend from his three sons. The Chief of the Name in 1560 was inaugurated chieftain of Carbery by the great MacCarthy Reagh.

The O Donovans were faithful to the Catholic and Stuart cause, and because of this allegiance they lost all their power and possessions. Many of them went to France where they joined the Continental armies in the service of the Irish Brigade. O Donovan's Infantry was one of the foremost of these many regiments of Irish exiles.

In 1843, after more than 150 years in exile, a descendant of the "Wild Geese", **Rhoderick O Donoven**, Lieutenant-Colonel of the 8th French Infantry, the old Regiment of Dillon and O Mullaly, was legally permitted to reside in Ireland. He married Marguerite Josephine Ida Lally-Tollendal of France, also a descendant of an illustrious family whose name had once been Lally of Tullaghnadaly from County Galway. Count Lally-Tollendal was of this family, a nobleman of both Ireland and France.

The Irish suffered from the excesses of the French Revolution, as they were classed as aristocrats. **Abbé Donovan**, a Capuchin friar from Cork, was chaplain to a noble Parisian family. The family fled from Paris, leaving the Abbé in charge of their palatial house. Holy orders gave him no protection and he was arrested and condemned to the guillotine. He gave spiritual consolation to his fellow-prisoners on the way to their execution. An officer of the troops guarding the guillotine called out in Irish, "Are there any Irish among you?" "There are seven of us," answered the Abbé Donovan. The officer used his influence and saved the lives of his fellow countrymen. The Abbé returned to Cork, where he is said to have devoted himself to preparing condemned prisoners to meet their death.

John O Donovan (1805–61), the fourth son of **Edmund O Donovan** and Eleanor Hoberlin of Attateemore, was born on a Kilkenny farm.

O Donovan

These O Donovans were proud of their lineage which they could trace back to Eoghan, King of Munster in about AD 250. On his deathbed, John's father reminded him of his aristocratic forefathers. Afterwards his eldest son took his brother John to Dublin and had him educated there. In Dublin John came under the influence of his uncle, **Patrick O Donovan**, who instilled in him a great love for Anglo-Irish history and tradition.

At first he worked in the Irish Record Office, then for the Ordnance Survey, where he examined ancient manuscripts in the Irish language. He checked no less than 144,000 ancient place names and his research was so thorough that he corrected the mistakes of many eminent historians of previous ages! In 1845, he published his *Irish Grammar*, having worked on it for twelve years. His finest achievement was the translation, annotation and editing of the first complete edition of *The Annals of the Four Masters*. It had been compiled in the reign of Charles I by Michael O Clery with monks of the Franciscan order. In recognition of this scholarly work, John O Donovan was awarded an honorary law degree by Trinity College, Dublin.

John O Donovan

The great Gaelic scholar, Eugene O Curry (1796–1862), said of it: "The translation is executed with extreme care—an immense mass of notes contain a vast amount of information, historical, topographical and genealogical... There is no instance of a work so vast being undertaken and completed in a style so beautiful by the enterprise of a private publisher". The Irish type for the *Annals* was cast from designs by George Petrie and printed in Dublin by the still extant firm of Michael H. Gill. It has been said of the scholarly John O Donovan that "no man has done so much for native Irish history".

Literary gifts of a different order were passed on to his son, **Edmund O Donovan** (1844–83). He studied medicine and science at Trinity College, Dublin, but did not graduate. For a while he worked as clerk to the Registrar, and then as Assistant Librarian. He showed a keen interest in heraldry and was chosen by Sir Bernard Burke, Ulster King of Arms, to carry the banner at the installation of the Duke of Connacht as Knight of St Patrick in Dublin Castle.

By the time he was 22, Edmund was contributing to the *Irish Times* and other Dublin newspapers. He went to France and America and in 1870, during the Franco-German war, his adventurous temperament led him to join the French army. After the battle of Sedan he transferred to the Foreign Legion, which provided him with many adventures about which he wrote for the London and Dublin newspapers. He was in Spain during the Carlist rising in 1873, from where he sent back reports which were published in *The Times*. In 1876 he was in Bosnia and Herzegovina during the battle against the Turks. When he was appointed war correspondent for the *Daily News* in the same year, he went to Asia Minor to report on the war between Russia and Turkey.

Representing the *Daily News*, he made a celebrated journey to Merv and penetrated, undisguised, into the midst of the Turks, who thought him an emissary of the Russians and kept him in captivity. An excellent linguist, he managed to talk himself out of this situation and, on reaching home, he wrote an account of it in his book, *The Merv Oasis*. In 1883 he was attached to the army of Hicks Pasha which was annihilated at Obeid in the Sudan. He was killed in the battle of Kashzil when the Egyptian army was ambushed by the Mahdi. Edmund O Donovan was one of the first and most daring of war correspondents.

A famous O Donovan in Irish political history was known as O Donovan Rossa. He was born **Jeremiah O Donovan** (1831–1915) at

Jeremiah O Donovan Rossa

Rosscarbery, County Cork. He worked for a while as a relieving officer at Skibbereen, but soon became deeply involved in the Fenian movement. He was imprisoned, though eventually released, for complicity in a subversive plot known as the Phoenix Conspiracy. From 1863 to 1865 he was business manager of the *Irish People*, the newspaper of the Young Irelanders. With O Leary, Kickham and other Fenians, he was sentenced to penal servitude for life by the notorious Judge Keogh. In prison in England he was remarkably badly treated, but wrote so effectively about it that he received an amnesty. He was given no option but to emigrate to America. There he edited the *United Irishman* and wrote about his prison life. He was 84 when he died in New York. When his body was brought back to Dublin, it was the focus of one of the largest, most political funeral ceremonies ever seen in Glasnevin cemetery. It was shortly before the outbreak of the 1916 rising, and Patrick Pearse, one of its instigators, gave a rousing oration at the graveside.

Gerald O Donovan (1871–1942), a Catholic priest, left the Church in 1904 to become a successful novelist in London. Although his books are now out of favour, they were highly regarded by Frank O Connor. They provide an original account of Ireland at the turn of the century as seen through the eyes of a very critical priest. While still a priest, he had been responsible for attracting Lady Gregory and Edward Martyn into Sir Horace Plunkett's co-operative movement. Only since his wife's death in 1958 has Gerald O Donovan been revealed as the lifelong friend, possibly lover, of the English novelist Rose Macaulay, whom he met in the Italian Department of the British Ministry of Information in 1918.

A marked literary vein runs through the O Donovans. **Michael O Donovan** (1903–66) was born in Cork, educated by the Christian Brothers and began work there as a librarian. In his early years he had been greatly influenced by Daniel Corkery, a nationalist writer and Professor of English at University College, Cork. He wrote under the pseudonym Frank O Connor and his first story, *Guests of the Nation*, published in 1931, is a classic which recounts the conflict between England and Ireland from the viewpoint of a group of men who, rather than killing each other, would have been friends had it not been for their history and politics. A scholarly writer, his strength was rooted in the Gaelic language and culture. He translated many works, including Brian Merriman's poem *Midnight Court*, wrote plays for Dublin's Abbey Theatre and travelled many times to the USA to lecture. He could be trenchantly critical of progress that involved the destruction of the human environment. His private life was often tempestuous. By the time he died he was the foremost writer of modern Irish literature and was even compared to Chekhov and de Maupassant.

One family of O Donovans who emigrated to the USA in the nineteenth century distinguished themselves during the Tailteann Games in a form of athletics called the *roth cleas* which means weight throwing. It is a sport in which the Gaels reputedly competed as far back as 1829 BC! In 1914, **P. Donovan** set a world record for throwing the 56-pound weight for height with a distance of 16 feet 11 inches.

John O Donovan (1836–1912), a Waterford-born priest, sailed for Sydney in September 1861, but was shipwrecked in the Bass Strait and did not arrive until January 1862. He soon established a reputation as an orator and was described as "an athlete of no mean character", particularly in the handling of horses. Not only did he build churches and convents, he designed them. He was made a fellow of St John's College at the University of Sydney. He lived in a style that his Sydney colleagues assumed he had enjoyed in his paternal home. He was looked after by a sister, then a niece, and a staff which included a Chinese cook and several maids. His fine horses were greatly admired, and while riding he never opened a gate if he could jump it instead. He never missed the Mudgee races, where he took an interest not only in the horses but also in the "big boys" of his flock, whom he chastised with his riding whip if they transgressed. He was parish priest, later Monsignor, at Mudgee for 44 years.

Harry O Donovan (1896–1973), a Dubliner, edged his way into show business as an artisan-actor. When he met up with Ireland's supreme comedian, Jimmy O Dea, they formed O Dea–O Donovan Productions, a partnership which, for thirty years, produced variety shows and Christmas pantomimes. They also supplied radio and television scripts. Harry O Donovan was manager, actor and dresser, and it was he who invented the character "Biddy Mulligan, the Pride of the Coombe", which was to make Jimmy O Dea Ireland's best-loved comedian.

Irish-Americans took part in the First World War in the famous Fighting 69th. One of their outstanding officers was **Colonel William Donovan** (known as Wild Bill). It was he who, during the Second World War, directed America's first intelligence organization known as the Office of Strategic Services. This was to be the forerunner of the CIA.

O Farrell
ó feARghAill

Farrell

More O Farrell

O Ferrall

The Ó Fearghaile were a very ancient and powerful sept which spread from Annaly in County Longford into County Westmeath. Their chieftain was Lord of Annaly and his headquarters was known as Longphuirt Uí Fhearghaill, meaning O Farrell's Fortress, which is how the town of Longford acquired its name.

From the personal name Fearghaill (meaning super valour) came the Ó Fearghaill surname. As the family grew in numbers it divided into two septs known as O Farrell Boy (from *buidhe*, meaning yellow) and O Farrell Bane (*bán* meaning white).

The More O Ferralls descend from the illustrious Mordha (Moore or More) family. As with the Nugents and the O Reillys, it was marriage which amalgamated the two names, but, unlike the Nugents, the O Ferralls kept the More name.

Lysagh O More, in about 1340, wrested his territory and title of Lord of Leix (Laois) from the usurping Mortimers. It is recorded that "He stirred up to war all the Irish in Munster and Leinster by persuasion, promises and gifts, and expelled nearly all the English from their lands by force, for in one evening he burned eight castles of the Englishry, and destroyed the noble castle of Dunamase belonging to Roger Mortimer, and usurped to himself the lordship of the country. From a slave he became a lord, from a subject a prince".

Caech MacDonnell O More was Chief of Leix from 1542 to 1545. In 1555 his brother, **Patrick O More**, supported by the O Connors of Offaly (the neighbouring county) invaded Leix. His brother **Rory Óg**, who opposed him, was killed. In England this invasion was regarded as Rory Óg's rebellion and, as a result, his land was forfeited and colonized by the English, and its name was changed from Leix to Queen's County. In 1567, twelve years too late, it was established that it was Patrick and his allies who had been the "rebels", while Rory Óg had been the defender. In the meantime the O More territory had been parcelled out among English adventurers and it was deemed politically inadvisable to uproot them. Instead, by way of compensation, Queen Elizabeth I granted Rory Óg's surviving son, **Charles O More**, the Balyna estate near Moyvalley in County Kildare. He had no alternative but to accept and Balyna became the home of the O More chieftains and their descendants for the next 400 years.

In October 1641 **Rory O More** (1592–1655), a nephew of Rory Óg, plotted with Conor Maguire, Baron of Enniskillen, and others to seize Dublin Castle. They were betrayed by Owen O Connelly. Rory, who had been suspicious of the traitor, escaped, but the others were executed. Rory hid in the thick woods then surrounding Balyna. When surprised by his pursuers he is said to have plunged his stick into the ground before fleeing. This stick took root and grew into a conifer. There was a family legend that when the tree died the family would leave Balyna. In 1957 the tree died and, shortly afterwards, Balyna passed from the More O Ferrall family.

Rory O More managed to rally the Irish and the Old English into forming the Confederate army in which he was a colonel. It represented the four provinces and its aim was a united Ireland and to drive out the usurpers. It was an inspired idea which had the support of many of the influential Irish in Europe. There were many differences of opinion however, and, after several years, the army came to a sad end.

Colonel Charles O More was the commander of a troop of horse in Owen Roe O Neill's army. In 1688 he raised a regiment of foot in which all barring two of its members were natives of the Queen's County. All the officers, except for these two odd men out, were killed at the battle of Aughrim on Sunday 12 July 1691, after quarter had been granted.

The Ó Fearghaile are well recorded in the genealogical archives, having a variety of spellings. The Catholic Confederation of Kilkenny which endured from 1642 to 1649 had **Father Richard O Farrell**, a Capuchin friar, as one of its members. In 1709, **Roger O Farrell** completed his admirable *Linea Antiqua*, a genealogical manuscript which is now in the custody of the Genealogical Office in Dublin.

Ceadaigh O Farrell, who was killed at the battle of the Boyne in 1690, left three sons who emigrated to Picardy in France. The lists of the Irish regiments who served in France in the early eighteenth century contain at least 21 O Farrell officers. In 1780 there was an O Farrell regiment.

Francis Thurot O Farrel (1726–60) was born in Burgundy, France. He adopted the name of his maternal grandfather, a Captain O Farrel who had fled with the Jacobites to France where he had married a French lady named Thurot and assumed her name. A headstrong youth, Francis tried many ways of earning a living. With England and France at war, he turned his hand to privateering and became very wealthy. Later he got a commission in the French naval service where he had many adventures during the Seven Years' War. In 1760 he was aboard one of the frigates that broke through the English blockade in Belfast Lough, but he was killed shortly afterwards when they met a British squadron.

Among the many O Farrell papers abroad is an account of an "Act for naturalizing the children of **Colonel Francis Fergus D. O Ffarrell** who was born in Holland in 1694". In 1799, **Gonzalo O Farrell**, who was Spanish Minister to Berlin, exchanged diplomatic letters with the French Foreign Minister, Talleyrand.

In Ireland, despite the difficult times in the seventeenth and eighteenth centuries, at least one of the O Farrells was prospering. In his book *Dublin 1660–1860*, Maurice Craig, the architectural historian, considered the rising social class of Dublin brewers and mentions an English traveller who in 1790 "dined with the most eminent of the Dublin brewers, **Mr James Farrell**, who had his brewery in the Black Pitts but his dwelling house in Merrion Square East"—a fashionable residential area.

Like Rory or Roger, Letitia is a name that appears frequently, and often potently, in the O Ferrall lineage. **Letitia**, daughter of **Ambrose O Ferrall** of Balyna, who was a nun in the Sisters of Charity order, gave £3,000 to purchase a house in St Stephen's Green, Dublin, which grew to be one of Dublin's largest hospitals, St Vincent's, now moved to the suburb of Donnybrook. It was the **Letitia** (b. 1732) who married Richard Ferrall of Dillon's Bank in Dublin who joined the More name to O Ferrall. A descendant of theirs, **James Ambrose O Ferrall** (1753–1828), was a major-general in Austria's Imperial army, which he entered when he was twenty. He had a long and adventurous military career and was also a Royal Chamberlain. A Miss Ambrose, a connection by marriage, left him a fortune and the family seat, Balliane House, in County Wexford, on condition that he change his name to Ambrose. He died unmarried, which saved further confusion with names.

The Balliane estate went to his kinsman, **Charles More O Ferrall**, who entered the Sardinian service in 1791 when he was 23. When the monarchy was overthrown by Napoleon in 1798, Charles's appointment with the Sardinian army came to an end and he went to Piedmont in northern Italy.

At Novi Liguri, on the southern bank of the River Po, the scene of a French defeat in 1799, he was made a captain of the horse on the field of battle by the king's viceroy. Subsequently the king made him first equerry, gentleman of the bedchamber, major-general of cavalry and adjutant-general. He retired to Ireland where he died at Balliane House in 1831. Balliane had previously been the home of his eldest sister, Mary, a widow.

Charles's son, **Victor Emmanuel More O Ferrall**, named after his godfather, the King of Italy, returned to Ireland to manage the Balliane estate. Despite the efforts of the More O Ferrall family to help him, he mismanaged it so badly that it had to be sold. He emigrated to America where he died.

Major Ambrose O Ferrall (1752–1835) of Balyna had his early education at Dublin's popular Fagan's Academy before going to the Jesuit College at Bruges. In 1770 he entered the Military Academy in Turin, where he was taught to ride by the famous Chevalier Capitolo. He also served for some years in the Royal Sardinian army. He married twice and had ten children.

His eldest son was the **Right Honourable Richard More O Ferrall** (1797–1880), who was a Member of Parliament for Kildare and Longford. In 1832 he was a member of the parliamentary committee set up to report on the situation in Ireland. When a Royal Commission was issued in 1833 to report into the condition of the poor in Ireland, Richard More O Ferrall and the Archbishop of Dublin were its two Catholic members.

He was an adviser to the Catholic University and was a friend of Cardinal Wiseman and a supporter of Daniel O Connell. In 1835, under the administration of Lord Melbourne, he became Lord of the Treasury, First Secretary of the Admiralty and, in 1841, was Secretary to the Treasury. In 1847 he was the first civilian to hold the post of Governor of Malta. Four years later he resigned because he would not serve under the Prime Minister, Lord John Russell, who had championed the Ecclesiastical Titles Act of 1851 in opposition to the Papal Bill of 1850 to restore a Catholic hierarchy in England.

Richard's brother, **John Lewis More O Ferrall** (1800–81), was educated at Acton Burnell and Stonyhurst College in England. He graduated from Trinity College, Dublin, and was called to the Irish Bar. He became Commissioner of the Dublin Metropolitan Police on its establishment in 1871. He declined a baronetcy.

George Anthony More O Ferrall (1907–82) joined Sir Phillip Ben Greet's Shakespearean Company and later won a scholarship to the Central School of Dramatic Art. In 1936 he joined the first BBC television team and was joint producer of the very first television programme. Following four and a half years of service with the Royal Artillery during the Second World War, he was put in charge of all BBC broadcasts to Allied Forces, including the American Forces Network.

From 1946 to 1950 he was a senior BBC television producer, but he left when told he had reached his salary ceiling. He went into films and directed for 20th Century Fox, ABC, Korda, Rank and British Lion. In 1959 he joined Anglia Television as Head of Drama. He had more television plays to his credit than any other producer and was awarded the Baird Medal for outstanding contributions to television. From 1964 to 1968 he directed for ATV. He retired to live in Spain.

Following the More O Ferrall lineage can be confusing, especially in the case of the long and sometimes catastrophic history of Kildangan, near Monasterevin in County Kildare. Kildangan was originally a FitzGerald castle but they sold it, in about 1705, to the brothers Edward and Edmund

Reilly, originally from County Cavan, but now prosperous merchants in Dublin where Edmund was an alderman of the city. In 1849, Kildangan passed into the More O Ferrall family with the marriage of Susan O Reilly (1826–54) to **Charles Edward More O Ferrall**. She died in childbirth aged only 28, leaving a son, **Dominick**. During his lifetime he considerably extended the estate, with the advice of the eminent British landscape gardener John Sutherland, who laid out the celebrated gardens. He dynamited the remains of the ancient castle and used its stones to build the present house.

Kildangan Stud in County Kildare, home of the More O Ferralls

Dominick's son, **Roderic** (1903–90), was known internationally as a successful breeder and trainer of bloodstock. He was president of the Bloodstock Breeders Association. His brother **Francis** (d. 1976) was a chairman of the Anglo-Irish Bloodstock Agency in London and his youngest brother, **Rory**, is chairman of the advertising firm of More O Ferrall which works on an international scale.

In Victorian Dublin, **Sir Thomas Farrell** (1827–1900) was a popular sculptor whose numerous statues of its leading citizens adorn the city.

James Gordon Farrell (1935–79), who was born in Liverpool, won the 1973 Booker Prize for literature with his novel *The Siege of Krishnapur*. In the same year he wrote a best seller, *The Singapore Grip*, and was forecast by the critics to be on the way to a promising career. Unfortunately, he died dramatically, washed into the sea by a freak wave while fishing in County Cork.

In the nineteenth century, many Farrells left Ireland for Australia and the Americas. **Charles F. O Farrell** (1840–1905), born in Virginia, was a lawyer, a Confederate cavalry colonel and Governor of Virginia from 1894 to 1898. It was this son of Irish immigrants who, as a Virginia legislator, worked vigorously to stamp out lynching.

The parents of **John Farrell** (1851–1904) emigrated during the Famine to Buenos Aires. Some years later they sailed for Australia where the family farmed and went into brewing. John became a minor poet and an excellent journalist, especially as a contributor to the *Sydney Daily Telegraph*.

James A. Farrell (1863–1943) is a classic example of the American-born Irish who did well for themselves, and for America. Born in Connecticut, he married Catherine McDermott and rose from labourer in a New Haven steel mill to developing its foreign trade sales figures to an astonishing degree. He became president of the US Steel Corporation in 1911. Later he held directorships of the American Bridge Company, Federal Steel, the Tennessee Coal and Iron Railroad, Minnesota Steel and many other related companies. He was also vice-president of the American Iron and Steel Institute and founder and chairman of the National Foreign Trade Council.

The grandparents of **James T. Farrell** (1904–79) emigrated from Athlone and Mullingar to the USA. He became a best-selling writer in the 1930s with the *Studs Lonigan* trilogy, in which he wrote of the social inequalities of the Irish artisan community in Chicago. He visited Ireland several times.

Charles Farrell (b. 1906), a Dubliner, went first to Canada and then to the USA where, during the boom years of the Hollywood film industry, he appeared in many films and was Janet Gaynor's leading man in the classic film *Seventh Heaven*. He also acted on radio and television and was a founding member of the British Actors' Equity Association in 1930.

O Flaherty

ó flaithbheartaigh

Flaherty

O Laverty

The O Flahertys are a very old Irish family and are thought to have been in Ireland before the time of Christ. Their armorial bearings depict their history. The red hand indicates their dealings with the Ulster O Neills, the black galley signifies their ships and the lizard warns the sleeping O Flaherty warrior of an approaching enemy.

In County Donegal a different dialect of Irish was spoken which corrupted the name to O Laverty. The O Lavertys were a minor sept of the O Flahertys and their chieftain was styled Lord of Aileach (Elagh) in Donegal.

To this day the O Flaherty clan is most numerous around Galway, though, happily, they are no longer "the ferocious O Flahertys from whom God defend us", an exhortation the citizens of Galway felt impelled to fix over their city gate in the Middle Ages.

The early history of the O Flahertys was one of constant warfare and some very dark deeds. For decades they fought with, or against, their O Conor neighbours. The Norman Burkes who overran Connacht had intermarried with the Irish, but they could not feel secure while the O Flahertys were rampaging, so they retaliated until the O Flahertys had to capitulate and make a treaty with the Burkes. Then, as allies of the Burkes, they both attacked the O Conors! It was a period when many lives, and much land, was lost.

At Annaghdown, near Lough Corrib in Connemara, the O Flahertys founded a church on the site of the monastery where St Brendan the Navigator is said to have died in the sixth century. Between 1976 and 1978, Tim Severin sought to verify the legend that the saint had crossed to the New World, by constructing a leather boat and sailing it to Newfoundland. His book describing this enterprise has been translated into many languages.

Although the O Flahertys are listed in various pedigrees, there are no outstanding characters until the thirteenth century, when the English drove them to the south side of Lough Corrib where they built their castle at Moycullen and were styled Lords of Iar (west) Connacht.

When **Morogh O Flaherty** and his brother, **Roderick**, were once again attacked by the belligerent Burkes they took their complaint to Henry III, but they received little help and had to do their own fighting. They finally succeeded in quelling the Burkes, which made them undisputed masters of 250,000 acres of Connacht, from Lough Corrib to the Atlantic, which kept them quiet for several centuries.

They were mostly on good terms with the O Malley clan of County Mayo. However, when they killed an O Malley, his son, Connor, retaliated by plundering their rich castles and sailing away with the bounty. Connor did not get far, for he and his son foundered with their ships off the Aran Islands.

The impressive O Flaherty castle at Aughnanure near Oughterard in County Galway has been restored. A description of it in an old manuscript related that "the domestic staff of the castle included a physician, a master of the horse, a standard bearer, two brehons or legal advisers, attendants on ordinary visitings, a poet and an ollave in genealogy, a master of the revels, two keepers of the bees, a steward, and a collector of revenue". The names of these people and their exact duties are all recorded. For centuries this palatial castle was the O Flaherty home and fortress. It was here that they entertained a young Burke who had come to collect a long-overdue rent. They sat him down to dine, but as soon as he mentioned rent the stone floor yawned beneath his chair and he fell into the river underneath. Retrieving his body they cut off his head and sent it back to the Burkes with the message: "This is O Flaherty's rent".

Not even Grace O Malley (Granuaile), the greatest seafaring woman of all time, could quell the fighting O Flahertys—even though she married one! She was about fifteen when she was wed to **Donal O Flaherty**, known as Donal an Chogaidh (Donal of the battles). They lived in his castle at Dunowen, an inlet of the Atlantic. He was rich and powerful and she had a couple of sons and possibly some daughters by him. Irish law did not recognize descent in the female line, which makes it difficult to follow the female half of most Irish families. Donal waged war as today he might have engaged in motor racing. He was duly killed and, with some deliberation, Granuaile married MacWilliam Burke, nicknamed Richard in Iron, possibly because he wore chain mail, or maybe because there was ore on his land.

Queen Elizabeth I, whom they dubbed Cailleach Granna, meaning the ugly hag, was constantly trying to subdue them. When the sons of the Earl of Clanrickard (*see* Burke) rebelled and tried to enlist O Flaherty's aid against the queen, **Morogh O Flaherty** betrayed their plans. For this she rewarded him with the patrimony of the man who was their rightful chief, **Crone O Flaherty**.

Morogh O Flaherty was eventually plundered by the ruffianly soldiers who came with Elizabeth's detested governor, Bingham. Morogh and his twelve sons were forced to surrender their castles and Irish customs, but not the O Flaherty succession. So disillusioned was Sir Morogh—he had been honoured with the English title by the "ugly hag"—that he joined with the O Neills and O Donnells of Ulster to fight at the battle of Kinsale.

His descendants were on the losing side in the insurrection of 1641, and again at the battle of the Boyne in 1690, so that by the seventeenth century the O Flahertys who had once lorded over vast tracts of Connacht were landless. It was the end of the "ferocious O Flahertys".

The last of the O Flaherty chieftains, **Roderick** (1629–1718), was only two years old when his father Hugh died, leaving him the O Flaherty estate at Moycullen near the city of Galway. Roderick was taught by Alexander Lynch, who aroused his interest in Irish literature. He also came under the influence of the great Dubhaltach MacFirbisigh (1585–1670), who was compiling his massive *Genealogies of the Families of Ireland*. When Cromwell devastated Galway, he confiscated all Roderick's possessions. So little was returned to him that he ended his long life in poverty. He left behind an invaluable contribution to Irish letters, *The Ogygia*, an accurate history of Ireland which was written in Latin and published in London in 1685.

Monsignor Hugh O Flaherty was born in Kerry and ordained in Rome. He earned the name "The Scarlet Pimpernel of the Vatican" for being one of the priests who organized escape routes for thousands of Allied soldiers out of German-occupied Italy during the Second World War. After a lifetime spent abroad, he returned to die in his native Kerry in 1963.

The O Flahertys who went to Europe and the USA served in the Irish Brigades. Despite their martial inclinations at home, they do not appear to have had their names inscribed in military or administrative records abroad.

One of their clerics who emigrated to the USA, **Colman E. O Flaherty** (1874–1918), was from Carraroe in Connemara. In 1901 he was ordained in South Dakota and worked for eighteen years at Columbus College and Notre Dame Academy. He organized the building of many churches. When America entered the War, he went to France as chaplain with the 28th Infantry of the American Expeditionary Force and died on the battlefield.

Robert J. Flaherty (1884–1951), known as the father of the documentary film, was born in Black Mountain, Vermont, where his family had come from Ireland and had prospered in mining. While still in his teens, mining was hit by a recession and the young O Flaherty joined his father and became a cartographer and prospector for the US Steel Corporation. He travelled widely in north Canada and must have made an impression in the Hudson Bay area, where there is a small island named Flaherty Island.

He was fascinated by the life of the Eskimos and bought a movie camera, took a crash course in how to use it and made one of the great classics, *Nanook of the North*. He followed this with many other films on the lives of primitive people, including *Man of Aran*.

Liam O Flaherty (1897–1984) was born on the Aran Islands into a community which spoke only Irish. His education was sponsored by a priest up to university level, when he discovered he did not have a vocation. He served in the British army during the First World War, then returned to take part in the revolution and Civil War in Ireland. Afterwards, unhappy with Ireland, he moved to London and began writing. In 1925, his novel, *The Informer*, established him as an important writer. Although he wrote many novels, the short story is regarded as his forte. He returned to live in Dublin, where he died.

Stephen O Flaherty (1905–82) was born in County Waterford. He was one of the first native Irish millionaire industrialists. Son of an Aran Islander, he was the first to assemble the Volkswagen car outside of Germany when he introduced it to Ireland after the Second World War.

Unlike their forebears who were forbidden entrance to the city of Galway, the twentieth century has seen the city with two O Flaherty mayors: **Michael O Flaherty** of Carraroe was Mayor of Galway in 1949, while his son, **Patrick**, filled the office in 1964.

Liam O Flaherty

Aughanure Castle, County Galway, built by Morogh O Flaherty

184

O Grady

ó gráða

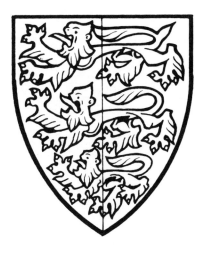

Brady

The O Gradys are an ancient aristocratic family, kinsmen of their neighbours the O Briens of Thomond in Limerick. The original O Grady stronghold was Inis Cealtra (Holy Island) on Lough Derg. Ó Gráda means illustrious, and the name goes back to the Dalcassian sept who had their territories at Killanasooghlan, by the River Fergus in County Clare. The tower of a ruined O Grady castle can still be seen in their former territory in Cineal-Donghaile near Tuamgraney, County Clare, where the O Briens granted them a generous acreage of land. A little further north, near Scarriff, there is a Lough O Grady. The O Gradys were prominent churchmen and filled high ecclesiastical office, including the bishoprics of Cashel, Tuam and Killaloe.

Towards the close of the thirteenth century they were at war with their former allies, the O Briens, who drove them from Clare to Limerick. **Hugh O Grady** acquired the lands of Kilballyowen when, in 1309, he married the daughter of the chief of the O Kerwick or Kirby clan. Kilballyowen, near Bruff, County Limerick, has been in the O Grady family ever since. It is close to Lough Gur, a small lake around which there is a rich concentration of ancient monuments, including stone circles, forts, dolmens and other megalithic remains. The O Gradys multiplied and formed new septs at Cappercullen, Elton Grange, Lodge, Cahir and Mount Prospect, and many other Munster holdings.

In 1543, **Donagh O Grady**, styled Captain of his Nation, was knighted by Henry VIII, who also granted him titles to secure his land. To win favour with the king, some O Gradys changed their Gaelic name to the innocuous-sounding Brady. Sir Donagh's son, who called himself **Hugh Brady**, was the first Protestant Bishop of Meath. His descendants are the Bradys of Raheen in County Clare. Sir Donagh's other son, **John**, was the forebear of the O Gradys of Kilballyowen, who have long since reverted to their original name.

On the estate of the O Gradys who settled at Cappercullen, there was a tree-lined avenue. One particular tree was known as the Ilchester Oak, because it was here that the beautiful **Miss O Grady** was said to meet her lover, Lord Stavordale, whom she had first met at a Limerick ball. He was the son of the Earl of Ilchester, but her father was poor and too proud to approve of their courtship. Ilchester approved however, and persuaded her father to give his blessing. The Benedictine priory of Glenstal, one of Ireland's leading boys' schools, is on the former O Grady estate.

Standish is a traditional O Grady first name. It expresses their gratitude to a good neighbour during the worst of the penal times in the seventeenth century, when **Darby O Grady**, son of **Donogh O Grady**, got into serious trouble with the authorities on account of his religion. He pretended to be a Protestant but was caught innumerable times attending mass. Finally, he was caught once too often and his lands were confiscated. In nearby Bruff lived Sir Thomas Standish, who had an only daughter, Faith. As if by divine intervention, Darby fell in love with Faith, married her and had his lands restored.

For several generations religion was a thorny issue in the family. When **John O Grady** married Mary Elizabeth de Courcy in 1751, he promised her solemnly that he would change to her religion. However, on his deathbed he called for the priest. Mary barred the way, but the priest pushed her aside and John died, the last Kilballyowen Catholic.

Standish O Grady, by John Butler Yeats

Standish O Grady (1766–1844), born at Mount Prospect, County Limerick, graduated in law from Trinity College, Dublin. He became Attorney-General and it was he who prosecuted at the trial of the patriot, Robert Emmet. For many years he was Chief Baron of the Exchequer of Ireland. In 1831 he was created Viscount Guillamore and Baron O Grady, both in County Limerick. The title is now extinct.

His nephew, **Standish Hayes O Grady** (1830–1915), was the son of **Admiral Hayes O Grady** (d. 1864). He was born at Castleconnell, County Limerick, and went from fosterage in an Irish-speaking family to Rugby School in England and Trinity College, Dublin. There he divided his studies between engineering and copying ancient Irish manuscripts under the guidance of John O Donovan and the Clare scholar, Eugene O Curry. In about 1857, he went to the United States of America, where, for thirty years, he worked as a civil engineer. He retired home to spend the rest of his long life working on ancient Irish manuscripts. He made a valuable compilation of old folk tales, *Silva Gadelica*, but his principal work, *Catalogue of the Irish Manuscripts in the British Museum*, was delayed because of difficulties with his publishers. It was completed by another scholar, Robin Flower.

Tom O Grady, a cousin of the scholarly Standish, had served abroad in the British army and was a poet with a wicked sense of humour. He was known as Spectacles O Grady. He said of Standish that he "sent his children to church [Protestant] thro fear of his wife and went to Mass himself for fear of the devil". He satirized a Limerick banker in a notorious poem, "Nosegay". The repercussions led to Spectacles O Grady exiling himself to France rather than pay £500 damages and 6d costs in a £20,000 libel suit.

Standish James O Grady (1846–1928), a cousin of Spectacles O Grady, was born at Castletown Berehaven, where his father, Viscount Guillamore, was Church of Ireland rector. He was educated locally and followed the family tradition, studying law at Trinity College, Dublin. He too, like his scholarly namesake, was fascinated by the ancient Irish tales which, at that time, had not had the benefit of much research. Drawing on the rich vein of Celtic mythology and heroic incidents from Irish history, he wrote a stream of novels and children's books including *Red Hugh's Captivity*, *Fin and His Companions*, *The Chieftain's Last Rally*, *The Coming of Cuchulain* and *The Flight of the Eagle*. He influenced the younger generation, imbuing many of them with a strong sense of nationalism.

There are so many Standish O Gradys that it is understandable that, when **Standish O Grady** the engineer and scholar died in 1915, some of the obituaries in the English newspapers confused him with the living, romantic writer, **Standish James O Grady**. This family, who were Viscounts of Guillamore, a junior line, are commemorated in the church of St John of Knockaney, County Limerick, by a series of stained glass windows.

It was a family tradition to join the army, and many O Gradys had fine service careers. There was an O Grady admiral and naval commander. **Lieutenant-Colonel Gerald Vigors de Courcy O Grady**, who died in 1993, served in India and in Burma in the Second World War and was awarded a Military Cross. His wife, Holly, was from Maryland, USA. Their son Brian de Courcy, who lives in England, is now The O Grady of Kilballyowen. The O Grady mansion is no more. It was dilapidated and impossibly expensive to repair and maintain. It was quietly "put down" and replaced with a modern house nearby. The O Gradys have meticulously preserved the invaluable historic family archives. The late O Grady named his daughter **Faith Standish O Grady**, and their coat of arms and the 1632 deed guaranteeing their land through the original Standish is still in their possession. Callers often come from abroad seeking family roots, not all of them authentic O Gradys!

Henry Woodfin O Grady's antecedents were Irish. He was born in 1850 near Atlanta, Georgia, and his father, a colonel in the Highland Guards, was killed during the American Civil War. Henry O Grady graduated in law from the University of Virginia. Prevented from exposing corruption in local politics by the newspaper on which he worked, he left it and bought up all the other newspapers, hoping to use them as a weapon to clean up politics. Nobody bought O Grady's newspapers, however, and he lost all his money.

In New York his journalism found a more appreciative audience and he was employed by the *New York Herald*. His reporting did much to alleviate the misery that followed the Civil War. He achieved great popularity as an orator on the subject of negro rights. He died at the early age of 39.

Australia also lays claim to yet another O Grady writer, **Frank O Grady**. Born in 1909 in Sydney, he has been a vice-president of the Royal Australian Historical Society and has published many novels.

Even Rudyard Kipling knew of the O Gradys. He wrote: "For Rosie O Grady and the Colonel's lady, are sisters under the skin".

Generations of schoolchildren doing physical training have been ordered "O Grady says knees bend. O Grady says feet apart. O Grady says quick march", and so on. It can only be supposed that the original O Grady instructor was of the numerous O Gradys who served abroad with the army.

An O Grady who emigrated from Clare a century ago married a black American woman. They kept the Irish name proudly in their family and his great-grandson is **Cassius O Grady Clay**, or Muhammad Ali!

Iniscealtra on Lough Derg, the original O Grady stronghold

O Keeffe
ó caoimh

Cuif

Ó Cuiv

The O Keeffes who descend from the kings of Munster were kinsmen of the MacCarthys and the O Callaghans. Fionghuine was King of Munster in the tenth century and it is from his son, Art Caom, that the surname derives. *Caom* means noble or gentle.

Donncad Ó Caoim was the first to use the name during the reign of King Ceallachán of Cashel. The family had their earliest settlement at Glanmore, County Cork, and their former domain near Fermoy, County Cork, has since become known as Roche's Country. When they were driven out by the Norman Roches, they settled in Duhallow, County Cork, and became so entrenched and numerous that the district was called Pobble O Keeffe (by then their name had been transformed to O Keeffe).

Father Eoghan (Owen) O Keeffe (1656–1726) of Glenville, County Cork, was president of the bards of north Cork and a Gaelic poet of considerable achievement. He entered the Church after the death of his wife and was parish priest of Doneraile until his death. Many of his songs are still sung in his native County Cork.

Until the disruption of the Gaelic order in the sixteenth century, the O Keeffes remained a distinct clan. Following the sad exodus of so many of their compatriots, they also sought a new life and opportunities in Europe, mostly in the armies of France.

One of the many O Keeffe officers in the French army, **Constantine O Keeffe** (1691–1745) served with remarkable valour in the Irish Brigade. In order to be admitted to the very conservative nobility of France, he had to procure records from Ireland to prove his aristocratic Irish lineage.

In the eighteenth century, another **Constantine**, a later emigrant, was a lieutenant with the Regiment of O Brien. **Patrice O Keeffe** was chef de brigade of the regiment of Dillon from 1793 to 1794.

General Patrick O Keeffe of the next generation served for forty years in the Irish Brigade and was wounded many times. Some of the O Keeffes of Retigny in the province of Champagne, France, were descendants of men who served in the Swiss Guards and the English service between 1530 and 1797. In France the name was spelled Cuif, and there is a record of a baptismal certificate issued in the fourth year of the Republic of France for **Jeanne Cuif** from the parish church of Alligny in the diocese of Rheims.

In the eighteenth century in Ireland, when some of the penal laws were relaxed, the O Keeffes were among the Old Irish who began to distinguish themselves as artists and writers.

Daniel O Keeffe (1740–86) of Dublin trained at the Dublin Society's drawing school, where he won several prizes. He went to London and began a promising career with an exhibition at the Royal Academy. Such acclaim for an Irishman gave him the confidence to restore the Gaelic O to his surname. "Few of us Old Irish ventured to sport our 'O' at that period", his brother John, the dramatist, had said.

This **John O Keeffe** (1747–1833) was a prolific writer of almost every kind of comic drama. He, too, had studied at the Dublin Society's school and had exhibited at London's Royal Academy. His talent turned towards the stage. He made his début as an actor at the Smock Alley Theatre in Dublin, in a comedy written by himself. He acted a dozen years with considerable success but, when still quite young, became almost totally blind. He moved to London where he found an outlet in writing, assisted by his daughter, **Adelaide**, who was herself a novelist and poet.

His plays and songs were so popular that they were performed in all the playhouses around Britain. As recently as 1978, London's National Theatre staged his play, *Wild Oats*. For his comic opera, *Merry Sherwood*, he wrote the popular song "I am a Friar of Orders Grey". His plays included such great favourites as *Tony Lumpkin in Town* and *The Castle of Andalusia*. A critic described his turn of phrase as being "a contrivance of significant gibberish".

In 1798 he published a collection of his comedies and farces which ran to four volumes. His amusing *Recollections* were published in 1826, just a few years before his long and busy life came to a close at Southampton.

His portrait by Thomas Lawrenson, painted in 1786, was hung in London's National Portrait Gallery. This Irishman, who had no O to his name to begin with, was awarded a royal pension.

Another **John O Keeffe** (1797–1838) is little known today. He was born in Fermoy, County Cork, where he was apprenticed to a coach painter. There he developed into a skilled heraldic artist. Moving to Cork city he specialized in portrait painting, and many of his altar pieces are to be seen in local churches. He also exhibited at the Royal Hibernian Academy, but he died too young to have developed his art to the full.

Glenville Park was one of the original O Keeffe homes but it has passed through many hands. This splendid mansion is now the home of Mark Bence Jones, the writer, architectural historian and contributor to the Burke series on families, houses and the peerage.

Belle Isle, Lorrha, County Tipperary, has also housed the O Keeffes. Elizabeth Yelverton of Belle Isle, who was born about 1780, married an O Keeffe of Marble Hill, County Cork. Their son, **Charles O Keeffe**, who was one of the registrars of the Court of Chancery in Ireland, married Letitia Yelverton of Belle Isle. With the marriage of their daughter, Cecilia, to the 3rd Viscount Avonmore, Belle Isle reverted to another branch of the Yelverton family.

An O Keeffe family of Richmond, County Tipperary, assumed the additional name of Lanigan when John Lanigan (b. 1800), Member of Parliament of Glenguile, County Tipperary, married **Frances**, only daughter of **Charles O Keeffe**. The Lanigan O Keeffe family, many of whom have settled in Australia and Rhodesia (now Zimbabwe), continue a tradition of practising law.

Eugene O Keeffe (1827–1939) from Bandon, County Cork, emigrated with his parents to Canada in 1832. At first he worked as a bookkeeper in the Toronto Savings Bank. He left to go into business on his own and, by 1861, had founded the Victoria Brewery, later to become the O.K. Brewery Company Ltd. In 1904 he was elected president of the Home Bank and, in acknowledgement of his many charitable works, he was appointed as private chamberlain to the Pope.

Shán Ó Cuiv (1875–1955), who was born at Macroom, County Cork, was a journalist who wrote for all the leading Irish language newspapers. He also wrote children's stories and textbooks in Irish.

A distinguished American woman artist who came into prominence in the 1920s, in New York, and lived to a great age, was **Georgia O Keeffe**.

A most numerous clan, the O Keeffes have remained remarkably faithful to Munster, particularly to County Cork.

Mrs John O Keeffe, painted by John O Keeffe

O Kelly

ó ceallaigh

Kelly

Kelly, now mostly O Kelly, is the second most numerous name in Ireland, surpassed only by Murphy. The first bearer of the name was **Ceallach**, son of Finnachta, a chief of the Hy Many people in about AD 874. *Ceallach* means war or contention.

The O Kellys were for centuries one of the most powerful Connacht families. They ruled over 80,000 acres of Hy Many, an area named for a fourth-century invader from Ulster known as Maine Mór. Hy Many country, counties Galway and Roscommon, was once known as "O Kelly's Country".

Their chieftain in 1014, **Tadgh Mór Ó Ceallaigh**, was killed at the battle of Clontarf when Brian Boru defeated the Vikings. The enfield, a strange heraldic beast borne as the crest on the armorial shield of some of the O Kellys, is said to have come out of the sea at Clontarf to protect Tadgh Mór's body until his kinsmen could collect it for honourable burial. St Grellan, a contemporary of St Patrick, was their patron saint, and his crozier, lost comparatively recently, was always used as their battle standard.

Although they lived up to their warlike reputation, the O Kellys were also constructive. **Conor O Kelly**, their chief for forty years, endowed thirteen churches, including, in 1167, O Kelly's Church at Clonmacnoise. Traces of their many castles can be seen at Aughrim, Garbally, Gallagh (i.e. Ceallach), Monivea, Moylough, Mullaghmore, Castlekelly and Screen. The Abbey of Kilconnell, near Ballinasloe, County Galway, was founded in 1400 by an O Kelly, and there the legendary enfield can be seen carved on many of their tombstones.

As the population increased, at least eight distinct O Kelly families developed, not all in Connacht. The more important ones were lords of Breagh, a large area of Meath and North Dublin. The Cinel Eachach O Kellys are still in County Derry. There were O Kelly chieftains in counties Laois, Wicklow, Sligo and Cork. They have all dispersed far and wide now, so in only a few cases would it be possible to pinpoint the origins of a particular sept.

Until Elizabethan times the dominant family were the O Kellys of Galway and Roscommon, the Hy Many sept. In 1351, **William Boy O Kelly**, Chief of Hy Many, sent an invitation to all poets, musicians, jesters and artists to join him in a feast at the Castle of Galway which he had built himself on Galway Bay. This lavish feast was such a success that it was called "the welcome of all welcomes". Since then, "O Kelly's Welcome" has come to mean great hospitality.

In the fifteenth century, **Murtough O Kelly**, Archbishop of Tuam, County Galway, commissioned the compilation of *The Book of the O Kellys*, an amazingly comprehensive manuscript synchronizing the reigns of Roman emperors and Irish kings. It is preserved in the Royal Irish Academy.

Malachy O Kelly, who succeeded as the 28th Chief of Hy Many in 1499, was greatly angered when his newly-built castles at Monivea and Garbally were destroyed by the Earl of Clanrickard. He called on Garret Mór, the great Earl of Kildare, to help him to get his revenge. Garret Mór went willingly because of Clanrickard's ill-treatment of his wife, Kildare's daughter. All the principal chiefs joined in—some on O Kelly's side, others on Clanrickard's. On the O Kelly side were O Donnell, O Neill, MacMahon, O Hanlon, Magennis, O Reilly and O Farrell. In opposition

Ulick Burke, Earl of Clanrickard, had the O Briens, MacNamaras, O Carrolls and O Kennedys. For the first time in Ireland gunpowder was used, and in 1504, at Knocktoe near Galway City, Clanrickard was horribly defeated. This lamentable inter-clan fighting, when some 10,000 Irish men faced one another in battle, contributed significantly to the later downfall of native Irish supremacy. Together they could probably have wiped out the English usurpers. Instead, the wily English regarded it as a great victory for them—and awarded Kildare the Garter!

In 1583, an O Kelly, with the assistance of Owen O Moriarty, cut off the head of the old and ailing Earl of Desmond and sent it to Queen Elizabeth who spiked it on London Bridge. However, it was O Moriarty who got the £1,000 reward in silver!

O Kellys have shaped the course of history in many curious ways. It is thought to have been O Kelly who fired the gun that killed Garret Mór, who, ironically, had been the one to introduce gunpowder at the battle of Knocktoe.

The 39th and last chieftain of the O Kellys was **Aedh** (Hugh), son of **Donnchadh**, who died in about 1600. Aedh's death heralded the break-up of the Gaelic order.

Defeat at Kinsale in 1601 left the Irish little choice but to flee abroad, especially to Europe, where they joined the various regiments of the Irish Brigade. The O Kellys of Belgium are descendants of **Captain John Kelly** (c. 1672–1753) of Galway, who advised the Austrian Emperor on the administration of his army. The important Irish College in Paris, founded in 1578 for the education of Irish priests who could not study at home, was headed in 1684 by **Father Malachy O Kelly**.

John O Kelly, 8th Lord of Screen, County Galway, educated his son, **Charles** (1621–95), at Saint-Omer, France. In 1642 Charles returned to the aid of Ormond the Lord Lieutenant, whose elevated appointment came from Charles I of England. When Charles I was executed and Cromwell came to devastate Ireland, Charles O Kelly and many of his kinsmen fled to Spain. At the restoration of the monarchy, Colonel Charles O Kelly, aged 68, returned to Galway to take part in the battle of Aughrim. "So glorious to Ginkell, so fatal to St Ruth and the Irish…" he wrote of it afterwards, when he had retired to Castle Kelly where he died in 1695. He left an enigmatic manuscript, *Macariae Excidium*, which historians now believe to be an oblique account of the struggle between James II and William III of Orange, with Ireland as pawn in a European power game.

The O Kellys who were formerly of Galway found great favour with the astute but benevolent Empress of Austria, Maria Theresa (1717–80). They served in her army and in her Court. She conferred the title Reichgraf on **Dillon John Kelly**, making him a Count of the Holy Roman Empire. As Dillon John had no children, his brother, **Conor**, succeeded to this illustrious title which has gone down through that O Kelly family to the present day. The Empress decreed that the title would be held by "All descendants, male and female, the female to bear the title until marriage with no rights of transmission". This is a very old European title which is in no way connected with the papacy.

In the O Kelly family of Gurtray, Portumna, County Galway, there were, until comparatively recently, six brothers, all Counts of the Holy Roman Empire, all styled **O Kelly de Gallagh et Tycooly**. The third brother, **Gerald** (1890–1968), following school and university in Ireland, travelled widely and was badly wounded in the First World War. He entered the Irish Diplomatic Service in 1919. Arthur Griffith, then acting as head of the Republic of Ireland, sent him to Switzerland to the League

Kilconnell Abbey, County Galway, founded by the O Kellys in 1400. This tomb depicts members of the family

of Nations to help promote Irish independence. In 1921, Count Gerald was Ireland's representative at Brussels. From 1923 to 1935 he represented Ireland in France. During the Second World War he helped negotiate the release of many Irish citizens from occupied France. In 1948 he was Irish Minister in Lisbon. Although he had retired in 1955, the Irish government named him honorary counsellor to the legation at Lisbon, where he remained until his death. He was a Knight of Malta, Grand Officer of the Legion of Honour and of the Order of Christ of Portugal.

Brendan O Kelly of the Gurtray family of County Galway was in the United States for over 25 years as North American vice-president of Aer Lingus, the Irish international airline. Although he is a Count of the Holy Roman Empire he does not use his title. **Walter Lionel O Kelly of Gallagh and Tycooly** (b. 1921), who served in the Second World War, is 8th Count of the Holy Roman Empire, and also the current representative of the old Gaelic title O Kelly of Gallagh.

The easing of religious restrictions in the eighteenth century enabled the O Kellys to divert their energies away from war to literature and the arts in general, to administration, diplomacy and sport. **Dennis O Kelly** (1720–87), who was born to a poor Irish family, went to England where he made a fortune in horse-racing. He began by buying a share in the famous racehorse Eclipse. He acquired a commission in the Middlesex militia, reaching the rank of colonel. He bought a country house. He also had a talking parrot who could whistle the 104th psalm. A professional gamester, he was never short of money, but when he died a rich man, in London, he left a clause in his will that for every time his heir made a bet he must forfeit £400!

Michael Kelly

Michael Kelly (1764–1826) of Dublin, a child prodigy, could play intricate piano pieces when he was eleven years old. At that time Dublin was a flourishing capital, and the young Michael had an excellent musical grounding before being sent for training to Italy. For four years he was principal tenor at the Vienna Opera house. He was very friendly with Mozart, who wrote the part of "Basilio" in *The Marriage of Figaro* especially for him. He was drawn towards the London theatre, where he had great success. When he was appointed musical director at Drury Lane Theatre in 1797 under Sheridan's management, his musical settings of plays filled the theatre for many seasons. Hoping to consolidate his finances, he opened a shop for the sale of his compositions, but soon became bankrupt. He suffered intensely from gout for many years. In 1975, Roger Fiske edited Kelly's reminiscences which were made into a serial for Radio Éireann.

The popular ballad, "Kelly the Boy from Killann", was inspired by **Captain John Kelly** of Killann, County Wexford, who died while leading the insurgents at New Ross in the rising of 1798. **Catherine Kelly** had a brief public life. Known as "the Irish fairy", she was only 34 inches tall and weighed a mere 22 pounds. **Patrick O Kelly** (1754–1840) was a highly respected mathematician and astronomer. In 1813, the London House of Commons consulted him on the currency question.

Mary Eva Kelly (1826–1910) of Headfort, County Galway, married the Young Irelander revolutionary, Kevin Izod O Doherty. She wrote patriotic poems and essays for their newspaper, the *Nation*. Until her death in Brisbane, Australia, she was always known as "Eva of The Nation".

Over the last century the innumerable Kelly writers, dramatists and journalists can cause considerable confusion.

James O Kelly (1845–1916) had an adventurous career as soldier and war correspondent. He was educated in Dublin and France, joined the

Foreign Legion and went with it to Mexico. Later he served with the domestic French army until the fall of Paris in 1870. He then joined the *New York Herald* newspaper and was immediately sent to report the revolt in Cuba. Escaping imprisonment by the Spanish, he joined the US troops in their campaign to eliminate the Sioux chief, Sitting Bull. In the 1880s he returned to Ireland, where he pursued an active political career as Member of Parliament for Roscommon. He also represented the *Irish Independent* newspaper in the House of Commons in London.

J.J. O Kelly (1873–1957) wrote about Irish language and history using the name "Sceilig". He was president of the Gaelic League, and succeeded Eamon de Valera as president of Sinn Féin.

The family of **Sir Gerald Kelly** (1880–1972) lived in London for several generations, so it would be correct to describe him as a leading British painter of his time. He travelled widely and admitted to preferring the Spanish people to the Irish. However, he was proud to trace his lineage back to Tadgh who was killed at the battle of Clontarf in 1014. **Festus Kelly**, his grandfather, had been appointed Her Majesty's Inspector of Letters in 1837. Festus also founded the international firm of publishers known as Kelly's Directories. In 1921 it was taken over by the Amalgamated Press, which, in the 1950s, merged with the International Publishing Corporation. Sir Gerald Kelly was president of London's Royal Academy and was accorded an honorary LLD by Trinity College, Dublin.

Seamus O Kelly (1881–1920) left Loughrea in County Galway to become a journalist in Dublin, where he took part in the 1916 rising. His plays were produced at the Abbey Theatre. A radio version of his short story, *The Weaver's Grave*, won the Prix Italia for Radio Éireann in 1961.

Seán T. Ó Ceallaigh (1881–1966) of Dublin was the second President of Ireland, a position he held for fourteen years. In 1905 he was one of the founder members of the Sinn Féin party and took part in the fight for independence. He was Speaker in the first Dáil (the Irish Parliament) and held a number of ministerial appointments.

James Plunkett Kelly (b. 1920) first worked as a trade union official in Dublin before becoming a radio and television producer. When he turned to writing novels he dropped the Kelly, probably to avoid confusion, and as James Plunkett wrote the best-selling novel, *Strumpet City*. Set in Dublin during the infancy of trade unionism before the First World War, it has been made into a successful film.

In the 1980s, **Seán Kelly** of Carrick-on-Suir, County Tipperary, worked his way up in the tough sport of international cycling and lives close to the action, in Brussels. He won the prestigious Paris to Nice cycle race three times in succession.

There have been many well-known Kellys in the United States. **Patrick Kelly** (1779–1829) left Kilkenny to become the first Bishop of Richmond, Virginia. In 1863, **Colonel Patrick Kelly** commanded the Irish Brigade at Gettysburg. **Michael Kelly** (1857–94) was a US baseball champion. In New York in 1893 he was the subject of the popular song, *Slide, Kelly, Slide*.

"Honest John" Kelly was the first Catholic Irishman to head Tammany Hall, New York. He was elected Congressman in 1857 and Sheriff of New York City. He suffered a tragic bereavement in the death of his wife, his son and two daughters and was too grief-stricken to accept the offer to stand as mayor of New York. It was when he returned from a recuperative trip to Europe that he began a clean-up of Tammany Hall. He organized the Irish immigrants into a political force and is credited with being the pioneer of the party machine that has become the model for

J.J. O Kelly

Seán T. Ó Ceallaigh in Paris in 1919 as Ireland's envoy to the Peace Conference

American politicians. It was said of him that "he found Tammany a horde and left it an army".

James Edward Kelly (1855–1933) was known as the "sculptor of American history". He was born in New York of Irish immigrant parents. One of his most famous sculptures was of a fellow Irish-American, General Philip Henry Sheridan. Kelly's busts of leading military men, as well as of Thomas Edison, Paul Revere, Theodore Roosevelt and others, would fill a hall of fame.

John Henry Kelly (1857–1944), an unskilled labourer, left County Mayo for Philadelphia. There he married the seventeen-year-old Mary Costello. Their family became one of the most famous Irish-American families, the Kellys of Philadelphia. He made his money in insurance, and of the Kelly's six sons, **Jack Kelly** was outstanding. In 1920, he was the first American oarsman to win an Olympic Gold Medal. He developed a profitable construction company and helped in the building of the United Nations headquarters in New York. Jack's brother, **George Kelly**, following service in the Second World War, became a successful writer and won a Pulitzer Prize for one of his plays.

Princess Grace (Kelly) with Prince Rainier

Jack's daughter, **Grace Kelly**, the award-winning film star, married Prince Rainier of Monaco in 1956. Princess Grace's death in a car crash in 1981 deprived the prince, his family and the principality of a loved and honoured personality. In 1984, Prince Rainier set up an Irish library in Monaco in memory of Princess Grace.

Captain Colin Kelly (1915–1941) was the first United States hero of the Second World War. He was the pilot of a bomber which destroyed one of the battleships that attacked the American fleet in Pearl Harbour. His aircraft was damaged and he ordered his crew to bail out, and died when it crashed. He was posthumously awarded a Distinguished Service Cross.

The Congressional Medal of Honour, the United States of America's highest award, has been awarded to nineteen Kellys since 1864.

Australia is yet another country where the Kellys are numerous and, in the case of one outstanding Kelly, notorious! **Ned Kelly** (1854–80), the outlaw whose parents came from Ireland, was head of the Kelly gang of bushrangers and bank robbers until he died on the gallows in Melbourne. Writers, film and television producers and even the distinguished Australian painter, Sydney Nolan, have found him an engrossing subject.

Although the Kellys, like other Irish families, have not produced an Australian Prime Minister, they did produce a bishop. He was **Michael Kelly** (1850–1940), who came from Waterford and was Bishop of Sydney in 1911.

Sir David Kelly (1891–1959) was the son of Irish parents. His father left his post in Trinity College, Dublin, to emigrate to Adelaide, Australia. After his death, David Kelly went to London where, following graduation from Oxford, he entered the British Diplomatic Service in 1919. From 1949 to 1951 he was British Ambassador to Moscow. On his retirement he went with his wife, the writer **Marie-Noel Kelly**, to live in Inch, County Wexford. He wrote several popular books about his career as a much-travelled diplomat.

The Kellys abroad, particularly in the United States of America, are far more numerous than in the home of their ancestors. The many who have added a spouse's or other relative's name to the O Kelly root have considerably simplified the task of tracing this multitudinous family, not only in the Genealogical Office, but also in the telephone directory! Some of these are de Pentheny O Kelly, Blake Kelly, Roche Kelly, Harvey Kelly, Aliaga Kelly, and possibly a score more.

O Mahony
ó mathúna

Mahony

Ó Mathghamhna

Tracing the history of the O Mahony (Mahony) family is comparatively simple. The *O Mahony Journal*, published annually, gives an account of many aspects of the ancestry of this ancient family.

According to Peter Tynan O Mahony, *Eagrai agus Cartlannai* (Organizer and Archivist), "The O Mahony surname is derived from **Mathghamhan**, son of Cian Mac Mael Muda, the tenth-century warrior-prince, and Sadbh, daughter of the High King of Ireland, Brian Boru. Mathghamhan's ancestors were known as the Eoghanacht Raithline, a branch of that great group of dynasties claiming descent from Eoghan Mór, son of Oilioll Olum who, in the second century was reputedly first King of Munster".

The O Mahonys occupied a huge tract of Munster, stretching from the environs of Cork city to Mizen Head. The sept owned this land until the seventeenth century when, in common with other Gaelic families in those stormy times, they were dispossessed. Today, many of their descendants continue to thrive in the land of their ancestors. Many more are scattered across the face of the earth with little or no knowledge of their origins, only recognizing a link with Ireland through their surname.

During the clan wars of the Middle Ages, the O Mahonys divided into eight separate septs and at one time they owned fourteen castles in west Cork. Among their strongholds were Castle Mahon, Castle Lac, Dunmanus, Laemcon, Rosbrin, Ardintenant, Ballydevlin, Dunbeacon and Templemartin, the cradle of the clan near Bandon. Dún Lacha, near Mizen Head, was built in 1212 by Donagh na hImrice (Donough of the pilgrimages), so called because he went to the Holy Land. Ardintenant Castle beside Roaringwater Bay was the seat of the chief of Iveagh.

At Rosbrin in the fifteenth century, the scholar-prince **Finghin O Mahony** translated Sir John Mandeville's book *Travels in the Holy Land* into Irish. Finghin's manuscripts were discovered in 1869 in the public library at Rennes in Brittany, where many Irish families fled following the catastrophic defeat by the English at the battle of Kinsale in 1601.

According to an account by the O Mahonys of Lota Beg, Cork, "they held distinguished military and diplomatic appointments in the service of Continental sovereigns, and became allied by marriage with the nobility of France, Italy and Spain".

The most renowned of the Continental O Mahonys was **Count Daniel O Mahony** (d. 1714), the hero of Cremona who commanded the Regiment of Dillon in the absence of its commander, Colonel Lally. Daniel, a direct descendant of **Teigue O Mahony**, the sixteenth century seneschal of Desmond, later gave a graphic account of his victory to an appreciative King Louis XIV.

It was **Colonel John O Mahony** (1815–77) who gave the name Fenian to the revolutionary brotherhood founded in the United States to assist in the liberation of Ireland. Descended from the O Mahonys of Kilbehenny in County Limerick, his political views forced him to flee to America. In New York he translated the great documentary record of Irish history, Geoffrey Keating's early seventeenth-century manuscript, *Foras Feasa ar Eirinn* (History of Ireland), indebting himself to future scholars. John O Mahony was the leader of the Fenian Brotherhood, and, during the American Civil War, he organized a regiment of Fenians, the 99th Regiment of the New York National Guard, of which he was appointed colonel. Despite his patriotism, he was too scholarly to be a successful

Colonel John O Mahony

leader, so he devoted his life to scholarship and campaigning on behalf of his beloved country, raising £8,000 for that cause. He died in poverty in New York, too proud to ask for help for himself.

Probably the most celebrated O Mahony was known as Father Prout. He was born **Francis Sylvester Mahony** (1804–66), second son of **Martin Mahony** of the woollen manufacturing dynasty of Blarney. Educated in France and Rome, he was destined for the Jesuit priesthood, but was rejected on grounds of ill health. Instead he became a literary and somewhat Bohemian priest who wrote verse and became a journalist, using the pseudonym Father Prout. A traveller and *bon viveur*, he numbered among his acquaintances Thomas Moore, Charles Dickens, Lady Blessington (*see* Power) and William Makepeace Thackeray. He wrote the words of the haunting song about Cork city:

> *The bells of Shandon,*
> *which sound so grand on*
> *the pleasant waters*
> *of the River Lee.*

Canon John O Mahony (1844–1912) wrote the *History of the O Mahony septs of Kinelmeaky and Ivagha.*

The O Mahony of Kerry moved to County Wicklow, where he established his family at Grange Con. His son, **Pierce Gun Mahony**, barrister and Herald of Arms, was unwittingly involved in the scandal of the Irish Crown Jewels which disappeared from the Genealogical Office in Dublin Castle just before the visit of Edward VII in July 1907. It was a most unsavoury affair. Pierce Mahony's uncle, Sir Arthur Vicars, Ulster King of Arms, was dismissed ignominiously and, in 1921, his home was burned down and he was murdered. Pierce Gun Mahony was found drowned in Grange Con Lake in 1914. While there were many suspects, no one was brought to trial for the theft and there is little hope that the jewels will ever be found, although occasionally people come forward announcing that they know where they are!

In 1870 a farmer's son, **John O Mahony**, ran away from Kilcrohane in west Cork, at the age of 17, and emigrated to America to seek his fortune. He rose to become the "Senator from Wyoming" and, for his enterprise as a rancher, engineer, oil prospector and banker, was dubbed "King of the West".

David J. Mahoney, chief executive of the Norton Simon Corporation, whose personal wealth has been put at £10 million, was born in the Bronx, the son of an Irish crane driver. He progressed, via a basketball scholarship, an army commission and advertising, to become a leading businessman in the United States. He is nicknamed "the Kissinger of Commerce".

The twentieth century produced the most lovable O Mahony—**Eoin O Mahony** (1904–70). One of the O Mahonys of Dun Locha, Douglas, County Cork, he was barrister, Knight of Malta, genealogist, raconteur and a world traveller. It was he who originated the annual O Mahony rally in 1955. He has been described as "a maker of epics, an interpreter of history, an incurable romantic, the avowed champion of lost causes, a sterling protagonist of the social values of rural Ireland with a mission of preservation of resistance to materialism; he was a modern crusader".

The O Mahoney name, originally the Irish word for bear, has been modernized to Ó Mathúna. **Pádraig Ó Mathúna**, the Cashel artist who works in silver and enamel, made a commemorative cup for Eoin

Eoin O Mahony

196

O Mahony and described him as "a catalyst fusing ages through scholarship and genealogy, linking our continuity with our oldest past". Alas, Eoin left little of written family history, only the tapes of his weekly programme for Radio Éireann, *Meet the Clans*.

An unexpected, and probably unsuspected, member of the clan is the audacious television comedian, Dave Allen. Born **David Tynan O Mahony**, he was the third son of the Dublin newspaper journalist **G.J.C. (Pussy) Tynan O Mahony** who became general manager of the *Irish Times*.

The clan's chief representative on the Continent, **Vicomte Yves O Mahony** of Orléans, France, retains links with Ireland. A barrister, he is directly descended from **Seán Meirgeach** (freckled) **Ó Matgamma** of Dunloe, who died about 1720.

Fishermen, farmers, teachers, shop owners, priests, doctors, lawyers, nuns, nurses, journalists—the numerous O Mahonys are scattered all over west Munster. On the Bandon (County Cork) electoral role there are 800 O Mahonys.

The O Mahony Records Society sponsors an annual scholarship of £1,000, administered by The Royal Hibernian Academy, to enable scholars to go abroad to research sources of Irish family history.

Dunmanus Castle, West Cork, built by Donogh Mór O Mahony, is seen here during the 1971 clan gathering

O Malley
ó máille

Melia

The O Malleys are true Gaels from the west coast. Malley is thought to have come from the old Celtic word for chief, *maglios*. They held the chieftainship of two *umhalls*, or baronies, in Connacht known as Burrishoole and Murrisk, both in west Mayo. Their exploits are well recorded. In an island like Ireland it is remarkable how few have made the sea their element and ironic that their most famous seafarer should be a woman! The Four Masters (*see* Cleary) who wrote the *Annals* as well as compiling the *Book of Lough Cé*, generally ignored women and made no exception for a female sea captain. It is mainly in Elizabethan state papers that we find reliable information about this intrepid woman.

Owen O Malley, "strong in galleys and seamen", traded in fish with Spain and England. Great quantities of salted herrings were exported and there was more fishing off the south-west coast than there is now. English and foreign vessels had to pay a high toll for fishing in Irish waters. In 1556, Philip II of Spain paid £1,000 for leave for 21 years to fish off the Irish coast.

His infamous daughter **Grania (Grace) O Malley** is the sea captain mentioned above. She is sometimes called Granuaile (Grania the bald) because she is supposed to have cut her hair short so that she could pass as a boy. She was reared on the sea, and throughout her long and tempestuous career she could never be parted from it.

At about 15 she was married to Donal an Chogaidh (Donal of the battles), the tanist, or heir apparent, of the O Flahertys of Ballinahinch. These O Flahertys were the most contentious of all the bellicose clans of Ireland. She had three or four children by him before he was killed in battle.

Grania was well able to look after herself. She raided the territories of the neighbouring chiefs and even as far afield as the coast of Scotland. To strengthen her territory Grania married Richard Burke, another Connacht chieftain. She stipulated it was only "for a year certain". She waited until she had his lands and was safely installed in his castle, and when he returned from a fighting expedition she yelled down at him from inside his battlements, "I dismiss you", and that was the end of the alliance.

With Richard Burke she had a son, Tibod, who had been born at sea in the middle of an attack from pirates. Grania had to rise from her bed to inspire her men to massacre the pirates. When Tibod grew up she went with him to London to get him a peerage from Queen Elizabeth. She was not successful, but years later Charles I bestowed on him the now extinct title of Viscount Mayo.

Once when she was detained by an English government official and questioned about how she maintained herself, she curtly answered, "maintenance is by land and sea", her ruthless method of commerce. She was constantly harassed by the cruel Bingham, President of Connacht, who was always looking for an opportunity to eliminate the Irish "rebels". One of his men sought hospitality from Grania's son, Owen, and got it generously. Then, calling his troops, he murdered Owen and his men.

Grania fell foul of the powerful FitzGeralds, and the Earl of Desmond of that family imprisoned her for a while in Dublin Castle. She was released, only to be captured by Sir Richard Bingham who had the gallows ready for the woman he had described as, "for forty years the stay of all rebellions in the West". She was, however, rescued by her son-in-law, another Richard Burke.

From September to December 1588, thousands of men from the Spanish Armada were washed up on the shores of the west coast. Grania and her crewmen must have been witnesses to this disastrous epic. Unable to return to her stronghold in Clew Bay because of the loss of all her ships, Grania fled to Ulster to seek refuge with the O Neills and the O Donnells. Despite her rebel status in Ireland, she corresponded with Queen Elizabeth and is recorded as having visited her in London in August 1593, when she described herself as "a Princess and an equal", though the Queen addressed her as Lady Burke. Elizabeth must have had some regard for her, because she granted Grania a pension which supported her in her later years. The Queen and the "pirate queen" died in the same year, 1603.

The O Malley motto, *terra marique potens* (powerful on land and sea), was not always true. When, after the battle of Kinsale in 1601, the old chieftaincies were broken, the O Malleys also began to leave Ireland. For many Irish, life became impossible in their own country.

Charles O Malley and his five brothers all went to France, "disdaining from the turn affairs then took in that Kingdom to live or serve therein… some of whom went up to the frontiers of Hungary to fight against the Turks and were never heard of again. One became a Count of the Empire…", wrote a chronicler of the time. Charles O Malley, who settled in France, commented that none of his family "were ever known to follow any trade or profession but arms, the cause of not accumulating any considerable fortune since they forfeited their hereditary one".

This Captain Charles O Malley, who was at James II's court at Saint-Germain-en-Laye, wrote to his son in Ireland, **Captain Teig O Malley**, late of Colonel Brown's Regiment, telling him how James II had offered to create him a Lord Baron, but that he had answered, "I was already Prince as O Malley, Chief as O Malley, and the honour his majesty was so graciously pleased to offer could be no addition to me". He prudently advised Teig, who "desired the patents, parchments and titles relevant to our properties in Ireland to be shown to the Court of Claims in Ireland", that it would be safer to keep them in France, not only because of the uncertainty of the Irish political situation, but also because "some of our lands were added to the estate of the Protestant archbishop, and the clergy of every persuasion are in general too fond of property to part from what they once get while they can".

George O Malley (1711–1843) was a volunteer in the Castlebar Yeomanry when that town was attacked by the French under Humbert in 1798. In recognition of his services against the "rebels"—his fellow countrymen—Lord Cornwallis made him a lieutenant. Abroad he served with Henry Augustus, 13th Viscount Dillon, who raised the 101st Foot Regiment in which George O Malley was appointed major. Because of his local connections in County Mayo, George was recognized as having materially assisted in the formation of the regiment. He served with it in Ireland and in Jersey and was dispatched with 300 men to St John's, New Brunswick, in 1808, when war with America was imminent. He soldiered in Jamaica and at Quatre Bras, and he was at Waterloo where he commanded a battalion of infantry, was twice wounded and had two horses shot from under him. In 1817, when the regiment was disbanded, his repeated application for employment in Europe was unsuccessful. He returned forthwith to the British army!

When the French, led by General Humbert, were attacking Castlebar, **Austin O Malley** was with the United Irishmen, fighting against the Yeomanry in which George O Malley was a volunteer on the English side. Austin's son, **Patrick O Malley**, became a general in the army of France.

Soldiering was a professional career, with little thought given to which side one fought on, or against whom one was fighting.

From earliest days there were many O Malley churchmen, including several archbishops of Tuam. The best recorded of them were not of the Mayo line of the family, but of the O Malleys who had settled in Limerick.

Thaddeus O Malley (1796–1877) of Garryowen, County Limerick, went to America after his ordination. He was suspended by his superior for being "strong-willed and independent". Back in Dublin, he wrote a series of public letters resolutely demanding a Poor Law for Ireland. He also disparaged Irish education and supported a system of national education. Considered to be too dangerously progressive, he was sent off to be rector of the University of Malta, where he drastically reformed the discipline and was posted back to Dublin once again. Soon he was denouncing the enforced celibacy of clerics.

Thaddeus O Malley also disagreed with Daniel O Connell on the question of a complete repeal of the Act of Union. He urged the establishment of a federal parliament for Ireland. This proposal was hotly debated, and many former disciples of O Connell flocked to O Malley's standard. He started a newspaper, the *Federalist*, and tried to unite Old and Young Ireland—the former, headed by O Connell, favoured moral pressure while the Young Irelanders advocated arms and deserted O Connell. After an abortive rising and O Connell's death, Father Thaddeus O Malley lived for twenty years in retirement in a back lane in Dublin. In 1870, Isaac Butt's new movement for Home Rule found in O Malley a zealous and energetic ally. Though bold in urging changes in ecclesiastical discipline and social justice, O Malley was unswerving in his faith. His tragedy was that he was ahead of his time.

Sir Edward O Malley (d. 1932), a direct descendant of Grania O Malley, the pirate queen, spent nearly all his life in the British Colonial Service. He was Attorney-General and Chief Justice of various colonies, and judge of the former extra-territorial court of Egypt and the Ottoman Empire.

His son, **Sir Owen St Clair O Malley** (1887–1974), was a British diplomat who served in China, Mexico, Spain, Hungary, Poland and Portugal. On retiring he wrote his biography, *The Phantom Caravan*, which was published in 1953. He wrote nostalgically of Belclare and Clew Bay, where he had made Rockfleet his home. **Lady O Malley**, the author Ann Bridge, wrote a stream of best sellers in the 1930s and 1940s.

Frank Ward O Malley (1875–1932) of Pittsburgh, Pennsylvania, was one of the *Morning Telegraph's* greatest reporters. He wrote with insight and some humour. In 1929 he wrote about the Irish in the United States for the *American Mercury*. He achieved success with his book *The Swiss Family O Malley* and also with several plays. He retired to France.

Ernest O Malley (1898–1957) was born in County Mayo. A medical student at the time of the 1916 rising, he joined the Irish Volunteers. During the Civil War he fought against the Treaty which had been accepted by the Free State government. He was severely wounded, yet recovered and was able to travel widely, collecting funds for the establishment of the *Irish Press*, the paper founded by Eamon de Valera and his Fianna Fáil party. At various times he was a schoolteacher in New Mexico and a cab driver in New York. His autobiographical account of the Civil War, *On Another Man's Wound*, was published in the United States as *Army Without Banners*.

Donogh O Malley (1921–68), who came from a prominent Limerick family, was a member of the Fianna Fáil government. As Minister of

Education he shocked the establishment when he unveiled plans for the amalgamation of the 400-year-old Trinity College, Dublin, with the comparatively new University College, Dublin. He died suddenly before he could carry out the plan and it was abandoned a few years after his death.

O Malleys are to be found in the Indian Civil Service, as colonial governors, doctors and lawyers, but no reference book or genealogy contains the famous "Charles O Malley", the character who is supposed to typify the devil-may-care Irishman who rollicks through the novels of Charles Lever (1806–1872), a Dublin doctor and consul at Trieste.

Ellen O Malley of Malahide, County Dublin, for many years was leading lady in plays by George Bernard Shaw, Somerset Maugham and other leading dramatists. When she retired from the stage she turned to teaching, at which she had great success with the Webber Douglas School in London.

Major Hamilton Joseph Keyes O Malley (b. 1910) is recorded fulsomely in *Burke's Irish Family Records 1976*. He claims descent from "Flanafra, Lord of Umhall in AD 670, from Owen O Malley who was killed at Killybegs in 1513 and from **Edmund O Malley** of Cahir, their last chieftain, who died about 1610". These were the O Malleys of Ross House situated on Clew Bay near Newport in County Mayo. Major Keyes O Malley's antecedents are dispersed through America and Europe and his father, **Middleton Joseph**, was with the Munster Fusiliers in India. Major Keyes O Malley, who lives in Spain, has had three wives. The third, whom he married in December 1970, he designates as "Betty Saunders, bullfighter".

Charles Conor O Malley (1889–1982) of Kilmilken, County Galway, was the youngest of fourteen children. His father intended him to run the family sheep farm, but by his own efforts he followed his brothers into the medical profession. He was an excellent all-round sportsman and wrote a book about fishing in Ireland. He was a surgeon on an aircraft-carrier during the Second World War, then returned to Galway to specialize in ophthalmology. He founded the Irish Order of Malta Ambulance Corps. For five years he was president of the Galway Archaeological Society. When he died, at the age of 93, he had been Guardian Chief of the O Malley clan rally for many years.

Tomás O Máille, a much admired Professor of Irish language and linguistics at University College Galway during the 1920s and 30s

O Neill

ó néill

Creagh

Neill

Nihill

Nial Glún Dubh (Niall of the Black Knee), who became King of Ireland in AD 890, was killed in battle against the Norsemen near Dublin in 919. It was his grandson, **Domhnall** (*c.* 943) who adopted the surname Neill, meaning champion. From the fifth to the eleventh century, and from the twelfth century to the death of Red Hugh in 1608, this dominant family were monarchs of all Ireland, kings of Ulster, earls and princes of Tyrone, statesmen and soldiers. They claim descent from the legendary **Niall Of The Nine Hostages** and his Red Branch Knights. In the tenth century, Brian Boru wrested the throne of Ireland from **Maoilseachlan**, leader of the northern O Neills. Also known as Malachy, he was King of Ireland from 988 to 1002. His descendants, who remained in Munster, adopted the name MacLoughlin and set up a new chieftaincy in Meath. The O Neills are the oldest family in Europe with unbroken descent in the male line. Since 1740, the O Neills of Clanaboy in Ulster have been living in Portugal, where they proudly continue their ancient Gaelic designation O Neill, Chieftain.

There were also O Neills in Thomond, County Clare, and some scholars believe that the Clare Nihills were of Ulster origin, left behind after the battle of Kinsale when many survivors adopted the name of their chieftain. The name Creagh, which is found in this area, is also thought to derive from O Neill ancestry. Creagh comes from the Irish word *craobh*, meaning branch, and in a battle with the Norsemen at Limerick they camouflaged themselves with green branches, which is why the laurel is incorporated in the Creagh coat of arms.

The O Neills of the Decies, who are to be found in counties Waterford, Tipperary and Cork, claim descent from the dynastic Ulster O Neills.

Today there are at least 29,000 of the name in Ireland—and probably ten times that number abroad. There are many legends as to how the O Neills acquired their motto, *Lamh Dearg Éirinn*, which means The Red Hand of Ireland. One story is that when their ancestors sailed close to the north-east tip of Ireland they agreed that whoever landed first would have that area of land. A quick-witted warrior named Nial chopped off his left hand, threw it onto the shore—and claimed his reward! In fact, this red hand which is now incorporated in the arms of the Province of Ulster is a universal image of ancient origin and symbolizes God blessing mankind, but with his right hand!

From the sixth to the twelfth century, the Grianan of Aileach, which overlooks the Inishowen Peninsula in County Donegal, was an O Neill stronghold. It was plundered many times and Murtough O Brien demolished it in 1101 in revenge for the destruction of the O Brien royal seat at Kincora in County Clare. It is recorded that he ordered his soldiers to carry away the stones with their provisions. In the last century, the Grianan was imaginatively restored by a local citizen.

At Tullahogue, near their castle at Dungannon (Gannon was the fort of the Red Branch Knights in the first century), the Tyrone O Neills held a very impressive coronation ceremony for their elected chieftain. The O Hagans, who owned the land thereabouts, performed the ceremony, putting O Neill's foot into a golden slipper. The last inauguration held there was of the great Hugh O Neill, in 1593. A few years afterwards, the Elizabethan General Mountjoy obliterated the Tullahogue stone. It has recently been found and reassembled in the Ulster Museum in Belfast.

In the fourteenth century, the O Neills divided into two houses. The Tyrone O Neills descend from **Niall Ruadh** (the red), Prince of Tyrone. The Clanaboy O Neills of counties Antrim and Down descend from his elder brother, **Aodh Dubh** (the black), King of Ulster.

Conn Bacach (the lame), the 1st Earl of Tyrone (*c.* 1484–1559), was the first of the great warrior O Neills. When his territory was invaded, he went to London to submit to Henry VIII who created him Earl of Tyrone. His family did not approve of an English title and there was much feuding, which led to the murder of one of his sons. Conn took refuge in Dublin, inside the Pale, where he died.

Conn was succeeded by his son, **Seán an Diomais** (Shane the proud). Shane's followers murdered his half-brother, **Matthew**, and Shane himself was murdered by the MacDonnells of Antrim in revenge for the destruction by Shane of their Scottish settlements in the county.

Conn Bacach's grandson, the great **Hugh O Neill** (1550–1616), 2nd Earl of Tyrone and son of Matthew, lived for six years at the Court of Queen Elizabeth as Baron of Dungannon. She hoped to tame him and win the allegiance of the O Neills and for a long time he appeared to be loyal to the Crown. Ireland was in a chaotic state, it lacked any government except inside the Pale, and constant warring had led to famine and disease. Given his experience in England, Hugh was aware of the wider political issues, and at times it must have been difficult for anyone to know, including himself, which was the right side to support. He began a series of intrigues with the local chiefs and also with the English, and was harassed by Elizabeth's spies. Endlessly suing for peace or pardons, he played for time, waiting for the promised help from Spain.

His marital arrangements were equally unstable. He divorced his first wife, his second wife died, and, at 45 he eloped with Mabel Bagenal, the sister of his arch enemy, Sir Henry Bagenal. She left him when she discovered he "affected two other gentlewomen". She did not live long and, after her death, he married Catherine Magennis.

In 1595 he had a successful encounter with the English at the battle of Clontibret. At the battle of the Yellow Ford, near Armagh in 1598, the Irish had one of their greatest triumphs and Bagenal was killed.

Hugh O Neill now began to be regarded as Prince of Ireland—The O Neill—a title which meant much more to him and the Irish than Earl of Tyrone. This arrogance alarmed Elizabeth who sent over her favourite, the Earl of Essex, with a vast army. However, Essex was tricked by O Neill and returned, unsuccessful, to London, where Elizabeth had him executed.

She sent another expensive army with more efficient leadership. Many of the Irish chiefs, thinking only of their property, joined the English. When the Spanish army finally landed, it was at Kinsale rather than at an Ulster port. Hugh O Neill had to lead his army in hazardous winter conditions from the north to the extreme southern tip of Ireland. He wanted to attack at once, but was, it is thought, restrained by Red Hugh O Donnell and Del Aquila. When they finally attacked on Christmas Eve 1601, it was too late, and the best opportunity in centuries was lost. The defeat at Kinsale marked the end of the Gaelic order and ushered in the exodus to Europe. In 1607, Tyrone and his family and many other chiefs sailed from Lough Swilly, an event to become known as The Flight of the Earls. Tyrone died, homeless and penniless, in Rome.

Although they fought continuously, either between themselves or against their neighbours, they also sought valiantly to drive out the colonizers. When Hugh O Neill, Earl of Tyrone, and O Donnell, Earl of Tirconnell, fled to Europe, they left Ulster open to the Protestant plantations of

Hugh O Neill

James I, contributing to the continuing conflict in this area of Ulster which remained British when the rest of Ireland became independent.

Owen Roe (the red haired) **O Neill** (1590–1649), a nephew of the great Hugh O Neill, Earl of Tyrone, was a professional soldier who had served thirty years in the Spanish army. He returned to Ireland and, in 1642, joined the new movement styled the Confederate Catholics of Ireland. He defeated the Scots under Monro at Benburb in County Tyrone in 1646. When Cromwell landed to wreak vengeance, Owen Roe, on his way to join the royalist army led by Ormond (*see* Butler), died. Owen Roe's nephew, **Daniel O Neill** (1612–64), was a Protestant Cavalier and a favourite of Charles II who, in 1663, appointed him Postmaster-General, an appointment which an O Neill of Clanaboy, **Charles O Neill**, was to hold in the nineteenth century.

Sir Phelim O Neill (1604–53), a lawyer, soldier and *bon viveur*, took part in the disastrous insurrection of 1641 where he was Commander-in-Chief of the northern forces. He was betrayed by a kinsman and executed as a traitor.

Arthur O Neill

The O Neills of Ulster were a fiercely proud, sometimes arrogant clan. Although their royal dynasty is long gone, their fame still lives on in many parts of the world, particularly in Europe, where O Neills fought in the armies of Spain, Austria and the Netherlands. There were also distinguished O Neills in the Church and the arts. The wandering, blind harper, **Arthur O Neill** (1737–1816), is recorded as having said, "wherever an O Neill sits he is always the head of the table". This Arthur was the root stock from which has sprung some of the best in Irish traditional music.

The junior branch of the O Neill sept, the Clanaboy, sprang from King Aodh Dubh (black Hugh) whose grandson, **Aodh Buidhe** (fair Hugh), was 27th in descent from Niall Of The Nine Hostages. Aodh Buidhe acquired counties Antrim and Down for his clan, hence the name Clanaboy from Clan Aodh Buidhe. Despite much strife, the Clanaboy held on to these lands until dispossessed by the Cromwellians.

Sir Niall O Neill (1658–90), the eldest son of Sir Hugh O Neill of Shane's Castle at Antrim, had the dangerous assignment of stopping the first wave of King William's troops crossing the Boyne at Rossnaree in 1690. He was fatally wounded and was later buried in Waterford.

Shane O Neill was the last Gaelic Lord of Clanaboy. In 1740 he sailed for Lisbon in Portugal, and the aristocratic O Neill dynasty continues there to the present day. After his departure, the O Neill castle, Edenduffcarrig in County Antrim, was renamed Shane's Castle. Today, **Raymond, 4th Lord O Neill** of the English creation of 1868, lives there. An ancestor of his, **Mary O Neill**, married the Reverend Arthur Chichester, rector of Randalstown. Because these O Neills had died out in the male line, he adopted the illustrious O Neill name, and the numerous descendants of Mary and Arthur have kept the name an active one in Irish public affairs.

Sir Niall O Neill

Shane's Castle on the edge of Lough Neagh has suffered many vicissitudes. In the nineteenth century, Earl O Neill had almost completed the restoration of the splendid mansion designed by Nash, when it was destroyed by fire. Some say the fire was caused by Kathleen, the family banshee, who had been disturbed by the rebuilding. It was later burned by Sinn Féin, with the irreparable loss of historical family papers. Raymond O Neill includes among his wide-ranging activities the preservation of steam trains; he runs a railway system on the estate at Shane's Castle which is open to the public. There is also a nature reserve, and the rebuilt conservatory houses a unique collection of camellias which are over 100 years old. Lord O Neill is also chairman of the National Trust in Northern Ireland.

John O Neill, a member of the old Irish Parliament, supported Catholic emancipation. He was one of the delegates who, in 1789, went from the Irish Parliament to request George, Prince of Wales, to assume the regency. He was killed at the outbreak of the 1798 rising, while travelling home to help restore order to his Ulster homeland.

Terence O Neill (1912–90) was Prime Minister of Northern Ireland from 1963 to 1969, the year in which he resigned. He made staunch efforts to reconcile unionists, nationalists and republicans. He was created a life peer in 1970, taking the title Lord O Neill of the Maine.

Hugo O Neill, son of **Jorge**, whose family has been in Portugal since the eighteenth century, is officially recognized by the offices of arms throughout Europe as titular Prince and Count of Tyrone and Clanaboy, but he refuses to use this title. He believes a direct descendant of the senior Tyrone branch must exist and have a better claim to the title, if only it could be authenticated. Hugo is, in fact, a Portuguese nobleman who prefers to use his Irish title, O Neill Buidhe of Clanaboy. Because of the diversity of opinion regarding the rightful chieftain, Lord Raymond O Neill diplomatically stressed to the assembly that this was not "the inauguration of an O Neill Mór, since no one is currently recognized as such, but we hope research will find him".

In the eighteenth century, a few O Neill women came to the fore. **Eliza O Neill** (1791–1872) was born in Drogheda, County Louth, where her father, an actor manager, encouraged her early acting career. When she appeared on the Dublin stage, her dramatic talents were immediately recognized. Soon afterwards she played Juliet at Covent Garden. Her beauty, splendid voice and versatility made her a favourite, and she earned an enormous salary during five very successful years. In 1819 she retired to marry William Wrixon, an Irish Member of Parliament from Mallow, County Cork. His uncle left him a fortune and he assumed his name, Becher. Later he was knighted and Lady Eliza Wrixon Becher's many children married into the Munster gentry.

Early in the seventeenth century the O Neills, together with other leading Irish families, were pioneers in the exodus to America. They sailed with Leonard Calvert and began the settlement of Maryland, which became a haven for these early Irish and English Catholic settlers.

The O Neills had an abundance of Irish talent for drama. **James O Neill** (1849–1920) was only five when he left Kilkenny with his parents for America, where he became an outstanding actor. He played Edmund Banton in *The Count of Monte Cristo* 6,000 times in twenty years, and was thus frustrated from developing his acting talent.

He was the father of the great Irish-American dramatist, **Eugene O Neill** (1888–1953), who was born in New York. Having worked as an actor, gold prospector and seaman, to name but a few of his occupations, he began to write plays when he was confined to hospital with tuberculosis. He won the Pulitzer Prize for drama in the 1920s and the Nobel Prize for literature in 1936. He was very aware of his Gaelic heritage and many of his plays reflect this, particularly *Long Day's Journey into Night* and *Moon for the Misbegotten*.

"Sweet Peggy O Neill" (1769–1879) almost caused the break-up of the United States. Daughter of a Washington tavern-keeper of Irish origin, she had beauty, wit and vivacity. Her second husband, John Henry Eaton, a Tennessee politician and member of the US Senate, was a close friend of President Jackson. In 1829, he appointed Eaton as Secretary of War. This sudden elevation of Sweet Peggy O Neill was bitterly resented by the other politicians and more so by their ladies, so Jackson was forced to reorganize his cabinet! Eaton became US Minister in Spain where Peggy was happily accepted and they were very successful. He died leaving her a wealthy widow, but she was tempted into a third marriage by a man who relieved her of her wealth. She spent the last years of her life in Washington in penury.

John O Neill (1834–78) from County Monaghan carried his nationalism with him when he emigrated to America. First he served with distinction in the army. Then he joined the Fenian Brotherhood in an abortive attack on British Canada, in the cause of Irish freedom. He survived and returned to civilian life to work for a company of land speculators. The chief town of Holt County is named after him.

Captain Francis O Neill (1848–1936) of Bantry, County Cork, became a senior official of the Chicago police at the beginning of this century. Encouraged by his mother, he listened to, and made notes on, the many traditional Irish singers living around Chicago. A fellow police officer, **James O Neill** from County Down, collaborated with him. Together they published a number of volumes of folk music and dances of Ireland. They left their great contribution to Irish musical heritage to the University of Notre Dame in Indiana. Subsequent Irish folklorists have been enriched by their research.

Congressman Thomas P. ("Tip") O Neill

Rose O Neill (1874–1944) was born in Wilkes-Barre, Pennsylvania. Her father's people were Irish, and he kept a bookstore and encouraged Rose in her writing and illustrating. She was the creator of the amazingly popular Kewpie (Cupid) doll, a forerunner of the Walt Disney industry. For 25 years, her "jolly little elves" disported themselves on the pages of *Ladies Home Journal* and other women's magazines. The Kewpie doll image was used to decorate nurseries, wallpaper, fabrics, china, even radiator caps. She made a fortune, but was careless, and generous, with her money and ended up penniless.

Congressman Thomas P. O Neill was born in Boston in 1912. President Jimmy Carter appointed him Speaker of the House of Representatives. Known as "Tip" O Neill, he was regarded as one of the most powerful advocates of the Irish cause internationally. He died in 1994.

Britain's entry into the European Economic Community was spearheaded by an O Neill. **Sir Con O Neill** (1912–88), who was born in London, went from Eton to Oxford to service in the Diplomatic Corps. When Britain was officially admitted to the EEC in 1973, part of the credit was due to Sir Con, who had headed the team that conducted the negotiations.

O Reilly
Ó Raghailligh

The O Reillys are a numerous clan who, both with and without the O prefix, fill about a dozen pages in the Irish telephone directories. Their name came from **Ragheallach** (*ragh* meaning race, *ceallach* meaning gregarious), who was the great-grandson of Maolmordha, said to be a descendant of the O Conor kings of Connacht. Maolmordha, simplified to Myles, is a popular O Reilly first name. Ragheallach lived at the time of King Brian Boru and was slain with him at the battle of Clontarf in 1014.

The O Reilly's original territory was around Lough Oughter in County Cavan, the most southerly of the Ulster counties. It was in this network of lakes and islands, stretching south from Upper Lough Erne, that, in pre-medieval times, they built their fortress on a *crannóg* (lake dwelling). O Reilly chiefs were inaugurated on the hill of Shanteman, not far from the standing stones known as Fionn McCool's fingers.

In 1237 **Cathal O Reilly**, Prince of Breifne, founded the monastery of Lough Oughter. The Franciscan abbey there was founded in 1300 by **Giolla Iosa Ruadh O Reilly** and it contains the tombs of several O Reillys. From AD 243 to 1523, there were 39 O Reilly abbots at Kells, County Meath. Saint Oliver Plunket, canonized in 1975, is among their family connections. Since the sixteenth century, five O Reilly bishops have held the primacy of Armagh, as well as five other bishoprics. The chief fortress of the Breifne O Reillys was on Tullymongan Hill, just outside the town of Cavan.

The ruins of the O Reilly castle of Cloughoughter can be seen on a small island on Lough Erne. It was here that Owen Roe O Neill, an O Reilly kinsman, died in 1649. A few years later the Cromwellians destroyed the castle.

Apart from feuding with the O Rourkes, the O Reillys lived remarkably peacefully, extending their territories into parts of County Meath. They also branched out into counties Longford and Cork.

Aodhagan Ó Rathaille (1670–1726) was the outstanding O Reilly poet who was born in County Kerry. He specialized in the genealogy of the leading families of Munster, glorifying them in his poems. During his lifetime the old Gaelic order was swept away, following William of Orange's suppression of the Irish at the battles of the Boyne, Aughrim and Limerick. There was no longer any place for Irish literature, and Ó Rathaille endured fearful poverty, but continued to write poetry until his dying day.

The chief of this numerous sept was styled Breifne O Reilly. When the Breifne O Reilly's were driven from their lands, as aristocrats they could offer credentials as exalted as any demanded by the courts of Europe for senior service in their armies. Few other families can boast such variety in the spelling of their name. There are at least seventeen different dialectical variations, including Oreigle, Oragill, Oreille, Orely. The countries in which they settled transformed their name to accord with local pronunciations, for example, Orely in Spain, Oreille in France.

Is any other Irish name found more frequently in the army lists of Europe? In the 1700s, **Colonel Edmond O Reilly** had no less than 33 O Reilly officers under his command, while Colonel Mahon had sixteen in his. In the complicated religious and territorial wars of two centuries ago, there is no doubt that O Reillys fought on every side: French,

Oragill

O Rahilly

Ó Rathaille

Oreigle

Oreille

Orely

Reilly

Austrian, Prussian, Spanish, Italian and Russian. They were professional soldiers who preferred to put their swords at the disposal of the monarchs of Europe than to fight for the colonizers who had overrun their country.

The exploits of the O Reillys abroad span many continents. **Count Alexander O Reilly** (1722–94) was born in Baltrasna, County Meath, and fought for Spain with the Irish Brigade. He was a Field Marshal and Governor of Madrid, Captain General of Andalusia and Governor of Cadiz.

"Was it for this that General Count O Reilly, who took Algiers, declared I used him vilely?" is asked in Byron's poem *Don Juan*. "General Count O Reilly did not take Algiers", writes Lord Byron, "Algiers very nearly took him". His failure to capture Algiers in 1775 had been a great humiliation.

In 1769, Count Alexander O Reilly sailed for New Orleans with a strong military force. His affability allayed all suspicion and, after investigating the popular leaders, he invited them to a reception where he had them arrested. Five were put to death and others were imprisoned in Havana, which put an end to the revolution. Count O Reilly's rule was regarded as liberal and enlightened. He had such a high regard for his Irish heritage that, not long before he died, he sent home 1000 guineas to have an Irish genealogist set out his pedigree for him.

General Count Alexander O Reilly

Descendants of the O Reillys of Baltrasna have been in Cuba for two centuries where, as Counts of Castillo and Marquis of San Felipe y Santiago, their lineage is to be found in the archives of Havana. One of Havana's main streets is the Calle Orely. There are also streets in Madrid, Barcelona and Cadiz bearing their name. It was an O Reilly of the St Patrick's Brigade in Mexico who induced Texas, in the 1840s, to join the USA.

Colonel Myles O Reilly fought courageously as a cavalry officer during the terrible war from 1641 to 1653, when the old Gaelic Ireland was crumbling and its soldiers were being driven abroad. He too was forced to flee, but he received high honours and distinctions from the King of Spain as well as from the French monarch. Leaving France for Flanders to serve as Maestro di Campo, he fell suddenly ill and died. A descendant of his, Captain Cyril Beresford Mandy of England, whose mother was an O Reilly, donated a wealth of family papers and portraits to Trinity College, Dublin.

Hugh Reilly of Cavan supported the luckless Stuarts. He was Master of Chancery and Clerk of the King's Council for Ireland under James II, and followed him into exile. In 1693, he published *Ireland's Case Briefly Stated*, which had a wide circulation during the penal times. It was the only published history of Ireland written by an Irishman at that time.

Count Andrew O Reilly of County Westmeath was a Field Marshal in Empress Maria Theresa's Austrian army. He fought a duel and killed his opponent to win his wife, a Bohemian heiress. He gained battle honours at Marengo and Austerlitz. In 1809, when he was Governor of Vienna, he had the humiliation of having to surrender the city to Napoleon. He completed his Austrian service as Chamberlain to the Emperor.

Sir John O Reilly, 3rd Baronet, born in 1800, entered the Austrian service, where he became Major of the Hungarian Hussars and Chamberlain to the Emperor. In 1845 he returned with his wife, Maria Roche, to his Ballinlough home where their first son, **Hugh**, was born (the first O Reilly to be born there in more than 100 years).

The O Reillys suffered greatly for their Catholic faith during the penal times, and those who managed to retain their houses and land became targets of anti-landlordism in the nineteenth century and the anti-Ascendency nationalists of the twentieth century who ignorantly believed that all the

Count Andrew O Reilly

fine houses were British-owned. Ballinlough Castle in Clonmellon is over seven hundred years old and has evolved from fortress to castle to mansion. In 1812, as part of a marriage settlement, **Hugh Andrew O Reilly** (b. 1795) changed his name to Nugent. A measure of Catholic emancipation had recently been conceded and Ballinlough was able to continue as one of the rare Irish houses still owned by the Irish Catholic aristocracy. In the 1930s, Sir John's great-grandson, Sir Hugh Nugent (1904–83), with Lady Nugent, rescued it from demolition by the Irish Land Commission. They restored it to its original grandeur and preserved a wealth of O Reilly memorabilia, including a contemporary portrait of Count Andrew O Reilly. Conscious of the ancient O Reilly lineage, the present Nugent owners like to make a pun about their being "New Gents".

John Roberts O Reilly (1808–73) was one of the Meath O Reillys. He lost his eyesight in a naval battle, but, despite his blindness, he entered the coastguard service and saved many people from shipwreck. He invented the distress flare, for which he was made a naval knight of Windsor.

John Boyle O Reilly (1844–90), poet, novelist and Fenian, was born at Dowth, near Drogheda in County Louth. At the age of eleven he was an apprentice printer with a local newspaper. Later he joined the Fenians and enlisted in the British army in Dublin intending to persuade serving Irishmen to join the Fenians. He was discovered and imprisoned, and spent a year in solitary confinement. In 1867, he was transported to Australia and, two years later, he escaped from a road gang and sailed to the United States, where he settled in Boston and married an Irishwoman. He became joint proprietor of the *Pilot*, a newspaper which attracted contributors as distinct and varied as Lady Wilde and W. B. Yeats. An accidental overdose of sleeping tablets led to his premature death.

John Boyle O Reilly

Christopher O Reilly (1835–1910), born in Ballybeg, County Meath, emigrated to Victoria in 1854, and went from there to Tasmania. A mining engineer and farmer, he called his estate at Scotsdale, Brefney, to remind his family of his ancient Irish lineage. He became a politician and was elected to the Tasmanian Parliament's House of Assembly in 1906.

The O Reillys were, and still are, prominent financiers. In the fifteenth century they created their own coinage, by "clipping" English coins—a form of counterfeiting which was later outlawed. The memory of this rebellious enterprise remains in the language. People living remarkably well are described as "living the life of Reilly", or, in the opposite context, there is the man "who hasn't a Reilly to his name". The warrior O Reillys of Ireland have long since diverted their energies into commerce, and, though they no longer manufacture their own coinage, they could be said to generate it!

Frank O Reilly (b. 1922) is a director of the Irish Distillers Group. Graduating from Trinity College, Dublin, in engineering, he joined the family firm of John Power & Sons. He was instrumental in merging Ireland's three main whiskey distilling companies in 1966. He is also chairman of the Ulster Bank and a director of the National Westminster Bank.

A.J.F. (Tony) O Reilly was born in Dublin in 1936. Tony O Reilly, of the unbeatable Lions rugby tour of the 1960s, qualified as a solicitor and, following experience in a variety of industries, became president and chief executive officer of Heinz in 1979. He divides his time between Pittsburgh and his Irish home at Castlemartin, a historic County Kildare mansion. He has also initiated a philanthropic Irish American Association.

Listowel, County Kerry, was the birthplace of two leading scholars. **Thomas Francis O Reilly** (1883–1953) was Professor of Irish at Trinity

College, Dublin, and the first Director of Celtic Studies with Dublin's Institute for Advanced Studies. He published books on Irish history, mythology, dialects and the two St Patricks.

Dr Alfred O Rahilly (1884–1969) was a dynamic intellectual. At University College, Cork, he was Professor of Mathematical Physics. He was registrar and president of the college until his retirement at the age of seventy, when he entered the priesthood. In his youth he had suffered imprisonment during the War of Independence. He spoke eight languages and disagreed with Einstein's theory of relativity. He arbitrated in industrial disputes, increased the College's library from 50,000 to 5 million volumes, and was a member of a banking commission.

There are also prominent O Reillys in England. **Sir Patrick D'Arcy O Reilly** was a diplomat who was British Ambassador to Russia from 1957 to 1960. Afterwards he was appointed chairman of the Banque Nationale de Paris. **Paul O Reilly** (b. 1912), son of **Professor Sir Charles O Reilly**, former head of Liverpool's School of Architecture, was in the vanguard of post-war British design. In recognition of his work, he was created a life peer in 1978.

On the whole, the O Reillys mostly emigrated to Europe, but several have also made their mark in the USA. **Henry O Reilly** (1806–86), who emigrated from Carrickmacross in County Monaghan to New York, was a pioneer in the development of telegraphic communication. He edited a variety of newspapers while still very young. He campaigned for the improvement of the Erie Canal, but was frustrated by the outbreak of the Civil War. With financial backing he later erected 8,000 miles of telegraph line, part of a scheme to link Pennsylvania with St Louis on the Great Lakes, but litigation and technical problems sank this promising enterprise.

Alexander O Reilly (1845–1912), descendant and namesake of the Austrian Field Marshal from Baltrasna in County Meath whose descendants are now Spanish, was born in Philadelphia. From 1902 to 1909 he was surgeon general to the US army. He was personal physician to President Cleveland. After the Spanish American war he helped reorganize the army medical system.

Ballyjamesduff in County Cavan, in the heart of O Reilly country, was immortalized in Percy French's lighthearted song, *Come back, Paddy Reilly, to Ballyjamesduff*.

O Rourke

Ó RUAIRC

In the tenth and eleventh centuries, the kingship of Connacht was held by three members of the O Rourke family. Their name is said to come from the Norse, Hrothrekr, which was Gaelicized to Ruairc. Until the confiscations by Cromwell, their chieftains were lords of Breifne—at that time composed of counties Leitrim and Cavan. The Breifne O Rourkes ruled from Kells in County Meath to the northern tip of County Sligo.

Noted for their hospitality, their stronghold was at Dromahair (the Ridge of the Two Air Demons) in County Leitrim. Possibly it got this whimsical name because it looked out over the legendary Lough Gill. On the banks of the nearby River Bonnet are the ruins of Breifne Castle, another of the O Rourke fortresses. In about 1626 its remains were built on by Sir William Villiers, an English settler, but his castle has long since been levelled. The Franciscan abbey of Creevelea, also on the banks of the Bonnet, was founded in 1508 by the wife of Owen O Rourke. There are O Rourke relics all over their former territories. The modern town of Manorhamilton was once Cluain Uí Ruairc, meaning O Rourke's little field.

As the clan Uí Bruiuin, or as a race, the Aedh Finn, they were absorbed into Gaelic culture and they followed the old unhappy pattern: clan jealously warring against clan, O Rourkes fighting their own kin, the O Reillys.

In the O Rourke pedigrees there are nineteen chiefs, all called Tiernan. Recently the O Rourkes have successfully researched their authentic chieftain. This is **Philip O Rorke**, a London stockbroker, who is a direct descendant of the Gaelic kings of Breifne and Connacht and is 32nd in descent from **Tiernan**, King of Breifne, who died in AD 892. Another **Tiernan O Rourke** (d. 1172) ravaged Meath in 1022 and then extended his warfare into Connacht, which was then O Brien and O Conor territory. Dermot MacMurrough Kavanagh, King of Leinster, who was also striving to subdue Connacht, encountered Tiernan O Rourke's wife, Dervorgilla, there. Theirs was one of the most unusual affairs in Irish legend. He is reputed to have been 42 and she was 44 when they ran off together, she with most of her dowry. In less than two years they separated. MacMurrough was forced to pay O Rourke 100 ounces of gold in compensation. Dervorgilla later returned to her father's estates at Mellifont and built an exquisite little church at the famous monastic settlement at Clonmacnoise.

MacMurrough had made an implacable enemy. O Rourke allied himself with O Conor, King of Connacht, and deposed MacMurrough, who went in search of assistance from Henry II, King of England and France. Some time later, Henry II sent the Normans to Ireland, for which Dermot MacMurrough has never been forgiven. Dermot died soon afterwards and Tiernan O Rourke was killed by the Norman, Hugo de Lacy, who decapitated him and sent his head to Dublin to be impaled on a gate.

Looking down from the flat-topped hill known as O Rourke's Table near Dromahair, the poet Thomas Moore wrote his fanciful and moving poem about Dermot and Dervorgilla, of which the opening line is "The valley lay shining before me".

Like all the Gaels, the O Rourkes suffered heavily during the Elizabethan wars. **Sir Brian O Rourke** (Brian na Murtha, meaning Brian of the ramparts), although inaugurated as chieftain of the O Rourkes in 1564, accepted

O Rorke

Roark

Rooke

Rourke

an English knighthood at Athlone in 1578, which enraged the Gaelic Maguires and the O Donnells. A decade later he changed his allegiance, and when the Spanish Armada was wrecked off the west coast he was remarkable in his humane treatment of those who were shipwrecked, clothing them, feeding them and helping them to escape. For such a grave offence against the English, his territory was ravaged and he had to flee to Scotland where he sought help from James VI. Instead of helping him, James handed him over to Queen Elizabeth and collected the reward. A proud and independent man, he refused to face the humiliation of trial by jury and went to the scaffold at Tyburn, London, in 1591.

His natural son and successor, **Brian Óg na Samhthach** (of the axes), had been a prisoner, in his youth, in Oxford where he got into debt far beyond his father's ability to pay. He was returned to Ireland and fought with the Maguires and the O Donnells in their campaign to oust the English. Constantly embroiled in warfare, he kept a huge army, including 500 Scots. He took part in the siege of Kinsale in 1601 and died in 1604 in Galway.

From his time onwards, the history of the Breifne O Rourkes is predominantly centred on Europe, where they were distinguished as churchmen, statesmen or soldiers of fortune.

Colonel Tiernan O Rourke, who fought at the battle of the Boyne, afterwards served with the Irish Brigade in France and was killed at Luzzara in 1702.

His brother, **Dr Thady O Rourke** (b. 1658), was chaplain and domestic secretary to the Austrian general, Prince Eugene of Savoy (1663–1736), for a while. He returned to Ireland as Bishop of Killala. In the eighteenth century there were a succession of O'Rourke bishops of Killala.

Manus O Rourke (1660–1741) was educated for the priesthood in Paris and was one of a number of Irish-speaking priests at the Jacobite Court of Saint Germain-en-Laye.

Eugene O Rourke, Viscount and Baron of Breifne, followed James, the Old Pretender, to France and was entrusted with the task of sounding out whether the Elector Palatine might consider James as a son-in-law. The Elector was unwilling, but nevertheless James made Eugene O Rourke his minister plenipotentiary at the Court of Vienna where O Rourke died in 1742.

John O Rourke, Prince of Breifne, was born in 1735. Because of his excellent pedigree and his prowess at duelling, he was given a commission in the Royal Scotch Regiment by Louis XV soon after his arrival in Paris from County Leitrim. His French colleagues were incensed by this rapid promotion and he transferred to Russia where, as a major in the Czar's regiment of Body Guards, he fought valiantly against Prussia. Returning to France, he served with the cavalry and received the title of Count. In London, in 1778, John Count O Rourke published *Treatise on the Art of War*, which was favourably compared to Maurice de Saxe's classic on the art of warfare. O Rourke's treatise was ahead of its time in its advocation of "proper man management". He died, a bachelor, in London. Many papers relating to the O Rourke family are kept in the Austrian Record Office.

John Count O Rourke's brother, **Cornelius O Rourke**, settled in Russia. He was the father of the famous **General Count Iosif Kornilievich O Rourke** (1772–1849), one of the Russian generals who defeated Napoleon.

A kinsman, **Count Moritz O Rourke** (1804–78), was also in the army, while another was a chief of police in Russia. There are portraits and

Count Iosif Kornilievich O Rourke

papers relating to the Russian O Rourkes in the Hermitage Museum in St Petersburg where Russian army lists of the Czarist times record many O Rourkes. Irish writers mention meeting officers and ecclesiastics in Russia bearing the O Rourke name who spoke not one word of Irish or English.

Maria Nikolaievna, Countess Tarnovska, née O Rourke, was born in 1877. She was to become the central character in a notorious trial held in Venice in 1910 attended by reporters from all over the world. She was sentenced for complicity in the murder of her lover.

William Michael O Rourke (1794–1847) became famous in the musical world as William Rooke. He taught music, and had Michael W. Balfe, the Dublin-born composer of the opera *The Bohemian Girl*, as a pupil. He moved to England where he composed and produced several minor operas.

Edmund O Rourke (1814–79) was another member of the art world who changed his name. As Edmund Falconer he went on the London stage and was the first to play the part of Danny Mann in the long-running *Colleen Bawn*. He was a dramatist as well as an actor.

Bishop Count Edward O Rourke, born in Poland in 1876, was apostolic administrator of the Free City of Danzig until its disruption by the Nazis in the Second World War. A kinsman of the O Rourkes who fled Ireland in the previous century, he was known as the Irish Bishop of Danzig. Apart from Russian, English and German, he could also converse in Irish. In the 1920s he went in search of his family roots at Dromahair in County Leitrim. He published *Documents and Materials for the History of the O Rourke Family* from his Danzig home. A namesake in Dublin has a copy of this manuscript.

John Dennis O Rourke founded the Galway Blazers hunt in 1844. His great-great-grand-niece, **Molly O Rourke**, now Lady Cusack-Smith of Bermingham House, Tuam, County Galway, was the first woman Master for Hounds of the legendary Blazers, a hundred years later.

Although the O Rourkes have been most evident in Europe, in more recent times they have joined the drift to Australia and America.

Patrick O Rourke (1837–63) left County Cavan for New York when he was only a year old. He graduated from West Point Military Academy, became a colonel of the 104th New York Volunteers, and was killed at Gettysburg.

Timothy Murphy of the US army, and **Simon O Rourke** of the US navy, were the first chaplains to be killed in the First World War.

John F. O Rourke planned and took a major part in the construction of New York's subway system.

Miceál O Rourke of Dublin (b. 1947) is one of a galaxy of young Irish pianists. He is unique in his study of Mozart, having played all of his 22 piano concertos in a single session of concerts. He has also acquired an international reputation as a performer of Chopin. He lives in Paris.

Today in Ireland the O Rourkes, Rourkes or Roarks are listed among the 100 most numerous names in Ireland.

O Sullivan
ó súilleabháin

Sullivan

Whether Ó Súilleabháin, O Sullivan or Sullivan, the name fills seventeen pages in the Irish telephone directories and is the third most numerous in Ireland. Scholars agree that Súilleabháin means one-eyed or, maybe, even hawk-eyed. The O Sullivans deduce their origins from Eoghan, the eldest son of the third-century king of Munster, Oilioll Olum, from whom descend the Eoganacht, the clan name of many prominent families of south Munster.

The O Sullivan territory was originally in County Tipperary. Later the family branched out to counties Cork and Kerry. **O Sullivan Mór**, their chieftain, had his castle at the head of Kenmare Bay in County Kerry. **Donal O Sullivan Beare** (1560–1618), next in importance, occupied Dunboy Castle overlooking Bantry Bay, one of the finest harbours in Ireland which later became the site of an oil storage depot. Between the tragic dispersal of the O Sullivan Beare family in the seventeenth century and the ceremonial opening of this international commercial enterprise in 1969, there is a wealth of Irish history, an epic awaiting an Irish Homer.

Following the disastrous battle of Kinsale which changed the Gaelic order forever, Donal O Sullivan Beare managed to regain Dunboy Castle with a force of 143 men, including a few Spaniards. Carew, with 4,000 men, attacked from sea and from land and for 21 days Dunboy held out, until hardly a stone remained. Then, while O Sullivan Beare went to meet a Spanish ship which had landed too late and on the wrong side of the peninsula, his constable, MacGeoghegan, was killed and the castle was breached. Carew and his men killed every man, woman and child inside the castle. O Sullivan Beare decided to make his way north to Leitrim with his remaining people to seek refuge with his ally, O Rourke. At the end of December 1602, with 400 fighting men and 600 civilians, they began their 200 mile trek—two weeks of appalling cold, hardship and bitter tragedy. *The Annals of the Four Masters* said of O Sullivan, "He was not a day or night during this period without a battle, or being vehemently and vindictively pursued; all of which he sustained and responded to with manliness and vigour". Sadly, his main enemies were Irish chieftains anxious to win approval from their new masters.

Day by day the party struggled on. At the wide River Shannon, they killed some of their horses and crossed with boats made from their skins strengthened with osiers. At Aughrim they were attacked by the Anglo-Irish. They fought back and killed both leaders, Sir Thomas Burke and Captain Malby. Eventually, they reached Brian O Rourke's castle at Leitrim. Of the original 1,000 who had started out, only 35 reached their destination.

Elizabeth I died the next year. Her nephew, James I, came to the throne and the Irish chieftains, full of hope, went to London. They got no welcome there from James and no restitution of their territories. There was nothing for them at home and so they were forced to go abroad.

Donal O Sullivan Beare, whose wife and children had been guarded by the MacSweeneys, took flight with his family to Spain in 1604. Here, Philip III treated him kindly, created him Knight of St James and Count of Bearhaven, and gave him a monthly pension of 300 pieces of gold. He was killed, accidentally, in Madrid in 1618, aged 58.

His son, **Donal**, had been killed at the siege of Belgrade. **Dermot**, his brother, and Dermot's wife—the only woman to survive the epic march

Donal O Sullivan Beare

214

from Dunboy—had also gone to Spain. Dermot, who lived to be 100 and had been Lord of Dursey Castle at the entrance to Bantry Bay, had a son who had been in Spain since childhood. Together with other Irish youths he had been sent there as a hostage (the kings of Spain gave no aid to Ireland without collateral).

Philip O Sullivan Beare (1590–1660) was destined for the Spanish navy and served faithfully, even if his mind was more occupied with the study of Latin, history and polemics. Fortunately, he left a most useful contemporary account of the Elizabethan period in Ireland, which was published in Latin in Lisbon in 1621.

From then on, the story of the O Sullivans is diffuse, exemplified by characters pursuing diverse careers both at home and in the old and new worlds: soldiers, sailors, poets and writers predominate. In Brady and Cleeve's 1985 *A Biographical Dictionary of Irish Writers* there are no less than fifteen O Sullivans.

John O Sullivan (1700–46), born in Kerry, was sent to Paris and Rome to be educated for the priesthood but, changing his mind, he returned to Ireland. The penal laws presented him with the choice of forfeiting his estates or changing his religion. He chose the former and returned to France, where he joined the army and saw much service. When Prince Charles Stuart was planning his assault on Scotland in 1745, John O Sullivan was chosen as his adjutant and quartermaster-general. From then until Prince Charles' escape after Culloden, when he boarded a French frigate captained by another Irishman, Antoine Walsh, John O Sullivan was by the Prince's side. Despite the defeat at Culloden he was knighted for his services by James III, the Old Pretender.

Tadgh Gaolach O Sullivan (1715–95) was a poet born in County Kerry. His work was mostly political or sentimentally religious and Dr Douglas Hyde, the Gaelic scholar, has described it as "very musical and mellifluous".

Owen Roe O Sullivan (1748–84) was also born in Kerry. He abandoned farm labouring to become a teacher. His weakness for women, and theirs for him, disrupted his life so much that he had to give up teaching. He joined the army, but eventually returned to schoolteaching. He wrote many poems and songs, some of which still linger on today. He has come to be regarded as a great lyric poet.

Two O Sullivan brothers were in France at the time of the Revolution. **Charles O Sullivan**, grandson of an Irish *émigré* who had settled at Nantes, was a royalist. He had saved his brother, **John**, an ardent revolutionary, from the militant Vendeans. Later, John, a former fencing master, became a notorious terrorist. With the cruel pro-consul, Carrier, he organized the sinking of barges filled with priests and other citizens—a diabolical way of bypassing the guillotine or the expense of gunfire. John even betrayed his own royalist brother, Charles, who was guillotined. When the inevitable revulsion against the horror set in, John O Sullivan came before the Revolutionary Tribunal, which found him guilty of many atrocities and murders, but set him free "because he did not act with criminal revolutionary intention". He was, they averred, "merely a revolutionary with a perverted moral sense".

Morty Óg O Sullivan, a dispossessed O Sullivan of Berehaven, was a captain in the Irish Brigade in France. He served in Austria in Maria Theresa's army and was at the battle of Fontenoy in 1745. The following year he was another of the many Irishmen who supported Prince Charles Stuart at the battle of Culloden. After the defeat of the Scots, he went to sea to earn his living smuggling to and from France, from the conveniently indented Munster coast. He also smuggled "Wild Geese", young men escaping from the frustrations of English rule in Ireland who wanted to join the Irish Brigade in France. The export of Irish wool was also forbidden, but Morty Óg smuggled it to France to finance his adventures, until he was caught and shot dead. Many ballads have been written in remembrance of Morty Óg O Sullivan.

"If you can't beat them, join them", has long been the motivation of the many Irish who travelled no further across the sea than to England. Many went on from there to take part in the expansion of the British Empire. One of these pragmatic Irishmen was **Sir Richard Sullivan** (1752–1806), born in Dublin, the son of **Benjamin Sullivan** of County Clare. These Sullivans made a life for themselves in India. Benjamin Sullivan was a Supreme Court judge in Madras. Another member of the family, **Lawrence**, was chairman of the East India Company. The climate did not agree with Richard, who returned to England where he began writing political history, including a history of Ireland. One of his three sons, **Charles Sullivan**, was Admiral of the Fleet.

Another Sullivan, **Rear-Admiral Ball Sullivan** (1780–1857), had fourteen children; four of his sons were in the British navy. In the First World War, **Vice-Admiral Norton Allen Sullivan** took part in the battle of Jutland in 1916. **John O Sullivan** of Bantry won the Victoria Cross in that same war.

An impressive number of O Sullivans were literary. Their diaries, political treatises, poems, plays and songs are testimony to the endurance and versatility of this great clan.

In the eighteenth century, Bantry in County Cork was a seed bed of brilliant, if impoverished, O Sullivans. **Alexander Martin O Sullivan** (1830–84) worked as a government clerk while still a teenager, during the terrible Famine of 1845 to 1849. Moved by this experience, he joined William Smith O Brien's Young Ireland movement. Afterwards, he worked as a reporter on the *Liverpool Daily Post*, and when he returned to Ireland he got a job as assistant editor of the *Nation*. Inevitably there was conflict between those who sought an Irish republic by peaceful means and those who wanted instant and violent action. A.M. O Sullivan joined the Home Rule movement and was elected to Parliament and, as editor of the *Nation*, he began an unpopular temperance campaign. His legal studies led to his being called both to the Irish and English Bar. He handed over the *Nation* to his brother, Timothy Daniel O Sullivan, but over-exertion had damaged A.M.'s health and he did not live for much longer.

Timothy Daniel Sullivan (1827–1914) was a politician, journalist and poet. He wrote many popular nationalist songs, including *God Save Ireland*, and *Ireland, Boys, Hurrah*, which was sung by both sides during the American Civil War.

Alexander Martin Sullivan's second son, also **Alexander Sullivan** (1871–1959), was a distinguished barrister. He was the last to hold the title of King's Serjeant in Ireland. Because he was a constitutional nationalist, opposed to physical force, his life was threatened, as was his father's before him, by the men of violence who also burned his County Cork home. He was practising successfully at the English Bar until 1949, when the Costello coalition government repealed the External Relations Act. Feeling himself to be an alien in England, he retired from the English Bar.

Perhaps because of their rich Kerry literary background, many of the O Sullivans have been dedicated folklorists. **Muiris Ó Súileabháin** (1904–50) was born on the Great Blasket Islands off the Kerry coast. He joined the Gárda Síochána (the Irish police force) and, while stationed in

Connemara, he wrote *Fiche Bliain ag Fás* (Twenty Years A-Growing), an account of his childhood on the Blaskets, which became an international classic.

Seán O Sullivan (1906–64) studied art in Dublin and London and, at the age of 21, was the youngest artist ever to be elected to the Royal Hibernian Academy. He had a genius for portraiture and painted leading politicians, painters and writers.

In England the Sullivans mostly dropped the O prefix. **Joseph Sullivan** left Ireland to become a bandmaster at the Royal Military College at Sandhurst. He was the father of the great **Sir Arthur Sullivan** (1842–1900), whose music, coupled with W. S. Gilbert's witty lyrics, was to fill theatres, with amusing light operas such as *The Pirates of Penzance*, *The Mikado* and *The Gondoliers*. Arthur Sullivan was also a composer of hymns: particularly well-known are his *Onward Christian Soldiers* and *The Lost Chord*.

Barry Sullivan's (1821–88) father left Ireland to join the British army and was invalided out after the battle of Waterloo. Barry soon abandoned his law studies to tour Ireland with a theatre company. He made his first important appearance in London, playing Hamlet. From then on he toured Europe and America as Hamlet. In Australia, his acting in Shakespearean drama was so popular that he remained there for three years. For twenty years he was confined to two principal roles, Hamlet and Richard IV. He said he appeared 3,500 times in each part.

In the United States of America, notable Sullivans appear with great regularity. **General John O Sullivan** (1744–1808) opened hostilities in the American Revolution by capturing a fort and taking a cannon. He was a personal friend of George Washington and, at the siege of Boston, he watched the English sail away. He and his brother **James** were lawyers by profession and helped in the establishment of the new nation. James was twice elected Governor of Massachusetts. There were, in fact, four Sullivan boys, all sons of **Owen Sullivan**, who had emigrated from Limerick in 1723 and had founded an exclusive school in New England.

Louis Henri Sullivan (1856–1924) always referred to himself as "of mongrel origin". His father was a musician who, in the course of his European wanderings, married a French-German wife. In Chicago, where they lived during his youth, Louis Henri had the benefit of grandparents of three nationalities. He became one of America's visionary architects, pursuing his "form follows function" theory. He designed many of Chicago's important public buildings, including the Auditorium.

Building sites and boxing gloves were outlets for the poor who had the physical strength but lacked education. Irish immigrants were highly rated in the boxing ring, particularly **John L. Sullivan** (1858–1918), who was born in Boston of parents who had come from Tralee, County Kerry. His father was a small man, but his mother weighed 180 pounds and it was undoubtedly from her that John L. inherited his prodigious physique, which led him to become one of the most famous boxers in the history of the sport. He began to live recklessly and was reduced to making vaudeville appearances. His second wife reformed him and he ended his career as a temperance lecturer.

James Edward Sullivan (1860–1914), whose parents were from Kerry, was self-educated. He became a successful publisher in the United States and started the Amateur Athletic Union of the United States and New York's Public School Athletic league. He also opened the first public playground. He was American director of the Olympic Games and represented President Theodore Roosevelt and President Taft at the Olympic Games of 1908 and 1912.

General John O Sullivan

Timothy Daniel Sullivan (1862–1913), son of emigrants to New York, progressed from Tammany Hall politics and saloon-keeping to leadership of the Democratic Party in the Bowery. His commercial enterprises, which embraced theatres and gambling, made him a millionaire. He turned down leadership of Tammany Hall in favour of his good friend, the incorruptible Charles W. Murphy. He donated generously to charity and was elected to Congress. When his wife Helen Fitzgerald died, he lost interest in life and died soon afterwards.

Irish construction workers contributed to the dangerous job of erecting the Statue of Liberty, while the dedication speech for its opening ceremony in 1886 was delivered by **John L. O Sullivan**, the Irish-American statesman and editor who coined the phrase "Manifest Destiny".

Annie Sullivan (1866–1936) taught Helen Keller, who was deaf and blind from the age of nineteen months, to talk by lip-feeling. She was so successful that Helen Keller graduated from Radcliffe College, became a writer and linguist and worked for the physically handicapped.

It was **Pat Sullivan**, an Australian cartoonist, who created "Felix the Cat" for the *New York Herald* in 1919, while **Ed Sullivan** (1902–74) brought the Sullivan name into millions of American homes with his weekly variety show which ran from 1948 to 1971.

Irish-Canadians feature among the Sullivans of North America. **William Henry Sullivan** (1864–1929) started as a lumberman and ended up as a civic leader. Born of Irish parents at Port Dalhousie, Ontario, he moved to Louisiana where he founded the town of Bogalusa and became its mayor.

O Sullivans visiting the lakes of Killarney in County Kerry will find their name commemorated in the names of places such as, for instance, a stretch of water known as O Sullivan's Punch Bowl. At Muckross Abbey there are tombs of many distinguished O Sullivans of past centuries.

Annie Sullivan (left), with Helen Keller

O Toole

ó tuathail

The O Tooles were one of the great Leinster septs. Their surname comes from **Tuathal**, King of Leinster, who died in AD 956. According to Father Woulfe in his *Irish Names and Surnames*, *Tuathal* means prosperous, which the O Tooles undoubtedly were. They owned the southern half of the rich plains of County Kildare. But, in about 1172, they were driven out by the Anglo-Norman usurpers. With their neighbours in north Kildare, the O Byrnes, they found shelter in the hills and valleys of Wicklow, resisting Anglicization for more than 500 years.

Saint Laurence O Toole (*c.* 1130–80) was the first Irish Archbishop of Dublin. Son of **Murtough (Maurice) O Toole**, Prince of Hy Murray of south Kildare, his mother, Inian Ivrien, was the daughter of an O Byrne chieftain. He was twelve when his grandfather was killed by Dermot MacMurrough, who brought him to his fortress palace of Ferns in County Wexford, and treated him as a slave. Some years passed before his father succeeded in getting MacMurrough to release the boy and send him to the monastery of Glendalough in County Wicklow, where Laurence found his vocation. He so impressed his brethren that, on the death of the Abbot and Bishop of Glendalough, Laurence, aged only 25, was chosen to succeed him.

In 1161 he was made Archbishop of Dublin. This was just before the Anglo-Norman invasion, the start of a long and troubled period for Ireland. He was an able administrator who carried out a series of reforms in the Irish church. He travelled several times to Rome to papal conferences. *En route* to meet Henry II in Normandy to mediate between him and the deposed High King of Ireland, Roderick O Conor, he caught a fever and died at Eu in 1180.

The O Tooles had many castles in County Wicklow: at Imail, now Talbotstown; at Castle Kevin, Annamoe; at Powerscourt, Enniskerry, then called Fearcuallan. During the time of James I, the lands and castle at Fearcuallan were confiscated from the O Tooles and granted to Sir Richard Wingfield, and they remained in this family until about thirty years ago. The house was accidentally burned down in 1974. The landscaped grounds, Powerscourt Gardens, are among the most beautiful in Europe and are open to the public.

Castle Kevin was razed by Cromwell's army *en route* to Wexford. Set on a small hill surrounded by 1,544 acres of fertile fields, enough of it remains to recognize the palatial building it must once have been. In the 1500s it was "granted" to Art O Neill's family by Henry VII (1457–1509), "on consideration that they use the English language, habit, education and the like".

Laurence O Toole (d. 1823) of Fairfield, County Wexford, an officer in the Irish Brigade in France, had eight sons, all of whom served in the French army. The eldest, **Colonel John O Toole**, was ennobled, and from his family descends the present Count of Limoges in France.

Another of Laurence's sons, **Lieutenant-Colonel Bryan Burrough O Toole**, had a remarkable army career. He served with the Austrians at the time of the French Revolution and fought against the French in the Low Countries. In 1794 he was with the 6th Regiment of the Irish Brigade in the British army, one of the *émigré* Irish Brigades which, ironically, were received into the British army during the French Revolution.

Toal

Toale

Toole

Arthur Severus O Toole, a sixteenth-century warrior chieftain

Afterwards he served in the West Indies. Such was the career of a professional soldier that he also fought with the Hompesch Hussars against the Irish at the battle of Vinegar Hill, and against the French during the "Year of the French", the Castlebar–Ballinamuck rising of 1798, about which a film has been made. He was later decorated during the Peninsular war and went from there to join the Portuguese army, where he lost the use of an arm.

He was an ardent correspondent, writing comical letters to his mother and his sweetheart, Norah, in County Wexford. "Norah", he wrote, "lived convenient to his mother", which was why "The Noshuns of Bryan O Toole on the Goings on of the Irishtocracy in London" all went in the one letter. He penned reams of shrewd, amusing criticism about London's Royal Academy Exhibition. He lived long enough to retire to Fairfield for a few years before he died there in 1825. What happened to his Norah is difficult to discover.

When Sir Charles Wogan of Dillon's Regiment of the Irish Brigade in France rescued Princess Clementina, granddaughter of Jan Sobieski, King of Poland, from parental confinement in Innsbruck, he was ably assisted by **Luke O Toole**. Overcoming great obstacles they got her to Italy where, at Bologna in 1719, she married the Old Pretender to whom she had become engaged, two years previously, against the wishes of her family. For this romantic abduction, which became the subject of many novels, Luke O Toole was decorated by Pope Clement XI.

O Tooles are still numerous in counties Mayo and Galway while, as Toal or Toale, they survive in the Monaghan, Dundalk, Cavan and Athlone areas. Some went to Canada, where they eventually dropped the O prefix. **Laurence O Toole** (1874–1957) emigrated to Kenora, Ontario, but in 1917 it was an **Archer Toole** who became Mayor of Kenora.

James St Laurence O Toole, who died in 1990, divided his time between Venice and Madison Avenue, New York, where he was an art dealer. His family left Ulster several generations ago. His father was an American diplomat and his nephews have served in the US armed forces (and one is an astronaut). He claimed descent from the family of St Laurence O Toole, and had a life of the saint published.

Peter O Toole the film actor who was born in Connacht is probably this century's most famous O Toole.

The designation O Toole of Fer Tire, the Chief of the Name, has been dormant since 1965.

Plunkett
pluincéid

Plunket

Plunkett, whether spelled with one t or two, is a name seldom found outside Ireland, except when it applies to Irish exiles. According to some scholars the name is of French origin, a corruption of *blanchet*, from *blanc* meaning white, referring to the fair Plunketts who arrived in Ireland with the Normans. The present head of the Plunkett family, **Lord Randal Dunsany**, the 19th Baron, thinks that their roots are Danish.

It is uncertain as to when exactly they settled in Ireland. What is certain is that they have produced a succession of notable people: bishops, soldiers, diplomats, admirals, lawyers and even a saint! Despite centuries of war they managed to hold on to most of their estates and remain to this day in their territories in counties Meath and Louth. A glance at the Irish telephone directories will confirm that the greatest concentration of Plunketts is north of Dublin.

Dunsany, the palatial and beautifully maintained home of Lord and Lady Dunsany, is but one of the many splendid castles and mansions which emphasize the Plunketts' progress from medieval times. The Plunketts all share the same motto on their heraldic crest, *Festina Lente*.

Beaulieu, in County Louth, now regarded as one of the finest and best preserved, unfortified country houses in Ireland, was an early Plunkett estate. **John Plunkett**, who lived at Beaulieu towards the end of the eleventh century, was the ancestor of two brothers, **John** and **Richard Plunkett**. The elder was the ancestor of **Sir Oliver Plunkett** of Kilforan, who became the 1st Baron Louth in 1541. From Richard came the lords of Fingall and Dunsany.

In 1593 **Oliver**, 4th Lord Louth of the Plunketts of Ardee, is reputed to have brought six archers on horseback to the general hosting on the hill of Tara in County Meath. Another **Oliver**, 6th Lord Louth, a royalist, was at the siege of Drogheda in 1639. He led a meeting of the Catholic gentry, hoping to raise a force in County Louth to dispel the usurpers. He was outlawed for this in 1641.

His son **Matthew**, the 7th Lord Louth (d. 1689), also suffered for his support of the doomed Catholic Stuart cause. Not until 1798 was Matthew's great-great-grandson, **Oliver**, 11th Lord Louth, restored to his titles, enabling him to sit in Parliament.

In 1403, **Sir Christopher Plunkett**, ancestor of the earls of Fingall, married Joan Cusack, heiress to Killeen Castle in County Meath, from which her husband took his title, Lord of Killeen. A grandson of theirs, **Broughton Plunkett**, was with the Irish army which went to Nottingham, in 1487, to fight at the battle of Stoke for the Yorkist pretender, Lambert Simnel.

From this branch of the Plunkett family came many distinguished soldiers. **George Plunkett** fought at Drogheda when Cromwell savagely attacked it in 1641. **Christopher**, 2nd Earl of Fingall of Killeen, who was taken prisoner at the battle of Rathmines, died in Dublin Castle in 1649.

Robert, 6th Earl of Fingall, was a captain in Berwick's Regiment in France. The Plunketts were numerous in the Irish regiments of Lally, Walsh, Dillon and Clare.

Luke Plunkett was killed in the service of Austria in Italy in 1794. This Killeen branch of the Plunketts voted for the Union and so was able to sit in the Parliament in London.

Christopher Plunkett was created 1st Baron Dunsany by Henry VI. **Robert**, 5th Baron Dunsany, attended the Parliament held in Dublin in 1541 with his kinsman, **Lord Killeen** of the senior branch of the family. **Patrick**, 9th Baron Dunsany, was an adherent of two ill-fated monarchs, James I and Charles I. He was imprisoned for a while in Dublin Castle.

Oliver Plunkett (1625–81), the younger son of Lord Dunsany, the 9th Baron, was born in Loughcrew Castle in County Meath. He spent more than twenty years in Rome, where he was ordained and represented the Irish bishops. Religious persecution was rampant in Ireland and, when Oliver Plunkett was appointed to the primacy of Armagh in 1669, he was quietly consecrated Archbishop at Ghent, *en route* home. Once in Ireland, he administered the sacraments to thousands of people deprived of their religion, set up a Jesuit school at Drogheda and worked tirelessly to restore discipline to the Church. Eventually he was forced to go underground, enduring great privation, his life always under threat. To quote from *Burke's Peerage*, "He was a clergyman of great virtues and ability, who fell victim to the times in which he lived, being most unjustly executed in 1681 as one of the conspirators in the pretended Popish Plot". His trial was a travesty: he was alleged to have conspired with Titus Oates, the notorious clerical perjurer. He was found guilty of high treason and was hung, drawn and quartered at Tyburn in London.

On 12 October 1975, in Rome, he was canonized, the first Irishman to be so honoured since St Laurence O Toole. Present in Rome for the ceremonies were Randal, the 19th Baron, and Lady Dunsany, who preserve many of his relics at Dunsany, including his ring and crozier. Hundreds of Plunketts from all over the world went to Rome for the ceremony. The many letters written by St Oliver Plunkett from Ireland and Rome have fortunately been preserved, and were published in book form in 1979 as *The Letters of Saint Oliver Plunkett, 1625–81*. The letters were translated and edited by Monsignor John Hanly of the Irish College in Rome and published by The Humanities Press Inc. of New Jersey.

William Conyngham, 1st Baron Plunket (1764–1854), son of a Presbyterian minister, was born in Enniskillen. He graduated in law from Trinity College, Dublin. In the aftermath of the 1798 rising, he defended the revolutionary Sheares brothers, although he had little hope of saving them. He was the subject of abuse when he led the prosecution of the patriot Robert Emmet, whose brother, Thomas, was a close friend. Of an independent turn of mind, he strongly opposed the 1801 Act of Union and was very much in favour of Catholic emancipation, despite disliking the methods adopted by Daniel O Connell. Among the many lofty legal posts he held was that of Chief Justice, the position he occupied when he received his peerage. He was considered to be one of the finest orators in the House of Commons. His eldest son, **Thomas Spen Plunket**, the 2nd Baron, was Bishop of Tuam in County Galway.

A grandson of the 1st Baron Plunket, **David Robert Plunket**, 1st Baron Rathmore (1839–1919), was Solicitor General, Paymaster General and Commissioner of Works in various Conservative governments. He wrote a *Life* of the 1st Lord Plunket. The 4th Baron Plunket, another **William Conyngham**, grandson of the 1st Baron, was Church of Ireland Bishop of Meath and Archbishop of Dublin in the latter half of the nineteenth century.

John Hubert Plunkett (1801–69) was born at Mount Plunkett, County Roscommon. He went to Australia where he became a statesman, Solicitor General of New South Wales and President of the Upper Chamber. He always campaigned for Catholic emancipation, both in

1625   1681

SAINT OLIVER PLUNKETT

ÉIRE   7

Saint Oliver Plunkett

Ireland and Australia, and was one of the first Catholics to be appointed to high civil office in the colony. Many of his kinsmen followed him to Australia.

George Noble Plunkett, a barrister, was born in Dublin in 1851 and educated in Ireland and France. Pope Leo XIII created him a Papal Count. He was a poet as well as director of the Science and Arts Museum in Dublin. His son, **Joseph Plunkett** (1887–1916), was a revolutionary poet and journalist. Despite poor health, he travelled extensively in Europe and America to promote the ideals of republicanism. The military plans for the 1916 rising were drawn up by him and he was a signatory of the Proclamation of the Republic. He was court-martialled and sentenced to death after the rising. A few hours before his execution in Kilmainham Jail, Dublin, he was married to his fiancée, Grace Gifford.

The farmers of Ireland must be grateful to **Sir Horace Plunkett** (1854–1932), third son of the 16th Baron of Dunsany. He spent his life working for the improvement of agriculture. He lived for a decade in Wyoming, but visited Ireland each year and eventually he returned to help organize dairy co-operatives. He was a member of the Congested Districts Board and a Unionist Member of Parliament for Dublin in 1892. In 1922, after the Treaty, he was made a Senator of the Irish Free State. He founded the Irish Agricultural Organisation Society. Although he had constantly laboured to improve the quality of Irish life, his politics were not agreeable to the extremists. He suffered shameful intimidation and his home at Foxrock, County Dublin, was burned down. Ironically, from the refuge of England he continued to write and work on Irish rural problems.

Edward Moreton Drax Plunkett, 18th Baron Dunsany (1878–1957), soldier, sportsman and patron of letters, wrote many books and plays and gave great encouragement to young Irish writers. As a broadcaster and lecturer he was very popular in the United States. He was a complete original, especially in his writing. He was interested in supernatural forces and many of his works follow that theme. His neomyths, *The Gods of Pegana*, *The Sword of Welleran*, *The Glittering Gate* and many more plays, novels and poems are now regarded as the forerunner of J. R. R. Tolkien's *Lord of the Rings*.

George Noble Plunkett

Sir Horace Plunkett

223

Power

ᴅᴇ ᴘᴀᴏʀ

le Poer

Poher

That the name Power is not originally Irish might surprise many an Irish person, for the family is thoroughly Hibernicized and very numerous. Originally from Brittany, the legends that have accumulated around their name are legion. In Brittany there is a story that a **Countess of Poher** was the fifth wife of Count Comorre, the original Bluebeard. Like his previous wives, she lost her head.

Around 1324, by which time the Powers had settled in Ireland, **Sir John de Power** almost became the fourth husband of that notorious husband-consuming Kilkenny witch, Alice le Kyteler.

Poher, le Poer, Power—the name stems from the French *pauvre*, meaning pauper, or poor. Edward MacLysaght the genealogist says, "the poverty implied was rather that of a voluntary vow than of destitution". The Powers landed in England in 1066 and a century later arrived in Ireland with Strongbow. They boasted that among their forebears there was royal blood, both French and English.

Henry II of England granted Lismore in County Waterford and Baltinglass in County Wicklow to **Sir Robert Power**. It seems possible that it was Sir Robert's son, **William**, who built the first castle at Powerscourt in County Wicklow, which was later taken from the Powers by the native O Tooles. Today the name lives on in Powerscourt Gardens, among the finest gardens in the world.

The le Poers, as some of the lineage were known, acquired many titles: Earl of Tyrone, Count de le Poer Beresford, Marquess of Waterford, to mention a few. They fought, sometimes for, other times against, the kings and queens of England, both in Ireland and on the Continent. They were variously imprisoned in Dublin Castle, executed in the Tower of London or buried with honour in Westminster Abbey.

It was Henry VIII who conferred the title of Baron le Poer of Curraghmore (County Waterford) on **Sir Piers Power**, Sheriff of Waterford. **John Power**, a generation or two later, entertained Sir Henry Sidney, Queen Elizabeth's Lord Deputy, at Curraghmore. Another member of the family was on the side of James II and took part in the siege of Limerick, of which he was the mayor.

Despite "treason, fire and sword", the Powers proliferated, serving their country not only in the army but also in the Church. A Power was Archbishop of Tuam in 1743, and early in the nineteenth century one of the aristocratic Powers was Archbishop of Armagh and Primate of all Ireland. There have been clerical Powers in both the Catholic Church and the Church of Ireland. In the nineteenth century, the **Reverend Edmond Power**, a Jesuit, wrote learnedly on Islam, and the **Reverend Patrick Power** was an antiquarian and historian. As recently as 1961, the **Reverend Michael Power** was created Bishop of Toronto.

In 1791 **James Power**, a Dublin innkeeper, founded a distillery in John's Lane. He was succeeded by his son, **John Power**, who was created a baronet in 1841. John developed the distillery and was High Sheriff of the city of Dublin and a close friend of Daniel O Connell. In 1854, it was he who laid the foundation stone of the national monument, a lofty round tower, to "The Liberator" at Glasnevin Cemetery, Dublin. The title became extinct in 1930, following the death of the 6th Baronet. Their close kinsmen, the O Reillys, succeeded to the chairmanship of the distillery.

In the 1870s, the company pioneered the miniature whiskey bottle. It required a special Act of Parliament to launch the "Baby Power", the bottle that caused their Gold Label whiskey to acquire its alias and logo, "The Three Swallows". In 1966, the company merged with the three main whiskey distilling companies under the title Irish Distillers Limited.

"The most beautiful Countess of Blessington", who began life as **Margaret Power** (1789–1849) of Knockbrit in County Tipperary, earned fame as a biographer of her friend, Byron. With her stepson-in-law, Count D'Orsay, painter and king of the dandies, she was the chatelaine of glittering, all-male intellectual salons both in London and Paris. When Lord Blessington died, to maintain this extravagant lifestyle and also to support her improvident Power family (her father, old "shiver-the-frills", was a profligate), she wrote for ten hours a day. She was in truth the first, full-time woman journalist.

Margaret Power

William Grattan Tyrone Power (1797–1841) was born in Waterford and may have been the natural son of a Marquess of Waterford. When he was a year old his mother took him to Cardiff. In his early teens he joined a touring company and was into his thirties before he found his *métier* at the Adelphi Theatre, London, playing an Irishman in a William Macready comedy. Handsome and good humoured, he was soon much in demand to fill Irish parts. He also wrote a number of plays himself. He toured the United States and invested his money there, but always returned for an annual visit to Dublin's Theatre Royal. In the spring of 1841, he was on his way from New York to Liverpool on the enormous ship, *President*, when it sank off Cape Cod with the loss of all its passengers.

Frank Power (1858–84) of County Laois was a war correspondent. He sent dispatches to *The Times* of London from Bulgaria and, later, from Khartoum, where he was joined by Edmund O Donovan. Falling ill, he missed the march on Obeid, led by Hicks Pasha, when everyone, including O Donovan, was annihilated. A year later, sent by Gordon on a mission down the Nile, Frank Power and his companions were massacred.

Albert Power (1883–1945) was a leading sculptor in the first half of the twentieth century. He graduated from art school in Dublin to win many prizes and take part in exhibitions abroad. His commemorative statues can be seen in Irish churches and institutions. He sculpted a memorial to the *Lusitania*, which was sunk off Cobh, County Cork, during the First World War.

Tyrone Power (1914–56), the much-married, swashbuckling Irish-American film star, was one of William Power's great-grandsons. Another was Sir Tyrone Guthrie (1900–71), broadcaster and theatre director of international fame who left his home in Newbliss, County Monaghan, as a haven for artists and writers. The well-known theatre in Minneapolis is named after him.

There are well over 11,000 Powers in Ireland, and very many more abroad. They are still to be found mainly in Munster. At Curraghmore, the miniature Versailles that the Powers built long ago by the Clodagh River a few miles from Carrick-on-Suir, the **8th Marquess of Waterford** and 12th Baronet lives with his wife and sons. It is a treasure-house of Power history and legend. The Shell House, which can be visited, was created by **Catherine**, Countess of Tyrone, who in 1717 married Sir Marcus Beresford and won the important right for Irish heiresses to inherit property through the female line. Her statue in marble is one of the features of the Shell House of Curraghmore.

Tyrone Power

Quinn

ó cuinn

Quin

Patrick Quin, a well-known nineteenth-century harper

Quinn, in Irish Ó Cuinn, comes from the personal name Conn, meaning a person of high intelligence, or, maybe, a freeman. There were a number of distinct families of the same name. In Ulster, where they are most numerous, they were centred in County Tyrone and the Glens of Antrim. There was an important sept that was driven out of County Longford by their kinsmen the O Ferralls of Annaly. In the mid-twelfth century, the Ó Cuinn of Clann Chuain near Castlebar were a subsidiary of the powerful MacDermotts of Moylurg.

The most prominent family was a Dalcassian sept of Thomond in the barony of Inchiquin in County Clare. Place names such as Inchiquin, Ballyquin and Glenquin are spelled with a single n, while in Irish they have a double n. In general Catholics spell their name "Quinn" while Protestants spell it "Quin", but this has never been a rigid rule.

Niall Ó Cuinn, the first of the Dalcassian sept to use the surname, was killed at the battle of Clontarf in 1014. In the thirteenth century, **Thomas O Quinn** was bishop of the monastery at Clonmacnoise, the famed Irish centre of medieval learning. In the early sixteenth century, during severe religious strife, **John Quinn**, a Dominican, was Bishop of Limerick.

The Quins, whose ancestors were Chiefs of the Clan Hy Ifearnan, gave their name to Inchiquin and also became Earls of Dunraven, and are one of the rare families of true Gaelic origin in the Irish peerage. **Thady Quin** (b. 1645), who settled in Adare, County Limerick, was the ancestor of **Valentine Quin** who, between 1720 and 1730, built the first Quin manor at Adare by the River Maigue. He was the grandfather of **Valentine Richard Quin** (1732–1824), 1st Earl of Dunraven. His heir, **Windham Henry** (1782–1850), married an heiress from Wales. Gout prevented him from following the gentlemanly pursuits of fishing and shooting. Instead, with his wife, he rebuilt his home, turning it into a colossal Tudor manor. They built the new house around the existing one, which had to be demolished when the work reached its final stages.

Valentine's son, **Edwin**, 3rd Earl of Dunraven, designed the garden. He was an eminent archaeologist and antiquarian with a great knowledge of Irish and medieval literature. When he died in 1871 he was succeeded by **Windham**, 4th Earl of Dunraven (1841–1926), a most remarkable Quin. Privately educated in Rome and Oxford, he was also a fearless steeplechaser and yachtsman. He was a war correspondent in Abyssinia and during the Franco-Prussian war, and afterwards went to Texas to hunt with Buffalo Bill! Unlike some of his predecessors who tended to base themselves in England, his home remained Adare, which he made into the prettiest of villages. He ran a successful racing stud and took an active interest in the affairs of his country. With his yachts *Valkyrie II* and *Valkyrie III* he twice failed to win the America's Cup and was denied membership of the club when he disputed the conduct of the races. During the First World War he ran his steam yacht as a hospital ship in the Mediterranean.

George Wyndham (1863–1913), a relative of the 4th Earl of Dunraven, persuaded the wealthy landlords to accept land purchase and thus made a laudable breakthrough in the centuries-old inequitable ownership of land. This meant that tenants could own their own land, and the Wyndham Land Purchase Act of 1903 is a tribute to his name.

Thady Wyndham Quin, 7th Earl of Dunraven (b. 1940), unable to bear the expense of maintaining Adare Manor, sold it and its contents in

1984 for a reputed £2 million. It is now a hotel and golf course. Thady Quin, who was crippled by polio while a schoolboy, lives with his family in a nearby house.

Although the Dunravens predominated for centuries, there were other Quins (and Quinns) of some distinction. **Walter Quin** (1575–1634), a Dublin-born poet, left for London to become a tutor and lifelong friend of Charles I. His son, **James Quin** (1621–59), who was expelled from Oxford for his royalist views, is said to have been reinstated when he charmed the uncharming Cromwell with his "fine singing voice".

Quinns served in the armies of James II and, following the collapse of the old Gaelic order, many fled to France. One Quin family settled in Bordeaux, where they are still numerous. They were influential citizens, as demonstrated by a street there called the Rue O Quin.

Acting was in the Quin blood and **James Quin** (1693–1756), who was born in London of Irish parents, acted in both Dublin and London, where he shared the stage with the much admired Garrick. He took his art very seriously, killing a fellow actor in a stage duel. He killed another colleague in a quarrel over the pronunciation of a word in a play!

In the twentieth century, **Edel Mary Quinn** (1907–44) was a prominent bearer of the Quinn name. Although she was the daughter of a bank manager, financial misfortune prevented her from following her vocation to enter a Poor Clare Convent. Rejecting marriage, she did secretarial work and, when Frank Duff formed the Legion of Mary in 1932, she became a dedicated member. Despite a prolonged bout of tuberculosis, she volunteered to go abroad and was the Legion's first envoy in Kenya, followed by Nyasaland and Mauritius. Dogged by persistent illness, she singlemindedly continued her work for the Legion throughout Africa, eventually dying in a convent in Nairobi. So great was her influence in the missionary field that she is being considered for canonization.

Feargal Quinn (b. 1936) has founded a chain of supermarkets all around the city of Dublin bearing his name, Superquinn. An imaginative personality with an international outlook, he has brought a new dimension to retailing. In recognition of his contribution to the progress of the business community and his interest in charities, he was elected Senator from the National University of Ireland panel in 1993.

Niall Quinn was born in Dublin. An outstanding goal scorer, his height (6 feet 4 inches) and ability have led soccer fans to name him "The Mighty Quinn". His goal against Holland in the 1990 World Cup in Italy helped Ireland progress to the knock-out stages of the competition. He plays football for Manchester City and also lives in that city.

Niall Quinn

Regan
Ó RIAGÁIN

Ó Raogáin

O Regan

Reagan

The Regan name does not come from an eponymous ancestor. Like many Irish names, it appeared spontaneously in a number of counties when the population was growing and surnames were coming into use. Some Regans, however, can claim (as many do) kinship with the great Brian Boru, 175th monarch of Ireland. According to John O Hart's book of pedigrees, Brian Boru had eleven brothers and one of these, Donnchadh, was the forefather of, among other families, the O Kennedys and the O Regans. They were of the Dalcassian sept whose territories were in the district of Thomond—present-day counties Clare, Limerick and Tipperary. One of Donnchadh's sons was **Riagan**, a nephew of the great Brian. Many scholars are of the opinion that they may also be kinsmen of the MacCarthys of Munster. The arms borne by the Regans of counties Cork and Laois are similar.

The Ó Riagáins of counties Dublin and Meath, who were part of the Four Tribes of Tara, were a more important sept. They were active in every battle aimed at driving out the Norsemen. However, with the arrival of the Anglo-Normans their descendants were in turn driven out of their territories and dispersed.

The Regans remain numerous in Ireland, particularly in Munster. Since Irish independence, it has become fashionable to restore the O prefix to Irish surnames that were outlawed during the persecutions. In Ireland, Reagan is usually pronounced Reegan. Dr Edward MacLysaght writes that "the pronunciation of the name by the Reagans of America is in consonance with that of much of Munster where Ó Raogáin, rather than Ó Riagáin, is the more usual form".

The first of the recorded O Regans was **Maurice O Regan** (born *c.* 1125), who was interpreter and herald to Dermot MacMurrough, King of Leinster (*see* Kavanagh). At this cataclysmic period of Irish history, Maurice, as poet and chronicler, was close to the seat of power and was sent by the King to Wales, in 1168, to seal the bargain Dermot had made with Strongbow to encourage him to come to his assistance in Ireland. Maurice O Regan's report of the subsequent Anglo-Norman invasion has been translated into French and English by seventeenth- and eighteenth-century scholars. Fragments of his history in the original Irish are preserved in the Royal Irish Academy in Dublin.

Irish gentry in the Middle Ages had their lands confiscated and were barred from becoming officers in domestic armies. Thus denied their traditional occupations, they followed a well-beaten path, joining the armies of Europe, and, later, America.

Major Teig Regan is mentioned as being among the retinue of Irishmen who followed James II, the Stuart king, out of France in 1690. A distinguished soldier who had fought in many battles, Teig was probably at the battle of the Boyne. In this period there is also mention of a **Surgeon Thady Regan** attached to James's army.

Among the many surviving Stuart manuscripts, there are letters dated 1694 from Queen Mary to the Archbishop of Bordeaux recommending Jeremiah O Regan, "the Irish priest". The National Archives in Paris have receipts dated between 1752 and 1768 for pension payments and certificates of Catholicity for **Jeanne O Regane**, widow of Charles O Reilly, and also for **Marie Dorothy O Regan**. In the Bibliothèque Nationale in Paris, an O Regan pedigree is among the many papers relating to the history and genealogy of individuals of Irish origin in France. In the National Archives in Madrid, there is an account of an O Regan family in the late eighteenth century.

The Regans established themselves in America well before the Famine decimated the population of Ireland, reducing it from eight million to less than six and a half million from death and emigration. **Mathew F. Reagan** served as a surgeon with Corcoran's Irish Legion, the 164th Regiment of New York. There was also a **William B. Reagan** who was a sergeant with the Volunteers.

Anthony O Regan of County Mayo studied for the priesthood at Maynooth College before going to Rome for ordination. In 1848 he was posted to America, where he was consecrated Bishop of Chicago. There was some conflict with the clerics of his see, which caused him to resign. He died in London.

John Henniger Reagan (1818–1905) was the son of **Timothy** and **Elizabeth Reagan**, who had a tanning yard and farm in Sevier County, Tennessee. He moved to Texas where he became in turn, surveyor, lawyer, jurist, Confederate official and Congressman. A moderate Democrat and a member of President Davis's cabinet, he served as Confederate Postmaster until the close of the Civil War. Afterwards he advised Texans to accept defeat and to give negroes their civil rights, for which he lost his political status. Later his foresight was acknowledged and he was returned to Congress to serve in the House of Representatives from 1875 to 1887. He was US Senator from 1887 to 1891, and afterwards was chairman of the Texas Railroad Commission. His greatest service to the state was his advocacy of the bill to establish the Interstate Commerce Commission.

John William Regan (1873–1945) was born in Halifax, Nova Scotia. A correspondent for the *Associated Press*, he was an authority on the history of his native city. Using the name "John Quimpool" he wrote *First Things in Arcadia*.

Ronald Reagan, who was born in 1911 in Tampico, Illinois, was elected 40th President of the USA in 1981. His Irish ancestors came from the townland of Doolis in the parish of Ballyporeen, County Tipperary. Some of them emigrated to London where they settled for a while. Later the Reagans emigrated *en masse* to Fairhaven, Illinois. Ronald Reagan's father, **John Edward Reagan**, born in 1883 at Fulton, was orphaned at the age of six and was reared by an aunt. He married Nettie Wilson, daughter of an English-born Protestant mother and a Scottish-born father. Ronald Reagan's brother, **Neil Reagan** (b. 1909), was an advertising executive in Los Angeles. He is married and has no children.

Ronald Reagan first made his name in motion pictures and as a television host. He served with the US Air Force from 1942 until 1945. He spent a five-year term as president of the Screen Actors' Guild during which he fought for the thousands of unpaid actors and actresses in Hollywood. His biography, written in 1965, is, perhaps prophetically, titled *Where's the Rest of Me?* From 1967 to 1974 he was Governor of California, where he has long had his home. He breeds horses and cattle on his ranch there.

In June 1984, he and his wife, Nancy, paid a five-day visit to Ireland, stopping off at Galway and the ancestral home at Ballyporeen. He paid a state visit to Dublin.

Roche
δє Róιsτє

de la Roch

The Roches were originally from Flanders and came to England after the Flemish were defeated by the Normans in 1066. They settled into Roch Castle near Fishguard in Pembrokeshire, where they had to be vigilant to protect themselves against the impoverished Welsh nobility who made constant attacks on the Norman conquerors. Hoping to keep the Welsh from insurrection while he was in Normandy, Henry II organized a Welsh-Norman army to invade Ireland. It was led by the Earl of Pembroke, popularly known as Strongbow. He invited three close friends to join him, **David**, **Adam** and **Henry de la Roch**, all brothers. They took their name from their castle, and from these three brothers descend the many Roche families in Ireland.

A priceless Irish manuscript, *The Book of Fermoy*, now in the safekeeping of the Royal Irish Academy in Dublin, was written about in 1457 for the 1st Viscount Fermoy who was given the Irish chieftaincy designation, An Roistach.

By the fifteenth century there were at least five distinct branches of the family holding land in counties Wexford, Cork, Tipperary and Louth. David's son, **Philip**, had settled in Kinsale where the Roches became important politically as well as being prosperous landowners and traders.

David had settled in what became known as Castletownroche in County Cork. From David's branch came the Roche who, in 1478, was created Viscount Fermoy. Kilshannig, one of their early seats, has had many owners and it is now a very fine house about seventeen miles north of Cork city. Like the Normans, the Roches married wisely, mostly into aristocratic Irish families.

Law and order did not exist in those early, unstructured times. Unemployment was an unknown word. The chieftains occupied their time and earned a living raiding each other's properties.

Most of the Catholic aristocracy—Irish, Old English and Norman—were leaders of the 1641 rebellion, and the 8th Viscount **Maurice Roche** was one of them. Known by the English as "an active insurgent", he was away with the army when Castletownroche was attacked by the Cromwellian army directed by Lord Inchiquin, a descendant of Brian Boru. For three days **Lady Roche** (born a Waterford Power) put up a spirited defence. When she surrendered, she was publicly hanged as a traitor for defending her property in her own country against the invading English army! Shortly afterwards, her husband laid down his arms in Ireland while all his estates were divided among Cromwell's supporters. He had no alternative but to go abroad, to Flanders, from where his family had originally come. He died there in 1670, a colonel in the Flemish army. He, or perhaps his son, are said to have given half their army pay to the impoverished King Charles II. They never received any compensation, nor even the return of their lands.

James Roche, a colonel in the Williamite army, became a hero during the siege of Derry in 1689. A boom had been placed to barricade the inlet from Lough Foyle to Derry. James Roche left the fleet, plunged into the water and carried dispatches to the garrison. On his return journey he was ambushed by the Irish troops lining the banks. He was handsomely rewarded by William III, and for the remainder of his life he was known as "The Swimmer".

Captain Philip Roche soldiered in Europe, where he also took an interest in the glass industry. He returned to Ireland and, in about 1690, set up the first business in the country to manufacture lead glass. It did very well and was bought by his partners the Fitzsimon brothers.

Another **Philip Roche** was one of the largest merchants in Munster. In 1781 he drained a swamp in Limerick known as the Mardyke and built a warehouse on it. Because Catholics were not allowed to buy property, he bought his in the name of a relative and good ecumenical friend, Dr Perry, the Protestant Bishop of Limerick. Among other goods, he traded very profitably in seeds with the Low Countries.

His son, **Sir Philip Roche**, amassed a fortune during the Peninsular wars, which he left to his two daughters, provided they did not marry an Irishman or a Spaniard. They both married English colonels.

Four sons, direct descendants of a **Maurice Roche** of Cork, were born in Limerick. To escape the prohibition on Catholic education they were sent to France, where they settled and became very successful wine merchants. But they found no peace there either, as, during the French Revolution, they were imprisoned and had their property confiscated.

It is possible that **Eugenius Roche** (1786–1829) was of that family. His father had been a Professor of Modern Languages at L'École Militaire in Paris. Because of the unsettled state of France, Eugenius went to London, where he made his mark in journalism. He was an editor, poet and playwright and was described as one of the best journalists of his day.

In the 1880s, the Roches of Cork had gone into banking and were very successful, profiting from the Napoleonic wars. At one time they owned half of Cork, and one of their banks became very famous because of the hanging gardens they had built behind it. Wellington's victory over the French at the battle of Waterloo was followed by an inevitable slump, causing unemployment and many bankruptcies. In 1820 Roche's bank failed: there were huge debts which the family sacrificed much of their personal property to pay, even though it had been a limited liability company.

James Roche (1770–1853), one of the four brothers sent to France to be educated, had joined the Revolution at its outbreak. He was arrested, but was released because he was British. He had established the Cork bank with his brother, **Stephen**. He sold his very fine library to help pay the debts. He went to London, where he began a new career as "J.R.", an essayist and contributor to the *Gentleman's Magazine*. Later he returned to Cork as local director of the National Bank of Ireland, where he also had enough time for his writing.

In 1779, when all troops had gone to fight in America and it was feared the French might fill the vacuum in Ireland, one branch of the Roche family was able to form a Volunteer Corps. This family had one seat at Kilshannig and one at Trabolgan, on the windswept east side of Cork Harbour. Roche's Imokilly Corps was the only one in which Catholics were allowed to become officers, and all the local Catholics flocked to join it. They especially enjoyed riding in military formation through the predominantly Protestant town of Bandon.

There were two particularly notorious Roche brothers. In fact the elder of the two, known as **Tiger Roche** (b. 1729), was outrageous. As a young man he had charm and money, and was popular with the Viceroy. But he became involved with the Dublin "bucks", a group of wealthy dissolute gamblers and drunkards. During one of their riots he killed a night watchman and fled to North America, where he fought with the French against the Indians. He was accused of stealing from a brother officer, falsely as it later proved, and was dismissed from the service. While he was in custody, he fought so ferociously with his guard that he earned the name Tiger Roche. When his innocence was established, he was reinstated in his regiment and welcomed back into fashionable society. He married a London heiress, spent her fortune and drove her away with his cruelty. He found another wealthy young woman and squandered her fortune too. Heavily in debt, he set off for India and while on the boat he was accused of murder. He escaped from the ship, was captured and escaped several times in different parts of Africa, before finally disappearing completely.

His brother, **Sir Boyle Roche** (1743–1807), who served seven years under Woulfe in the American war, returned to Ireland to become a prominent politician. An ardent government supporter, he was Chamberlain at the Vice Regal Court and, in 1782, was created a baronet. He was opposed to Catholic emancipation and backed the Act of Union which destroyed the Irish Parliament. A forceful speaker, he was famous for his Irish "bulls". At one time he declaimed, "Why should we do anything for posterity? What has posterity ever done for us?" To a friend he wrote, "My lord, if you come within a mile of my gate I suggest you stay there".

Because of the family's failure to register its arms and pedigrees with the Ulster King of Arms, a gesture of contempt towards the English Crown in the seventeenth century, there had been a regrettable gap in the delineation of the Roche family tree. Strangely enough, although the name Roche means rock, their coat of arms displays three roaches, small, freshwater fish! Their motto is *Mon dieu est ma roche* (My God is my rock) and their patron saint is St Roch, who is customarily invoked against the plague.

James Jeffrey Roche (1847–1908) of Mountmellick, County Laois, left Ireland for America as a child. By 1866 he had become a journalist, assisting John Boyle O Reilly with the *Boston Pilot*, the leading Irish-Catholic journal in the United States. James Roche reached the highest echelons of American political life when, in 1906, he was sent as a US Consul to Genoa, Italy and, later to Berne, Switzerland. His son, **Arthur Somers Roche** (1883–1935), born in Somerville, Massachusetts, was a popular novelist.

In 1856 **Edmund Burke Roche** was created Baron of Fermoy, which is the title inherited by the present 8th Baronet, also **Edmund James Burke Roche** (b. 1939). The Princess of Wales's grandmother was a daughter of the 4th Lord Fermoy, a direct descendant of **Maurice Roche** (d. 1593), the Mayor of Cork to whom Queen Elizabeth I presented the handsome gold mayoral chain which is preserved in the FitzGerald Museum in Cork city.

In more recent times, the Roches are proud of their great Irish scholar, **Liam De Roaste**, who was a prominent member of the Gaelic League. He played an active part in the struggle for independence and afterwards represented Cork in Dáil Éireann, the Irish Parliament.

James Michael Roche (b. 1906) of Michigan, was director general of the General Motors Corporation, of Pepsico Inc. and of the Chicago Board of Trade.

Irish women seldom appear in family history, so it is good to record that in 1979 **Maura Roche** of Tourmakeedy, County Mayo, was the first woman judge to be appointed in Ireland.

On 26 July 1987, following a gruelling twelve-day cycling race through France, **Stephen Roche**, who was born in Dublin, won the top sporting event in France, the yellow jersey of the Tour de France.

To show Ireland's appreciation of this great achievement, the Taoiseach (Prime Minister) Mr Haughey flew to Paris to join with the Prime

Minister of France to greet him and watch him do a lap of honour on the Champs-Elysées. Stephen Roche lives mainly in France and speaks the language fluently, which, combined with his quick wit, makes him a favourite with French television interviewers.

Kevin Roche is one of the world's leading architects. He was born in Dublin in 1922 and his father was manager of the highly successful Mitchelstown creameries in County Cork. Following graduation in architecture from University College, Dublin, he worked briefly in Dublin and London before setting off for the USA on a post-graduate course. He was taken up by the great Finnish-American architect, Eero Saarinen (1910–61), with whom he worked in close association until Saarinen's early death.

He now works with ninety associates from his office in Hamden, Connecticut. Celebrated for his imaginative and innovative approach, he has designed six extensions to New York's Museum of Modern Art and has also worked on the Guggenheim Museum. He is interested in buildings for people rather than just buildings, and General Foods at Rye, New York, and the Ford Foundation, also in New York, are a few examples of his dedicated approach to the human aspect of architecture. In 1982 he was awarded the Pritzker Architecture Prize.

Almost every year since the renaissance of the Roche clan in the 1960s, they have held a rally during the last week of June at one of the many sites historically connected with their clan. There are, for instance, no less than sixteen Rochestowns, and innumerable castles, not all in ruins.

Ferrycarrig Castle, near Wexford. This eighteenth-century illustration depicts one of the earliest settlements of the Roche family

Ryan
ó RIAIN

Mulryan

Ó Maoilriain

O Mulryan

T he Ryans are a very ancient Gaelic family who claim descent from the second-century King of Leinster, Cathaoir Mór. They branched out into several septs. The Ó Riains, who were chiefs of Idrone, settled in counties Carlow and Wexford. The Ó Maoilriains, chiefs of Owney, held the rich pasture lands of the Golden Vale bordering counties Tipperary and Limerick. The name, which may mean illustrious, came from an ancestor, **Maoilriain** (meaning follower of Riain), who settled in County Tipperary in the thirteenth century. The clan motto is "Death before Dishonour". The O prefix disappeared and, until recently, the O Mulryan or Mulriain form was to be found only in Spain.

The Ryans are not much recorded until the seventeenth century, when **Cornelius O Mulryan**, a brother of the Chief of Owney, was a Franciscan friar. For 41 years, until his death, he was Bishop of Killala and also of Cloyne and Ross. He took scant care of his bishoprics, spending most of his time in Europe seeking help for the FitzGeralds of Desmond. He died in Spain in 1617.

It is not only in the distant past that the Ryans held high rank in the Church. Two O Ryan abbés were guillotined during the French Revolution. **Finbar Ryan** was Archbishop of Port of Spain in the West Indies. **Edward Ryan** (d. 1819) was prebendary of St Patrick's Cathedral, Dublin. **Vincent William Ryan** (1816–88) of Cork was the first Anglican Bishop of Mauritius. **Abram Ryan** was chaplain to the American Confederate army and also wrote rousing songs. **Stephen Ryan** (1826–96) was Bishop of Buffalo and **Patrick Ryan** (1831–1911) was Archbishop of Philadelphia. During the Second World War, **John Ryan**, a Jesuit priest, helped Allied prisoners in Rome to escape. **Hugh Edward Ryan** was Bishop of Townsville, Australia, in the 1940s. **Dermot Ryan** (1924–84) was Bishop of Dublin until his transfer to Rome, where he died shortly afterwards.

The celebrated Ryan poet, **Eamon Ó Riain** (*c.* 1680–1724), a former gentleman whose lands were confiscated, was a Jacobite soldier. His life was constantly at risk and he became an outlaw, leading a band of robbers. In his Irish love song, "Eamon an Chnuic" (Eamon of the Hill), he symbolized his love of Ireland. The treachery of one of his friends led to his murder.

Daniel Frederick Ryan (*c.* 1762–98) was a blot on the Ryan escutcheon. Son of a Wexford doctor, he graduated from Trinity College, Dublin, and became a British army surgeon. He was one of those who went with Major Sirr to arrest the United Irishman, Lord Edward FitzGerald. In the struggle, FitzGerald stabbed Ryan, who died shortly afterwards.

The insurrection of 1641, followed by the violated Treaty of Limerick in 1691, forced many of the Irish aristocracy and their followers to go abroad. The Ryans found a haven in Europe for their military and administrative genius. **Captain Luke Ryan** (*c.* 1790), once of Dillon's Regiment, commanded French privateers during the American War of Independence, destroying many British vessels and taking hundreds of prisoners. When he was captured and imprisoned by the British, the French shipowner would not pay his ransom. The bank in Brittany where he had lodged his private fortune failed and he is said to have died in prison. A French version has it that when the war ended he was released from prison and became a French citizen with the title Captain *de navires par le roi*.

Early in the nineteenth century, **Juan Francesco O Ryan**, of Irish parentage, went to Chile, where he served for 38 years in the Chilean navy, reaching the rank of vice-admiral and later holding the posts of Minister for Defence and Minister of the Interior.

Captain Denis Ryan of Inch House, County Tipperary, lost an arm serving in the Austrian army during the Napoleonic wars. He died a prisoner of war in Hamburg in 1804.

Sir Edward Michael Ryan of the 4th Dragoon Guards in Austria fought bravely during the siege of Cambrai and was given an Act of Nobility and the Knight's Cross of the Military Order of Maria Theresa. He died in 1812 on a ship carrying dispatches from Java to India.

As soldiers and statesmen the Ryans in Spain have been outstanding. The Spanish records have innumerable accounts of their deeds and pedigrees under the different versions of their name.

The family of **Lieutenant-General Tomás O Ryan Y Vayquez** (1821–1902) has been in Spain since the eighteenth century. Specializing in engineering and administration, Tomás was given many responsible appointments in Spain's overseas military establishments, often being sent abroad by the Minister of State for War, General O Donnell. He was in France when Queen Isobel II was exiled. She entrusted the care of her 13-year-old son, who later became King Alfonso XII, to him. With the restoration of the monarchy, O Ryan was summoned to Madrid to be made Field Marshal and aide to the King. His wife, **Sofía O Ryan** of Seville, was of a different Ryan sept. They had three children and his descendants are still in Spain, although the O Ryan surname died out there in 1946.

Captain Luke Ryan

Inevitably, the Irish were to be found on both sides in every battle, at home and abroad. **William Abbot Charles Ryan** (1843–73) was one of four children born in Canada, where his parents had emigrated. He came from a long line of soldiers who had fought all over Europe in the Napoleonic and Peninsular wars. He himself fought in the Civil War and afterwards he had some success mining quartz in Montana. In 1868, during a business trip to Washington, he met the leader of the Cuban insurgents who were planning to overthrow their Spanish rulers. Ryan sold his business and went off to fight for Cuba. His task was to ferry men and military supplies between New York and Cuba. After completing many successful expeditions, the Spaniards captured his corvette, *Tornado*, and Ryan and his men were executed and their heads paraded through Santiago. There was an outcry in New York and much embarrassment in Madrid. He was only 30 when he died. His brother, **John George Ryan**, had fought on the opposite side in the Civil War, but they had remained loyal friends and W. A. C. left him a generous legacy.

In Ireland, **Frank Ryan** (1902–44) of Limerick represented a new type of Republican Socialism. He fought on the Republican side in the Irish Civil War and afterwards graduated in Celtic studies from University College, Dublin. He turned against the IRA, seeing it as Fascist. He went to Spain to fight with the International Brigade. He was imprisoned and later released and allowed to go to Germany, where he died in a sanatorium in Dresden. In 1979, his body was reinterred in Glasnevin Cemetery, Dublin.

A remarkable family of twelve children from Tomcoole in County Wexford was known as "The Ryan dynasty". **Dr James Ryan** (1891–1970) was a Senator and also held a number of ministerial positions in de Valera's Fianna Fáil government, including Minister for Finance from 1957 to 1965. There were farmers, priests and a reverend mother in the

Irish Family Histories

Dr James Ryan

family. **May Ryan**, a sister of James, was Professor of Romance Languages at University College, Cork. Several of the women of the family married into medicine or politics. **Josephine** married General Richard Mulcahy, leader of the opposition Fine Gael party. **Kate** married Seán T. O Kelly and **Phyllis** became his second wife after Kate's death and First Lady when Seán T. O Kelly became President of Ireland. Phyllis (d. 1983) was also Dublin's first city analyst.

The Ryans of Knocklong, County Limerick, have records going back to the seventeenth century, when **Thaddeus Ryan** fought at the battle of Aughrim and the Siege of Limerick. Today's **Thady Ryan** is Master of the Scarteen Hounds, the noble black and tan foxhounds which his family has bred for over 300 years. He was *chef d'équipe* of the Irish Olympic team at Tokyo and Mexico, and asserts that the great hunting country at the foot of the Galtees is the nursery of all good Irish horses. The Knocklong point-to-point, which has been meeting for the past seventy years, attracts participants from all over Europe and America. Point-to-point, which originated in Ireland, involves horses racing in a direct line across open country and jumping all the natural hazards they meet on the way.

The premier Ryan in athletics was **Patrick J. Ryan** (1883–1964) of Limerick, an Olympic hammer-throwing champion who rarely threw less than 175 feet. In 1901 he emigrated to America to join the New York police force. His world record throw of over 189 feet, set in 1913, was not surpassed until 1937. He won the US championship every year until 1917, when he went to France with the US forces. He won a gold medal for the United States at the Antwerp Olympics of 1920. He retired to Limerick to farm.

If in earlier centuries the dominant Ryan occupation was fighting, in the twentieth century it has to be writing. Few families have produced such a wide range of journalists. **William Patrick Ryan** (1868–1942) of Templemore, County Tipperary, learned his trade in London. He returned to found the *Irish Peasant*, which was disapproved of by the clergy. He changed its name to the *Nation* and it prospered. Later he returned to London where he involved himself in journalism, as well as in writing fiction, poetry and plays in Irish and English, all with a Gaelic theme. He was editor of the *Daily Herald*, the radical English newspaper.

His son, **Desmond Ryan** (1893–1964), although London-born, was educated at Dublin in Patrick Pearse's School. He took part in the 1916 Easter rising. He followed his father into journalism and wrote many biographies and novels.

Another Ryan, **A.P. Ryan** (b. 1900), was literary editor of the *London Times*. During the Second World War he edited the BBC News.

Cornelius Ryan (1920–74), who was born in Dublin, also went to London and was 23 when he covered the D-Day landings in Normandy for the *Daily Telegraph*. He set up its Tokyo office and reported on the War in the Far East. He moved to New York, where he worked for *Time*, *Newsweek* and *Collier's Magazine* before joining the *Reader's Digest* as their roving correspondent. At the same time he produced an astonishing variety of books on subjects as diverse as General MacArthur and space.

In 1959 he published *The Longest Day*, an account of the Normandy landings. It was an instant best seller and a great financial success. Ten years of intense research, and grinding work to keep his family, went into it. He was greatly encouraged and supported by his wife, a magazine editor. He became an American citizen and wrote two more best-selling war books before he was stricken by cancer. Some of his books have been filmed.

236

Judge George Edward Ryan (1810–80) of County Meath was an astute lawyer who practised at the Bar in Wisconsin. He took care of the legal business of the railways and various other commercial enterprises. New York's floodlighting and its high-intensity street lighting were developed by **Walter D'Arcy Ryan** (1870–1904), an engineer of Irish stock.

Thomas Fortune Ryan (1851–1928) was born to Irish parents on a farm in Virginia. Despite being left a penniless orphan at 13, he saw the opportunities offered by the burgeoning commercial world of New York. It was not long before he was able to buy a seat on the New York Stock Exchange and he joined Tammany Hall. He made money on the New York railways until the subways replaced them. Undeterred, he branched into banking and public utilities. King Leopold of the Belgians invited him to the Congo to set up commercial enterprises. It was estimated that he was the wealthiest man in New York. His home at 858 Fifth Avenue encompassed one-third of a block and included gardens, an art collection and a spacious church. He was described by his colleagues as "the most adroit, suave and noiseless man of American finance".

The Spirit of St Louis, which Charles Lindbergh flew across the Atlantic in 1927, was built in the USA by Ryan Aviation.

Many Ryans emigrated to Australia and New Zealand. **Thomas Joseph Ryan** (1876–1921), a classics master at the High School, Melbourne, and a lawyer, became leader of the Labour Party in 1912. He was Prime Minister of Queensland, and a statue in Brisbane commemorates him.

Sheridan

ó sioradáin

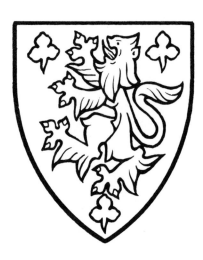

In Irish the name Sheridan is O Sioradáin (descendant of Sioradáin), but no record remains of who this individual was. Little is known about this ancient Gaelic family except that they have not used the O prefix to their name since the seventeenth century, and, although they are now widely dispersed through every province, they all originated from County Cavan.

Denis Sheridan (b. 1612) was ordained in 1643. He was a friend of the benevolent Bishop William Bedell, Provost of Trinity College, Dublin, who persuaded him to abandon the Catholic priesthood to embrace Protestantism. Together they translated the Bible into Irish. Denis's son, **William Sheridan** (1636–1711), was Protestant Bishop of Kilmore.

Thomas Sheridan (1647–1712), author and Jacobite, was born near Trim in County Meath. He was a fellow of Trinity College, Dublin, when he met James II, then Duke of York, in Brussels. Thomas served a period in prison for his participation in a "Popish Plot". After his release, James II proposed him as Chief Secretary and Commissioner of the Revenue in Ireland, but opponents prevented the confirmation of his appointment. He accompanied James II into exile and is believed to have married James's natural daughter, by whom he had a son and a daughter.

A son, **Thomas Sheridan** (1684–1746), was tutor to Prince Charles Edward, the Young Pretender. He was one of the famous "Seven Men of Moidart" at the Scottish battle of Falkirk. After the defeat at Culloden, he escaped to Rome where he wrote *Some Revelations of Irish History*. His nephew was the **Chevalier Michael Sheridan** (c. 1715–55) who took part in the "Forty-five Rebellion" and was later a major-general of cavalry in the Regiment of Dillon in France.

Thomas Sheridan (1687–1738) of Cavan, possibly a grandson of Denis, was a pensioner of Trinity College, Dublin. He married Elizabeth, the only child of Charles MacFadden of Quilca House, County Cavan. Originally a Sheridan property, this house had been confiscated by William III and given to the MacFaddens. Thomas, a clergyman, opened a school in Dublin for the sons of good families. Jonathan Swift became Dean of St Patrick's Cathedral when Sheridan's reputation was very high. He was no mean scholar and he and the Dean became close friends. When he went to visit Quilca, the Dean accompanied him, though he found it far from comfortable.

This Thomas was sometimes dangerously absent-minded. In 1714, on the Sunday following the death of the controversial Queen Anne of Great Britain and Ireland, the text he chose for his sermon was "sufficient unto the day is the evil thereof". As a result of this indiscretion he was accused of Jacobinism and was struck off the chaplains list! This left him almost penniless, but his good friend Jonathan Swift helped him to obtain a living near Cork. By fulfilling an old promise to tell Swift if he ever saw him showing signs of avarice, Sheridan unwittingly ended their friendship. Lacking the Dean's patronage, he sadly lapsed into poverty.

His son, **Thomas Sheridan** (1719–88), became one of the leading actors of the day and was manager of Dublin's Theatre Royal. He married Frances Chamberlaine who, despite her father's refusal to educate her, had been secretly coached by her brother. She became a considerable novelist and dramatist, and an ardent supporter of her actor husband. Thomas was also deeply involved in writing and in developing a new education system.

With the opening of Spranger Barry's theatre in Dublin, playgoers were attracted away from the Sheridan theatre. This was a serious loss and the Sheridans had to go to England, where Thomas began a career lecturing on education.

The second son of this literary alliance was the great playwright and politician **Richard Brinsley Sheridan** (1751–1816), who was born in Dublin and educated at Harrow School. He married Elizabeth Ann, the daughter of the musical composer Thomas Linley of Bath. Sheridan had neither capital nor income to begin with, but the tremendous success of his comedy, *The Rivals*, enabled him to enter fashionable London society. Afterwards, he became a partner in the Drury Lane Theatre, where he put on his own plays, *The School for Scandal* and *The Critic*, which were both outstandingly popular.

Almost overnight, this master of the comedy of manners turned to politics, and for the next thirty years held ministerial posts. In 1788 he played a major part in the impeachment of the former Governor of India, Warren Hastings. His parliamentary leader and friend was James Fox, the Whig statesman, and he also moved in the Prince Regent's circle.

Sheridan's wife, the former Miss Linley, was a fine singer, and a beauty who was pursued by the nobility because of her good looks and charm. She was also a competent wife who helped with his accounts and took an interest in his political life. After her death in 1792, he married a rather less gifted woman. His final years were less auspicious. Drury Lane Theatre burned down, James Fox died, Sheridan lost his seat in Parliament. Nevertheless, he was accorded a splendid funeral in Westminster Abbey.

His son, **Thomas Sheridan** (1775–1817), was a poet of some merit who went to the Cape of Good Hope to take up an appointment in the colonial administrative service. He died there while still quite young, leaving six children. His wife, Caroline, was a novelist whose books were very popular. She gave her three beautiful daughters as good an education as her three handsome sons.

One of these daughters, **Helen Selena Sheridan** (1807–68), became Lady Dufferin, who wrote that enormously popular ballad *The Irish Emigrant*, which begins, "I'm sitting on the stile, Mary, where we sat side by side, on a bright May morning long ago, when first you were my bride". The music was composed and sung at the Theatre Royal, Drury Lane, by G. Parker.

Lady Helen Selena Dufferin's daughter, **Caroline**, married the Honorable George Norton, a barrister, when she was 19. He proved to be a poor husband and she had to support him and their children by her writing. In 1836, in a bid to acquire what money and effects she had earned from her novels, he falsely accused Lord Melbourne, the Prime Minister, of having an affair with her. Lord Melbourne was acquitted, but this incident led to her becoming the model for a character in Meredith's novel, *Diana of the Crossways*. The Sheridan family could not keep out of literature!

Caroline was an independently minded woman at a time when this was considered unfeminine. She shocked society in London by publishing a book demanding the rights of women to their own property and equal rights before the Courts of Justice. It was one of the campaigns that led to a greatly needed reassessment of justice for women.

Joseph Sheridan LeFanu (1814–73) was a Sheridan on the female side; his father came from a Huguenot family. Sheridan LeFanu specialized in ghost stories and wrote sixteen novels of the supernatural, including *The House by the Churchyard*, *Uncle Silas* and *In a Glass Darkly*.

Richard Brinsley Sheridan

Caroline Sheridan Norton

239

It was not only in Dublin or London that the Sheridans made their name. **Richard Bingham Sheridan** (1822–97) went from Castlebar, County Mayo, to New South Wales in 1842. He progressed from farm manager to the Customs department of the Steam Navigation Company at Moreton Bay. He won a seat in the Legislative Assembly at Maryborough and helped found the Botanic Gardens and the School of Arts. He tried to reform the Polynesian labour system, and was Postmaster General.

John Felix Sheridan (1825–97) of Athboy, County Meath, went to the Benedictine monastery of Ampleforth in Yorkshire to study for missionary work. In 1848 he sailed for Sydney in Australia where he was to play a prominent part in Lyndhurst College. With great dynamism he built churches, cared for the youth and the unemployed, and established a home for immigrant girls. Occasionally he experienced a conflict between his role as a Benedictine monk and that of parish priest. Although he revelled in work he would relax by playing a tune on the fiddle.

There is a town called Sheridan in Wyoming, USA, and the family also had a distinguished military hero, **General Philip Henry Sheridan** (1831–88). Like most of the Sheridans, his roots were in County Cavan. He was educated at West Point Military Academy in the United States. During the American Civil War, as a result of his handling of the decisive battle in the Shenandoah valley, he was appointed major-general in charge of a cavalry corps. Sheridan's famous twenty mile ride to rally his troops has become part of American folklore. This dashing Irish soldier has been ranked with Grant and Sherman, whom he succeeded as commander-in-chief. After the Civil War, he was Military Governor of Texas and Louisiana for a while.

Martin Sheridan, who was born in Bohola, County Mayo, in 1881, emigrated to the USA when he was 17. Representing his adopted country, he won his first Olympic gold medal at St Louis in 1904. During the 4th Olympiad in London in 1908 he won three gold medals and one bronze, setting an Olympic record for discus throwing of 134 feet 2 inches.

Margaret Burke Sheridan (1889–1958), Ireland's first prima donna, also came from County Mayo, this time Castlebar. Her father was a postmaster and she was orphaned at only four years of age. She was sent as a boarder to the Dominican Convent in Eccles Street, Dublin. Her devotion to music was soon recognized by the Sisters, who encouraged her and were rewarded when, at 19, she won the premier prize in the mezzo-soprano competition at the Dublin Feis Ceoil. Marconi, who had Irish connections, sent her to study in Rome, where she soon learned Italian and became one of the leading members of Milan's La Scala Theatre, an extremely rare honour for a non-Italian. Under the baton of Toscanini, she sang in many operas and had great success as *Madam Butterfly*. The Italians called her the "Irish nightingale". She toured Italy and sang at London's Covent Garden, but would not sing in either the United States or in Ireland. In 1936, still at the height of her career, she dramatically retired to live in Ireland and never again sang in public.

General Philip Henry Sheridan

Smith
mac Gabhann

Mac an Ghabhainn

MacGowan

Mageown

O Gowan

Smyth(e)

It is perhaps little wonder that Smith is the most common surname in England, and the fifth most common in Ireland, as, until the invention of mechanized travel, the horse was an essential adjunct for anyone who wanted to travel. In Ireland, Smith can be a synonym for MacGowan, meaning son of the smith, but it can also come from the Englishmen who came to settle in Ulster or Cromwellian soldiers who were disbanded in Ireland.

In medieval times the Ghabhainn clan families of counties Clare and Tipperary were hereditary historians to the O Loghlins of Burren and the O Kennedys of Ormond. A branch of the family known as Cruthnean Dáil h-Araide of counties Antrim and Down, of which **Hugh O Gowan** was chief in the reign of Queen Elizabeth I, was transplanted to County Cavan because they aided the O Neills. Other families remained in County Down, Anglicizing their name to Smith or Smythe.

In Ballygowan, County Down, an O Gowan sept Anglicized its name to Smith, and a distinguished descendant of this family reintroduced the original O Gowan name, with the full agreement of the Irish Genealogical Office, in 1949. This was **Major-General Eric Dorman-Smith**, a brilliant military tactician, who was born in 1895 at Bellamont Forest, Cootehill, County Cavan. His nephew, **Sir Reginald Dorman-Smith**, was Governor of Burma at the time of the Japanese invasion during the Second World War.

Numerous Smiths and MacGowans served in the Irish armies in the seventeenth century. They also served with Charles I, and were soldiers of the Commonwealth in Ireland and, later, in the French and American brigades.

An Ulster O Gowan family, sometimes known by the name Smyth, included many ecclesiastics. One such was **Edward Smyth** (1662–1720) of Lisburn, who was a fellow of Trinity College, Dublin, and was expelled by James II in 1689. He was Dean of St Patrick's, Chaplain to William III (of Orange) and, in 1699, Bishop of Down and Connor.

Charles Smith (1715–56) of Waterford wrote histories of the countryside and pioneered Irish topography. **James Smith** (*c.* 1720–1806) emigrated to America with his father and was educated in Philadelphia. He was a lawyer, and also raised the first volunteer company in the state to resist the British. He lost all his money supporting the revolution. He was one of several Irish-Americans who signed the Declaration of Independence.

Henry John Smith (1826–83) of Dublin was educated at Rugby and Oxford. He lectured at Balliol College until 1861. He was made a fellow of the Royal Astronomical Society and, despite many commitments, came to be acknowledged as "the greatest authority of his day on the theory of numbers". **Vincent Arthur Smith** (1848–1920), born in Dublin, entered the Indian Civil Service. He retired early to devote himself to writing and was renowned for his *History of India, Ceylon and their Fine Arts.*

Brigadier-General Thomas Smyth served under the former Irish patriot, Major-General Thomas Meagher, in the American Civil War of 1861 to 1865.

Smithson is yet another variant of Smith. **Harriet Smithson** (1800–54) of County Clare, daughter of a theatrical family, had great success on the Paris stage, where she caught the eye of the composer, Berlioz. He fell madly in love with her and pursued her for several years. His *Symphonie Fantastique* was written for her. Alas, seven years of marriage was as much as their clashing temperaments could endure.

Annie Smithson (1873–1948), born in Dublin, was a district nurse for many years. A republican sympathizer, she nursed the wounded during the 1916 rising. When she retired from nursing to write romantic novels, she produced a series of best sellers including *Her Irish Heritage* and *The Walk of a Queen*.

Although the Smiths—Smythes, MacGowans or O Gowans—have not towered in the pages of Irish history, a study of *Burke's Guide to Country Houses, Vol. 1* reveals a remarkable number of country estates belonging to various wealthy bearers of the name. Like the innumerable Kellys, the Smiths have assumed a variety of extra names to make it simpler to distinguish one family from the other, for example: Cusack-Smith of Bermingham, Tuam; Dorman-Smith; Murray Smith of Belline; Quan-Smith of Bullock; Holroyd-Smith of Ballynatray; Smith Barry of Fota—and many more.

There was also "Smyth of the Gates", whose eighteenth-century house, Glananea, in County Westmeath, had such a flamboyant triumphal arch at the entrance to his demesne that he became known as Smyth of the Gates. Growing annoyed with this name, he sold the arch to a neighbour, whereupon he was dubbed "Smyth without the Gates".

Harriet Smithson

Taaffe

táth

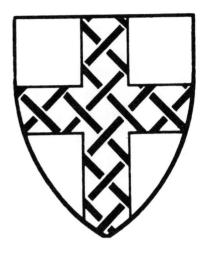

Taaffe (the Welsh name for David) is the name of a remarkable family who came to Ireland in 1196, shortly after the Anglo-Norman invasion. They settled in County Louth, the smallest of Ireland's 32 counties, and a richly historic one also. Smarmore, their castle near Ardee, was built in about 1320. Smiranair, its ancient Irish name, is said to mean a marrow bath. The folk hero, Ceithin, is supposed to have soothed his wounds in this exceptional concoction after his fight with the warrior Cuchullain at the fort of Ardee. The founder of this influential Irish family was **Sir Nicholas Taaffe**, whose grandson, **Richard Taaffe**, was Sheriff of Dublin in 1295, and also Sheriff of County Louth.

Sir William Taaffe's family branched out to Ballymote, County Sligo, where he was sheriff in 1588. Fighting on the government side, he won distinction for his attempts to subdue the great Hugh O Neill. After the siege of Kinsale in 1601, when the Irish, and the Spanish who had come to reinforce them, were routed, William received his knighthood. To quote a conciliatory account of the time, "he had not the least share in ensuring the confiscation of the territory of the MacCarthys". He died in 1630. His son, **Sir John Taaffe**, the 1st Baron Ballymote and 1st Viscount Taaffe, was created a peer in 1628.

John's eldest son, **Theobald Taaffe** (d. 1677), 2nd Viscount Taaffe and Baron Ballymote, was a Member of Parliament for County Sligo in 1639. As he did not share the allegiance of his grandfather, Sir William, he joined the Catholic Confederacy at Kilkenny and commanded the Irish forces in Connacht and Munster until their defeat by Lord Inchiquin (*see* Murrough O Brien) at Knockanass near Mallow, County Cork. When the Cromwellian ferocity had abated and the English monarchy was reinstated, Theobald had his estates restored to him and was created 1st Earl of Carlingford, taking his title from the County Louth town where the remains of Taaffe's Castle are still to be seen.

Theobald's brother, **Lucas Taaffe**, was also in the army of the Catholic Confederacy and was Governor of New Ross in County Wexford in 1649. **John**, one of Theobald's sons, an army major, was killed at the siege of Derry in 1689.

The Taaffes were ardent Jacobites. **Nicholas**, 2nd Earl of Carlingford and 3rd Viscount Taaffe, was killed at the battle of the Boyne. There is a family legend that this Colonel Taaffe (or possibly his brother) and his thirteen sons, all mounted on white horses, were killed in this tragic turning-point in Ireland's history.

The migration to Austria began with **Francis Taaffe** (1639–1704), 3rd Earl of Carlingford and 4th Viscount Taaffe, who was sent to study at Olmutz in Moravia. First he was given a commission in the army of Charles V, Duke of Lorraine. Later he was appointed Chamberlain and Councillor of State. He was so highly thought of by European royalty that when he succeeded to his hereditary titles, which had been granted to his forbears by the English colonial power against whom his kinsmen had later fought, a special Act was passed in the London parliament to remove the charge of "high treason" from the Earl of Carlingford and Viscount Taaffe. He was unmarried and his titles passed to his nephew, **Theobald**, 4th Earl of Carlingford and 5th Viscount Taaffe, who also died without heirs, and the Carlingford title then became extinct.

Viscount Nicholas Taaffe

The 6th Viscount **Nicholas Taaffe** (1677–1769) was born at O Crean's Castle, one of the family's County Sligo estates, which was confiscated as a result of the penal laws. He followed the family to Austria, where he distinguished himself as a lieutenant-general in the army at Belgrade. He was Chancellor to Leopold, father of Francis I of Austria. He did what he could to promote Catholic emancipation in Ireland. Because of his "unchanging attachment to an unfortunate country", his colleagues described him as "the German statesman and general, the Irish sufferer and patriot". In his eightieth year, this man of two countries rallied the Austrian cavalry at Köln. He was created Count of the Holy Roman Empire by the Empress Maria Theresa, a title that continued as Taaffe succeeded Taaffe in the service of the Habsburgs. In their earlier days in Ireland they had married aristocratic Irishwomen, now they married into the European aristocracy. He died, aged 92, in his palatial castle, Elischau, in Bohemia.

His grandson, **Rudolphus** (1762–1830), 7th Viscount Taaffe, who was born in London and became a captain in the Irish Yeomanry, was summoned to Parliament in 1798, but did not take his seat. Instead he went to Austria, where he served with distinction in the Imperial army.

Francis, 8th Viscount Taaffe (1788–1849), an Imperial Chamberlain, was a captain in the Austrian army and aide-de-camp to Field Marshal Archduke Carl at the battle of Wagram. He saved the life of General Wimpffen. He died childless at Baden, near Vienna.

Eduard Franz Josef (1833–95), 11th Viscount Taaffe, Baron of Ballymote and 6th Count of the Holy Roman Empire, was Imperial Prime Minister of Austria for fourteen years. Among the many honours he held was that of Knight of the Golden Fleece, one of the highest orders in Christendom. He was born in Vienna, and as a child was one of the chosen companions of the future Emperor, Franz Josef (1830–1916). All his life he enjoyed the Emperor's unlimited confidence. There were those who thought him "essentially an opportunist", maintaining himself in office by the employment of the principle, *divede et impera* (divide and rule). He was disliked by the Crown Prince Rudolph (1858–89), a frustrated progressive stifled by the autocracy of the imperial court. After the dark tragedy at Mayerling, when Rudolph and his mistress, Marie Vetsera, were found dead, the Emperor entrusted the documents concerning the post-mortem to Count Taaffe. He imposed a heavy burden of secrecy on the Count and his successors. His son, **Heinrich**, the 12th Viscount Taaffe, was removed from the roll of Viscounts because he fought against Britain in the First World War.

Group-Captain Rudolph Taaffe (1902–85) kept a comprehensive Taaffe archive in his County Dublin home, and went to visit his cousin Heinrich before the Second World War. He found him sitting magisterially at the top of a flight of stairs lined on either side by powdered footmen through which he deigned to come down half-way to meet his Irish cousin. Gambling rather than the War contributed to the decay of Heinrich's palace at Elischau. The Nazis plundered it and when the USSR annexed Bohemia it was turned into a Czechoslovakian military school.

Heinrich's heir, **Count Edward Taaffe**, came to live in Ireland in the 1930s. He was said to have been offered $200,000 for the Habsburg file by, among others, William Randolph Hearst. Although his property had been destroyed by the War and he earned a modest living in Dublin as a gemmologist, he held fast to the family secret. He fobbed off his cousin, Rudolph Taaffe, with all sorts of stories and all he would say was that what had happened at Mayerling was more hideous than he could imagine.

Taaffe family papers have been stored in the Vatican archives since the time of the Barberinis, and it is possible that a competent researcher who could penetrate that fortress might be able to unlock the secret. A number of journalists have tried, but without success. Several films and a musical have been made about the Mayerling incident.

Meanwhile, there are Taaffes who are not Viscounts or Counts of the Holy Roman Empire. In Europe they have died out, but in Ireland they have grown more numerous, particularly in their original stamping ground, the Ardee area of County Louth.

When Dr Edward O Reilly, Primate of Ireland, was forcibly exiled by the Cromwellians, a **Father James Taaffe** conceived the audacious scheme of putting the Irish Church completely under his control! He forged a Bull from the Holy See, making him Vicar Apostolic of all Ireland with absolute power. He was exposed in 1668, and duly dealt with.

The **Reverend Denis Taaffe** (1753–1813) of County Louth, a Catholic clergyman, was educated in Prague and sent back to Ireland as a missionary. However, his disorderly behaviour obliged his superior to defrock him and so he joined the Protestant religion and fought with the United Irishmen at Wexford in 1798. He survived to found the Gaelic Society and publish many historical papers. He died in Dublin, reconciled to the Catholic Church.

John Taaffe (1787–1862) of County Louth was the poet of the family. He lived in Italy, where he kept company with Byron and Shelley and is remembered for his commentaries on Dante. He died at Fano in Italy.

The most famous Taaffe of this century lived in Kildare. This was **Pat Taaffe**, who died in 1992. He rode the Duchess of Westminster's famous horse Arkle, which dominated the National Hunt racing scene in the 1960s. His brother **"Toss" Taaffe** is also a trainer and his daughter, **Noreen**, is a promising rider.

Walsh

Breathnach

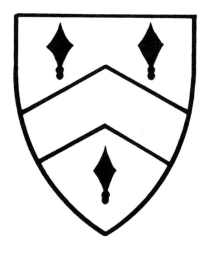

Walshe

Welsh

Walsh ranks alongside Murphy, Kelly and Sullivan as one of the most numerous names in Ireland. Yet its origins are not Irish at all. The name was simply used to designate the wave of Welsh people who arrived in the wake of the Cambro-Norman invasion, which is why the Walshes do not have a common ancestor. They were many and they were mostly unrelated. Those who wanted to feel thoroughly Irish changed their name to Breathnach. They spread all over Ireland, giving their name to many townlands, such as Walshtown and Walshport, and there is a range of mountains in County Kerry known as the Walsh mountains.

Philip came from Wales in the twelfth century. He and his brother, **David**, are thought to be the ancestors of the Walshes who settled in the counties of Kilkenny, Laois, Waterford, Wicklow and Dublin. In 1958, six different Walshes were recorded in *Burke's Landed Gentry of Ireland*. In 1976, when land was no longer synonymous with gentry, one Walsh and one Walshe were recorded in *Burke's Irish Family Records*.

Many articles on this extensive family were published in the *Genealogist* magazine at the beginning of this century. Books and articles have been published about the Walshes of Austria and France. In France they are represented today by the **Count de Serrant**.

In 1588, **Lawrence Walsh** compiled a pedigree of the Mayo Walshes, showing them to be descended from **Walynus**, who accompanied Maurice FitzGerald to Ireland in 1169. Walynus had a brother, Barrett, from whom descend the Barrett family of Mayo, where they were lords of the territory known as Tirawley.

While the Roches, who also came to Ireland via Wales, were essentially businessmen, the Walshes consistently entered the Church. **William Walsh** was appointed Bishop of Meath in 1554. When Queen Elizabeth I asked him to conform to the Anglican rite, he refused and was imprisoned. After a long time he managed to escape to France. The Pope ordered him to return to Ireland but, finding his priestly duties there untenable, he went to Spain where he became suffragan Archbishop of Toledo and probably met the young painter El Greco. He died in Spain in 1577.

Nicholas Walsh, Bishop of Ossory, the son of the Protestant Bishop of Waterford, was consecrated in 1567. He introduced Irish type so that church services could be printed in Irish which, he believed, "proved an instrument of conversion to many of the ignorant sort of Papists". His translation of the New Testament was cut short when he was stabbed to death by a man he had publicly accused of adultery. He was buried in St Canice's Cathedral at Kilkenny.

In very troubled times, **Thomas Walsh** (1580–1654), a Franciscan, was Archbishop of Cashel in County Tipperary, once the seat of the Munster kings. **Peter Walsh** (1618–88) of County Kildare studied at Louvain. He returned to Ireland having taken his vows as a Franciscan. He joined the Ormonds (*see* Butler) in opposing the Papal Nuncio, Rinuccini, and the Catholic Confederates. He was expelled by the Franciscans when he published his "Loyal Remonstrance", addressed to Charles II, promising the allegiance of Irish Catholics to the English Crown and repudiating papal infallibility. He argued that he was trying to alleviate the suffering of the Catholics, but the Pope excommunicated him. He went to London where he lived on the pension awarded him by his friend, James Butler, Earl of Ormond and Lord Lieutenant of Ireland.

John Walsh of County Tipperary was Legal Adviser to Cromwell and Agent to the Duke of Ormond. Not surprisingly, he was the only Walsh left alive in Clonmel, County Tipperary, after the siege by Cromwell's soldiers in 1650.

Thomas Walsh, born at Limerick in 1730, was a schoolteacher at the age of 18. At the time, Wesley, the founder of Methodism, was touring Ireland on horseback. Thomas was inspired to join him and, following his methods, developed into a rousing preacher in both English and Irish. His excessive zeal wore him out and he died at the early age of 28.

Antoine Vincent Walsh (1703–65), son of a Waterford shipbuilder who had emigrated to Saint-Malo in France, was in charge of the *Doutelle*, the ship that landed Charles Stuart, the "Young Pretender", in Scotland in 1745. He was knighted for this enterprise. He went to Austria and became yet another Irishman to find favour with the Empress Maria Theresa and was appointed her Chamberlain.

Robert Walsh

It was the eldest of Antoine's seven sons, **Count Walsh de Serrant**, who founded the family that is still in France. The first Count was instrumental in having him appointed Superior of the Irish College in Paris, which had a bad time during the Revolution, especially as its superior was a royalist appointment.

Captain Oliver Walsh, the tenth and youngest son of **John Walsh** (1720–85) of Ballymountain, County Kilkenny, served in the British navy and was at the battles of Copenhagen, the Nile and Trafalgar. He was one of Nelson's youngest officers. In 1813, when he was only 36, he died from yellow fever.

Robert Walsh (1772–1852) came from a distinguished County Waterford family. A graduate of Trinity College, Dublin, he was both a clergyman and an author. He was chaplain to the British Embassy at Constantinople (now Istanbul), which inspired his many travel books. He travelled in Turkey and further afield in Asia, as well as studying for a medical degree. For a brief period he was a chaplain at St Petersburg. Following a visit to Rio de Janeiro, he sat on a committee of the Society for the Abolition of Slavery. He returned to Ireland and was rector at Finglas vicarage in Dublin. He developed his interests as historian, physician, botanist and antiquarian, and collaborated in writing the book, *History of the City of Dublin*. His son, **John Edward Walsh** (1816–69), was also a writer, Attorney-General for Ireland and Master of the Rolls.

Walter Hoyle Walsh (1812–92) of Kilkenny, who was a professor at London University, was the first to describe the condition known as floating kidney.

In the 1920s and 30s, one of the most popular Irish novelists was **Maurice Walsh** (1879–1964). He was Kerry born and worked for twenty years in the Customs and Excise service in the highlands of Scotland and northern England. This experience provided him with a connoisseur's palate for whiskey and a rich narrative source. With the granting of self-government he transferred to the Irish service and wrote a novel, which was first rejected and then accepted by another publisher for £100. *The Key Above the Door* sold hundreds of thousands of copies and was the beginning of a stream of very popular novels, culminating in *The Quiet Man*, which was made into a successful film. Despite being criticized as too stage-Irish, it helped promote tourism in the west of Ireland.

Like so many Irish families, the Famine in the 1840s drove the Walshes to seek the hospitality and opportunities of America. **Robert Walsh** (1784–1859) went earlier than most others. He was born in Baltimore, County Cork, the son of an aristocratic family who, it is believed, had

Maurice Walsh

connections with France. He read law and worked for a while in journalism. In the War of Independence he fought on the Federalist side. Afterwards he settled in Paris. He was a man of some wealth and it was he who opened the first of the American literary salons there.

Michael Walsh (1815–59) was born near Cork and was taken to America by his parents. He worked as a reporter in New York City and attempted unsuccessfully to publish his own newspaper. He got the working men of New York city to join the Spartan Association, aiming to break the hold of Tammany Hall by demonstrating the principles of democracy. He was imprisoned twice for his anti-establishment oratory and wrote bitingly of the squalor and poverty he saw in New York. He was described as "a maverick Irish-American politician".

John Walsh (1830–98), formerly of Mooncoin, County Kilkenny, went to Toronto, Canada, where he was ordained and became its first Catholic archbishop. He kept in close touch with Ireland and suggested holding the Irish Race Convention in Dublin, with the idea of healing the political rift caused by Parnell's liaison with Katherine O Shea.

William John Walsh (1841–1921) was appointed Archbishop of Dublin in 1885. A distinguished scholar, he was the first chancellor of the National University of Ireland.

Thomas James Walsh (1859–1933), a Senator from Montana, was the son of Irish parents. He followed a legal career and made his reputation in copper litigation.

Thomas Walsh (1871–1928), the son of gentry in County Longford, went to Brooklyn. A man of many parts, he was an accomplished pianist, painter, writer and lecturer. His main interest was literature, particularly that of Spain. He could afford to be philanthropic and he is esteemed for his enhancement of Catholic culture in America.

Blanche Walsh (1873–1915) was the daughter of an Irish saloon-keeper who was also a Tammany Hall politician. She was one of the most popular actresses of her time and played most of the leading roles in the contemporary theatre including Little Billy in *Trilby*. In the 1940s, **David I. Walsh**, a Boston man of Irish ancestry, was the first Catholic Governor of Massachusetts.

Dr Tom Walsh (d. 1988) was a scientist of international standing whose work for the rural community led to his being described as "the father of modern Irish agriculture".

Dr T. J. Walsh of Wexford, who also died in 1988, graduated in medicine but later followed a musical vocation. In 1951, he was one of the founders of the Wexford Opera Festival, an annual event which has gone on to achieve an excellent reputation in the musical world. A fine scholar, Dr Walsh wrote a number of important books on the history of opera.

Michael Walsh

Woulfe

ꝺe ꞴhulꞴh

The Woulfes came to Ireland with the Normans. Some settled in County Limerick, while others became firmly rooted in County Kildare, where they were so numerous that a district near Monasterevan was called Crioch Bhulbhach, meaning Woulfe's Region. As they were not originally Irish, they did not found a sept in the Gaelic fashion. **Father Patrick Woulfe** (d. 1933), the Gaelic scholar who wrote *Irish Names and Surnames*, an Irish-English dictionary of Irish surnames and their origins, wrote: "Ulf, Wulf, Woulfe, Wofe son of Ulf, is a common personal name among all Teutonic races… and is descriptive of a rapacious disposition".

Pro patria mori (die for one's country) is the motto of the Woulfe crest—and many of them did die, particularly in the seventeenth century. Edward MacLysaght says that "Nix, MacNiocais, is an Irish patronymic assumed by some families of Woulfe in County Limerick, where the two names were used synonymously until recently. Wooley, from the Irish Abhula, was also used as a variant of Woulfe".

David Woulfe (1523–78) of Limerick was sent to Rome to be educated. He was ordained in the Jesuit Order where Ignatius Loyola and Francis Borgia were contemporaries. He was sent as apostolic legate to Ireland, his purpose being to set up schools, regulate the form of religious services and establish communication with the local Catholic aristocracy. Inevitably, he was arrested and suffered imprisonment in the dreaded Dublin Castle. After a number of years he escaped to Spain, but returned to Ireland to care for his flock. Constant warfare had devastated the country. Unable to carry out his apostolic mission, he fell ill and took refuge in a castle in Connacht. He died of starvation there, refusing food when he discovered that it had been stolen.

The Woulfes played an active part in Limerick city from the fourteenth to the middle of the sixteenth century. For their part in the Geraldine wars, **Patrick**, **John** and **David Woulfe**, and many other members of the family, were transplanted to Connacht. A Dominican priest, **Father James Woulfe**, was hanged in 1651 following the siege of Limerick.

For their resistance to Cromwell's rapacious army, many of the Woulfes had their lands confiscated, including **Captain George Woulfe**, grandfather of **General James Wolfe** (1727–59), the hero of the taking of Quebec. Like so many other Irish families, they joined the exodus to Europe, America and England. Captain George Woulfe changed his surname to Wolfe, and Wolfe it has remained in that family to the present day, both in Ireland and in Canada where his descendants now live.

Peter Woulfe (1727–1803) left Limerick for London. He was a chemist, a mineralogist and an eccentric. He searched, unsuccessfully, for the elixir of life. In 1766 he discovered tin, which brought prosperity to Cornwall. He invented "Woulfe's Bottle", an apparatus for passing gases through liquid, and was a fellow of the Royal Society.

John Woolfe of Kildare was of the same period as Peter. He was one of Ireland's early architects and, with James Gandon (1743–1823), revised the source book of English Palladian architecture, Colen Campbell's *Vitruvius Brittannicus*. This magnificent publication took four years to complete.

Theobald Wolfe of Blackhall in County Kildare was a freeman of Dublin in 1769. It was from him that Wolfe Tone, whose family were freehold tenants of the Blackhall estate, got his name.

Wolfe

Wooley

Woolfe

Arthur Wolfe

Arthur Wolfe (1739–1803) was of the family who owned the County Kildare mansion, Forenaughts, for generations until its sale in 1989. His portrait is in the dining hall of Trinity College, Dublin, where he was vice-chancellor in 1802. A Chief Justice of the King's Bench, he was raised to the peerage as Viscount Kilwarden for his support of the Union. Although not considered a brilliant lawyer, he was humane, and refused to strain justice in disfavour of those tried before him for their part in the insurrection of 1798. He helped save Wolfe Tone from the gallows in 1794, and tried to remove him from the jurisdiction of a military court in 1798.

On the evening of the rising of the young rebel Robert Emmet, 23 July 1803, Viscount Kilwarden, accompanied by one of his daughters and his grand-nephew **Richard Straubenzie Wolfe**, Rector of Kilbeggan, County Westmeath, drove into Dublin to attend a gathering at Dublin Castle. Nearby, in Thomas Street, his carriage was halted and a pike was plunged into his body. His daughter managed to escape, but Richard was killed outright. As Kilwarden lay dying, some officers swore they would hang those that they had taken prisoner. With his last breath Kilwarden admonished them, "Murder must be punished, but let no man suffer for my death but on a fair trial and by the law of his country".

The **Reverend Charles Wolfe** (1791–1823), also of Forenaughts, was one of eleven children, the youngest of eight sons. His father died when he was very young. His mother gave him an excellent education at Winchester and at Trinity College, Dublin, where he took Holy Orders. He was a curate first in County Tyrone and then in County Down. At the age of 31, in failing health and rejected by the young lady he wanted to marry, he gave up his curacy and shortly afterwards died of tuberculosis. He was a promising poet and is remembered for one poem, his ode on *The Burial of Sir John Moore after Corruna*. It was first published in the *Newry Telegraph* in 1817 and was hardly noticed until Lord Byron praised it highly. Then several poets, seeing its great popularity, tried to claim authorship, but there is no doubt that Charles Wolfe wrote it.

Stephen Woulfe (1787–1840), an Irish judge from Ennis, belonged to the family which had settled in County Limerick in the fifteenth century. They remained Catholic all through the penal times, and Stephen was one of the first Catholic students to be admitted to Trinity College, Dublin. He followed a career in law and politics, and shocked his fellow Catholics by criticizing Daniel O Connell's method of raising funds for his emancipation campaign. He was appointed Crown Counsel of Munster and was the first Catholic Chief Baron of the Irish Exchequer.

George Wolfe (1859–1941) of Forenaughts served with the Royal Irish Fusiliers in Egypt at the battle of Tel-el-Kebir. He was a member of Dáil Éireann (the Irish Parliament) from 1923 to 1932.

Maurice Wolfe (d. 1915) from Cratloe, County Clare, joined the United States army and saw much service during the Civil War in which many of his fellow Irishmen took part. He made friends with the American Indians and was given a pony in return for a "burning glass". He wrote home regularly during his time in the army. He described how "the Redskins capture and burn the mails which might account for any delay in communication with home!" His presents home (which got through) included moccasins for his mother and an Indian scalp for his brother. His letters, written between 1863 and 1874, were published in 1957 in *The Irish Sword*, the journal of the Irish Military History Society.

Key Dates in Irish History

c. 500 BC	The arrival of Heremon, son of Milesius, King of Spain, precursor of the Celts.
AD 350	Irish raids on Britain.
AD 360	Writing begins.
AD 377–405	Niall of the Nine Hostages is High King.
c. AD 400	Oilioll Olum is King of Munster.
AD 431	Palladius sent by Pope Celestine.
AD 432	St Patrick brings Christianity.
c. AD 590	St Columbanus begins Irish mission on Continent.
7th & 8th C	The Golden Age when the Tara brooch, the Ardagh chalice, the Book of Durrow and the Book of Kells were produced.
AD 795	Arrival of first Scandinavians—Norsemen, Vikings and Danes.
AD 841	Dublin founded by the Norsemen.
1002	Brian Boru becomes High King.
1014	Brian Boru dies at the battle of Clontarf having defeated the Norsemen.
1162	St Laurence O Toole becomes Bishop of Dublin.
1169	Arrival of the Anglo-Normans inspired by Dermot MacMurrough.
1170	Richard, Earl of Pembroke (Strongbow), lands and succeeds Dermot as King of Leinster.
1171	King Henry II of England comes to Ireland, granted to him by the Pope. About this time Irish surnames coming into use.
1172–1250	Normans gradually settle in.
1175	St Laurence O Toole negotiates the Treaty of Windsor with Henry II which leaves Rory O Connor as King of Connacht.
1224–1270	Dominican, Franciscan, Carmelite and Augustinian friars come to Ireland.
1224	Death of Cathal Crovderg O Conor, the last independent King of Connacht.
1235	Richard de Burgo conquers Connacht.
1258	Gallowglasses (mercenary soldiers from Scotland) arrive in Ulster.
1266	The battle of Downpatrick and the death of Brian O Neill.
1261	MacCarthys victorious at battle of Callan.
1264	Walter de Burgo created Earl of Ulster.
1297	First Irish Parliament.
1333	The last de Burgo Earl of Ulster, the Brown Earl, is murdered.
1366	The Statutes of Kilkenny, designed to prevent Norman and later settlers integrating with the Irish, are passed.
1376–1417	Art MacMurrough, King of Leinster.
1399	Richard II visits Ireland.

1462	Desmond defeats Butler at the battle of Piltown.
1468	Earl of Desmond executed.
1477–1513	Gerald, 'the Great Earl' of Kildare, rules Ireland.
1487	Lambert Simnel crowned as Edward VI of England in Christ Church, Dublin.
1491	Yorkist pretender Perkin Warbeck comes to Ireland.
1494	Poynings' Law enacted at Drogheda, subjecting Irish Parliament to English Privy Council, abolishing Gaelic Brehon laws.
1496	"The Pale", an area encompassing Dublin and parts of County Kildare, instituted to repel Irish raiders. Dissolution of monasteries begins. Anarchy reigns.
1504	At the battle of Knockdoe, County Galway, the Lord Deputy Kildare, a FitzGerald, defeats Ulick Burke.
1513	Lord Deputy Kildare dies from gunshot wounds and his son Gearóid Óg becomes 9th Earl of Kildare.
1534	Gearóid Óg recalled to England, dies in the Tower of London, succeeded by his son "Silken" Thomas.
1534–5	Rebellion of Silken Thomas, Lord Offaly.
1536–7	"Reformation Parliament" meets in Dublin.
1537	Silken Thomas and his five FitzGerald uncles are executed at Tyburn.
1540	Sir Anthony St Leger, the Lord Deputy, instigates the policy of "surrender and regrant" and forces submission of O Neills.
1556	St Leger prepares for plantation of Leix and Offaly.
1558	Accession of Elizabeth I. Restoration of Anglican Church. Reformation not accepted by Catholics.
1559	Shane O Neill (d. 1567), Lord of Tyrone, succeeds Conn as The O Neill.
1569–83	Revolt and suppression of Earls of Desmond.
1562–67	Shane O Neill wages war; defeats MacDonnells at Glenshesk, County Antrim; is defeated by O Donnell and killed at Cushendun, County Antrim.
1571	First book printed in Irish in Dublin.
1585	Hugh O Neill becomes Earl of Tyrone.
1586–92	Plantation of Munster.
1588	Spanish Armada wrecked off Irish coast.
1591	Trinity College, Dublin, founded.
1598	Hugh O Neill is victorious at the battle of the Yellow Ford in Ulster.
1601	Irish and Spanish under O Neill and O Donnell defeated at Kinsale by Lord Deputy Mountjoy.
1603	Death of Elizabeth I and accession of James I. Surrender of Hugh O Neill.
1603–9	English common law enforced throughout country, especially Ulster.
1607	"Flight of the Earls": O Neill and O Donnell lead exiles from Lough Swilly to the Continent.

1608–10	Protestant settlers begin to settle in Ulster's confiscated lands.
1632	Compilation of the *Annals of the Four Masters* begins in Donegal.
1641	Ulster rising against Protestant settlers commences and spreads south to include Old English Catholics.
1642–49	Catholic Confederation of Kilkenny in place.
1642	Presbyterian Church in Ireland organized.
1646	Owen Roe O Neill defeats Monro (Scots army) at Benburb, County Tyrone.
1649	Cromwell (d. 1658) devastates country, exiles Catholic landowners to Connacht.
1660	Restoration of monarchy with Charles II proclaimed King of Ireland in May.
1667	English Act excluding export of Irish livestock to English markets.
1677–85	James Butler, Duke of Ormond, becomes Lord Lieutenant.
1681	Archbishop Oliver Plunkett executed in London; canonized in 1975.
1685	Accession of Stuart king, James II.
1689	James II lands in Ireland, deemed to have abdicated throne of England. He is refused entrance to Derry and unsuccessfully besieges the town.
1690	William of Orange (King William III of England) defeats James II and his Irish allies at battle of the Boyne in County Meath. William had a force of 36,000 Anglo-Dutch and sustained 2,000 casualties. There were 23,000 on the Irish side and 1,500 casualties.
1691	Following defeats at the battle of Aughrim and the siege of Limerick, James's army capitulates and the Treaty of Limerick is signed.
1692	Catholics excluded from Parliament and high office, leading to the flight of the "Wild Geese", when 12,000 Irish sought refuge in Europe between 1690 and 1730.
1695	Act forbids Catholics from educating their children abroad or opening schools at home.
1704	Penal laws enacted against Catholics in violation of Treaty of Limerick between 1697 and 1704.
	British trade restrictions on export of Irish goods.
1719	Toleration Act recognizes the educational and religious liberties of Protestant dissenters.
1720	Declaratory Act asserts supremacy of the British parliament over the Irish.
1739	England at war with Spain.
1740	France at war with Austria.
1740–41	Unprecedented frost causes severe famine and kills an estimated 400,000.
1742	France under Louis XV declares war against Britain.
1745	France (60,000 troops) defeats England (50,000 troops) at the battle of Fontenoy.

1751	Act authorizing use of surplus revenue for reduction of national debt leads to dispute between Irish and English parliaments.
1759	Restrictions on export of Irish cattle removed.
1771	Relief for Roman Catholics begins.
1772	Rise of Patriot Party in parliament.
1775	American War of Independence begins.
1778	Volunteer companies start in Belfast, numbering some 40,000 by end of year.
1779	Repeal of most export restriction Acts.
1782	Legislative independence won from Britain by Irish parliament.
1784	"Peep O Day Boys", a Protestant peasant movement, founded in Ulster.
1789	Start of French Revolution.
1791	Society of United Irishmen founded in Belfast.
1792	Wolfe Tone appointed Secretary to the Catholic Committee.
1795	"Battle of the Diamond" at Loughgall, County Armagh, where Peep O Day Boys, who later form Orange Order, rout Catholics.
1796–97	French fleet, with Wolfe Tone aboard, fails twice to invade Ireland.
1798	Outbreak of rebellion throughout the country. Wolfe Tone arrested and dies by his own hand before death sentence can be carried out.
1800	Act of Legislative Union of Ireland with Great Britain passed by Irish and British parliaments.
1807	Daniel O Connell becomes leader of Catholics.
1815	Britain defeats France at the battle of Waterloo. The army was led by Wellington and had a large Irish contingent.
1829	Catholic emancipation granted.
1831	Commissioners of National Education appointed.
1842–48	First issue of the *Nation*, the organ of the Young Ireland movement, founded by Thomas Davis, Charles Gavan Duffy and John Dillon.
1843	Daniel O Connell campaign for Repeal. Irish ownership of land had fallen from 59% in 1641 to 7% in 1714.
1845–7	The Great Famine. This causes the population to drop from eight million to six and a half million through starvation and emigration.
1846	Breach between O Connell and Young Irelanders over use of physical force.
1847	Daniel O Connell dies in Genoa *en route* to Rome. Buried in Glasnevin Cemetery, Dublin.
1848	Abortive rising by William Smith O Brien and the Young Irelanders, many of whom are deported to Australia.
1849	Visit of Queen Victoria and Prince Albert. Queen's Colleges at Belfast, Cork and Galway opened.

1850	Tenant Rights League formed.
1859	Irish Republican Brotherhood formed in Dublin, Fenians formed in New York, both dedicated to form an Irish republic by force.
1867	Unsuccessful Fenian rising. Allen, Larkin and O Brien, the "Manchester Martyrs", are executed.
1869	Church of Ireland disestablished and disendowed.
1870	Prime Minister Gladstone's first Land Act. Home Government Association formed by Isaac Butt and John Martin.
1872	Ballot Act introduces secret voting.
1879	Irish National Land League formed.
1880	Sectarian rioting in Belfast. Charles Stewart Parnell leader of Irish Parliamentary Party at Westminster.
1891	Downfall and death of Parnell.
1893	Gladstone's second Home Rule Bill defeated. Gaelic League founded by Douglas Hyde who becomes its first president.
1896	Irish Race Convention held in Dublin.
1900	John Redmond elected leader of re-united Irish Parliamentary Party.
1903	Wyndham Land Act, headed by Lord Dunraven (*see* Quinn), abolishes landlordism.
1905	Sinn Féin formed by amalgamation of societies.
1909	Irish Transport and General Workers' Union formed by James Larkin.
1912	Irish Home Rule Bill passed by British House of Commons due to come into effect in 1914; its provisions are defied by Ulster Volunteers. Bill suspended for duration of First World War in which 200,000 Irish enlisted.
1916	Irish Republic declared during Easter Week Rising. The insurrection is crushed and its leaders executed.
1921	Treaty with Britain establishes a 26-county Irish Free State, the six counties of Ulster having voted themselves out.
1922–23	Civil War between Free Staters and Republicans.
1922	Treaty approved by Dáil Éireann. General election majority pro-Treaty. Republicans led by de Valera disagree and Civil War begins.
1923	End of Civil War. Ireland (Free State) joins League of Nations.
1926	Inauguration of radio service, 2 RN, later Radio Éireann.
1939–45	Second World War, in which Ireland remains neutral. However, thousands of Irish men and women enlist in British services and over 50,000 are killed in action.
1948	The Taoiseach (Prime Minister) John Costello confirms that the External Relations Act will be repealed. Ireland leaves the Commonwealth.
1955	Ireland joins the United Nations.
1960	Ireland sends troops to serve with the United Nations in the Congo.

1961	Ireland joins UNESCO. Television service inaugurated.
1973	Ireland joins the European Economic Community.
1985	Anglo-Irish Agreement signed between Dublin and London in an effort to solve continuous conflict between unionists and nationalists in the six counties of Ulster.

Bibliography

Heraldic bibliography

(courtesy of the Chief Herald, Donal Begley)

Brooke-Little, J.F. (rev). *Boutell's Heraldry*, London and New York, Frederick Warne, 1973

Fox-Davies, Arthur Charles (ed). *Armorial Families: A Directory of Gentlemen of Coat of Arms*, 2 vols., Newton Abbot, David and Charles Reprints, 1970

Franklyn, Julian and John Tanner. *An Encyclopaedic Dictionary of Heraldry*, Oxford, Pergamon Press, 1970

Kennedy, Patrick. *A Book of Arms*, Canterbury, Achievements Ltd., 1967

Lynch-Robinson, Christopher. *Intelligible Heraldry*, London, MacDonald, 1948

MacKinnon, Charles. *The Observer Book of Heraldry*, London, Frederick Warne, 1972

Pine, L.G. *Heraldry and Genealogy*, Teach Yourself Books, London, English Universities Press, 1974

Pine, L.G. *The Story of Heraldry*, London, Country Life, 1953

Woodward, John and George Burnett. *Woodward's Treatise on Heraldry*, Newton Abbot, David and Charles Reprints, 1969

'A Sketch of the Gaelic Elements in Irish Heraldry', *Proceedings of Heraldic Congress*, Vol. 1, Madrid, 1982

General bibliography

Bence-Jones, Mark. *A Guide to Country Houses*, London, Constable, 1988

Begley, Donal F. (ed). *Irish Genealogy, a Record Finder*, Dublin, Heraldic Artists Ltd., 1981

Boylan, Henry. *A Dictionary of Irish Biography*, 2nd edn., Dublin, Gill and Macmillan, 1988

Brady, Anne M. and Brian Cleeve. *A Biographical Dictionary of Irish Writers*, Mullingar, The Lilliput Press, 1985

Burke's Landed Gentry of Ireland, London, Burke's Peerage Ltd., 1958

Burke's Irish Family Records, London, Burke's Peerage Ltd., 1976

Curtis, Edmund. *A History of Ireland*, London, Methuen, 1968

The Dictionary of American Biography, 22 vols., New York, Scribner, 1935

The Dictionary of Canadian Biography, 12 vols., University of Toronto Press, 1991

The Dictionary of National Biography, 30 vols. and supplements, Oxford University Press. Several editions.

Doherty J.E. and D.E. Hickey. *A Dictionary of Irish History since 1800*, Dublin, Gill and Macmillan, 1987

Dudley-Edwards, Ruth. *An Atlas of Irish History*, London, Methuen, 1973

Fitz-Simon, Christopher. *The Arts in Ireland: a Chronology*, Dublin, Gill and Macmillan, 1982

Griffin, William D. *A Portrait of the Irish in America*, Dublin, The Academy Press, 1981

Harbison, Dr Peter. *Guide to the National and Historic Monuments of Ireland*, Dublin, Gill and Macmillan, 1992

Hayes-McCoy, G.A. *Irish Battles: A Military History of Ireland*, Harlow, Longmans, 1969

Moody, T.W. and F.X. Martin (eds). *The Course of Irish History*, Cork, Mercier Press, 1984

O Hart, John. *The Irish and Anglo-Irish Landed Gentry*, Dublin, Irish Universities Press, 1968

MacLysaght, Dr Edward. *Irish Families, their names, arms and origins*, 4th edn., Dublin, Irish Academic Press, 1985

MacLysaght, Dr Edward. *More Irish Families*, Dublin, Irish Academic Press, 1982

MacLysaght, Dr Edward. *The Surnames of Ireland*, Dublin, Irish Academic Press, 1982

Paor, Máire de and Liam de Paor. *Early Christian Ireland*, London, Thames and Hudson, 1967

Reader's Digest, *Illustrated Guide to Ireland*, 1992

Searle, Percival. *The Dictionary of Australian Biography*, Sydney and London, Angus and Robertson, 1949

Who's Who in Ireland, Dublin, Vessey Publications, 1991

Woulfe, Revd Patrick. *Irish Names and Surnames*, Dublin, Gill, 1923

Periodicals

The Irish Ancestor

The Irish Genealogist

The Irish Sword

Journals of the historical and archaeological societies in Ireland.

Glossary

Anglo-Irish   People of English origin living in Ireland.

Ascendancy   Usually people of English origin owning large estates. Also known as the landed gentry.

Brehon Laws   Gaelic legal system in force before the Norman invasions and, to a lesser degree, until the seventeenth century.

The Fenians   A republican organization founded by John O Mahony in New York in 1859.

Flight of the Earls   Following the Irish defeat at the battle of Kinsale in 1601, Rory O Donnell, 1st Earl of Tirconnell (1575–1608), and Hugh O Neill, 2nd Earl of Tyrone (1550–1616), sailed with other chiefs and their families to Italy. Their flight marks the end of the native feudal aristocracy.

Gaelic   It is used to denote the Irish language or to denote Irish people, as opposed to people of Norman or English origin.

Gaelic Athletic Association   Commonly known as the GAA. A powerful amateur sporting association founded in 1884 by Michael Cusack.

Gaelic League   Founded in 1893 by Dr Douglas Hyde and other Irish language enthusiasts dedicated to the revival of the Irish language.

Gallowglass   An armed mercenary soldier, usually of Scottish origin.

Irish Volunteers   In the eighteenth century England was threatened by the armies of Europe. Realizing that Ireland had no protecting army and was vulnerable to European invasion, the Irish Volunteers were formed, mostly manned by the Protestant ascendancy.

Ollave   A learned man or teacher.

The Pale   Dublin and the surrounding countryside at one time under English rule.

Penal Laws   Laws enacted in 1695 to deprive Catholics of freedom to worship or enter the army or other professions.

The Plantations   There were a number of plantations dispossessing the Irish in the sixteenth century. In 1608 the British began colonizing Ulster with Scottish Protestant settlers who remain a separate entity loyal to the British Crown.

Seneschal   In medieval times, a steward to a noble or sovereign.

Sinn Féin   Meaning 'ourselves alone'. A movement developed at the beginning of this century inspired by Arthur Griffith and other patriots campaigning for Home Rule. Consolidated under Eamonn de Valera and Michael Collins for the rising of 1916. Following the Treaty in 1921 it split and Sinn Féin became the political wing of the IRA.

Tanaiste   Deputy Prime Minister, literally second-in-command.

Taoiseach   Meaning 'chief'. The Prime Minister.

Wild Geese   Leaders of the old Irish aristocracy who fled to serve in the armies of Europe following their defeat by the English in the seventeenth and eighteenth centuries.

The Young Irelanders   The 'Physical force' men who disagreed with Daniel O Connell's peaceful moves towards winning Home Rule.

Index

Page numbers in bold type indicate that the name is the subject of that chapter.

The h prefix is ignored alphabetically.

Mac and Mc are not differentiated.

Please note that the Genealogical Office has abolished the apostrophe after the O prefix.

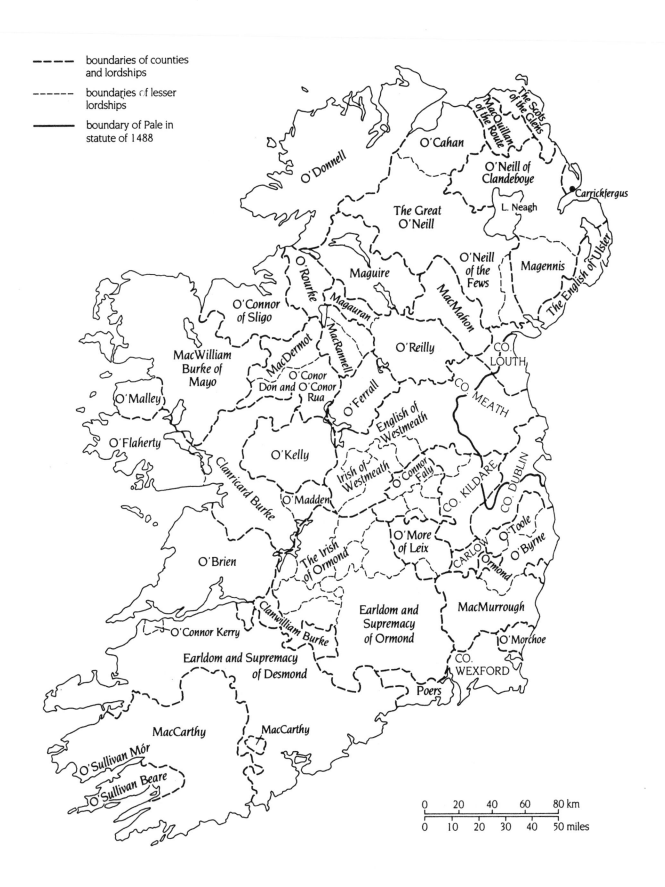

boundaries of counties
and lordships

boundaries of lesser
lordships

boundary of Pale in
statute of 1488

The Scots
of the Glens

MacQuillan
of the Route

O'Cahan

O'Donnell

O'Neill of
Clandeboye

Carrickfergus

The Great
O'Neill

L. Neagh

Maguire

O'Neill
of the
Fews

Magennis

The English of Ulster

O'Rourke

Magauran

O'Connor
of Sligo

MacRannell

O'Reilly

MacMahon

CO.
LOUTH

MacWilliam
Burke of
Mayo

MacDermot

O'Conor
Don and O'Conor
Rua

O'Ferrall

CO. MEATH

O'Malley

English of
Westmeath

O'Flaherty

O'Kelly

Irish of
Westmeath

O'Connor
Faly

CO. KILDARE

CO. DUBLIN

Clanricard Burke

O'Madden

O'More
of Leix

O'Toole

O'Byrne

CARLOW

Ormond

O'Brien

The Irish
of Ormond

Clanwilliam Burke

Earldom and
Supremacy
of Ormond

MacMurrough

O'Connor Kerry

O'Morchoe

Earldom and Supremacy
of Desmond

CO.
WEXFORD

Poers

MacCarthy

MacCarthy

O'Sullivan Mór

O'Sullivan Beare

0   20   40   60   80 km

0   10   20   30   40   50 miles

*The boundaries of Lordships in
fifteenth-century Ireland*

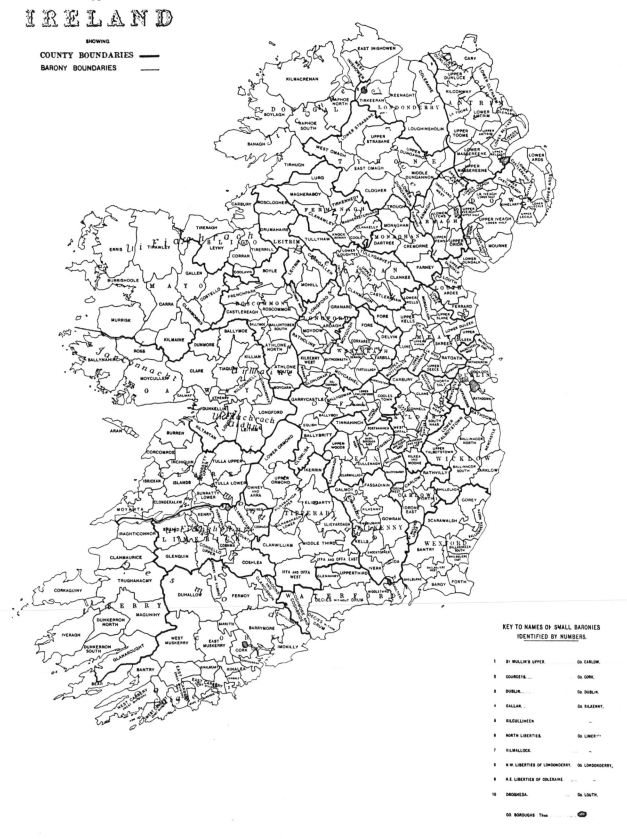

ORDNANCE SURVEY
OF
IRELAND
SHOWING
COUNTY BOUNDARIES ——
BARONY BOUNDARIES ——

KEY TO NAMES OF SMALL BARONIES
IDENTIFIED BY NUMBERS.

1	ST MULLIN'S UPPER.	Co. CARLOW.
2	COURCEYS.	Co. CORK.
3	DUBLIN.	Co. DUBLIN.
4	CALLAN.	Co. KILKENNY.
5	KILCULLIHEEN	"
6	NORTH LIBERTIES.	Co. LIMERICK
7	KILMALLOCK.	"
8	N.W. LIBERTIES OF LONDONDERRY.	Co. LONDONDERRY.
9	N.E. LIBERTIES OF COLERAINE	"
10	DROGHEDA.	Co. LOUTH.
	CO. BOROUGHS Thus	